THE NORMATIVE CLAIM OF LAW

This book focuses on a specific component of the normative dimension of law, namely, the normative claim of law. By 'normative claim' we mean the claim that inherent in the law is an ability to guide action by generating practical reasons having a special status. The thesis that law lays the normative claim has become a subject of controversy: it has its defenders, as well as many scholars of different orientations who have acknowledged the normative claim of law without making a point of defending it head-on. It has also come under attack from other contemporary legal theorists, and around the normative claim a lively debate has sprung up. This debate makes up the main subject of this book, which is in essence an attempt to account for the normative claim and see how its recognition moulds our understanding of the law itself. This involves (a) specifying the exact content, boundaries, quality and essential traits of the normative claim; (b) explaining how the law can make a claim so specified; and (c) justifying why this should happen in the first place. The argument is set out in two stages, corresponding to the two parts into which the book is divided. In the first part, the author introduces and discusses the meaning, status and fundamental traits of the normative claim of law; in the second, he explores some foundational questions and determines the grounds of the normative claim of law by framing an account that elaborates on some contemporary discussions of Kant's conception of humanity as the source of the normativity of practical reason.

Volume 1 in the series Law and Practical Reason

The Normative Claim of Law

Stefano Bertea

OXFORD AND PORTLAND, OREGON
2009

Published in North America (US and Canada) by
Hart Publishing
c/o International Specialized Book Services
920 NE 58th Avenue, Suite 300
Portland, OR 97213-3786
USA
Tel: +1 503 287 3093 or toll-free: (1) 800 944 6190
Fax: +1 503 280 8832
E-mail: orders@isbs.com
Website: http://www.isbs.com

© Stefano Bertea 2009

Stefano Bertea has asserted his right under the Copyright, Designs and Patents Act 1988,
to be identified as the author of this work.

All rights reserved. No part of this publication may be reproduced, stored in a retrieval system,
or transmitted, in any form or by any means, without the prior permission of Hart Publishing,
or as expressly permitted by law or under the terms agreed with the appropriate reprographic
rights organisation. Enquiries concerning reproduction which may not be covered by the above
should be addressed to Hart Publishing at the address below.

Hart Publishing Ltd, 16C Worcester Place, Oxford, OX1 2JW
Telephone: +44 (0)1865 517530 Fax: +44 (0)1865 510710
E-mail: mail@hartpub.co.uk
Website: http://www.hartpub.co.uk

British Library Cataloguing in Publication Data
Data Available

ISBN: 978-1-84113-967-8

Typeset by Hope Services, Abingdon
Printed and bound in Great Britain by
TJ International Ltd, Padstow, Cornwall

Contents

Introduction	1
PART I: MEANING, STATUS AND ESSENTIAL FEATURES	11
1. Meaning and Status	15
Introduction	15
The Semantic Question	17
The Metaphysical Question	28
Can the Law Make Any Claims at All?	29
Is the Normative Claim of Law Contingent or Necessary?	48
Conclusion	62
2. Generality and Moral Quality	67
Introduction	67
Inclusive Positivism and the Normative Claim of Law	69
Failure of the Inclusive-Positivist Account	78
Non-contingent Status of the Normative Claim of Law	78
Moral Nature of the Normativity of Law	85
General Scope of the Normative Claim of Law	94
Conclusion	96
3. Content-dependence and Discursive Character	99
Introduction	99
Reconstructing Raz's Account of the Normative Claim of Law	101
Engaging with Raz's Account	107
Main Argument	108
Objections and Counter-objections	114
The Normative Claim of Law and its Authority	121
Conclusion	131
PART II: GROUNDS	133
4. Why Grounds are Needed	139
Introduction	139
The Reductive Thesis	140
The Irreducible Core of the Normativity of Law	152
Legal-theoretical Considerations	152
Metaethical Considerations	160
Conclusion	169

5. Grounding the Normativity of Practical Reason — 171
Introduction — 171
Kant's Account of the Source of the Normativity of Practical Reason — 176
Relevance and Shortcomings of Kant's Account — 184
The Modified Kantian Account — 188
   Action and Human Agency — 189
   Human Agency and Normativity — 204
   A Reply to an Objection — 212
Conclusion — 223

6. Grounding the Normative Claim and Force of Law — 225
Introduction — 225
The Normativity of Law: the Fundamental Principle and its Implications — 227
The Normativity of Law in Detail — 250
   Normative Claim — 250
   Normative Force — 254

Conclusion — 271

Appendix: The Modified Kantian Account and Kant's Legal Philosophy — 277

Bibliography — 289

Index — 299

References to Kant's Works

References to Kant's writings will be given by the page numbers of the relevant volume of the Berlin Academy Edition (abbreviated 'AK') and take the following form. 'AK volume: page number'. The *Critique of Pure Reason*, however, is cited in its own standard way, by the page numbers of both the first (A) and second (B) editions.

For the editions and translations used, please see the Bibliography.

Introduction

SEVERAL LEGAL THEORISTS associate the existence of the law not only with the normative function of guiding conduct by generating practical reasons of a special kind but also with a claim, or contention, to do so. The possibility of attaching some normative claim to applications of the law is at the origin of theoretically relevant questions, amongst which are: How can this claim be precisely defined? What is its status? What are its exact features? and What entitles the law to make any such claim? These questions will provide the structure of this monograph, which can be understood as a systematic attempt to examine the main issues surrounding the normative claim of law and so contribute to dispelling some of the puzzles vis-à-vis its normative dimension. This search will involve subjecting the normative claim of law to analytical scrutiny with a view both to explaining and to grounding that claim.

The significance of the normative claim of law—what justifies our concern for that claim—is twofold. On the one hand, the normative claim of law owes its importance to the overall realm, the normative experience, of which it is a specific component. Normativity is widely regarded as an element lying at the very core of the law and so one that is to be accounted for by any legal theory seeking to be comprehensive. A theory that suppresses the normativity of law 'fails to mark and explain the crucial distinction between mere regularities of human behaviour and rule-governed behaviour' (Hart 1983: 13). This is a serious drawback for a general theory of law, for a distinctive part of the legal domain concerns rule-governed behaviour and so may be expressed only by the use of paradigmatic normative notions such as norm, obligation, duty and right. As a result, scholars of different orientations would hardly disagree with Stephen Perry's (2001: 330) statement that 'the provision of an account of the normativity of law is a central task of jurisprudence, if not the central task'. On the other hand, the significance of the normative claim of law is due to its being a necessary constituent of legality. Necessary elements of the law are intrinsically significant for legal theory, which at its core is the study of the invariable, and so defining, features of the legal enterprise.

The second source of significance is apparently subordinate to the recognition of the *necessity* of the normative claim of law. This necessity is acknowledged by contemporary legal theorists of different convictions, among whom Joseph Raz, Philip Soper and Robert Alexy figure prominently.[1] From the common assumption that 'necessarily law, every legal system which is in force anywhere, has *de facto* authority', Raz (1994: 199), a proponent of legal positivism, argues that for

---

[1] Further statements of the thesis that some normative claim is of necessity attached to the law can be found in Gauss (1981: 333–5), Detmold (1984: 31), Lyons (1987: 115–18), Postema, (1987: 92–3), Burton (1989: 1956–62), Gavinson (1991: 737), Postema (1998: 333) and Green (2002: 519–20).

conceptual reasons the law claims legitimate authority, and concludes that 'though a legal system may not have legitimate authority, or though its legitimate authority may not be as extensive as it claims, every legal system claims that it possesses legitimate authority'. In other words, the claim to authority, which in Raz's work refers to the property of providing people with exclusionary reasons for action and so is to be regarded as a normative claim, is acknowledged to be 'part of the nature of law' (Raz 1994: 199) and then a claim the law necessarily makes.

Soper too endorses the thesis that legal systems are necessarily characterised by some normative claim. Contrary to Raz, however, he defends a moderate version of natural law theory—moderate, for Soper takes the positivist theory as the main point of reference against which his view of the law unfolds, which carries the implication that Soper's natural law theory is at least rooted in the research horizon framed by legal positivism. In Soper's (1984: 55) view, legal systems make the normative 'claim to justice', which takes the form of 'the claim in good faith by those who rule that they do so in the interests of all'. This claim can be further characterised as the assertion that 'when the state acts, it does so in the belief that it has chosen morally appropriate norms for enforcement' (Soper 1996: 219). The reference to moral appropriateness allows us to regard Soper's claim to justice as a normative claim, that is, a claim that relates to how people *ought to* guide their conduct.

Finally, Alexy, who champions a species of non-positivism informed by discourse theory, assigns a normative claim to the law in his argument from correctness.[2] By means of a presentation of different ideal-types of wicked legal systems (the senseless order, the predatory or rapacious order, and the governor system), Alexy argues that no institutional arrangement can be regarded as legal unless it implicitly or explicitly lays a claim to correctness.[3] This claim, which incorporates an action-guiding and justificatory component and so is normative, sets the boundaries of legality: it is the inclusion of the claim to correctness that turns an order of social control into a legal system.[4] This means that for Alexy, a normative claim figures as a necessary element of legality.

However, the necessary status of the normative claim has not gone undisputed. Recently, Carsten Heidemann, Kenneth Einar Himma and Neil MacCormick, amongst others, have deployed different arguments to show that the law does not of necessity make normative claims.[5] As a result, the status of the normative claim of law has become a subject of controversy, an issue around which a lively debate has arisen, especially among scholars working in the analytical tradition of legal philosophy. In consideration of its impact on the significance of the study of the normative claim of law, in chapter one I will take a position in this debate. The aim of the first chapter is twofold. First, I intend to settle the definitional, or semantic, issue by establishing unequivocally the *meaning* of the normative claim, which

[2] This argument is deployed in Alexy (2002b: 40–83).
[3] On these ideal-types, see Alexy (2002b: 31–5).
[4] See Alexy (2002b: 34–5).
[5] See Himma (2001), Heidemann (2005) and MacCormick (2007b).

various scholars have defined differently, as Alexy's, Soper's and Raz's accounts clearly show. The meaning I take the normative claim of law to have is basic and so configures it as a 'minimal' contention summarising the core of the richer definitions championed in the contemporary literature, where the normative claim of law is connected to notions (legitimate authority, justice, moral correctness) that are indeed normative but exceed sheer normativity. Focusing on a thin definition is instrumental in avoiding the incorporation from the outset of partisan and controvertible assumptions that aprioristically exclude admissible definitions of the normative claim of law. This inclusive attitude frames the discussion of the *status* of the normative claim of law (and this is the second concern of chapter one) at a highly general level of abstraction. The question relative to the status of the normative claim of law leads one to tackle the problem as to whether that claim is possible, optional or necessary. Because this problem confronts us with the modality of the normative claim of law, its nature is metaphysical or ontological. The metaphysical question is twofold: it bifurcates into the two distinct subquestions as to (a) whether the normative claim of law is possible and, if it is possible, (b) whether that claim is optional or necessary. In chapter one I argue not only that the law can meaningfully make the normative claim—that is, the claim is possible—but also that the normative claim is one of the necessary elements of legality, an element distinguishing legal governance from other, non-legal, forms of pursuing the action-guidance function.

With the semantic question and the metaphysical question addressed, I turn to a discussion of the essential features of the normative claim of law. To this purpose, I engage with the dominant tradition in contemporary jurisprudence, analytical legal positivism, which provides an account of the normative claim of law that is illuminating but needs also to be revised in some key aspects. In chapter two, the critical discussion of the treatment the normative claim of law undergoes within inclusive legal positivism will make it possible for me to characterise the normative claim as the contention that legal institutions make of necessity in order to guide action by providing citizens with practical reasons, the nature of which is moral. This picture of the normative claim of law, which is understood as an initial statement fleshing out the basic definition laid out in chapter one, requires one to take issue with some fundamental aspects of the characterisation of the normative claim of law provided by inclusive positivism. Inclusive positivism is committed to the views, here argued to be mistaken, (a) that the status of the normative claim of law is merely contingent; (b) its object is a peculiarly legal kind of normativity, radically distinct and autonomous from moral normativity, to the effect that the practical reasons the law claims to create are conceived not as moral reasons but as distinctively legal reasons; and (c) that the normative claim of law is addressed to legal officials, as opposed to the generality of people concerned with the existence of a legal practice. The argument showing that these statements are untenable will also carry with it an important implication for the grounds of the normative claim of law: it rules out the possibility that such a claim is grounded on an appeal to the notion of endorsement, or commitment, and therefore shows that a non-cognitivist approach is ill-equipped to provide a theoretical justification of the normative claim of law.

These remarks, while falling short of an exhaustive account of the normative claim of law, do provide a sound beginning to it. Building on the results of the discussion of inclusive legal positivism, I turn in chapter three to Raz's writings concerning the concept of law and legal authority, which are argued to contribute further to the explanation of the normative claim of law. Bringing Raz's account into the picture contributes to the understanding of the normative claim of law in two ways. First, it provides further support for the theses (a) that the normative claim is a defining element of the concept of law; (b) that the practical reasons the law claims to create are moral reasons; and (c) that the scope of the normative claim is general. Secondly, the discussion of Raz's work makes it possible for us to elaborate on the distinctive traits of the reasons the law claims to produce. Raz depicts the reasons that the authoritative structures of the law claim to generate as content-independent and exclusionary. I argue that this view cannot be maintained. Legal provisions do not necessarily replace and pre-empt the substantive reasons they depend on. The relationship between legal directives and underlying moral reasons is not governed by an exclusionary logic on the basis of which a legal provision can be completely insulated from the moral arguments that justify it, but by a dialectical principle whereby legal authority and morality are mutually transparent and connected. This conclusion suggests that we should characterise the practical reasons the law claims to engender as reinforced reasons that hold valid only if they are not irremediably unreasonable or blatantly immoral. This leads us to characterise the normative claim of law further as the contention that, perforce, the law generates reinforced reasons to act, which, provided that their contents are not seriously flawed from a moral point of view, bind all citizens.

Once characterised—its meaning, status and essential features spelled out—the normative claim of law still remains partially unexplained unless it can also be theoretically justified, or grounded. Hence, determining the grounds of the normative claim of law, by addressing what is called here the grounding question, ought to be regarded as an essential element of any comprehensive study of the claim. This leads us to the subject matter of Part II, where an effort is made to offer a theoretical justification of the normative claim of law, namely, to put forward a theory elucidating what makes something normative: what entitles some objects or properties to (claim to) have the capacity to guide and justify conduct, and why, then, some objects or properties ought to be taken to be normative. Doing so requires two major changes in focus. First, we should look for assistance outside the debate among legal theorists, for legal theorists, with few exceptions, have shown little concern for theoretically justifying the normative claim of law. Secondly, the normative claim of law can be grounded only to the extent that the normativity of law, the notion shaping the very definition of that claim, is grounded. This means that in Part II I will be focusing the attention also on the *normativity* of law, not only on the *normative claim* of law. The shift in focus clearly distinguishes the argument laid out in Part I from the argument deployed in Part II, where I first discuss and reject the sceptical view depicting the normativity of law as a certain arrangement of social facts, and then go on to embrace a constructivist account, which has its roots in the Kantian strand of practical philosophy, in order to provide both the theoretical justification of the normative dimension of the law and the related claim associated with the existence of the law.

More specifically, chapter four takes up the sceptical view, according to which the problem of grounding the normative claim of law is not one that need worry us, for it arises only if normativity is viewed as a dimension of human experience distinct from, and irreducible to, the factual dimension. As long as the distinctiveness and peculiarity of the normative sphere are not established, one is entitled to disregard the grounds for the normative claim of law. The possibility of this objection suggests that in order to secure the relevance of the grounding question, the thesis that the normative is a declination of the factual, as distinct from an independent dimension, should be discussed in a preliminary way. The position denying the distinctiveness of the normative finds a wide assortment of statements in the existing literature. In its strongest version, however, the sceptical thesis takes the shape of a model viewing the normative dimension through its accompanying facts and, ultimately, equating normativity with certain arrangements of social facts and properties. This model can be described as *reductive*: it understands normativity as wholly enveloped in the 'is' dimension, rather than as designating the category of human experience known as the 'ought' dimension, the specific existence of which category is denied in consequence. I will argue that the reductive model comes with a considerable strain, for it is packaged with two glaring yet unaddressed problems. For one thing, since we are being asked to equate the normative with the factual, we have to solve the problem of how an identity can ever be established between two categories (normative categories and factual categories) that are described by different sets of predicates. Norms can be described as valid or invalid; in contrast, this predicate ('valid') does not apply to facts. This leaves reductionism with the hard task of showing how two categories characterised by different predicates can be reduced the one to the other without distortion. Moreover, I will be claiming that the reductive thesis cannot explain normativity in the sense that matters in legal contexts, where a standard is normative in the sense that it has an unqualified capacity to guide action, meaning that the standard in question does not allow for any 'opting out' once it has been set down. Reductionism cannot do justice to the non-contingent forms of action-guidance peculiar to the law, although it may do justice to some (weaker) forms of action-guidance.

Having cleared the way by showing the significance of the question relative to the grounds of the normative claim of law, I set out in chapters five and six to answer that question. In completing the task, I will rely on and elaborate on some recent contributions that are informed by Immanuel Kant's practical philosophy. Specifically, I will hold that if we are to ground the normative claim of law, we will have to look at some contemporary discussions of Kant's conception of humanity as the source of the normativity of practical reason. My argument in chapter five proceeds thus. First, I introduce the basics of Kant's account of normativity and clarify how, for Kant, the normativity of practical reason has its source in humanity. Kant's account applies to the normativity of *any* instantiation of practical reason and so of any practically rational requirement. Hence, in so far as we acknowledge the law as a specific, highly institutionalised, kind of practical reason, Kant's treatment of normativity applies to the normativity of law, too. Yet Kant's account proves problematic, for it relies on a peculiar and questionable metaphysics that is brought into play as a device by means of which a connection between normativity and humanity is established. Rather than defending this metaphysical view, I opt for a pragmatic reinterpretation of Kant's main ideas. Thus, we no longer have a metaphysical attempt to define the essence of *humanity*, but a pragmatic one that aims to single out the traits of *human agency*. I identify these distinctively human traits, which must be understood as necessary properties if a subject is to be regarded as a human agent, namely, one who is capable of performing action and who therefore has a distinctive existence in the practical realm, as reflectivity, rationality and autonomy. They frame human agency, understood as a broad basis without which individuals could not give content to any conception of themselves as acting beings. Hence, we can describe these traits as the minimum condition for the construction of a practical self-conception, and as an enabling condition for the process of identity-making in the practical sphere.

In this role, the self-conception stemming from human agency acts at the same time as a precondition and a product of human acting selves. A kind of weak dualism is thus established. The necessary self-conception exists before and beyond the agent as a deep conception enjoying a good measure of independence from this or that particular human agent, which is to say that it cannot be disposed of without thereby giving up one's distinctive existence as a human agent. At the same time, however, that self-conception is the outcome of the capacity for self-reflection that enables each human agent to move about in the practical sphere and makes every individual human agent capable of recognising herself as such. In this deep and dual role as constitutive of practical identity and as a product of the self, the self-conception stemming from human agency importantly explains the emergence of normativity. For the deep level at which this conception operates makes it possible not only to *describe* what human agents come to (describing the minimal, necessary features that everyone in the class has) but also to *prescribe* how human agents ought to behave, and so, by virtue of defining a model that no human agent can afford to ignore, ends up carrying normative force. It is in this prescriptive function that human agency—the identity rooted in it and shaped by it—accounts for, and grounds, normativity.

The conclusion that practical reason owes its normativity to human agency sets the stage for chapter six. There, I argue that the normativity and the normative claim of law can be grounded in the same way as we ground the normativity and the normative claim of practical reason, in that both normative kinds are grounded in human agency. I expand on these points by first looking at the main principle involved in the functioning of the normativity of law and then working out the scheme in details. My first step is the observation that the normative claim of law can be further specified as the contention that human agency be protected and can be seen as an essential ingredient of the concept of law. Building on this point, I illustrate the open-ended and flexible way in which the source of normativity works, observing that this imparts to the normativity of law the shape of an optimisation command: normativity in law functions as something requiring that it be fulfilled to the highest degree possible. I then point out that optimisation commands cannot be accurately determined in their content except through a concrete argumentative process. This brings into view a necessary link between the normativity of law and legal reasoning and invites attention to the important role of legal argument in establishing the normative dimension of the law. There are, too, specific features of the normativity of law and the normative claim of law that depend on a number of distinctions I introduce and clarify in chapter six, including, importantly, the distinction between direct and indirect normativity, and between the normativity of individual legal provisions and the normativity of the legal system as a whole.

I go on in chapters five and six to defend an account of the normative claim of law that is undergirded in Kant's practical philosophy. I do so, working for the most part from his *Groundwork of the Metaphysics of Morals* and his *Critique of Practical Reason*. While these two sources contain the core of Kant's practical philosophy, however, neither of them deals specifically with the law, a topic that Kant addresses in *The Metaphysics of Morals*. This might lead one to wonder why an essay putting forward a Kantian account of *the normative claim of law*, however modified the account may be, should pay so little attention to Kant's primary discussion of the law. I address that concern in the appendix, answering the suspicion that my account of normativity requires an unorthodox reading of Kant's philosophy of law. In particular, by confronting the interpretation of Kant's legal philosophy defended, inter alia, by George Fletcher and Ernst Weinrib, I argue that my construction assumes nothing that Kant would reject. *The Metaphysics of Morals* offers no textual evidence for the view that a sharp line of demarcation should be drawn between the law and other practical realms. This line of argument is supported by Kant's thesis of the unity of practical reason, a thesis entailing the view that different spheres of practical reason are not separate but contiguous, with significant conceptual overlap. I conclude on this basis that Kant's philosophy of law in no way prevents us from conceiving the normativity of law as a special case of the normativity of practical reason.

As the reader might have observed from the foregoing introductory remarks, this study is primarily concerned with the normative claim made by the law *qua* legal system or domain. In the existing literature, 'law' is a term used to refer to single legal provisions or norms (a single statutory provision, a regulation or a judicial holding) as well as to the legal system as a whole, understood as the institutional context or domain within which individual legal provisions are found. The distinction matters, for the thesis that the law makes claims will mean one thing if we are referring to an individual legal provision, and will mean quite another if we are taking up the legal domain as a whole. In the latter case, the law includes not only legal norms but also the machinery that is employed to create and apply them, including people, institutions, procedures, and the like. When the law as a *system* or *domain* is said to advance a claim, the thesis being argued is that this claim stems not simply from legal norms but from the ways in which different parts and constituents of the system come together and interact. There are different forces at play here (officials, norms, institutions and procedures) and the claims that the law makes stem from various combinations of such forces. A study of this nature, in which different kinds of entities are taken into account, brings up issues different from those that arise when one is considering legal provisions alone. For this reason, any account of the claim-making capacity associated with the law that seeks to be exhaustive will have to treat this as a twofold question, discussing this capacity with respect to both single legal provisions and the legal domain as a whole.

It is, moreover, the claims of the legal domain as a whole rather than those of single legal provisions that I will be primarily concerned with: this is in keeping with the current debate, in which greater theoretical importance is accorded to the claims made by the law understood as a system. The discussion that follows will therefore keep this focus front and centre, and the choice of vocabulary will reflect this, which is to say that unless otherwise specified, I will be using 'law' to refer to the legal domain as a whole rather than to individual legal norms. As an additional terminological detail, I will favour, throughout the monograph, the locution 'the law' over 'law' in order to point to the legal domain; the only exceptions being those phrases of wide currency that have the status of idioms, for example, 'concept of law', 'nature of law', 'normativity of law' and '(normative) claim of law', which all employ 'law' and not 'the law'.

I have worked over this project for a long enough period of time to warrant its qualification as a long-term project. As with any such project, it would not have been possible without the support of a number of institutions and people.

Funding for the completion of this monograph has been provided by the Alexander von Humboldt Foundation through a generous fellowship that enabled me to spend the academic year 2005–06 and part of the academic year 2006–07 at the Christian-Albrechts University of Kiel, and by the British Academy, which granted me a Small Research Grant in the academic year 2006–07. In addition, from September 2006 I have been a New Blood Lecturer at the Law School of the University of Leicester. The research-friendly orientation of the New Blood Lectureship, granting a sabbatical year and further three years with reduced teaching load, enabled me to complete this book within a reasonable span of time. Finally, my gratitude goes to the University of Antwerp: my appointment to a Senior Research Fellowship at the Centre for Law and Cosmopolitan Values at the School of Law in September 2008 has meant a significant increase of my research time.

For comments on the overall project as well as on early drafts of some specific chapters, I am grateful to Kola Abimbola, Robert Alexy, Zenon Bankowski, Jason

Beckett, Giorgio Bongiovanni, Marco Braga, Bob Brouwer, Bartosz Brozek, Thomas Casadei, Emilios Christodoulidis, Maksymilian Del Mar, Gabriele Fedrigo, Marco Goldoni, Carsten Heidemann, Aileen Kavanagh, Christoph Kletzer, Massimo La Torre, Neil MacCormick, Panu Minkkinen, Colin Perrin, Pablo Quintanilla, Janice Richardson, Veronica Rodriguez-Blanco, Antonino Rotolo, Jon Rubin, Emmanuel Voyiakis, Veronique Voruz and Gianfrancesco Zanetti. I must apologise to each of them for this collective acknowledgement, which falls well short of doing any sort of justice to their essential contributions. Special credit is due to Francesco Belvisi, George Pavlakos and Corrado Roversi, with all of whom I have carried on a far-ranging discussion concerning certain theoretical topics in law for several years. Not only have they been kind enough to discuss several parts of this book with me, thereby contributing significantly to improving my argument and to eliminating serious misunderstandings, but they have also been constant sources of encouragement and inspiration. In addition, I want to express my deepest thanks to Filippo Valente, who was initially involved in this project to help with matters of English language and style, and in the end has also contributed enormously to clarifying several important conceptual issues. Finally, I am most grateful to Stanley L Paulson, who went through the whole manuscript and helped enormously to clarify crucial points, as well as to improve the overall argument deployed here, thereby making an invaluable contribution to this work.

This book is dedicated to Luciano, Miranda, Simone, Fiore and Linda, my bedrock and only protection against the vagaries of a life that has radically parted ways from my hobbit-like ideal. Others will find other defects in this work. My own chief complaint is that it has kept me away from my loved ones for far too long.

Part I

Meaning, Status and Essential Features

The centrality of the normative dimension in legal experience has meant that theorists working in the traditional schools of legal thought have put forward different explanations of the normative claim of law. These accounts make up the subject matter of Part I, where I establish the meaning and status of the normative claim of law and also address the problem as to how, by means of a specification of its essential features (which I identify in generality, moral quality, content-dependence and discursive character) the normative claim of law should be characterised. Part I will be at the same time critical and constructive, for I point out what I see as being the inherent weaknesses of the existing approaches, and then lay the groundwork for treating the normative claim in such a way as to make it possible to attack the problems singled out in the critical discussion.

In chapter one, I argue that before a discussion of the normative claim of law can begin, the meaning of this claim needs to be set out and its status to be established. Each of these issues, relating to what I call the semantic and the metaphysical question, respectively, is taken up in turn. The *semantic question* requires careful analysis for two reasons. On the one hand, there is wide disagreement on what the normative claim means in the first place; on the other, the claim has waxed larger, becoming richer than its minimal content would otherwise warrant. There is nothing inherently wrong with having a richer conception, but keeping our focus on the minimal content of the normative claim will enable us to have a genuine starting point from which to discuss it and to steer clear of arbitrary definitions. Once the minimal content of the normative claim of law is defined, I look at the *metaphysical question* of its status, which involves taking up the two problems of its possibility and its necessity. In this context, I will defend the capacity of the law to make claims against the objection that the law *cannot* meaningfully lay any claim, lacking the power to do so, and so the normative claim of law is at best fictional. This leads me to clarify how the law can make a normative claim and establish such a claim as necessary.

With the semantic question and the metaphysical question answered, in chapters two and three, I spell out the fundamental traits of the normative claim of law. First, I argue that the normative claim of law is a general claim, addressed to legal officials and citizens alike, and it has a moral quality, to wit, it concerns reasons for action that not only enter into competition with, but also are ultimately reducible to, moral reasons. This means that the normative claim of law can be characterised as the contention that legal systems non-contingently make in order to guide conduct, namely, by providing the *generality* of their addressees with *moral* reasons for action. Then, I bring to a close my characterisation of the normative claim of law by eliciting the remaining traits that I regard as essential to it. These are, I argue, content-dependence and discursive character: the practical reasons that the law claims to generate are reinforced reasons conceived of as standards following a *discursive logic* and holding to the extent that their *contents* do not collide egregiously with those of rational critical morality.

The argument for this characterisation will take shape by means of a critical confrontation with the writings of legal theorists working within the tradition of analytical legal positivism. This tradition is at once well-suited to address the questions surrounding the normative claim of law, and ill-equipped to find convincing answers to them. This kind of paradox originates from the distinctive approach to the law devised by analytical legal positivism. The advocates of analytical legal positivism, especially since Herbert Hart's work, have expressly acknowledged the practicality of the law and have duly emphasised the relation existing between the law, on the one hand, and guidance and assessment of conduct, on the other. Because an account of the normative claim of law is part and parcel of the study of the practical side of the law, it is reasonable to expect that we will find elaborate treatments of that claim in the positivist camp. Yet, we should also expect that legal positivists will have some difficulty in making sense of the normative claim of law in the course of their endorsement of the thesis, a core thesis of analytical legal positivism, that the law is an arrangement of social facts. Since, by themselves, social facts do not provide reasons for action, it is then far from obvious to explain from a positivist standpoint how the law, with an eye to guiding conduct, can impinge upon the reasons to act that individuals have.

This tension between the practical dimension and factual component of the law is at the origin of the different accounts of the normative claim of law defended by the champions of analytical legal positivism. Far from disqualifying those accounts, this tension renders them sophisticated and intriguing. Their discussion, therefore, has the potential to shed light on important aspects of the normative claim of law. The assumption underlying the argument carried out in this part is, then, twofold. On the one hand, analytical legal positivism is regarded as a theory that provides an excellent starting point for a characterisation of the normative claim of law. On the other, however, one's overall stance towards analytical legal positivism needs to be critical. Because the positivist accounts of the normative claim of law are in need of revision in key aspects, it is by confronting analytical legal positivism from a critical point of view, rather than by sharing its basic theses and contributing to the positivist tradition, that we can arrive at a comprehensive characterisation of the normative claim of law.

Before I can commence with the argument, clarity of exposition requires that I define the notion of analytical legal positivism, at least by adumbrating its fundamental tenets. Analytical legal positivism is a theory of the nature of law (a study of the necessary and universal conditions for something to qualify as the law) that rests on two fundamental views: the separability thesis and the social fact thesis. The *separability thesis* can be framed as a negation, a jurisprudential statement in the negative: it denies any object-level conceptual connection of content between the criteria of legality and critical morality.[1] As Hart (1994: 185–6) puts it, 'it is in no sense a necessary truth that laws reproduce or satisfy certain demands of morality'. The *social fact thesis*, a positive contention, makes a claim about the conditions for the existence of the law, saying that the law is grounded in social facts, not in moral values. In other words, the criteria of legality are established by social facts, and this stands in the way of the view that critical morality enters as a condition of legality. Thus, on the reasoning that existence of the law depends exclusively on complex facts (such as the officials' practice of accepting a certain kind of rule), the social fact thesis construes the law as an artefact, a social construction.[2]

The separability thesis and the social fact thesis get plied together in such a way as to frame the conceptual space of analytical legal positivism, grounding its concept of law on two defining elements, namely, authoritative enactment and social efficacy: what the law is depends on what the authorities have enacted and on what is socially efficacious.[3] But analytical legal positivism cannot be reduced to these two core claims alone, for that would oversimplify what is actually a sophisticated view. Different varieties of legal positivism bring to light further tenets, tenets that are not all compatible: witness the sources thesis, the practical difference thesis, the conventionality thesis (in both its weak and strong versions), and the incorporation thesis.[4] These varieties can be reduced, albeit not without simplification, to two fundamental positions: inclusive positivism (also known as soft positivism or incorporationism) and exclusive positivism (or hard positivism). It is to these two species of analytical legal positivism that I will turn in my search for an adequate characterisation of the normative claim of law.

---

[1] In Coleman's words, the separability thesis amounts to 'the claim that there exists at least one conceivable rule of recognition (and therefore one possible legal system) that does not specify truth as a moral principle among the truth conditions for any proposition of law' (Coleman 1982: 141). The separability thesis constitutes the core of 'negative positivism'. On the separability thesis, see also Coleman (2001: 151–2) and Himma (2002: 135–6). On the notion of negative positivism and the distinction between negative and positive positivism, see Coleman (1982).

[2] The social fact thesis is paradigmatically defended in Hart (1994: 82–91). On the social fact thesis, see also Himma (2002: 126–9).

[3] This is how legal positivism is characterised in Alexy (2002b: 3–4), for instance.

[4] The *sources thesis* amounts to the claim that 'what is law and what is not is a matter of social fact' (Raz 1979: 37), that is, the law depends entirely on conventional sources for its validity, and hence is all based on sources. The *practical difference thesis* says that legal norms must be capable of making a difference in our practical deliberation as individuals: they must be able to motivate us to act differently from the way we would otherwise act. The *weak conventionality thesis* says that the criteria of legal validity are specifically established by the social convention that obtains among the officials of a given community: the standards of legality are social facts and so are conventional. The *strong conventionality thesis* means that this convention—the rule of recognition—can create an obligation to act on it. And last we have the *incorporation thesis*, which states that the criteria of legal validity *may* include moral standards, and so that this inclusion is only a possibility. These theses are so named in Coleman (1998), Coleman (2001), Shapiro (2001), Himma (2002) and Marmor (2002).

1
Meaning and Status

INTRODUCTION

ESTABLISHING CONTENT, STATUS and the theoretical significance of the normative claim of law is the initial move that constructing a comprehensive account of that claim requires. This is the immediate task at hand, which involves, first, clarifying the content of the normative claim; secondly, showing how this claim can actually be asserted by institutions charged with functions pertaining to the law and its operation; thirdly, qualifying the status or modality of the claim as merely contingent or necessary. The first step concerns a semantic or definitional question, in that the content of the normative claim depends on the way its meaning is defined. This is preliminary to the second and third steps, which concern what I will call a metaphysical or ontological question. Together, the semantic and the bipartite metaphysical questions, which I will take up in turn, make up the subject matter of this chapter.

The semantic question reveals the very basic level at which the normative claim of law begins to occasion disagreement, even among its main proponents, namely, Robert Alexy, Joseph Raz and Philip Soper. None of these scholars regards his definition of the normative claim of law as bearing any significant kinship to that of the others.[1] This disagreement makes it all the more important to start out with a definition of the normative claim that clearly specifies its content and boundaries, for this will help to frame the discussion and render it perspicuous. It can be observed in this regard that the normative claim of law, as contemporary legal scholars have expounded it, departs to various extents from the 'minimal normative claim', meaning by this expression the claim as it derives from the concept of normativity alone. The most widely discussed accounts of the normative claim deeply embed certain key ideas (such as correctness, legitimate authority and justice) that show a clear connection to normativity yet cannot be equated with normativity as such, or 'sheer normativity'. So, to the extent that those ideas are brought into play, we end up with a richer account than the minimal conception would warrant. There is nothing inherently wrong with having a richer conception, to be sure, but keeping our focus on the minimal content of the normative

---

[1] Soper (1989), for example, finds fault with the theory of authority on which Raz bases his definition of the normative claim. And Raz, in turn, uses his account of the normative claim of law to ground a view of the nature of law radically different from that of Alexy.

claim will enable us to steer clear of circular, and hence arbitrary, definitions. We will have a statement offering a genuine vantage point from which to assess the broadest range of theories of the normative claim of law and bring to light their underlying assumptions. Thus, if we are comprehensively to treat the thesis that the law makes a normative claim, we must first be clear about what this claim basically is and what it basically states. To this end, we need to set out the minimal claim and keep it distinct from the more elaborate versions of the normative claim that have been associated in the literature with the existence of the law. This I will do in the second section, where I formulate the normative claim as it derives directly from the bare meaning of normativity (normativity considered without regard to companion ideas), thereby singling out the common core of meaning shared by different accounts of the normative claim of law.

Once this is done—with a clear statement of what the normative claim of law means in its most basic form—we can move on to a discussion of its metaphysical status. This will require determining whether the law can make claims to begin with, and then whether some normative claim so made is contingent or necessary. The first part of this metaphysical question I take up in the third section, where the capacity of the law to make claims will be defended against the objection (voiced by such writers as Carsten Heidemann, Kenneth Himma and Neil MacCormick) that the law *cannot* meaningfully lay any claim, simply lacking the power to do so; this alleged power of the law is at best fictional, and drawing conclusions from any fiction is going to be problematic, if not arbitrary. This is a general objection. If it holds up, it will show that it is not just the normative claim that the law fails to make, but any claim whatever.

To be sure, if we can rebut this general objection, we can conclude that the law does indeed have the ability to make claims—which means that the normative claim is possible—but we will still not know anything about the status of the normative claim: we will not know whether the normative claim is contingent or necessary, that is, whether the law might choose *not* to make this claim even though it *can* make it. This will take us to a further stage in the argument, a stage in which it is to be established what import the normative claim bears. For if the claim is merely contingent, we should not expect it significantly to change our view of the law, but if the claim is necessary, it will entail such a revision. The claim will become entrenched in the very concept of law, from which it follows that any general account of the nature of law (the province of legal theory) will also have to include an account of the normative claim. At the same time, we will have a new analytical tool that can help us to compare different legal theories by looking at how they account for the normative claim and to work this into the concept of law. This discussion will take up the whole of the second part of the third section, where I will use the theory of speech acts, together with the widely shared view of the law as a practical enterprise, to show that the ability of the law to make the normative claim corresponds to a role or function the law *has* to exercise, in such a way that the normative claim becomes an essential component of the law rather than an optional one.

THE SEMANTIC QUESTION

The semantic question is the question of the content, or meaning, of the normative claim of law. Since we are dealing with a definition, we should not want to pack too much content into it from the outset, for we may otherwise end up begging the question of why ought the law and how can the law make a claim so specified in the first place? To avoid this kind of recursive process, we will need to state the normative claim in its plainest, least demanding form, by establishing the minimum content of the claim: the common core shared by all the different accounts of the claim as these are found in the literature. The claim in its minimal form is that whose meaning derives directly from the concept of normativity. So, in this section, I will primarily be concerned with tracing out this derivation, showing how the normative claim of law comes straightaway from the concept of normativity as such, that is to say, normativity not infused with any other supporting ideas. In this context, I will focus on the practical side of normativity rather than on its epistemic side. This limitation is justified by the practical nature of the normative claim of law—a claim widely understood as primarily concerning human conduct rather than human beliefs and theory. Hence, throughout this book, and unless stated otherwise, the words 'normative' and 'normativity' will be understood as designating practical concepts used in reference to 'practically normative' and 'practical normativity'.[2]

What brings the semantic question into prominence is at the same time what makes it intractable, namely, the manifold existence the normative claim of law reveals in contemporary legal theory, with Joseph Raz, Philip Soper and Robert Alexy, among many others, giving the claim markedly different contents and degrees of force. Thus, Raz understands the normative claim as the claim to legitimate authority, meaning that the law can exercise of right the power to bind the subjects under its purview, a right with respect to which the same subjects have a corresponding duty of obedience.[3] Soper, for his part, understands the normative claim as the claim to justice, meaning 'the claim in good faith by those who rule that they do so in the interests of all' (Soper 1984: 55). Alexy disagrees with both Raz and Soper, framing the normative claim (a criterion he takes to distinguish law from non-law) as a claim to moral correctness: the legal system as a whole, and its constituent legal provisions individually, explicitly or implicitly contend that their contents are morally correct, or not wrong.[4] The ideas of legitimate

---

[2] The assumption here is that of normativity as an umbrella concept capable of accommodating multiple specific meanings, each of which can be worked out in such a way as to bring out appreciable differences from other meanings. The argument being developed in this section is specifically framed to apply to normativity understood as a practical concept and not also as an epistemological concept. So even though the argument may support just such an extension, either in full or in part, I am neither showing how that should happen, nor am I making an assumption to this effect.

[3] See Raz (1994: 199–204).

[4] See Alexy (2002b: 34–9).

18 *Meaning and Status*

authority, justice and moral correctness are all interlinked, to be sure, but their overlap is partial and does not imply coincidence.[5]

What ultimately accounts for the overlap between the different forms the normative claim of law may take is the link that the normative claim in each such form establishes with justice, despite all the differences between forms. This link is quite explicit in Soper, in his thesis that the law makes a claim to justice, but it also informs Raz's notion of legitimate authority and Alexy's notion of moral correctness, since both ideas relate conceptually to justice. In fact, legitimate authority, as Raz constructs this idea, combines two meanings, in that the authority it designates commands obedience, exerting a de facto binding force, which, in addition, incorporates a justificatory dimension, an aspiration to bind people *by right*.[6] Justification and the right are understood by Raz as moral ideas, and they confer that quality on legitimate authority.[7] That is how a necessary connection is established between (the claim to) legitimate authority and (the claim to) justice: both are shaped by morality. Similarly, Alexy understands moral correctness as a kind of justifiability: 'correctness implies justifiability. Therefore, in raising a claim to correctness, law also raises [a claim] to justifiability'.[8] In this way, the practice of justifying is made a necessary element of the law. Moreover, Alexy defines justification as the practice of backing up a statement with reasons, at least some of which will either be moral themselves or will otherwise bear a connection to morality.[9] Justifiability, then, relates correctness directly to justice and it, too, is a moral standard.[10]

In defending the connection between law and justice, the advocates of the different versions of the normative claim of law neither assume nor argue that such a connection necessarily obtains in fact. The connection between law and justice underlying the different theories of the normative claim of law is deployed at the level of mere assertion.[11] Yet even on this weaker reading, whereby the law only

---

[5] There is more on these theories in the chapters that follow, with a dedicated analysis of Raz's view in particular in chapter three.

[6] The argument establishing the connection between legitimate authority and justification is stated in Raz (1986a: 23–37).

[7] On the moral nature of justification and the right, see Raz (1984) and Raz (1986: 53–7).

[8] Alexy (1998b: 208); see also Alexy (1989b: 180).

[9] This point is stated most clearly and succinctly in Alexy (1989b: 180–2).

[10] On the relation between correctness and justice, see Alexy (1998b).

[11] The necessary connection between law and justice requires a specific argument in support of it, and not everyone who ascribes a normative claim to the law is prepared to put that argument forward. In fact, the connection tends to occasion much disagreement, especially between legal positivism and non-positivism, since it can stand only if moral values can be shown to form a necessary part of the law. Opposing theories of the nature of law cannot be expected to accept the necessary connection of law and justice as a matter of fact, but they *can* be expected (less demandingly) to accept it as an assertion, in the sense that the law necessarily *claims* such a connection. Indeed, a claim or assertion need not be true: it can simply be understood as a social fact involving our use of the language without thereby entailing a commitment to any moral view, and hence without entailing a connection between law and morality. This latter thesis (the connection thesis, establishing a conceptual connection between law and morality) forms the core of a view regarding the nature of law: it sets non-positivism (which subscribes to it) against legal positivism (which rejects it), and it does condition the more specific connection between law and justice, but not if this latter connection is claimed on the level of a mere

claims a necessary connection with justice without necessarily *obtaining* it, thus qualifying as law even if the connection fails to obtain, the normative claim of law cannot be understood as a minimal claim, not in any of its variants as found in contemporary legal theory.[12] The normative claim of law can aspire to any minimum only to the extent that it derives its content directly from the definition of normativity, that is, only to the extent that what shapes it is (not justice, but) plain normativity, namely, normativity unaccompanied by ideas elaborating on normativity by adding content to it, making it more specific than it would otherwise be, or by changing its scope. The ideas of justice, legitimate authority and moral correctness can each be *woven* into the concept of normativity, but none can be *equated* with it: they are not normativity per se but additions to it, serving not to *define* normativity but to expand its basic idea. Hence, it is the basic idea of normativity, its core meaning, that we must get at and stay close to if we want a genuinely minimal statement of the normative claim of law.

Plain normativity is such that the normative claim deriving from it cannot be further simplified or resolved into any more basic normative components. But how does one arrive at this elemental level? And how does one make it workable? We need a *concept* of normativity common to its manifold *conceptions* (these last consisting of the different ways in which the concept may be articulated or specified).[13] The concept will form the ground layer of normative meaning, a core set of theses and assumptions about what it means for something to be normative, theses and assumptions that make good sense from within any of the more content-rich conceptions of normativity, and that are not called into question by these conceptions, at least not for reasons inherent in the conceptions themselves. But we do not want this overlap or wide agreement to come too easily, with a concept of normativity so vague and general that it makes no practical difference to any of the specific conceptions whether or not they adopt it. In short, the concept of normativity should be sufficiently abstract to yield a core meaning of normativity common to all conceptions, but should not be so abstract as to deplete that core meaning of all substance and content, in effect making it meaningless. This requires a careful gauging of the abstraction that goes into the concept. Plain normativity should express an umbrella concept capable of encompassing different content-specifying theories of normativity and of the normative claim. The concept must therefore carry uncontroversial content only and so must be able to

---

assertion or proposition. A merely *asserted* connection between law and justice remains neutral to different, or even conflicting, views of the nature of law (including different or conflicting views of the conceptual connection between law and morality), so the assertion can equally be espoused or rejected by legal positivists and non-positivists, without their having accordingly to rewrite their concepts of law.

[12] To be sure, some contemporary legal theorists do present their statement of the normative claim of law as a minimal statement, and Soper (1996: 218–20) is one example, but that does not thereby *make* it minimal, as I propose to show.

[13] The distinction between 'concept' and 'conception' is one of abstraction: a concept is kept at a very basic level of abstraction; a conception, instead, is carried to a further level, moulting its abstraction as it picks up content, thereby becoming increasingly specific and situated. This is a distinction I am borrowing from Rawls (1999a: 6–10) and Dworkin (1986: 70–2).

embrace any of the richer theories—richer precisely because they work into their construction such theses and assumptions as may prove controversial. But, its umbrella coverage should also have enough substance in it to yield practical conclusions.[14]

Crucially, at the core of normativity we find a dimension that cannot altogether be reduced to the way we would understand a natural phenomenon; that is, we find a dimension that cannot be constructed as 'the immediate result of what lies *in* the world' (Delacroix 2004: 503). This core dimension or idea singles out a component of our experience extending beyond or outstripping the world as it is or as we perceive it to be.[15] This means that normativity sets itself up as an idea having the potential to question the given. As such, normativity gives rise to a tension in the existent, with a striving to shape the existent into something other than what it is. This lends to normativity a certain point of view: that of critique and judgement, describing the attitude of the reviewer and assessor of the reality sensed, experienced or comprehended, rather than the attitude of the explainer, describer, reproducer or reporter of that reality. In this sense, normativity can be said to delimit a sphere apart from that of actuality, a sphere pertaining not to reality such as we find it but to reality such as we ought to find it. So, at a general level of abstraction we can therefore think of normativity simply as 'ought',[16] which configures the 'ought' as 'the central normative concept' (Broome typescript: 8), such that at a very basic level the 'normative' can be understood as that which has 'to do with ought' (Broome typescript: 10). Normativity conceptually is, therefore, akin to a family of ideas that, for all their diversity and specificities, can all be said to share the characteristic of incorporating an 'ought': exemplary in this regard are the notions of model, paradigm, standard, guideline and rule.

The first point to note here is that understanding normativity in terms of 'ought' makes it different not only from 'what is' but also from 'what must be': the 'ought' gives expression to criteria and demands that we ponder over and reject, or that we need not take into account and act on; this in contrast to 'what must be', which in this description expresses a natural necessity, or unconditional requirement, that we cannot choose to disregard, for it is not subject to exception or discussion.

---

[14] While the *concept* of normativity is being developed here for general application (a concept unburdened by controversial content and assumptions, in such a way as to run the gamut of legal theory, in its every specification, or at least its main specifications), the rest of the book will instead be concerned with deriving from that concept a *conception* of normativity carrying the initial abstraction into one such level of specification. The outcome will be an account of the normative claim of law that, while it descends from a plain concept of normativity, will not be intended to have the same wide descriptive power as that concept and so will not necessarily have the same wide appeal.

[15] Cf Korsgaard (1996b: 1–5). The view being defended here—that normativity cannot be reduced to our experience of the world—should not be confused with the view that normativity resists explanation as a factual phenomenon or as a phenomenon supervening upon a certain constellation of hard facts. This latter view, that normativity cannot be reduced to fact, suggests a critique of reductionism; but this is not something that will be taken up in this section, for we are reasoning here at the *concept* level of abstraction, and reductionism should rather be understood as a *conception* of normativity. The relative discussion (in which I criticise reductionism) will therefore be deferred to chapter four.

[16] Dancy (2000: vii), for instance, describes it as 'the characteristic common to everything that appears on the "ought" side of the distinction between what is and what ought to be'.

As an 'ought', what is normative only *guides* us; that is, it does not properly force or compel us, as does 'what must be'. Normative statements therefore affect our judgement in a specific way, in that they can guide us only if we *accept* their guidance: like the 'must', 'ought'-statements need not necessarily *come* from us, but unlike the 'must', they do have to be *endorsed* by us—their status is determined by a *choice*. The point can otherwise be expressed in terms of 'willed normative statements', that is, statements 'whose status as such is not the product of our will even though they can act as guides only if we consent to and endorse them' (Dancy 2000: xv). Normativity unfolds in a context of willing and is yet not 'wholly within the scope of direct willing' (Railton 2000: 5): while agents play a role in their acceptance of normative standards, this does not mean that they can choose to disregard such standards whenever that seems convenient.

In what way, exactly, the questions of choice and endorsement come into play in the normative 'ought' is yet to be seen. Already, however, there begins to emerge here, in broad outline, the basic idea of normativity as a force that can point out something that ought to be other than it is. We know that this takes place in a fundamentally different way than with natural necessity, for whilst it is the point of normativity to say something about what ought to be done, this does not come in as the final word, as a statement independent of what we might think in regard to what is being prescribed. Yet, even with this important qualification, we are still looking at normativity in silhouette: we have described as a single block what is actually a manifold phenomenon. Let us try, therefore, to break this idea down a bit further and see what goes on inside. We can begin this analytical exercise by thinking of normativity as the result of two more primitive constituent elements forming a complementary pair, these being (1) directiveness and (2) justification.

(1) The notion of *directiveness* sits at the very core of normativity. The normative can direct action in two basic ways, the one by putting forward what I will call evaluative considerations and the other by appeal to deontic considerations.[17] On the one hand, normativity is what moulds behaviour by showing it to be good, valuable or attractive; on the other hand, normativity is what does so by showing it to be right, required or obligatory. Thus, the evaluative class covers the whole area of value, populated by the ideas of the good, the advisable, the recommendable, the appropriate, the sensible and the reasonable. The guiding force that these ideas exert upon us is that of attraction: something qualifies as normative in an evaluative sense if it directs us by the gravitational pull of a quality that we find inviting or appealing, this in such a way that any turning away from it would be tantamount to our acting unwisely or unreasonably, even thoughtlessly or foolishly. By contrast, the deontic class covers an area populated by the ideas of requirement, precept, duty, obligation and permission, among several others. The guiding force these ideas exert on us is a binding force or *vis directiva*, meaning that it drives action by virtue of its being not so much appealing as compulsory. At the

---

[17] For a narrower definition of normativity framed exclusively in terms of its deontic properties, without also taking into account its evaluative component, see Broome (typescript: 8).

core of deontic normativity, we find not what is prudent or advisable but what is binding or demanded of us; we find a demand, the rejection of which would render us not imprudent or injudicious, but blameful or even guilty.[18]

Having laid out this contrast between two forms of directiveness (the one exerted by invoking what is *valuable* for us, the other exerted by invoking what is instead *required* of us) we can now consider a further difference, one concerning not the different kinds of practical guidance but the ability of such guidance actually to make a difference in how people will behave. I will thus introduce at this point an idea of proffered (purported or potential) guidance in distinction to what might be called guidance actualised or realised. This further distinction cuts across the earlier one (between evaluative and deontic guidance), since both evaluative and deontic guidance can be actualised or fall short of this more demanding standard and exist as merely an unfulfilled capacity or tendency to guide.

In a basic sense, normativity merely singles out a *propensity* to govern behaviour, to wit, a potential for action-guidance, or an attitude that is predisposed to guiding conduct. Something is normative in this sense if it can be used for the purpose of guidance and can generally be regarded as a standard that can be used to shape our practical choices. On this view, what is normative is equated with what is *prescriptive*. The central normative idea is therefore that of *proffered guidance*, making normativity a realm delimited by a purport or a disposition to guide conduct. On a more ambitious interpretation, a prescriptive purport will not suffice to summarise the core of normativity, at least not within the context of law. As Andrei Marmor (2001: 25) puts it, 'the idea that law is a normative social practice suggests that law purports to give rise to reasons for action, and that at least some of these reasons are obligations.' Normativity, on this more ambitious interpretation, means that a certain standard becomes normative by virtue of its being *obligatory* rather than merely prescriptive. What is normative in law conclusively determines a course of conduct, as opposed to constituting one among several factors having a potential to make a difference in our practical choice-making. A conceptual connection is thus established between normativity and obligation: normativity is equated with obligatory force, understood as an ability to establish obligations that achieve actual compliance and compel action; thus, if a standard purports to direct behaviour without making such behaviour obligatory, it still cannot be counted as a normative standard. Far from merely *contributing* to practical guidance, what is normative weighs in decisively on the conduct to be performed; it acts as a factor strong enough or conclusive enough to shape our practical choice-making. So instead of making normativity *co-extensive* with prescription, this stronger view makes it a *subset* of what is prescriptive: not every prescriptive paradigm is also normative; only when prescriptive paradigms are binding do they carry normative force. The idea central to the normative realm—what distinguishes the normative

---

[18] The distinction between evaluative and deontic directiveness is loosely based on the distinction that Thomas Pink makes between the notion of 'recommendation' and that of 'demand', respectively, on which point cf Pink (2004).

from the non-normative—can therefore be described in this case as *guidance actualised*. The guidance of a normative standard is actualised when, instead of singling out an action as merely possible or preferable to any alternatives, it makes this action required and so non-optional.

It emerges from this treatment that normativity is not the monolith that its name might otherwise suggest. Even if we confine ourselves to the directive element conceptually associated with normativity, which is but one of the two basic elements of normativity (the other being justification) we find two alternative ideas: proffered guidance and guidance actualised. The question therefore arises as to which of the two ideas of guidance is essential to the directiveness of law and so figures in the very concept of normativity in law. Let us start from proffered guidance, understood as guidance carrying prescriptive force only, or as practical guidance that is merely offered. This is a primitive idea of guidance, and since normativity is itself a basic and abstract concept, we may be tempted to anchor the concept of the normativity of law to this ground level of guidance, thus equating the normativity of law with the prescriptivity of law. This would mean that a standard becomes normative in the law simply by virtue of its figuring among all the other standards that can provide practical guidance. This may strike us as an attractive proposal, but it commits us to the conclusion that a mere gesture at directing conduct is enough to make the law normative. The implication here is that a law or any legal framework can be considered normative even if, overall, it never succeeds in making a difference in the conduct of the people under its purview for the reason that its directives consistently fail to prevail over non-legal guidance and requirements. The problem here is that it is hard to bring this conclusion into line with the widespread understanding of the law as a practical endeavour. The law is primarily thought of as a device by means of which acts are channelled, and it owes a significant part of its justification to its ability effectively to shape, organise and order social relationships. A law that never succeeds in guiding the conduct that ought to be performed is largely condemned to practical insignificance. Accordingly, such a law could hardly be described as a component of a practical endeavour. In sum, most of the point of having the law seems lost if we define normative standards in terms of a mere disposition to govern action, thereby allowing for the possibility that these standards have no practical import. These remarks suggest that a mere purport to guide action does not suffice to define the concept of normativity in such a way as to make it expressly relevant to the law. An ability to prescribe conduct can *begin* to explain the normativity of law but cannot account for the whole of it.

The alternative idea, where seeking a role as an elemental part of normativity is concerned, is that of guidance actualised. What makes this a fitting choice intuitively is the affinity that guidance actualised bears to duty and obligation. If we consider the two main areas into which the normative is extended—the evaluative and the deontic—we find ourselves very much within the deontic sphere, and that places us fairly comfortably within the legal domain. Indeed, the law is traditionally understood as operating mainly not in the sphere of advisability but in that of requirement: this can safely be regarded as its 'home ground', and rights, duties and obligations as its 'stock in trade'. This in turn seems to warrant an understanding of the law as conceptually connected and primarily concerned with duty and obligation, suggesting that the normative question in law be framed exclusively as the question of what makes an action mandatory, or what it is that gives rise to an obligation we are bound to perform. This conclusion points strongly in the direction that in order for law to count as normative, it must show an inherent ability to determine conclusively the actions of those who fall within its purview, which is to say that normative legal statements become ipso facto effective at guiding action. But this standpoint is too narrow, for 'it ignores the way in which the punctual questioning of law's normative force may actually contribute to its renewed vigour' (Delacroix 2006: xiv). A paradigmatic example of such questioning is civil disobedience. If we interpret normativity as guidance actualised, civil disobedience cannot be distinguished from ordinary law-breaking, since in both cases the law has been violated, and nothing else counts toward a judgement of the normativity of law: anytime anyone carries out an act of disobedience or breaks the law, there the law has ceased to be normative because it has failed to obligate materially and guide conduct. A view of this kind, whereby what it means for something to be normative is reduced to a single criterion, namely, the power to bind and coerce, cannot accommodate the contribution that civil disobedience makes to specifying and fine-tuning the normative dimension of the law, namely, by making legal requirements cohere with extra-legal directives. The normativity of law as we know and recognise it through the actual functioning of legal institutions is far more manifold, producing as it does a wide range of legal situations and effects. So it is a distortion to equate the normativity of law with the activity of setting out obligations, or with the power thereto, or with monitoring whether these obligations are invariably complied with, or actualised.

It seems, then, that neither proffered guidance nor guidance actualised can serve as the sole criterion of the normativity of law, the former being too weak and the latter too strong and demanding. In combination, however, they do point the way; that is, by their failure they highlight how the normativity of law might more accurately be framed. More specifically, they illustrate that the concept of the normativity of law occupies an intermediate position between bare prescriptive force and full obligatory force. This is to say that something will count as normative in a sense relevant to the law if it does more than merely purport to guide action, while at the same time stopping short of setting forth an obligation that its addressees cannot choose but to comply with under any circumstances whatever. Normative force in law might thus be described as something carrying a reinforced prescriptive force or, from the opposite angle, a weakened or pliant obligatory force, a force whose power to bind and compel action is real yet neither absolute nor unappealable.

In summary, we have thus far considered guidance on a sort of graduated scale, from proffered to actualised, as if all that mattered in law were its ability to exert some degree of influence on behaviour. Now, however, we need a more powerful tool, a language more effective at moulding the whole idea of guidance and bringing out its different forms. This is the language of reasons, which is more flexible than what has thus far been taken into account. But before this language can be used, the specific connection needs to be further worked out and established between normativity and reasons, which in turn makes it necessary to focus on the other basic component of normativity, namely, justification.

(2) To see how *justification* turns out to be a necessary component of normativity, figuring into the very concept of normativity, we need to backtrack a bit and work from the idea of normativity itself as introduced earlier, namely, normativity as an 'ought' exhibiting an action-guiding force. It was observed that normativity exerts this force by pointing out a possibility, that is, by showing how the 'is' (what is given) might be different from what it actually is, thereby putting the situation at hand into perspective and introducing a tension into it that accounts for our disposition and ability to shape what exists into forms other than those in which it is presently found. This tension is at the origin of the justificatory component of normativity. That is, if normativity is to make good on its promise of imparting some sense of direction to a situation and delimiting a realm differing from the reality of the situation at hand, then normativity must be accompanied by some kind of ideal, principle or standard—a criterion in light of which to judge or evaluate what exists—that is, indeed, embedded in it. That critical stance which the normative introduces begins to convey the sense in which normativity implies a justificatory element: it does so by virtue of its special calling, which is to urge or at least to suggest a certain course of conduct without thereby *forcing* behaviour in any brute way. Whence the fundamental role of justification: justification is what make it possible to guide action without simply saying that this is what you must do; it is what marks off the normative 'ought' from the unconditional 'must' previously considered, which admits of no discussion and simply calls for and demands compliance.

This conclusion—that there is a justificatory component in the very concept of normativity—is of the utmost importance. For, if the critical stance of normativity makes normativity amenable to justification, then a space is opened up for deliberation. Stated otherwise, if normativity incorporates a critical element laden with value, and so an element calling for justification, then normativity becomes permeable to reasoning, thereby delimiting an ambit of human experience and understanding that coincides with the dialectical space of discourse. This connection between normativity and deliberation, or reasoning, can be further specified by turning to Ralph Wedgwood's analysis of the meaning of 'ought' in practical context. Wedgwood's analysis of the 'ought' proceeds on a method known as conceptual role semantics, by which the meaning of a word is determined by its conceptual role as framed by the rules governing the use of the word by a competent speaker.[19] As far as 'ought' in the practical sphere is concerned, this role is expressed by the rule stating that the practical 'ought' commits us to acting on its

---

[19] This method comes in many varieties. Wedgwood offers an overview of his own version in Wedgwood (2006: 128–30).

own prescription, on the content of the proposition embedded in the 'ought' sentence itself, in such a way as to make this content part of our plan about what to do. This is reasoning in a specifically practical way, aimed at assessing what ought to go into my plan about what to do (as well as what ought to remain outside this plan), and then acting consistently with that determination. The conceptual connection exhibited here, whereby reasoning about plans of conduct plays a defining role in giving the meaning of the practical 'ought', can be extended to other kinds of 'ought'. Wedgwood lists the 'political ought', the 'purpose-relative ought', the 'information-relative ought' and the 'epistemic ought'.[20] None of these will be taken up here, but the important thing to note is that their respective meanings can be analysed in connection with their respective roles in different kinds of reasoning and deliberation, all of them involving an assessment made against a larger background consisting of a body of information relevant to the kind of 'ought' in question. So there is a general conceptual connection between 'ought' and reasoning that can be specified in different ways between different kinds of ought and different forms of reasoning. Hence the conceptual connection between normativity and practical reasoning: whatever 'ought' is considered, it will derive its meaning from some form of reasoning, practical, political, purpose-relative, and so forth, which can be shaped in any number of ways according to the kind of guidance in question and the sort of problem this guidance is meant to solve.

The connection established between normativity as 'ought' and reasoning at large makes it possible to cast the concept of normativity in the language of reasons, since reasons are the basic units of reasoning. Reasoning has us assessing and weighing reasons for and against proposed alternative states of affairs, as well as reasons for and against alternative courses or modes of action, all this against the background of what we believe to be true about the world. Hence, deliberation about what to do involves assessing reasons for and against a proposed activity as such, primarily with an eye to its worth.[21]

Introducing the notion of reason has the advantage of preserving the uniformity of reasoning and decision-making, by showing there to be, at bottom, a single activity that can be taken up by going in either of two directions, that of the good and advisable or that of the right and obligation. This approach, which uses reasons and reason-giving as the basis on which normativity is explained, can be found in Raz, among others, for whom such an undertaking—explaining normativity—requires that we make recourse to an explanation of 'what it is to be a reason, and of related puzzles about reasons', thus establishing a basic connection between 'ought' and so normativity on the one hand, and reasons on the other.[22] Raz finds himself in a good company here, with several contemporary philoso-

---

[20] See Wedgwood (2006: 153–9).

[21] In any such process, the reasons assessed and brought into comparison may lie on the same level or on different levels of practical reasoning: in the former case, the assessment is said to involve direct comparison and in the latter case, indirect comparison, as when weighing first-order against second-order reasons.

[22] Raz (1999: 67). The overall approach is introduced in Raz (1999: 67–75).

phers ready to endorse the view that to address normativity is to address reasons, for presenting a standard as normative presupposes an argument showing that the conduct required by the standard is a conduct that ought to be performed, and any argument of this sort is going to involve a showing, at some point, to the effect that that conduct is governed by reasons.[23] From this reason-centred perspective, normativity in law is an instance of what makes something compulsory by requiring or demanding something of us, and nothing can be required or demanded unless there is a reason for it. So we can see here a clear connection that normativity in law establishes with reasons, for if normativity in law is not entirely independent of justification, and justification ultimately does not stand apart from reasons, then we have a view of normativity in law as related to reasons, and in fact as responsive to them. But this is not enough to render a demand normative, for the reason involved cannot be just *any* reason, anything lending support to what is demanded, but rather a reason *of a special kind*, a highly exacting reason that is susceptible to support the force of duty and obligation and their emergence.[24] Hence, the normativity of law can be understood as a dimension delimited and characterised by reasons of a special sort: reinforced or entrenched reasons for action protected from some of the potentially outweighing factors. What it means for a normative standard to require someone to do something is that there is in this standard a special reason, a reason carrying extra weight and strength with respect to countervailing reasons, or enjoying a certain insulation from them.[25]

Here is what can be extracted from the foregoing discussion. Under the minimal normative claim, the law contends that it can (a) guide conduct (it can get us to act in certain ways in certain circumstances), and (b) do so by bringing to bear justificatory reasons for action of a special kind, or practical reasons endowed with extra force. Subjects, institutions and statements making the normative claim are

[23] Now, while this connection between normativity, ought, and reasons is widely recognised as indisputable, its articulation into a full conception does present something of a philosophical conundrum, with a debate as to whether or not the ought should be constructed as an elemental component—one that, in articulation with other concepts, plays the larger part in explaining normativity. Broome (typescript: 48–76), for example, treats the ought as fundamental. But this debate does not immediately concern us here: what matters for our purposes is rather that both sides recognise normativity and reasons as connected, in one way or another, and that neither rejects the view of normativity as responsiveness to reasons.

[24] On the connection between obligation and reasons, see Pink (2004).

[25] The reader will have noticed that reasons have not yet been defined here, other than by pointing out their role in guiding action and in justifying such guidance. This has to do with the method adopted: we are still working on a level of abstraction in which we are seeking to account for normativity as such, framing a *concept* of normativity capable of embracing normativity in its many conceptions, and the moment we specify what a reason is (in practical discourse), we will have stated not a concept but a conception. In fact, depending on how a reason is defined (morally, as pertaining to the good and the right; naturalistically, by reference to natural properties; or procedurally, as a convention, that is, as the outcome of a discussion based on criteria that participants agree to, and, indeed, however a reason is defined, that definition will be reflected in a corresponding *conception* of normativity as responsiveness to reasons, a conception now moral, now naturalistic, now conventional, as the case may be. So we cannot yet have a statement of what a reason is, because we have yet to transit from concept to conception in normativity, and because we want the concept to be malleable enough that it can cover, and be fashioned into, the widest possible range of conceptions.

thus subjects, institutions and statements that purport to influence conduct by introducing (some special kind of) reasons for action. This claim derives directly from the concept of normativity, understood as responsiveness to reasons offered under a general scheme seeking to establish obligations. We can see these two elements (namely, offering reasons aimed at giving rise to corresponding obligations) reflected in a twofold articulation of the claim. Indeed, the capacity that the law is claiming under the minimal normative claim really amounts to two capacities: both are *directive*, to be sure, rather than descriptive, but one is aimed at moulding *action* and the other refers to practical *reasoning*. Action in normative legal settings is guided by seizing on the reasons one may have for action, and practical reasoning is correspondingly affected (or at least engaged in) through the activity of offering reasons why certain obligations should stand. Under the normative claim, therefore, the law claims a directive capacity to hold us duty-bound to act or refrain from acting in certain ways given certain conditions for certain reasons. All the statements in which the minimal normative claim of law has just been expressed can all be understood as equivalent; thus, any of them can be taken to constitute the standard form of that claim, which from here on out will simply be referred to as the 'normative claim' of law.

THE METAPHYSICAL QUESTION

As was mentioned above, the metaphysical question involves two tasks. The first of these consists in determining whether the normative claim as just specified is possible (whether the law *can* make that claim in the first place), and the second is whether that possibility is actually a necessity (in contradistinction to being an option of the law, a matter of choosing to make the claim or not). I will argue that the normative claim is both possible and necessary, appealing to the idea that the law has the ability to make claims, and that making the specifically normative claim is essential to the law; that is to say, it is a claim failing to make which the law would no longer be such.

The question as to the possibility of the normative claim of law is a special case of the question about the capacities that can be attributed to social institutions at large. The law can be understood in this sense as a social institution made up of different practices; so the problem will be to figure out whether it makes sense, with respect to each of those practices, to understand it as an inherent source of claims. The point, at this early stage, is not yet to state *how* exactly such claims are specified or *what* contents they take, but rather to assay the generic ability of the law to make any claim at all, of whatever nature. In fact, any such example of the law making a claim will show that there is no reason *in principle* why the law cannot make claims generally, and we will have then cleared the way, conceptually, for an argument showing how the law can make, specifically, the *normative* claim. Conversely, any argument purporting to show the impossibility of the law making a claim *generally* will thereby purport to show the impossibility of its making the normative claim *specifically*, thereby frustrating from the very start the effort to explain how the law might make a normative claim.

Having established the ability of the law to advance claims in general, as a matter of principle (or having otherwise rebutted the argument purporting to show this to be a general impossibility), we will then be able to key in on the normative claim specifically and see whether that claim is possible. At this point we will be ready to consider whether such a normative capacity is something the law can *choose* to exercise (the capacity is contingent) or whether the law *must* so proceed, to the effect that any failure consistently to do so would mean that the practice in question is not really law but some practice or institution *other* than law (the capacity is inherently connected with the law and is in this sense necessary).

The claim-making capacity of the law is something I take up below, showing this to be an actual rather than a fictitious capacity; its normative capacity I then take up immediately thereafter, in the following section, where I will adduce an argument showing this capacity to be a necessary component of the law.

Can the Law Make Any Claims at All?

As I mentioned in the Introduction, the law can be taken to refer to a single legal provision or to the legal system as a whole, and this distinction matters since the thesis that the law makes claims changes according to whether we are referring to a legal provision singly considered or to the system as a whole. In the former case, the thesis will be essentially propositional, meaning by this that it will be predicated of a linguistic entity (this being the legal provision in question), arguing that some claim is conveyed by a certain legal statement. Not so if the law designates the legal system as a whole, because in this case we will have to take into account a whole lot more than merely provisions. In fact, in this wider sense the law operates as a concretisation of different kinds of elements, which include not only the legal provisions but also the whole machinery that supports them, consisting of people, institutions and procedures; that is to say, people acting in any official capacity (as law-makers, law enforcers, judges, and the like) or otherwise carrying out a function entrusted to them under the law; institutions exercising a legislative, judicial, executive, administrative or regulatory power; and finally procedures, to wit, the formal processes by which officials and institutions design, enact and apply legal provisions.[26] Thus, when the law is said to advance a claim as a *system*, the thesis being argued is that this claim results from the way the different parts and constituents of the system come together and interact. There are different forces

---

[26] The items just mentioned do not make up an exhaustive list of the elements that might go into and define a legal system. In fact, whether or not an item gets on the list as a defining element of a legal system will depend on the legal theory one proceeds on, and that should give a measure of just how theory-dependent the idea of a legal system is. So any list is bound to be partial, depending on the theory in the light of which it is being considered, but it suffices here to observe that a legal system is made up of heterogeneous elements, not all of which can be regarded as presenting a linguistic nature.

at play—officials, norms, institutions and procedures—and the claim results from the combination of such forces. It is equally important here that not all of the constituents of the system are purely linguistic entities. A link is, therefore, being established between claim-making and a complex consisting of both linguistic and non-linguistic entities. A study of this sort, in which both kinds of entities are taken into account, brings up different issues than those involved when dealing with linguistic entities alone. For this reason, any account of the claim-making capacity associated with the law that seeks to be exhaustive should have to treat this as a twofold question, discussing this capacity with respect to both single legal provisions and the legal system as a whole. At the same time, however, it is the claims of the legal system as a whole (rather than those of its single provisions) that this discussion will be mostly concerned with: this is in keeping with the current debate, in which greater theoretical importance is accorded to the claims made by the law understood as a system. The discussion that follows will therefore keep this focus front and centre to the effect that the (normative) claim of legal systems and their normativity, rather than the (normative) claim of individual legal provisions and their normativity, will be the privileged subject matter of the rest of the book.

The answer to questions about whether the law can make claims, normative or otherwise, relies heavily on one's conception of which elements are entitled to make claims. In a strict sense, a claim-making capacity can be attributed only to people, that is, only to intentional agents, to 'subjects having the capacity to speak and act' (Alexy 1999a: 24), and not also to provisions, institutions, practices or procedures. These cannot properly be described as intentional, and without intention (a capacity properly ascribable only to individual agents) there can be no claim-making either. At first blush, then, it seems that neither legal provisions nor legal systems can make claims, in that neither can properly be understood as subjects of intention. Legal provisions are statements of the law having certain meaning contents, and neither statements nor meaning contents have intentions. Legal systems, for their part, face at least two related difficulties as subjects of intention. For one thing, they are compound and contain unlike constituents, only a few of which (namely, people acting in an official capacity under the law) can be described as subjects of intentional action. So the system as a whole cannot make a claim, even if there are people in it who can. For another thing, even if we were to consider the system as made up of people and nothing else besides, we would still have to explain the intentionality of a collective subject: certainly an individual can act intentionally, but can a collective body do so as well? The argument will at least have to answer the charge of committing the anthropomorphic fallacy of attributing human capacities to non-human entities.

Some legal scholars who have thought about this problem do in fact maintain that a connection has to obtain between claim-making and intention in law, but they tone this down by questioning whether the connection has to be a *direct* one: the law can be understood to make claims simply by virtue of the people issuing legal provisions or acting on behalf of legal systems; the law makes claims not through its written form but through those who take part in the processes by which laws are made, applied and enforced, in such a way that the claim-making capacity rests ultimately with the officials, with those who 'represent', 'speak for' or 'act on behalf of' the legal system.[27] This can be understood as a *subjectivist* reading of the thesis asserting the claim-making capacity of the law, for it equates the claims of law with those of some *subjects*, namely, officials and especially law-makers, rather than seeing these claims as inherent in the statements, acts, institutions, practices and procedures of law (in which case we would instead have an *objectivist* view, as here the claims are attached not to given subjects but rather to certain legal objects). The subjectivist view has been stated in more general terms by Soper (1996: 218), for whom something qualifies as a claim of law if it originates with an official or if it can otherwise be said to accompany an official's act, that is, if it ought to be regarded that way by 'any sensible individual, putting him- or herself in the position of a representative of the legal system—e.g. the officials who are responsible for the creation and implementation of the system's directives'.[28]

The subjectivist solution is strong on intuitive appeal, for it is able to account for the claim-making capacity of the law without discounting or even loosening the intuitive link found to exist between claim-making and intention. Everything seems to fall into place in the view that certain human agents make claims intentionally and that, under certain circumstances, these claims can be extended to the institutions on whose behalf the same agents are entitled to speak and act. But the intuitive appeal of this subjectivist account is also what invites attention to its weakness. A major problem in particular arises and suggests that the subjective element may be too controlling. The problem is how to account for the 'staying power' of the law if we are attributing this power to the intentions of those who participate in the legal practice.[29] If the subjectivist account explains the claim-making capacity of the law as derivative, as residing and inhering in the first instance in the people who accompany the law in the making and unfolding of it, we have to ask how the claims these people make or the acts they perform in an official capacity transfer or connect to the provisions, acts, institutions, practices and procedures of which the law is made up. In other words, the subjectivist account constructs the claim-making capacity of the law, and hence the content, scope and quality of

---

[27] This idea is especially associated with Alexy (1998b: 206), where the view is defended that 'law raises [the] claim [to correctness] through persons who work for and in it'.

[28] A similar view has been expressed by Mark Murphy, who lays out his argument as follows: on the one hand, the law cannot paradigmatically be considered a speaker, since 'for an entity to be a speaker, it must be susceptible of a certain range of belief and desire-states; it must be susceptible of a certain range of normative standings; it must be capable of producing a certain range of events', and none of these features can properly describe the law, for that would require a basic condition the law fails to satisfy, namely, a mind capable of belief and desire. But at the same time, even though the law cannot *itself* achieve goals, it can do so through 'the motivational systems of real, live, paradigmatic desirers' (Murphy 2006: 38), these being the operative agents of law, such as officials and citizens taking the internal point of view. So the cognitive and volitional states that cannot be ascribed *directly* to the law are instantiated through real people who, as agents of the law, 'lend' their own states to it, which therefore acquires those states by extension, an extension by virtue of which the law can be treated as a speaker in more than a metaphorical way.

[29] Cf Heidemann (2005: 128–31).

the claims of law, as revolving around the central unifying element of intention, consisting in the claim-maker's intention at the time the relevant legal statement was issued, or otherwise in the claim-maker's issuance of the relevant legal procedure. But this element (intention), however undeniable, tends, if overstressed, to turn the whole legal enterprise into a subjective affair: the objective, material existence and force of the law will seem less certain and reliable and, if we insist too much on viewing it as the expression of what officials think, do and claim, it might even turn psychological.[30]

The subjectivist account of the claim-making capacity of the law falls short in another respect, too; namely, even if it does explain this capacity with regard to single legal norms, it cannot adequately do so with regard to the legal system as a whole. As Heidemann points out in criticising Alexy's theory of the claim to correctness made by the law, it is far from clear who exactly is entitled to speak for an entire system of law and to make corresponding claims on behalf of this system. For, 'there seems to be no member of the legal staff whose acts could be regarded as representative of the legal order as a whole' (Heidemann 2005: 131). No single official can conceivably be empowered to make claims reaching beyond the scope of the activity which she carries out or is otherwise responsible for. Since the legal system extends far beyond that reach, it cannot possibly be construed as the product, issue or outgrowth of anything a single intentional subject does or claims. So nobody can be singled out as the person capable of or empowered to make claims for the legal system as a whole. Because the subjectivist account forces a reduction of precisely this sort, it looks like we must rest content, where the subjectivist approach is concerned, with explaining the claim-making capacity of single legal provisions but not of the entire system. This, however, falls short of expectations, especially in the context of a study concerning the normative claim of law, for the thesis that the law makes the normative claim would lose much of its interest if it could not be understood as a system-wide claim. That this is so can be appreciated from the way the main theories supporting the capacity of the law to make the normative claim present the argument, namely, they understand this capacity, and the argument for it, as pertaining to the whole system of law rather than to single legal provisions.[31] True, a legal system can be regarded as asserting a claim through its components, if enough of these components (or those understood to play a prominent role in the system) can be shown to assert such a claim.[32] But this

---

[30] It is arguably with a view to avoiding these difficulties that Alexy (2007: 334) has drawn a distinction between the personal and the objective claims of officials, the former being based on personal wishes or decisions and the latter being independent of such wishes, for in this latter case the claims are necessary to serve in a given role as a representative of the legal system: they are claims that 'everyone who performs an act-in-law or submits a legal argument necessarily has to raise'. Alexy explains that only in this latter case are the claims relevant to law in a discussion about the claim-making of the law. But notice that even an objective claim so construed belongs to a subjectivist view as here defined; that is, in either case, whether the claims are personal or objective, they are ascribed not to any objective elements of the law itself but to the people who use the law or manage it in an official capacity.

[31] This is clearly the case with Raz's authority thesis (Raz 1994: 199) and Soper's claim-to-justice argument (Soper 1996: 216).

[32] One theorist who can be interpreted as using this strategy is Alexy (2000b: 142).

extension would come at the cost of making the claim of law unreal.[33] In sum, the subjectivist solution may initially appeal to our intuitive understanding of what claim-making implies, but then stretches that solution to the point where it requires figurative language in order to hold up; and that seems especially weak when we move on to consider the legal system as a whole. MacCormick (2007b: 59), on this basis, concludes that the law should be considered a claim-making subject in neither a literal nor a metaphorical sense: 'to say law claims anything, meaning this literally, is a category mistake', because there is no entity 'law' capable of making claims; and to say law metaphorically does so is 'unhelpful', since there are clearer ways to express the same idea without suggesting any attempt to cover up the 'hidden implications about the character of law' that instead 'lurk in the metaphor'.

These shortcomings suggest that the subjectivist account is perhaps too stringent, for in making intention necessary to the claim-making of the law—an element without which no claim could properly be said to be made by the law—the account paradoxically forces us to resort to figurative language as a device by which to make full sense of the claim-making capacity of the law. So, in order to get out of this bind and explain without metaphor what it means for the law to make claims, I introduce a distinction between two senses in which claims are made: a performative sense and an attributive sense. In a performative sense, claims are made, namely, performed by an intentional subject and will accordingly be called performative claims.[34] Claims are performative in this sense as linguistic acts, that is, as acts broadly understood as anything *done* or *performed* through the use of words. A performative claim becomes a claim by virtue of its coming through as an act performed, or even an act performed intentionally with a purpose. This emphasis on the doing and performing involved in making a claim indicates that, as just mentioned, this is the work of *intentional agents*. Only an intentional agent can make a claim in the performative sense, since only an intentional agent can carry out an act and can do so intentionally. This is very much consistent with the subjectivist account thus far considered; therefore, for a different account we turn to the attributive sense of claim-making, producing claims that will accordingly be called *attributive* claims. What it means for a claim to be made attributively is not that someone is actually performing the claim, or that the claim would not exist but for this claim-making person, but that a situation exists that *calls for* such a claim: there is a state of affairs whose objective properties give rise to a claim that is ascribed to, or associated with, the situation in light of the basic conventions underlying our modes of life and thought. An example of a situation carrying with it such an attributive claim might be a state of extreme hardship brought about by forces other than human, as happened in the Ica and Pisco regions of Peru, struck by a devastating earthquake in August 2007. Situations like this are universally regarded as coming into existence with a claim attached to

---

[33] Heidemann (2005: 131) describes the extension as 'double figure of speech'.
[34] On this understanding of claims and claim-making, see Himma (2001: 275–83).

them: in this case, a call for help from other Peruvian municipalities as well as from the central government of Peru and the international community. To be sure, any disaster of such a scale is inevitably or at least very likely going to bring in its wake real claims performed by real people, the ones most affected. But the point is that alongside these people-specific claims (which might be called performative, in the sense of their being acts performed by intentional subjects) there will exist claims thought to be independent of any claim-making person and to have their source instead in the situation itself owing to its objective properties. Instead of being collapsed into the subjective claims of real people, these independent objective claims are regarded as inherent in the situation, or as arising in union with it, and thereby are attributed to it even though the situation (understood as a constellation of facts) could not by any stretch of the imagination be considered an intentional claim-maker. Attributive claims can thus be described as impersonal in the sense that they come about or are ascribed to a situation regardless of whether any claim has actually been performed by some person, and in the sense that they do so independently of any claim-maker's beliefs and intentions:[35] it is not these mental states that determine the emergence and ascription of an attributive claim, but the objective features of the situation to which such a claim is ascribed, a situation that, in combination with certain background assumptions explaining how we come to view all situations of the same kind as carrying the same claim, is capable of invoking the relevant claim.[36]

So the distinction being set up here gives us intentional agents, on the one hand, and non-intentional entities, on the other: the former are people engaged in the activity of making claims in the usual sense of making requests or calls for action based on whatever grounds; the latter are typically states of affairs out of which certain standard claims necessarily arise or to which such claims are necessarily attributed on the basis of criteria forming part of a foundational practice or set of assumptions. This distinction, between personal performative claims and impersonal attributive ones, makes it possible to appreciate that the *making* of a claim need not be understood in a strictly performative sense, in which subjects, capable of having the cognitive and volitional states necessary to *believe* that a request

---

[35] This last consideration makes it possible to appreciate the mutual independence of the two claims, the subjective one asserted by an intentional agent and the objective one attributed to the situation. This is to say that an objective claim can arise even if no subjective claim is ever made by anyone having a direct interest in the same situation, as indeed was the case with the Peruvian earthquake, in the wake of which the Peruvian president decided to make no appeal to the international community.

[36] As that general 'we' suggests, an attributive claim is impersonal not in the sense that no one is involved in giving rise to the claim, but in the sense that no specific agent *need be* involved, and that the mental states of any of the people actually involved are irrelevant to determining the claim. Hence, even though an attribution *is* made, with people ascribing claims to states of affairs, the scope and content of the claims so ascribed is not defined by any of those people's intentions, just as the same people cannot be considered the *sources* or *makers* of the relative claims. What brings about and defines an attributive claim is instead a combination of objective forces, these being the state of affairs (the one to which the claim is attributed) as assessed in light of the foundational practices guiding us as to what to make of that same state of affairs. The claim so attributed is thus very much constrained, since its ascription and content are guided by objective and public criteria rather than by anyone's personal choices.

should be made and to *want* it made, proceed to *carry out* the act of making it. Indeed, claims can be made in a non-performative sense, too, in which case no specific intention is required (nor any entities having any of the defining traits of intentional subjects, nor any intentional subject actually performing a claim on anyone's behalf) but only a state of affairs to which claims are attributed on the basis of the conventions framing our forms of life, thus making it so that certain states of affairs come to be understood in certain ways and so become associated with certain claims.

This connects to the thesis that the law can make claims, and most importantly can make the normative claim. This thesis need not be taken to mean that the law makes its claims through the people responsible for its operation, for it can be framed instead as the thesis that certain claims can be *attributed to*, or *associated with*, the law just as they are attributed to other states of affairs, whether natural or conventional. The law can therefore be described as a source not of personal performative claims but of impersonal attributive ones, thus making it possible to present the claim-making of the law as an activity in a literal sense. Otherwise stated: instead of viewing the law as an intentional claim-maker, that is, a maker of performative claims (a description that could only hold in the figurative language of metaphor), we can view the law as a source of impersonal claims, as something to which claims are attributed, and in a literal sense at that, in much the same way as other states of affairs become sources of non-performative attributive claims, except that the state of affairs in this case happens to be institutional. The law can thus be said to make claims in a literal way, without recourse to metaphor, and without our having to reduce the legal system to a community of officials understood as intentional agents making performative claims on behalf of the law.

This forms the basis for arguing that claims can ultimately be ascribed to, or made to inhere in, the law itself—in its constituent objective components—rather than in the officials acting on behalf of the law. The capacity of the law to make the normative claim is owed to the capacity of the law, *qua* state of affairs, to be ascribed to, or associated with, claims. The corresponding thesis can therefore be recast in terms of states of affairs and attributive claims; that is, the capacity of the law to make claims is, or rests on, the capacity to attribute claims to a legal state of affairs. This view has the advantage of making it possible to interpret the claims of law in a way that does not have us probing into the minds and intentions of the subjects making claims on behalf of the law. We can avoid the mentalism involved in determining what was going on in an official's head as she was making this or that claim, or enacting this or that statute, and hence can avoid the subjectivity that that effort tends to promote. Thus, this approach can secure objectivity in law, at least to the extent that legal states of affairs are acknowledged not to be private affairs. What makes this effort and its determinations objective is their publicity, in that states of affairs are there for *all* of us to see, understand and interpret, and not just for the officials to experience while making claims on behalf of the law: when the claims of law are attributed to some legal state of affairs, there will be an undertaking in which everyone can participate, for it is based on evidence that is open and public, such evidence consisting in the objective traits displayed by states of affairs.

The argument so far has been that claims need not come from an *intentional claim-maker*, and can therefore be made in an *attributive sense*, with claims associated with *states of affairs*. The argument extends to the law and claim-making in law by way of the objective elements of the law whose form makes it possible for them to make claims in an attributive sense. But now the question arises as to whether this extension to the objective elements of the law, considered individually, also holds when these elements are considered in the aggregate, that is, when the legal system is considered as a whole. The question can be restated thus. Although my treatment of claim-making shows that the law can make claims through its objective features and constituents, it does not yet show that these constituents give rise to any unitary claim, or to one single claim constructed out of the claims made through the different constituents of the law. A critic could therefore reply at this point: I accept that tokens of the law can make claims in a non-figurative sense when these tokens are understood as so many separate states of affairs, but can legal *systems* make the same claim? By contrast to single legal tokens as states of affairs, legal systems are states of affairs in quite a different way, for they are composed of heterogeneous elements (subjects, provisions, acts, practices and procedures) and it is doubtful that any aggregated or unitary claim can be ascribed to such congeries. In fact, the lack of unity in this heterogeneous compound, the legal system, is such that no claims can be attributed to the system as a whole, at least not in the way they can be attributed to its single constituents. The objection is relevant to this discussion, for the normative claim of law is being presented here as a *unitary* claim; it is therefore essential to show that the law, in addition to making claims in a non-metaphorical sense, can make these claims unitary despite its heterogeneous composition.

Doubts about unitary claims made by the legal systems have been expressed by Himma (2001: 278), who argues that 'to the extent that a legal system constitutes a unified institution', its functioning will be that of a *set* within which different elements operate and interact. But 'a set is a non-propositional abstract object', and no claim can be made by non-propositional objects if these contain heterogeneous elements that resist aggregation, as will be the case with legal systems. A legal system comprises elements of different kinds and so cannot, *qua* system, be considered a claim-maker. More to the point, Himma argues that the different elements of a legal system (officials, directives, acts, practices, procedures) can make claims in either a performative or an expressive sense, and the difference between these two kinds of claims is such as to prevent aggregation or compounding.[37] The reason

---

[37] This distinction should not be confused with the distinction (introduced above) between performative and attributive claims. While claims made in a performative sense are understood as 'linguistic acts' (Himma 2001: 278) in much the same way as they are here, claims made in an expressive sense cannot be compared to my attributive claims. Himma explains that claims become expressive not by virtue of their functioning as acts performed, or even as acts performed intentionally with a purpose, but by virtue of their conveying meaning and content. A claim understood in an expressive sense is a claim that can be attributed to *any* bearer of meaning, such as statements. Statements cannot *perform*

why we should want to aggregate or compound different kinds of claims is to attribute them to the system as a whole, as a single or unified source of claims, and, by definition, that would require treating these claims as a whole, as a single voice. Yet this is precisely the problem, for the required compounding can be achieved only between elements of the *same* kind and not between qualitatively different elements, that is, between claim-makers that can make claim only in a *performative* sense and linguistic entities (or language capable of expressing the meaning encapsulated in the claims of law) that can make claim only in an *expressive* sense. This heterogeneous character of the constituents of a legal system prevents one from constructing system-wide claims. Himma's argument, in other words, is that the mixed nature of legal systems precludes any all-embracing aggregation, summing up, or compounding of its claims, and this in turn implies a conceptual impossibility of making the system as such a source of claims. So, even on Himma's expressive interpretation, the legal system cannot be said to have as such a normative claim-making capacity. The thesis that the law makes certain claim has no grounding in fact. It is therefore false, or at best fictional, and it can only be maintained figuratively.

In arguing that legal systems cannot make claims—that their claim-making is at best a fiction—Himma acknowledges that this hardly poses a problem for lawyers, judges and legal practitioners, considering that these people make use of legal fictions as a matter of course and regard them as essential to the functioning of law. Thus, it is quite unlikely that this vast audience—those versed in the practical workings of the law, and indeed all those who rely on the operation of the law as users and consumers of the law—will find much point in the argument that legal systems can make claims only figuratively, or through a reliance on fictions. From which it follows that the force of Himma's argument is theoretical rather than practical. As a theoretical argument, however, it is worth taking up, for it reveals a basic misconception about the kind of 'oneness', or unitary character, required for a legal system to make claims.

---

anything (cannot perform linguistic acts) but clearly they are the medium for *expressing* meaning and content as that relates to the law, and so they can quite naturally express the meaning and content of a *claim*. It follows that all the components of the law capable of bearing meaning can thereby make claims in an expressive sense. This is a semantic understanding of claims, and it stands in contrast to the understanding of them found in my construction, which is pragmatic. On a semantic approach, the focus falls on meaning and content: on what gets expressed, regardless of *how* it gets expressed, and in such a way that any content (however conveyed) can be a claim by virtue of its meaning alone. Not so, on a pragmatic approach. Here we consider meaning *along with* its mode of expression, and we say that whether the meaning content expressed in a statement becomes a claim depends on whether the statement endows that content with the illocutionary force distinctive to claim-making. Indeed, the same meaning content (say, 'shutting doors') can be made into almost anything (into any linguistic act) depending on the illocutionary force it is given: it can be made into a command ('Shut the door!'), an assertion ('The door is shut'), a request ('Would you shut the door, please?'), a hope ('I wish the door were shut'), and so on. My construction, therefore, takes into account not one but two levels of discourse (a semantic one and pragmatic one) and so views expressive claims as something of a conceptual impossibility, since the only way an expressive claim can come about is if the pragmatic level is absorbed into the semantic one. I wish warmly to thank Corrado Roversi for bringing this point to my attention.

Himma is right to point out that the legal system contains components of different ontological kinds (like people, provisions, acts, and so forth) and that the differences between these components are such as to prevent us from adding them up to compose a single, ontologically homogeneous whole consisting of the 'legal system as such'. But this adding up is not what we should be looking to achieve after all. Indeed, the ontological make-up of the law can retain all its multiplicity and still make it possible to ascribe a unitary claim to the law, so long as the legal system is susceptible of being *represented* as a unified whole, and so long as this representation is *necessary* in the sense that the representation reflects the necessary features and components of the system. It is not through a unitary ontology of law that claims can be ascribed to the system but through a unitary representation of it: that is as much unitary character as we will ever need in the effort to explain the system's claim-making capacity. This makes ontological variety much less of an impediment: even heterogeneous collections that resist aggregation *in fact* can be made unitary *in representation*, so long as the components selected in representation are accurately described in their necessary relation to one another. Thus, Himma's reason for denying the claim-making capacity of the law is grounded on a misconstruction of the kind of singleness that that capacity requires: it requires not a unitary reality (oneness in fact) but a unitary understanding of it (oneness in representation), yielding an epistemologically correct unified account of the reality in question.

The reply to Himma, therefore, is to keep the reality of a phenomenon apart from its necessary representation and to focus on the latter. Two related reasons show why we can (and may even *have* to) do so. The first of these is that the reality of a phenomenon exercises a certain control over its necessary representation, and indeed stands in a strict conceptual relation to it. Necessary representations do not act as free and hence arbitrary renderings of the reality they represent: rather they account for that reality in a conceptually dependent and necessary way that is determined by reality itself, that is, by the nature of the objects being represented. This means that a necessary representation reveals something about the objects it represents to the effect that we can extract from it a knowledge of these objects and their ontology. The second reason accompanies the first one and proceeds from the observation that even the most systematic attempts to arrive at the ontology of an object may fail to make this ontology available to us (especially if the object in question is compound, having heterogeneous components and sources). In these cases, in which we have no direct access to reality, we have no choice but to approach the ontology of an object by a route other than ontological investigation proper, that is, by looking to the necessary representations by means of which the same objects are described. And the reason why we can and, indeed, have to do so is precisely that these representations relate in a necessary way to the reality they describe: they give us an understanding of this reality by describing it in its necessary make-up (rather than by departing from it), since this is what representation is *meant* to do and accordingly *tends* to do more and more as it progresses.

Let us see now how this discussion comes to bear on the question whether the law can make claims. It was argued that the necessary representation of a phenomenon, while conceptually connected to its ontology in a necessary way, can be considered apart from such ontology and become a focus of study in its own right. If this thesis is correct, it follows that in so far as a legal system can be *represented* as having a unitary character, despite the ontological complexity that marks it out, the system can be viewed as making system-wide claims even though the system's ontological plurality translates into claims of different kinds, performative and attributive. For these two kinds of claims can be made commensurate by addition and composition *in representation:* there is no need to make them *ontologically* commensurate, but only to find a medium capable of representing their plurality as well as making them meaningful and showing them to be the issue of a single system making an aggregate claim. This provides the general shape of the argument. Accordingly, the next step in the argument will be to identify the medium referred to: this will be presented as a necessary medium, and the task of making it possible to represent the manifold constituents of the legal system in a unitary way is entrusted to it.

The claim-making capacity of the law will thus be explained by establishing a necessary representation of the law as a uniform, systematic unity. What it means for this representation to be necessary is that (a) there is no way to conceive of the law except as a unitary entity, and the law must therefore be represented accordingly, and (b) there is only one medium capable of providing such a unitary representation of the law as a system. So what is necessary is, on the one hand, a unitary representation of the law and, on the other, the medium for such a representation. On top of these two conditions of representation, there arises a third condition, namely, that (c) the necessary medium making possible such a necessarily unitary representation of the law be capable of making claims, if not in a performative sense at least in an attributive sense. Once these three conditions are met, and in what follows it will be shown that they obtain, there is a justified basis for concluding that the law can make system-wide claims and so can make claims as a system. That, in turn, opens up the possibility for the law to make the normative claim, since this is in essence a system-wide or aggregated claim filled with a specific content. Let us then take up each of these three conditions in turn and see whether the corresponding theses are valid.

The first thesis states that the law must necessarily be represented as a unitary system. Of course, it is not *generally* the case that the law must be so represented: there are many purposes for which the law can be represented as less than a unitary system, namely, as a multiplicity of elements that need not, and indeed cannot, be reduced to any unity. In Raz's vivid words (1994: 280–1), the law builds up and exists as a 'higgledy-piggledy assemblage of the remains of contradictory past political ambitions and beliefs', as 'a hodgepodge of norms derived from the conflicting ideologies and the pragmatic necessities which prevailed from time to time over the many years of evolution'. Which is to say that the sources of law and the forces of its formation are plural. This accounts for the ontological plurality of the legal system itself, but it also means that it will take a theoretical effort to construct the law as a unitary system *in representation*. Thus, while there is no compelling reason generally to conceive of the law as marked by systemic unity, such a reason does arise in theory, and even more so when the aims and concerns driving the theoretical effort mark it as a case of general jurisprudence, understood as the study of fundamental legal concepts with an eye to arriving at a comprehensive concept of law. This is jurisprudence in the British tradition of John Austin and Jeremy Bentham, and the fundamental legal concepts it studies are those that turn up pervasively in law or apply to legal practices generally and in this sense are common to most legal systems, or at least to those having a significant degree of maturity. Legal theory, so conceived, is both analytic and synthetic, since it seeks to identify the distinctive properties of law as well as its shared ones. In this latter case, it will be necessary to construct general pictures and maps of the law, and at least some of this work proceeds on a view of the law as exhibiting some kind of systemic unity. Certainly, an assumption of this kind underlies any effort to arrive at a concept of law, as in general jurisprudence, for it makes little sense even to begin constructing such a concept if the law is viewed as no more than a congeries of disparate elements not amenable to any sort of reconstruction, synthetic in nature. This frames the activity of the legal theorist who is looking to a general account of the law. On the one hand, there will be an appreciation that the disparate elements of the law are not just appearance but reflect an ontological multiplicity, for otherwise there would be no need for a comprehensive account to begin with. But then, on the other hand, by the very nature of this enterprise, the effort will be to set out a unitary representation of the law wherein the disparate elements from which a legal system originates are traced to a common source and presented as different constituents of a single framework. Otherwise, that is, without such a unified source, it would prove impossible to have either a general theory or a concept of law.

This ability to construct the systemic 'oneness' of the law without either disregarding or discounting its diversified composition and ontology can be appreciated in Raz, whose account of the authority of the law shows this to be an aggregate authority that the law exercises as a unitary system. This is significant, for as the lines quoted above suggest, Raz by no means tends to idealise the law but instead puts forward a realist and unromantic philosophy of law. One would expect such a realist, unvarnished outlook to yield a pluralist conception. Instead, it yields a unitary conception. This can be taken to mean that any account of the concept of law makes it necessary to present the law as a unitary system, or to mean, at the very least, that an assumption of unity must precede any attempt to work out a concept of law, regardless of what kind of concept is being worked out, whether realist or idealist. In other words, there is no way to make progress toward a concept of law unless the law is acknowledged to be unitary in at least some non-trivial sense. Not to concern oneself with working toward a concept of law is to dismiss jurisprudence itself as senseless, ideological or illusory. Indeed, what defines jurisprudence as a single discipline is precisely its concern with a general, or comprehensive, account of the concept of law, and to the extent that such an account is general, it will have to assume some kind of unity of the law, or it will have to understand the components of the law as somehow intelligible as a unified whole.

In sum, it is not a general, all encompassing, point of view that brings about the necessary 'oneness' of the law in representation; rather, this is a local or 'bounded' necessity specific to jurisprudence. However, since this is primarily a study in jurisprudence, no broader kind of necessity is required. The sole initial assumption at work is that there is nothing especially senseless, ideological or illusory about jurisprudence—yet this is not an inert assumption, for it comes with a need to recognise as necessary the 'oneness' of the law in representation for any of the purposes central to jurisprudence and to this study in particular.

So, having considered the necessarily unitary character of the law in representation, we can now consider the medium of representation and see in what way this medium is in turn necessary, at which point we will have completed the two-step process of explaining what it means for the law to come under a necessary representation. The argument will be that of all the ways in which the law can be represented or accounted for as a unitary system, there is one, in particular, that stands out as primary, for it identifies a component—the language—that *any* representation of the law, whatever it might come to, will have to use both *in* and *for* the representation itself. Since neither the law nor any representation of the law is possible without language, language becomes a necessary medium of the law, and law-as-language a necessary representation or account of it.

This can be appreciated, to begin with, by taking note of the different ways in which one might represent the law and account for its unity: the law can be constructed as an aggregation of norms and sanctions; or as the institutionalised form of certain basic beliefs about the way social relations ought to be framed and governed; or as a systematised arrangement serving the interests of those in power; or again as a device of social control, in which latter case we have a causal conception of the law that disregards the validity of law and focuses exclusively on social behaviour, thereby exercising an effective influence on social behaviour. All of these and more are possible conceptions of the law and its unity, and they may differ in important respects. They have, however, one thing in common, namely, they must all be represented through the medium of the language, and they must all acknowledge that no form of law would be possible without such a medium. This is not to say that the law can be entirely reduced to a form of language, for there is far more to the law than the language of the law or the language that accompanies the practices framed by different legal forms. In fact, these forms coalesce with the very practices they frame, and since these practices define certain social forms, it follows that the law is itself a social construction and so is more than just language and discourse. Yet language and discourse are necessary elements of the law, not only because no representation or systematic account of the law would be possible without language, but also because the law itself could not exist or develop as a social reality without our capacity to use the language. A necessary link thus obtains between law and language. Whereas the two cannot be equated, whatever else the law is, it is also and in the first place to be understood linguistically. This language-based representation or conception of the law cannot account for the whole of the law—it cannot alone explain the workings of the law or make sense of the different forms, functions and features of the law—but it does provide the bedrock layer or skeleton for any account capable of taking up these aspects. Hence, law-as-language is not just one of several alternative representations of the law but the foundation on which any other representation must build in order to account for the law in any more specific way.

To see this, one need only consider that while different representations of the law can come into contradiction or can at least be mutually exclusive, none enters into any such relation with respect to the representation of the law as a system structured by the use of language. Thus, the law can be represented as a system of language forming an ordered set of valid norms with accompanying penalties for non-compliance, or as a system of language forming part of a device by which to influence social behaviour causally. Law-as-language can combine with either of these two other representations of the law: the norm-centred one, which focuses on validity and considers largely irrelevant to law its efficacy as a device of social control; and the sociological one, which considers validity at best a product of the causal influence the law applies on social behaviour. While both these representations combine with law-as-language—indeed they cannot but help combining with it—each rules out the other in that they cannot both be upheld at the same time without generating contradictions. For if the law is juridically represented as being in the first instance a set of valid norms, it cannot also be sociologically understood as being in the first instance a device by which to exercise a measure of effective control over social behaviour. The reason for this is that validity and efficacy belong to two different kinds of discourse, that of the normative sciences, on the one hand, that of the social sciences, on the other. The former is concerned with the *regulation* of behaviour, centring around the principle of imputation, while the latter is concerned, instead, with the *explanation* of behaviour, centring around the principle of causation.[38] Now, if inconsistency can arise between two representations of the law, as happens here between law as a system of valid norms and law as a device of social control, the reason is that neither of them is primary or necessary. This point can be generalised by observing that *all* representations not based on language can come into contradiction, and the reason they can do so with one another, but not with law-as-language, is that this latter representation is foundational and logically prior to any other representation. For only if the law is acknowledged as a form of language, or as necessarily coming about and developing through the medium of language, can any fuller account of the law then be offered, showing the law to be a unitary system in ways that cannot be explained by reference to the necessary language component alone. Thus, although law-as-language cannot as such fully account for the totality of the law and legal practice, it nonetheless functions as the necessary basis without which no such account could possibly be offered. This renders it unique both as a primary representation (the one that makes all other representations derivative) and as a necessary repre-

---

[38] For a distinction between the two kinds of discourse see Kelsen (1950), where it is argued that they should be kept entirely separate.

sentation, to the effect that any other representation not only *can* combine with it a full account of the law but also *must* combine therewith.

In summary, there can be found in the law different elements (including people, institutions, provisions, acts, practices and procedures), none of which can be reduced ontologically to any other, yet all of which, despite such irreducibility, can and do interact with one another and can accordingly be viewed and represented as parts of a single system: hence the thesis that the law must be represented as a unitary system (at least for the purposes of jurisprudence) through the medium of language.

Crucially, this feature of language—its ability to represent different legal objects—accounts as well for the claim-making capacity of the law, the subject of the third and final thesis in support of the view that the legal system can make normative claims. This third thesis works in combination with the first two, for if language does have a claim-making capacity, and if it does necessarily turn up in any representation of the law as a unitary system, then the system can act in its own turn as a source of normative claims. That is the general form of the argument. Clearly, it will not be a complete argument until we consider in what way language can make claims.

This capacity of language is something that can be appreciated by turning for help to the theory of speech acts, a theory, in its fully developed form, that offers a general account of how language works and how linguistic communication takes place. The basic premise of the greater theory is that there is more to language than words, and there is more to statements than their meaning content. Statements can be used to do a number of things besides describing reality or saying that something is the case, and in this sense the theory of speech acts can be presented (with, however, a great deal of simplification) as the systematic study of the different things that sentences can do, or of what we do and *can* do with our speech. These things we do in the sense that speaking a language is not just an ability but an activity we engage in, an activity that involves carrying out what the theory calls illocutionary acts, understood as acts *of* speaking as well as acts done *in* speaking.[39] And if these acts 'work'—if they do make it possible to do things, if they give pride of place to the daily transactions of communication—that is because there are rules and conventions (a common framework) governing the

---

[39] In what follows I will mainly be referring to John Searle's account of this theory (especially in Searle 1968; 1969; 1971; 1979; and Searle and Vanderveken 1985). Other significant contributions are Alston (1964; 1977; 2000), Austin (1975), Grice (1989), Schiffer (1972) and Strawson (1964). The reason for focusing on Searle is that his work expands on and generalises to a much greater extent than do other approaches the original insights found in John L Austin's pioneering study of speech acts. Indeed, Searle has consistently devoted himself over the past several decades to a broad study covering not just specific speech acts but the whole theory in its many connections, thus taking up questions such as how to accurately define speech act theory and tie together its fundamental notions, how this theory can find its ground in the philosophy of mind, and how to comprehensively formalise the theory using the tools of contemporary philosophical logic. The result has been a unified account showing how the fundamental notions of the speech act theory relate not only to one another but also to ideas and principles developed in other branches of knowledge, thus paving the way for further applications of speech act theory beyond the limits of linguistics and the philosophy of language.

activity by which the same acts are carried out. These rules structure the activity of speaking a language and make this a communicative activity that consists in more than blurting out sounds or even uttering meaningful and well-formed strings of words. This is to say that statements exchanged in the course of communication are not just made for their content alone but are made to present that content in a certain way, as content carrying a certain force. When we utter a sentence we express a meaning content: we refer to and represent something, or we predicate something about that thing, or we say anything that makes sense or can be understood in some way. But the content so expressed does not as such amount to an act of speech (it is not yet communication), for we have not yet *done* anything with that content: we have not yet specified *how* it is to be taken or understood, for example, as a description, a command, a request, a commitment, an expression of feelings.[40] These are all *further* things that we do in speaking (we describe, command, commit to something, and so on) and are called illocutionary acts. An illocutionary act consists, then, in expressing something (a meaning content) in such a way as to give it a certain force or an indication as to what to make of it.

Illocutionary acts owe their importance to their role as the basic units of linguistic communication, but this is a role they play on a fuller understanding of communication than just 'stringing together words that make sense in some language'; that is, they fit into a pragmatic view of communication as a rule-bound activity or practice that includes the use of words to express meaning contents, but that understands this use as taking place *in context*, in the context of what it is that we do and can do in the daily business of life whenever we are interacting with one another. Hence the idea of the communicative use of language as a necessarily performative activity, one that takes place through the performance of illocutionary acts.[41]

Speech act theory makes it possible to regard illocutionary acts (the most elementary units of language and communication) as also necessary to the representation of the law. For if the law takes language as the necessary medium for its representation, and language essentially comprises illocutionary acts, then these acts must be regarded as the essential and indispensable means for representing the law. When a legal system is constructed as a unitary whole, it must therefore be represented, in rough approximation, as composed of illocutionary acts of different types, forming sequences in which different illocutionary acts (so distinguished by type) interact in different ways depending on the mutual relationships that are set out by their different types.

This understanding of the legal system in terms of illocutionary acts does not deny the ontological complexity of the system itself; in fact, we are *representing* the

---

[40] Thus, a sentence like 'The door is shut' can be understood out of context as simply expressing the meaning content of a shut door. But *in* context (the context of linguistic communication) the same string of words becomes a speech act with a purpose, which might be to describe something (the door as being shut), or to state a belief (that the door is shut), or to issue a command (not to open the door) or a warning (about what might happen to anyone who should open the door), or again to express a feeling (such as fear of what might happen if the door were to be opened).

[41] Cf Searle (1969: 16–19; 1971: 39) and Searle and Vanderveken (1985: 1–8).

system through sequences of illocutionary acts, not reducing it to such sequences, much less to any single type of illocutionary act. This should not be mistaken, then, for the view that the legal system is not composed of anything other than illocutionary acts, for such a view would amount to deforming the reality of the law as an ontologically complex reality made of plural components. Illocutionary acts are only *one* such component, and they do not exhaust the law. They do, however, enjoy a special status as primary and hence necessary components: this is to say that, if the officials had no way of carrying out any illocutionary acts, they would have no way of discharging their function either; those responsible for the operation of the law could not possibly manage the law if they were not able to use the language in such a way as to do with the words they choose something more than simply convey meaning contents. For we would not even know what to do with such contents if they carried no illocutionary force, nor would we know how to position ourselves with respect to them, and in this sense they would remain inert with respect to anyone's practical choices and action. The bulk of the activities involved in maintaining a legal system thus necessarily involve the performance of illocutionary acts.

Hence the view being presented here, namely, that illocutionary acts play a necessary role with respect to the law. They do so in two ways: as indispensable constituents of the legal system and as the necessary means by which to conceptualise and represent the legal system and hence all the other constituents of which the system is composed. So, on the one hand, illocutionary acts are found *in* the law, making up its essential fabric; and, on the other, they are what all the diverse constituents of the law must primarily be represented or conceived as, that is, as sequences of illocutionary acts that interact and interconnect to form a single system.[42]

I have thus far argued that the speech act theory can help toward an understanding of legal systems by showing us how a mélange of elements, having different sources and produced through different procedures, can be made commensurate and reduced to unity *in representation*. This is to say that the different elements making up the law can all be viewed or represented as the outcome of a single activity, that of language and communication as it unfolds through the performance of illocutionary acts carried out in connection with the law and its operation. The law can thus be represented as a system through the lens of the illocutionary acts on which its functioning necessarily relies: the law is made, applied

---

[42] Using a theory of language to explain certain central features of the legal phenomenon does not ipso facto make the approach 'linguistic', and I reject such an approach if it amounts to understanding 'the enquiry concerning the nature of law' as 'an attempt to define the meaning of the word "law"' (Raz 1994: 180). No such attempt is being made here. In fact, my attempt is to reliably *represent* the legal system—this is an epistemological enquiry, and my use of a general theory of language (speech act theory) should be so understood. So I am not concerned with lexicography; that is, my working assumption is that 'philosophers are not lexicographers' (Raz 1994: 180), and I therefore reject the 'claim that the theory of the nature of law is simply an investigation of the meaning of "legally"' (Raz 1994: 182). Just as philosophy cannot be reduced to a lexicographical study of words and meanings, so the philosophy of law cannot tie the law down to its linguistic component alone and then proceed on this basis (by studying the meaning of legal terms and legal discourse) in an effort to uncover the nature of law itself.

and interpreted over time by officials and institutions on the basis of established rules and procedures that structure their activity; this structured activity takes place by way of illocutionary acts (performed by officials in making, applying and interpreting the law); and since this activity unfolds over time in process and is essentially interactive, the illocutionary acts through which it is carried out make up interconnected sequences that can be understood as forming part of a system, and through which the system can be represented. It is only in representation that the different components of a legal system can be rendered unitary as interacting components of a single system without thereby denying their ontological variety; that is, they can be represented as the outcome of a single activity, the use of the language for the production, application and interpretation of the law, that must necessary rely on illocutionary acts necessarily interconnecting in sequences. And there is a definite advantage to representing legal systems as sequences of interconnected illocutionary acts: since we are representing the system rather than explaining its ontology, we can grasp properties of the system for which we have no ontological accounts; in particular, we can understand the capacity of the legal system to make claims. This is because the illocutionary acts—the notion in terms of which the system is being represented—can themselves be understood as claim-making entities.

This property of illocutionary acts can be appreciated by considering their composition. This is to say, as discussed earlier, that an illocutionary act consists of a meaning content endowed with a certain force.[43] This force can be described as that on account of which we know how a meaning content is to be taken. There is a structural way in which illocutionary acts, as defined by their meaning content and illocutionary force combined, can be understood as claim-making entities. This structural claim can be appreciated by looking at the illocutionary force itself, noting that this force is, in turn, composite. The force of an illocutionary act is owing to a combination of seven components, these being the act's illocutionary point; strength of the illocutionary point; mode by which to achieve the illocutionary point; propositional-content conditions; preparatory conditions; sincerity conditions; and strength of the sincerity conditions. An example will shortly be provided below, clarifying what these components mean and how they all come together in a single illocutionary act; for the moment, however, it will suffice to point out that they specify the conditions of the successful (that is, non-defective) performance of an illocutionary act. Illocutionary acts are subject to two kinds of conditions: success conditions, failing which the act will not come into existence, and conditions of non-defectiveness, failing which the act (though it has come into existence) will not be ideal or faultless.[44] Thus, these conditions are determined by shaping the seven components of illocutionary force, on the one hand, and they determine when each kind of illocutionary act (as specified by its illocutionary force) can come into existence in an ideal way, on the other.

---

[43] So, too, an illocutionary act is entirely *defined* by these two components, that is, by its meaning content and its illocutionary force combined. On this aspect, see Searle and Vanderveken (1985: 8–12).

[44] We will look at these conditions shortly, below.

The conditions of illocutionary force thereby play at one and the same time two roles as both defining and enabling conditions. In the former role they define different kinds of illocutionary acts:[45] they do so by defining their force, for the force of an illocutionary act is 'uniquely determined once its illocutionary point, its preparatory conditions, the mode of achievement of its illocutionary point, the degree of strength of its illocutionary point, its propositional-content conditions, its sincerity conditions, and the degree of strength of its sincerity conditions are specified' (Searle and Vanderveken 1985: 20). Thus, by specifying the seven components of illocutionary force, we shape the conditions of illocutionary force and define different kinds of illocutionary act. In this role, each set of standard conditions for the successful and non-defective performance of an illocutionary act is constitutive of a type of act and defines it as being of that type. We can accordingly distinguish different types of illocutionary acts by matching them to different standard sets of conditions.

But in defining different types of illocutionary acts, these standard conditions also play an enabling role as conditions singly necessary and collectively sufficient for the coming into existence of any non-defective illocutionary act within each of the types defined.[46] This means that no illocutionary act can be said to have come into existence (to have been performed) unless it has satisfied the conditions for such existence within the relevant type. This means, in turn, that there is *implicit* in each illocutionary act a claim that the conditions have been satisfied for the existence and proper form of the same act relatively to its own type and, accordingly, that no illocutionary act can refrain from making the claim, at least implicitly, that these conditions have been satisfied.

Hence, for each type of illocutionary act there is a standard set of conditions that (a) defines an act as being of that type, and that (b) must be satisfied in order for the act to be able to achieve what it is supposed to achieve. It follows from this that with each act there comes a claim, whether implicit or explicit, that (a) the act falls within the type framed by the corresponding set of standard conditions, and that (b) the act does this by *satisfying* those conditions on which it is dependent for its success. Conversely, each set of standard conditions can be paired with a standard claim (defined by these conditions themselves), which any act corresponding to the same standard type cannot refrain from making implicitly, or which must be regarded as implicitly made by any corresponding act—failing which we would lose the very point of illocutionary acts, or of meaning contents carrying a force as to how the contents expressed are to be taken, which in turn would make language and communication futile.

In sum, it is part of the working of the language that each illocutionary act carried out is received as carrying a structural claim, or must be so received in order for communication to take place. And since communication involves an exchange of those acts that interconnect into sequences, it follows that these sequences, too,

---

[45] There are five such kinds in the mainstream account: assertives, directives, commissives, declaratives and expressives. See Searle (1979: 12–29).

[46] See Searle (1969: 54–6).

carry the same structural claim, or that such a claim can be *attributed* to each sequence (understood as what results from an exchange of illocutionary acts). Now, the legal system is being represented as a combination of such sequences (of interconnected illocutionary acts), and this makes it possible to ascribe to the system the very capacity ascribed to the sequences and illocutionary acts that the system is being represented as: this is the capacity to make claims in an *attributive* sense.

The argument has thus been completed showing that the law has a claim-making capacity. But this only means the law *can* make claims, not that these claims are *normative* or *necessary*. These two further questions have been touched on but not yet addressed. I will turn now to the task of showing how the claim-making of the law can be normative, and will consider, too, whether this normative claim-making is only possible (contingent) or whether it is necessarily associated with the existence of the law. This will take us to a further argument, as set out in the following section.

Is the Normative Claim of Law Contingent or Necessary?

The theory of speech acts can also help us settle the status of the normative claim of law, namely, whether it is contingent or necessary. The approach based on representing the law in terms of illocutionary acts has so far been used to understand the law as having the power to make certain system-wide claims: the structural claims framed by the conditions satisfying which the illocutionary acts themselves can be carried out. As we have seen, these conditions play two roles: an enabling or classifying role, as success conditions failing which the corresponding illocutionary acts could not come into existence in the first place, and a qualifying role, as conditions of non-defectiveness failing which an act of the corresponding type would count as such an act but only defectively so. In this part, where it is considered whether the law must *necessarily* make claims, it is the success conditions that take precedence.

Success conditions determine when each act can exist as an act of this or that type, and no act of any type can exist if its success conditions are not satisfied. Since each standard condition frames a claim (the claim that any act of the corresponding type satisfies that condition for its own success, or for the success of any act within the relevant type), it follows that an act not only *can* but also *must* make such a claim: the claim is necessary, for without it the act would present itself in a contradictory manner, as an act carried out even though it cannot be carried out (on account of its failing to meet its own success conditions). The same can be said of the law to the extent that we are presenting it as a complex sequence of interrelated illocutionary acts: the law necessarily makes the claims framed by the conditions for the success of the illocutionary acts in terms of which the law is represented, since a failure to do so would prevent such acts from coming into existence as acts of this or that type, and so would prevent the law itself from coming into existence.

Not so when the standard conditions play a qualifying role (over against an enabling one) as conditions of non-defectiveness. A failure to comply with conditions of non-defectiveness makes an illocutionary act not non-existent but only imperfect. Clearly, an act can exist in an imperfect state, and this means that no contradiction is involved in not making a claim to non-defectiveness: an act failing to implicitly or explicitly claim successful performance is simply faulty—one that exists as an act of a certain type but fails to meet the conditions for an ideal fit with that type.[47] Hence, the law can without contradiction be conceived of as not making the claims corresponding to the non-defectiveness conditions of the illocutionary acts in terms of which the law itself is represented, in which case the law does exist but in a less than ideal form. These claims, then, do not belong to a kind the law must necessarily make, but to a kind that the law *can* make: they are optional or contingent. In summary, certain claims the law simply *can* make, and certain others it not only can but also *has* to make. We therefore want to know how these necessary claims come about and whether, among them, there lies the normative claim as defined above. This will require some further discussion, as follows.

Let us begin by looking at the structure or make-up of the normative claim of law. Unlike the simple form of the claims framed by the single conditions (success conditions and conditions of non-defectiveness) of the different kinds of illocutionary acts, the normative claim of law is compound. This compound, the normative claim of law, can be analytically broken down into two components, the one establishing an *aim* for the law and the other a *mode* for achieving that aim. The *aim-specific* component says that the law should offer *guidance* in action, while the *mode-specific* component says that this action-guiding role is something the law should carry out *by providing people with certain distinctive kinds of reasons for action*. Both components are clearly *practical* in nature, and their conjunction therefore makes law an inherently practical enterprise: such is the normative aim of the law (guiding *action*), and such is the way to go about achieving that aim (by taking into account reasons for *action*). So there are two components to the normative claim, both of them practical, but one specifies an aim or point and the other a mode for achieving that aim or point. This means that the two components complement and complete each other in giving the law a normative status. It would be a mistake to conflate these components, obscuring their distinct roles.

The compound structure of the normative claim of law gives it a complexity surpassing that found in each of the single conditions failing which an illocutionary act would prove impossible. The two components making up the normative claim work in tandem, and they cannot, in their joint operation, be reduced to any of the single conditions making an illocutionary act possible as an act of a certain type. This makes the normative claim conceptually distinct from the individual claims associated with the conditions of possibility of the kinds of illocutionary act in terms of which the law is represented when such conditions are taken in isolation. We need a combination of such conditions to get at the normative claim.

---

[47] For a definition of ideal illocutionary act, see Searle and Vanderveken (1985: 22–3).

Accordingly, the normative claim of law is shown to be necessary only if its two components make up a combination of distinct conditions for the success of an illocutionary act. So, if the compound normative claim of law is to be proved necessary, it will require a matching compound argument, understood in such a way that each of the two components of the claim is backed by its own corresponding argument. It will thus be argued that the aim-specific and the mode-specific components of the normative claim of law correspond to two of the conditions for the success of a certain type of illocutionary act understood as necessary to the representation of the law. It is only when these two parts of the argument have both been presented (the aim-specific part and the mode-specific part) that the necessary status of the normative claim of law can be considered fully substantiated.

The aim and mode specified by the two components of the normative claim consist, as we have seen, in a purport to guide conduct by providing practical reasons. The aim-specific component of the normative claim can thus be described as directive in nature, since the point of the claim is to give direction, and its mode-specific component can be described as reason-based. Now, Searle has developed a specific kind of illocutionary act, whose components cover both the directive aim and the reason-based mode of achieving an aim so understood. This is what Searle has called the 'directive illocutionary act'. Indeed, two of the components making up this act (its illocutionary point and the mode by which to achieve that point) are so specified as to give rise to an overlap with the two components making up the normative claim of law. Let us see, then, how Searle specifies his directive illocutionary act and what it is about this specification that brings about its overlap with the normative claim of law.[48]

As was mentioned in the last section, the force of any illocutionary act can be defined by specifying its seven components, which so specified not only define an act as being of a certain type but also determine its conditions of possibility, those that make any act of the same type possible—that is, existent and non-defective. Here, in summary, is how Searle does this for the *directive* illocutionary act. Its *illocutionary point* (i) (this being the aim in pursuance of which an illocutionary act is carried out) is to have one or more other people take some future course of conduct. The *degree of strength* (ii) this point or purpose is presented as having varies according as the directive illocutionary act in question belongs to one subtype or another: the act could count as an order, a request, a plea, an entreaty, a recommendation, a piece of advice, and so on. So there is no way to say in general how strong the intended direction or guidance is for which a directive illocutionary act is carried out. The same goes for the *mode* (iii) by which such guidance is to be achieved: we might order someone to do something or we might beg this person to do it, and certainly these are two very different ways of achieving the same purpose (the same illocutionary point). Still, for all these differences, a common

[48] Searle's account of the directive illocutionary act proves useful because it forms part of an attempt to firm up and expand Austin's taxonomy of the different kinds of illocutionary acts, a taxonomy too heterogeneous and lacking a unifying classificatory principle. For a discussion of the relations between Austin's and Searle's classification of illocutionary acts, see Searle (1979: 1–29).

denominator does exist that ties together all these different modes by means of which a directive illocutionary point is achieved; namely, they must all in some way involve the use of reasons as to why the addressee should act as directed. These reasons may be more or less forceful or compelling, and may, to be sure, be either stated or implied; but they always play a role in the guidance at issue. This means that, while directive illocutionary points have no general strength, they do have a general mode of achievement, which consists in giving or implying reasons for whatever it is that makes up the content of the direction in question.[49] The *propositional-content conditions* (iv) can also be expressed in general terms: these conditions are simply summarised by the statement that the direction must be for some course of action to be taken in the future. The *preparatory conditions* (v) largely depend on the specific subtype of act in question, but they too can be expressed in general terms: the conduct specified in the meaning content must be feasible and not obvious. An action is feasible if it falls within the range of the addressee's capabilities and powers. It is not obvious if it does not come as a matter of course, as something the addressee would carry out quite apart from the directive: it must be an action that the addressee might choose *not* to perform, or might well not perform but for the directive itself. The *sincerity conditions* (vi) are mostly psychological and can be assessed by looking at the motive for carrying out the directive illocutionary act in question: this motive (the intent or desire behind the act) may vary in *degree of strength* (vii) depending on the specific subtype of act in question, but regardless of strength it must always translate into a genuine move toward getting one or more addressees to behave as directed. In a condensed formula, directive illocutionary acts are genuine attempts, of varying degrees of strength, to shape someone's future behaviour by creating practical reasons as to why this person ought to behave as directed, and by framing this direction in a meaningful way, in that the behaviour in question must be assumed to be both feasible and not obvious.[50]

We can see from this presentation that the directive point and its mode of achievement (items (i) and (iii) in the list) do more than simply overlap with the aim-specific and mode-specific components of the normative claim of law: they coincide. The directive point (that is, the illocutionary point of the directive illocutionary act) does exactly what the aim-specific component of the normative claim of law does: the aim or point in either case is to have one or more addressees behave in the future in keeping with a certain meaning content as expressed or represented by way of an illocutionary act, in one case, and by way of the law, in the other. So, too, does the mode of achieving the directive point coincide with the mode-specific component of the normative claim of law, in that both modes are based on the use of reasons: a directive point is achieved by creating practical reasons that need at least to be acknowledged by its addressees as reasons for

---

[49] That directive points are generally so linked to reasons, or to the reason-based mode of achieving them, is stated by Searle and Vanderveken only in passing (1985: 55–6). For a full argument see Alston (2000: 97–102).

[50] Cf Searle (1969: 64–71; 1979: 13–4), and Seale and Vanderveken (1985: 55–6).

acting as directed; likewise, the claim of law to action-guidance is achieved not by forcing people to act as stated in the law but by reasoning with them, or engaging with them in forms of practical deliberation, and so by setting up a framework within which to deliberate about the course of conduct to be undertaken.[51]

We can see, then, how speech act theory can be used to account for the normative claim of law: this claim of law is mirrored by two of the standard conditions framing the directive illocutionary act, and it can then be represented through these conditions. But this does not yet show that the law *necessarily* makes a normative claim so modelled, or that such a claim is an essential element of the law. There are two arguments that need to be made to this end. First, it will have to be shown that the point of the directive illocutionary act and its mode of achievement are success conditions of the same act; that is, nothing could count as such an act if it failed to satisfy either of these two conditions, which therefore define this type of act by stating how it can come to exist rather than by stating what makes it ideal. Secondly, it will have to be shown that this type of act figures *essentially* into any representation of the law, and that the law must accordingly be represented not as just any complex sequence of interconnected illocutionary acts of whatever kind, but as a complex sequence of interconnected *directive* illocutionary acts. Let us take up these two arguments in turn.

The first argument is devoted to a question arising within speech act theory, and I will accordingly base it on the account of this theory provided by Searle and Vanderveken. This, too, is a two-part question: whether (a) the illocutionary point of a directive illocutionary act and (b) its mode of achievement count as success conditions for this type of act. I will treat these two cases separately.

The first case can be viewed from the broader perspective of illocutionary acts generally (rather than from the specific standpoint of *directive* illocutionary acts), and it suffices to note here that the illocutionary point forms an essential part of *any* illocutionary act. For Searle and Vanderveken (1985: 14) describe the illocutionary point as 'internal' to any given type of illocutionary act, because the illocutionary point defines the 'purpose' of an act, and this makes it 'by far the most important component' of illocutionary force. Indeed, the purpose of an act 'is *essential* to its being an act of that type', and so close is the connection between point and purpose that 'if the act is successful the point is achieved' (Searle and Vanderveken 1985: 14). This makes the illocutionary point essential or indispensable to the existence of the illocutionary act for which it is a condition. Essential conditions are success conditions (in their defining role, they establish what is necessary for an illocutionary

---

[51] On law and reasons, see Postema (1991: 798–800). In particular, Postema (1991: 798) argues that 'law, not only typically but essentially, purports to direct action by addressing reasons to those falling within its jurisdiction'. Cf Soper (1989: 219). This means that the law relies not on external control but on internal appeal; that is, it appeals to what the addressees of law can appreciate as reasons for action, as reasons why they should act in certain ways, in the manner prescribed by the law itself. Rather than directly moulding a setting in which to act, thus drawing the boundaries within which to compel action, the law states reasons for acting within such boundaries: reasons offered, not measures aimed at constraining action, form the locus of the distinctive practical guidance of law. A contrary view, defended by Matthew Kramer, will be discussed in the next chapter.

act to exist) and whenever they are disregarded, the effect on an illocutionary act will not be technical, moral or conventional—it will be conceptual, which means that if anything will come to exist in consequence of such a defective performance, it will not be an illocutionary act. Specifically, a conceptual problem of this kind shows up as a performative contradiction, which takes place whenever the meaning content of an illocutionary act contradicts some necessary (however implicit) presupposition for that act.[52] The conceptual misstep involved in a performative contradiction—the contradiction arising whenever the meaning content of an illocutionary act conflicts with what is implied by the illocutionary force of that act— makes the illocutionary act in question pragmatically self-defeating. Illocutionary acts must therefore fulfil their success conditions if they are to function on a pragmatic level, that is, if they are to exist as such, or if they are to come into existence as illocutionary acts (rather than as something other than such acts).

The same reasoning applies to the *directive* illocutionary act, simply by virtue of its inclusion as a type of illocutionary act. But even more importantly, the reasoning applies to the law, and in particular to the aim-specific component of the normative claim of law. This component, on the argument being presented here, is modelled directly by the illocutionary point of the directive illocutionary act. This point functions as an essential condition, stating that the directive illocutionary act must count as an earnest attempt, successful or otherwise, to have something done. Since an essential condition is necessary, it confers the same quality on the aim-specific component of the normative claim, making this a necessary presupposition of the law. Following this essential condition, with its defining role, with respect to directive illocutionary acts and the law alike, any law that fails to offer a directive (that is, fails to make at least an implicit action-guiding claim) would give rise to a performative contradiction and would therefore not count as law, for it would fail to satisfy one of the conditions for the very existence of the law.

In sum, if the illocutionary point figures as an internal or essential condition of any illocutionary act, then the *directive* illocutionary point does so with respect to the directive illocutionary act, and this makes the aim-specific component of the normative claim of law necessary owing to the combination of two reasons: the first of these is that the directive illocutionary point corresponds to, or at least closely models, the aim-specific component of the normative claim of law; the second reason is that the directive illocutionary point acts as an essential condition,

---

[52] In a slightly different statement, a performative contradiction can be said to take place whenever the expressed meaning content of a illocutionary act (what one *says* in speaking) collides with its illocution (what one *does* in speaking): an inconsistency or logical incompatibility, then, arises between implicit presuppositions of an illocutionary act and its expression—between what is implied in *performing* the illocutionary act and what is *expressed* by it. For example, an assertive illocutionary act (one intended to represent a state of affairs, or to assert how things are) can only be performed by a speaker who has evidence of the truth of the statement he or she is making. This is a preparatory condition for this type of illocutionary act, and any instantiation of the same type that should fail this condition would give rise to a performative contradiction, as would have happened if in December 2005 I had said, 'Italy holds the 2006 world cup football title', since there could not have been any evidence in 2005 for a statement (meaning content) referring to the outcome of a tournament scheduled to take place only later, in 2006.

and essential conditions are necessary, since in defining an illocutionary act as being of a certain type, they also state what any act must do in order to count as a successful example of that type. This is to say that these are success conditions rather than conditions of non-defectiveness.

That explains why the directive illocutionary point should properly be construed as a success condition of a directive illocutionary act; so we can now consider why the same holds for the *mode* by which to achieve such a point. The argument for this second case will likewise proceed from the broader perspective of illocutionary acts (closing in on *directive* illocutionary acts only later), and here, too, the discussion will be based on Searle and Vanderveken's account of the success conditions of illocutionary acts. In their treatment, Searle and Vanderveken regard (some of) the preparatory conditions and the sincerity conditions as paradigmatic cases of non-defectiveness conditions of illocutionary acts. More specifically, Searle and Vanderveken (1985: 78) define the 'non-defective performance of an illocution' as 'a successful performance in which all the propositional presuppositions and the preparatory and the sincerity conditions are satisfied'. This remark should be read in combination with the definition Searle and Vanderveken (1985: 75) offer of the 'conditions of success of an illocutionary act', namely the conditions defining the notion of 'successful performance', which is central to Searle and Vanderveken's definition of the non-defective performance. In Searle and Vanderveken's account, an illocutionary act comes into existence if it achieves the illocutionary point with its characteristic mode of achievement and degree of strength, satisfies the propositional-content conditions, and is grounded on the presupposition that preparatory conditions and sincerity conditions obtain.[53] This statement makes it apparent that the conditions of an illocutionary point, mode of achievement and propositional content figure among the success conditions, whereas failure to satisfy the sincerity conditions brings about a flawed illocutionary act.

The qualification of the mode of achieving as a success condition finds a restatement in Searle and Vanderveken's discussion of a specific subtype of directive illocutionary act, the act of commanding. After claiming that in a command the specific mode of achieving the directive illocutionary point consists in 'invoking the position of authority of the speaker', Searle and Vanderveken (1985: 15–6) add that 'in order that the utterance be a *successful* command the speaker . . . must be using or invoking his authority in issuing the utterance' (emphasis added). This statement makes it explicit that the mode of achieving the illocutionary point (in the example: invoking one's authority) is a success condition of the illocutionary act (in the example: the order, understood as a specific instance of the directive illocutionary act). The argument can be generalised and so made to support the conclusion that an illocutionary act failing to pursue its illocutionary point by way of its typical mode of achievement does not constitute an illocutionary act of that type, as opposed to being a merely defective illocutionary act of that type.

---

[53] Cf Searle and Vanderveken (1985: 75–8).

In summary, the illocutionary point and its mode of achievement should both be understood as success conditions of illocutionary acts, and the same therefore holds as well for the *directive* illocutionary act. That is the first of the two arguments in support of the view that the law necessarily makes a normative claim. The second of these two arguments will be devoted to showing that the directive illocutionary act figures *essentially* in any representation of the law. Before turning to this second argument, however, we should take up a challenge originating in Mark Murphy's use of speech act theory to defend the weak natural law thesis, this being the view that any law failing to comply with the dictates of practical reason counts as a valid but defective law.[54] In defending the weak natural law thesis, Murphy proceeds on an understanding of the law as a speaker (in an extended but non-figurative sense) and so, as an entity capable of carrying out illocutionary acts. Let us therefore briefly consider Murphy's argument, bearing in mind that I am not concerned here to call into question the overall shape of the argument; instead, the focus will be on the use and understanding of illocutionary acts. The discussion will thus be geared toward bringing out what this understanding of illocutionary acts implies for the law and for its normative claim in particular.

Murphy conceives of the law as a speaker constructing norms as illocutionary acts of different types (chief among them the directive, commissive and declarative illocutionary acts). This construction of legal norms as illocutionary acts becomes the basis for the view that certain 'standards of defectiveness and non-defectiveness' exist that are 'internal to law' (Murphy 2006: 44). Indeed, these standards are framed by the very conditions accounting for the non-defectiveness of the types of illocutionary act in whose terms Murphy constructs legal norms. There are different kinds of legal norms that Murphy brings into his account (including power-conferring and rights-conferring norms), but let us for the sake of simplicity focus on mandatory norms, understood as norms that make demands on us and so count as instances of directive illocutionary acts: a legal norm so understood will thus present 'an act as to-be-done' and will do so by providing its addressees with 'decisive reasons' for so acting (Murphy 2006: 45). Thus, mandatory legal norms, so constructed as directive illocutionary acts, have both a point (to present an act as to-be-done) and a mode by which to achieve this point (by invoking decisive practical reasons). So far this is consistent with my own account. But then the point and its mode of achievement are both understood by Murphy to be conditions not of success (as I have argued them to be) but of non-defectiveness. Hence, a norm that makes a point but fails to back it up with decisive reasons will still exist as a valid norm, albeit a defective one: its lack of supporting reasons will render it not invalid but merely defective.

This stands in direct contrast to my own treatment of the normative claim of law. So let us see how Murphy comes to view the illocutionary point and its mode of achievement as non-essential conditions, such as do not compromise the existence of an act if unfulfilled, and so as conditions of non-defectiveness. Murphy

---

[54] See Murphy (2006: 37–57).

does this by setting up an analogy that the conditions for assertive illocutionary acts bear to the conditions for other types of illocutionary acts, and he then generalises from this analogy. An assertive illocutionary act is one that purports to say something true about the world, or to present a true meaning content; it must therefore count as an earnest attempt (sincerity condition) to state how things are (illocutionary point) and must rest on solid evidence showing that the state of affairs so described actually exists (preparatory condition). But as Murphy points out, it is not always easy to tell when someone is lying (unfulfilled sincerity condition) or is making an unjustified statement that lacks any basis or foundation (unfulfilled preparatory condition). Yet, despite these difficulties, we often take something to be an assertion so long as it *describes* a state of affairs as true or says anything about the world that makes sense and has the ring of truth to it, even if it turns out later that this was a lie or an inaccuracy. This forms the basis for Murphy's view that lies and unjustified assertions count as assertions even if they fail to satisfy what are ordinarily regarded as paradigmatic conditions of assertion: a lie and an unjustified, unsupported or unverified claim are defective *as assertions* rather than being non-assertions (their paradigmatic conditions are not success conditions but conditions of non-defectiveness). Hence the analogy that Murphy sets up by generalising from this case: just as anything we say still qualifies as an assertion even if we are lying or simply do not know what we are talking about, so any directive that gets issued still counts as a directive even if it fails to state a point (about what is required of us) or fails to state or imply a reason why we should act as required (assuming the requirement is clear enough that it can be acted on): in neither case has a condition been disregarded that makes the relative act (whether assertive or directive) some *other* type of act (something other than an assertion or a directive), but only makes it a *defective* act of the same type.

So how can we tell the two conditions apart? When does a failure to satisfy a condition yield something other than the type of act the condition is for, rather than yielding a defective act of the same type? In a word, how can success conditions be distinguished from conditions of non-defectiveness? Murphy (2006: 58) proposes a criterion, arguing that conditions of non-defectiveness 'require an appeal to epistemic and semantic values' in a way that success conditions do not, in that no evaluation other than a straight assessment of fact is involved in determining whether a condition has been satisfied which makes an act possible. So, on this criterion, a condition counts as a condition of non-defectiveness if it takes an evaluation to determine whether it has been satisfied: it takes a good deal of epistemic evaluation to determine whether an assertion is true and justified (preparatory condition) but none to determine whether it comes across as an assertion, for in this case we need only look at the plain facts of the situation (do the words make sense, is the context in which they are spoken a context in which we are likely take them seriously?, and so on).

The same criterion is made to apply to *directive* illocutionary acts. Just as it may not be immediately apparent whether someone has made an honest or a justified statement (sincerity and preparatory conditions of assertion), it may not be clear what the point of a directive is or whether a good reason has been offered for the directive. And since it may take a fair bit of evaluation to determine whether the illocutionary point of a directive act or its mode of achievement has been satisfied, it follows from this criterion that neither component counts as a success condition: they are both conditions of non-defectiveness, and neither, therefore, stands as a condition that must *necessarily* be satisfied. This implies for us the view that the normative claim of law is something the law might just as well do without. Indeed, the normative claim of law is being modelled here through its aim-specific and mode-specific components, coinciding with the point and mode of a directive act respectively, and if these specify conditions of non-defectiveness, then a law can still be valid without making a normative claim, for in this case we would simply have a *defective* (less than perfect) valid law rather than one that could not be qualified as law at all. Murphy's criterion would thus render the normative claim of law necessary not to legal existence but to legal perfection, and systems of law that should fail to make the normative claim would still retain their legal status.

Murphy's criterion for distinguishing between success and non-defectiveness conditions of illocutionary acts does, I think, have something going for it: it has the virtue of practicality, or of expediting the matter of getting illocutionary acts to do what they are supposed to do. Following this criterion we do not have to stop and ponder, every time an illocutionary act is made, about whether it really and genuinely is an assertion or a directive or whatever: we just receive it as the facts of the situation suggest we ought to receive it, and only later do we go back and enquire about whether any conditions it may have failed to meet (at which point they can only be conditions of non-defectiveness) are worth addressing. Thus, we do not have to seek out, investigate and weigh the reason behind a directive before realising that it is a directive that we face, for this was a plain fact to begin with.

So framed, the overall approach makes good sense, but when we bring it into operation we discover a problem, which is that Murphy's criterion fails to set a clear standard for determining whether something counts as this or that type of illocutionary act. Indeed, if we look at the way Searle and Vanderveken account for different types of illocutionary acts as framed by different success and non-defectiveness conditions, we can appreciate that this latter distinction is nowhere made to rest, even implicitly, on the distinction between factual and evaluative judgements. When we have to determine whether something counts as a success or a non-defectiveness condition for a certain type of illocutionary act, we proceed not by looking at the kind of judgement involved in deciding whether the condition has been satisfied, but by asking whether a failure to satisfy this condition would still make the relative illocutionary act recognisable as an act of that type. If the act is no longer recognisable as such, then the condition in question is a success condition; otherwise, it is a condition of non-defectiveness, even if it takes only a factual judgement to decide that the act was defective by virtue of its failure to meet this condition. A condition that makes an act unrecognisable as an act of a certain type thus serves as a sort of paradigm for determining what is essential to that type of act. Let us take declarative illocutionary acts, for example. A purported declarative illocutionary act that does not even make an attempt to bring about a change in the world solely by virtue of its performance (and so fails to have the characteristic illocutionary point of declaratives) is hardly recognisable as a declarative linguistic act and may be legitimately seen as an illocutionary act of some other kind or even as no illocutionary act at all. On this basis, the illocutionary point can be qualified as a condition of success. The same goes for the failure to present the characteristic mode of achievement of declaratives. Unless an appeal to authority is implied, the resulting act cannot be recognised as a declarative illocution and mistaken for some other kind of illocutionary act. To generalise the point, the lack of the typical illocutionary point, mode of achievement and propositional content sets success conditions, for the failure to instantiate these makes the act at stake unrecognisable as an act of the relevant kind. In contrast, an illocutionary act that fails to satisfy the non-defectiveness conditions of the relevant kind possesses the key traits of an act of that type, but there lies, hidden in it, some imperfection. The imperfection is not serious enough to have the act misunderstood for an act of another type. To continue with the example, an illocutionary act that constitutes an attempt to bring about a change in the world by means of an appeal to authority can be recognised promptly as a declarative act even if the subject performing it does not have the psychological state that is typically associated with declaratives. This more limited impact of the (lack of the) sincerity conditions characteristic of declaratives entitles us to qualify sincerity conditions as non-defectiveness conditions of a declarative illocutionary act. More generally, the lack of typical sincerity conditions and (some) preparatory conditions makes the illocutionary act at stake defective, since it renders the act less than ideal, but does not make it unrecognisable as an act of the relevant kind.

This framework also helps us make sense of Murphy's interpretation of lies and unjustified assertions. That a lie, or a unjustified assertion, can be treated as a defective assertion (namely, an assertion that is successful but less than ideal) depends on the fact that, by violating just the sincerity conditions, lies and unjustified assertions do not lose the external appearance of assertions whose essential structure they preserve, although on closer scrutiny they prove not to be fully-fledged examples of assertions. In other words, a lie, or a unjustified assertion, can be treated as a defective assertion, as opposed to no assertion at all, for it is susceptible of being taken (albeit mistakenly) as an illocutionary act that presents all the defining elements of the general category of assertive illocutionary acts; that is, it looks like an illocutionary act that represents an actual state of affairs (illocutionary point) and this representation appears to be backed by evidence counting in favour of its meaning content (preparatory condition). It is this appearance, however it be formed (resting on factual considerations or evaluative considerations) that justifies the qualification of a lie, or a unjustified assertion, as an assertive illocutionary act even in the face of its failure to comply with the sincerity conditions characteristic of assertions.

The upshot of these remarks is that the rationale behind the distinction between success conditions and non-defectiveness conditions has nothing to do with the factual character of the former as opposed to the evaluative nature of the latter. Contrary to Murphy's interpretation, there is no basis for formulating the distinction in terms of the opposition between facts and values. Indeed, it may be the case that when an illocutionary act lacks a factual element, such as when its constituent sounds are not words of a spoken language or when the context in which it is performed departs from the characteristic background of that kind of speech act, it completely loses its identity and thus becomes unrecognisable. However, this is not a conceptual necessity. There may also be cases where the lack of a factual element renders the act simply defective, not unsuccessful. For example, a (false) representation, echoing the picture given by the opposition parties, of the 2007 centre-left Italian government as unusually divided into factions when it is given by a political scientist during a prestigious public lecture can be mistaken for an assertion in good order, instead of detected as an unjustified assertion told as a result of careless analysis or, indeed, as a lie prompted by a programme of political propaganda. It is therefore a defective assertion, on the assumption (which in Murphy's framework is taken to be factual, not evaluative) that in prestigious public lectures, political scientists mean to make assertions, as opposed to dwelling on superficial remarks or making political propaganda. Then, factual features can arise both at the origin of a mere defect and as the source of failure. Similarly, there might be cases where evaluative impairments make an act unrecognisable as an act of the relevant kind and not just defective. Hence, contrary to Murphy's view, success conditions as well as non-defectiveness conditions can turn on evaluative considerations. This implies that the rationale behind the distinction between the two different sorts of conditions for the possibility of illocutionary acts (success conditions and non-defectiveness conditions) cuts across the fact-value dichotomy that Murphy relies on, and is grounded, instead, on the susceptibility of a given act to be recognised as an act of the relevant kind.

The argument so far has been that the aim-specific and mode-specific components of the normative claim of law correspond to two of the components that make up a directive illocutionary act (these being its illocutionary point and its mode of achievement, respectively) and since these two components frame the success conditions of illocutionary acts generally, they count as elements necessary to the existence of *directive* illocutionary acts specifically. It will now have to be shown that this specific type of act (the directive type) figures *essentially* in any representation of the law, or that legal systems must necessarily be represented as sequences of interrelated *directive* illocutionary acts. Once this is done, we will have a full argument showing that nothing can be regarded as a legal system unless a normative claim can be attributed to it. This is to say that the normative claim is a necessary, if only implicit, component of the law.

Central to this conclusion, whereby the law necessarily carries with it the normative claim, is that the law needs to be represented as the outcome of *directive* illocutionary acts rather than of other kinds of illocutionary acts. But this is an assumption that has to be supported, as even a quick survey of the law will reveal that its statements and issuances may result from any of several different kinds of illocutionary act. True, a good many of these issuances clearly count as orders, mandates, requirements, demands, and the like, that is, as clear examples of directive illocutionary acts. But it is equally clear that many other legal issuances instantiate *other* kinds of illocutionary acts: assertive, declarative and commissive ones, for example. There is a variety of instances and statements in law produced by illocutionary acts of non-directive kinds (assertive, commissive or declarative) that serve different purposes—not only guiding action or making people act in certain ways, but also asserting the truth of propositions, committing oneself to some future course of action, or bringing a state of affairs into being. Given this variety of purposes and instances, why is it that we can choose one such purpose (getting someone to do something, or directing behaviour) and give it prominence, treating it in such a way that *all* legal instances and statements (not just some of them) ought ultimately to count or to be understood as products of *directive* illocutionary acts?

To see why this is so, we have to take up the aforementioned difference between the legal system as a whole and its provisions singly considered and support the view that law is to be represented as the outcome of directive illocutionary acts with respect to both the legal system as a whole and its provisions separately considered. To begin with, while *legal provisions* singly considered do reflect different purposes and make different claims, the overall purpose of the system into which they are set is precisely to govern and guide conduct. And not only are all legal provisions shaped by this general purpose, and make sense within this overall framework and design, but they also contribute to its achievement, however indirectly. In fact, guiding conduct or having something done may well involve (in the sense that it may ultimately be achieved by) representing that thing, or committing to it, or constituting it and bringing it into being, or any combination of these. The assertive, commissive and declarative statements of the law embed a directive element, at least indirectly, that is understood as representing or stating what it is that we are required to do, or otherwise to constitute it, or again to commit to it. The *immediate* purpose and effect of these issuances may not be directive (it may be assertive, commissive or declarative), but the final purpose does carry a directive element, its point being to establish a course of action and to see that it is followed. In this sense, *all* legal provisions can be said to have a directive thrust, if not immediately and expressly so, at least obliquely or indirectly. All legal provisions, in other words, ultimately stem from a directive illocutionary act and can be restated accordingly: even legal provisions that do not immediately require or enjoin a certain form of conduct or behaviour, but rather establish a commitment to it, bring about or alter a state of affairs within the context of the law, or assert the truth of a proposition—even these provisions embody a directive aim, by playing a role within a directive framework, a framework meant to guide conduct. This feature of legal provisions—their forming part of a wider framework—necessarily equips each such provision with the aim-specific component of the normative claim.[55]

[55] My discussion of this point has benefited greatly from a series of conversations with Jason Beckett, whom I wish to thank here. The usual caveat applies; that is, responsibility for these views, and for whatever mistakes I may have made, rests entirely with me.

This mutual relation between the legal system and its provisions assures that the *legal system*, too, necessarily carries the normative claim. But there is also another reason why this is so, turning on the inherently practical nature of the legal system. The answer lies in the thesis that the law is not a theoretical enterprise but a practical one (in its concern with guiding action by offering reasons for it). It is widely agreed that what accounts for the interest the law has in conduct, behaviour and choice-making is not as such the question: What is action? or How is choice-making possible?, but rather: What is the best course of conduct? or What choices ought to be made, on the basis of what criteria, and how is that going to affect us? What is more, there is an explanation for the wide agreement about the law as an inherently practical endeavour. The explanation is that this broad, pliant view can readily be worked into a broad range of otherwise incompatible legal theories and conceptions of law. We can appreciate this point by looking at Steven Burton's illustration of it. In a comment on Raz's legal theory, Burton (1989: 755) fleshes out the idea of 'law as practical reason' through a definition of the law he presents as an umbrella concept seeking to 'speak meaningfully and usefully to a general legal audience while respecting the significant disagreements among the philosophers', that is, while providing a common ground for a variety of different conceptions of law. In his definition, Burton (1989: 758) depicts the law as 'a form of social organization through the systematic institution of supreme authoritative standards of conduct'. We can appreciate four basic elements in this definition, namely, social organization, systematic institution, supreme authority and standard of conduct, but the build-up is toward the fourth and final element—standard of conduct—which figures prominently in the set, and which Burton understands as meaning that the law is essentially concerned with providing its addressees with reasons for acting that are in keeping with this or that standard.

So the basic idea of guiding behaviour (providing standards of conduct) by offering reasons for action, as this idea is captured in the normative claim of law, survives even in the midst of deep disagreement among legal theorists as to what the law is and how it works. This premise is general enough to accommodate a wide range of theories, all of them understanding these reasons to be inherently connected with law as a practical enterprise. This places a strong directive stress on the law and explains the prominent role that directive illocutionary acts play in the making of the law. So, while the legal system cannot *entirely* be explained as the outcome of directive illocutionary acts (for this would claim too much), a system in whose production directive illocutionary acts played no role at all, either mediately or immediately, could not be regarded as a *legal* system at all, for this move would amount to emptying the law of its practical force. To be sure, the law comes into being as the result of several different kinds of illocutionary acts, but the system as a whole depends essentially on the use of directive illocutionary acts. This brings an element of necessity into the equation: it means that the legal system depends *as a whole* on the same success conditions as do directive illocutionary acts, and that the claim built into some of the success conditions of directive illocutionary acts—the claim to give practical guidance—forms an indispensable part of legal systems, too. Hence, explaining the legal system as the outcome of a sequence of illocutionary acts, some of them expressly directive, others only implicitly so, as parts of the larger design of the law, makes it possible to represent the system as necessarily carrying the normative claim, which in this sense becomes a necessary, though not necessarily explicit, condition of the system itself. A legal system that failed to make any claim to guide action by structuring the practical deliberation would contradict by virtue of its content the very conditions whose satisfaction is required for the existence of the system in the first place. Such a failure would amount to a performative contradiction, for it would contradict the conditions of existence of the very illocutionary act by means of which legal systems are represented, this being the directive illocutionary act.

That completes the argument showing the normative claim of law to be necessary. Indeed, it has been shown how just the directive illocutionary act shapes the features of the overarching aim and mode of the law (guiding conduct by providing practical reasons). These features are modelled by speech act theory through its account of the directive illocutionary act, and this type of illocutionary act purports to guide conduct by operating in a particular way, that is, by appealing to our practical reasoning. The directive illocutionary act can thus be used to explain both the *aim*-specific component of the normative claim and its *mode*-specific component: as with any directive illocutionary act, the law not only necessarily aims to guide action but also does so in a specific way, which consists in engaging the practical reasoning of those whose conduct the law aims to guide, by providing these persons with reasons for action, thus establishing practical reasons that these addressees would not otherwise have or recognise as having. In sum, speech act theory not only contributes to showing that the law can make claims, but makes it possible to see the normative claim of law as necessary rather than as merely contingent.

CONCLUSION

The starting point for this chapter was the widely shared but tacit and underdeveloped assumption that the law makes a normative claim of some kind. I tried to explicate this assumption and render it more compelling by giving a clear statement of it, that fashions it into the thesis whereby the law (not only its individual provisions but also the system as a whole) claims to guide conduct by providing its addressees with reasons for acting as directed. This claim, which I called the minimal normative claim, therefore specifies both an aim, that of guiding action, and a corresponding mode, that of offering reasons. The argument was that this claim is not only possible but also necessary; which meant that before this minimal claim could be shown to be necessary, it had to be clear how it was possible. It is so in the sense that the claims of law, regardless of whatever else may be true about them, and how complex the system is that produces them, can always be made in a way that does not involve any fiction. And this non-figurative possibility of claim-making of the law unfolds by way of an argument laid out in four stages, as follows.

First, a distinction was introduced between two senses in which how a claim can be made is understood: a performative sense and an attributive one. In the former sense, a claim is made by an intentional agent and could not exist but for that claim-maker. In the latter sense, a claim is simply attributed to a state of affairs on account of its objective features as considered in light of certain background assumptions that have gained general acceptance. This is to say that attributive claims (a) do not depend for their existence on any specific agent intentionally making the claim, and (b) they inhere in the situation to which they are attributed in such a way that in those cases where principles forming our shared ideology are called into play, these claims not only *can* but also *must* be attributed. This idea of an attributive claim makes it possible to find a way out of what is often considered a dilemma, that between the subjectivist view, under which the law can make claims only through its representatives, and the sceptical view, under which the law cannot make claims at all. But this is a false dilemma, for the denial of the subjectivist view (that the law needs intentional agents to make claims) does not imply the sceptical view (that the law has no way to make any claims at all). There is also a third way: the law can be understood as making claims in an attributive sense, and this is an objective sense of claim-making that needs to be taken into account before reaching the conclusion that there is no sort of claim the law can possibly make.

But before any claim can be attributed to the law, it must be possible to view the law itself as a unitary system rather than as a collection of independent elements, for the interest of the enquiry lies in understanding not how these different elements can make their own separate claims, but how a system-wide claim of law is possible. This takes us to the second stage in the argument. Here, we are dealing with the reality of the law as a complex system, whose different constituents (people, norms, interactions, practices, processes and states of affairs) cannot be ontologically reduced to one another, and we have to arrive at a means of bringing them together as a unitary whole. This was done not by denying the ontological complexity of the law, but by rendering it unitary *in representation*: the law can be *represented* as a single claim-making system without thereby reducing the diversity of its ontology to that of a single substance of some kind. What is more, seeing the law in representation makes it possible to understand certain properties of it, and indeed of any object being represented, which might well not be understood by conducting an ontological investigation alone.

With that argument in place, showing that the law can be made unitary in representation despite its complex ontology, I took the next step and argued that this is a necessary representation of the law, in the twofold sense that the law must necessarily be represented as a unitary system and that this must be done through the medium of the language: the unitary representation was needed, for it would otherwise have been impossible to understand law as a system and to arrive at a *concept* of law, this being the basic objective of any enquiry in general jurisprudence. And the reason why the language became the chosen (and necessary) medium for this unitary representation is that there proved to be no other way to make the different components of the law commensurate, thus making it possible for them to interact as parts of a system despite their ontological diversity.

Finally, this necessary representation of the law as a unitary system that uses language as its medium was further developed in order to show that the legal system can also be represented as a complex sequence of interconnected illocutionary acts. This was important because it is as such, as a sequence of illocutionary acts, that the law can be said to have a claim-making capacity. Indeed, there is a structural claim that illocutionary acts can be understood as making: the claim, namely, that the necessary conditions of their existence are satisfied, since by the very fact that an illocutionary act is at hand and can be used for the purpose specific to it, we know that it has met the conditions that make the act possible in the first place. Therefore, if the law can be represented as a sequence of interconnected illocutionary acts, it can also be understood as making the same claim of these illocutionary acts, this being the claim that the law is satisfying the conditions that make it possible to carry out the illocutionary acts in whose terms the legal system is represented.

In sum, it was the theory of speech acts that made it possible for us to see how the legal system can make claims. This was done by representing the law as a sequence of interconnected illocutionary acts. Three advantages stem from this strategy. First, I could conceive of the law as a unitary whole, this without thereby levelling out the ontological complexity of the diverse components of a legal system. Secondly, I could show how a legal system can make claims: it can make claims in an *attributive* sense, which does not mean in an imaginary or a fictitious sense but in the real sense that claims are ascribed to the law or associated with it in the same objective way that they are found as arising out of other states of affairs. This ties in with the third advantage to the approach, which is that the claims of law can be shown also to be system-wide claims and not only claims specific to any of the single constituents of the legal system to which a claim may be attributed.

This conclusion, that the law *can* make claims as a system, set the stage for the discussion of whether (a) the system-wide claims that the law can make include in their number the normative claim, and whether (b) this claim is necessary. The normative claim is a compound claim comprising an aim-specific and a mode-specific component that together model the idea of law as a system capable of guiding action by offering reasons for such action. So I first determined that (a) the conditions framed by these two components coincide with the conditions framed by two of the components making up the directive illocutionary act, and I then determined that (b) the latter two components, namely, the illocutionary point of the directive act and its mode of achievement, count as *success* conditions for this type of act, meaning that this act could not exist if it failed to satisfy these two conditions. These two arguments, in combination with the argument that the law must necessarily be represented as a sequence of interconnected *directive* speech acts, mark the completion of the overall argument that the law must necessarily make the normative claim. Ultimately, the argument was made to rest on the basic assumption of law as a practical enterprise. This idea of law as a practical enterprise is an independent source of support for the thesis in favour of the necessary normative claim of law, and it is, too, a well-established tenet that needs little backing of its own—it finds its way into a vast range of legal theories that differ in important respects except in their use of this assumption of reason-giving as a fundamental premise.

The thrust of the argument, as developed thus far, is that the normative claim is a defining and hence essential component of the law: the connection between the two (the law and its normative claim) is *conceptual* rather than simply contingent or factual. This means that no issuance of the law, or the legal system as a whole, can qualify as legal unless it at the very least implicitly makes the normative claim. Anything falling short of the normative-claim standard would have to count as a *non-legal* system of social control, or as a system for the plain enforcement of a rule. The normative claim, therefore, establishes a condition for the very existence of the law: it forms part of the very nature of law, to the effect that no concept of law can be adequate that fails to make some reference to the normative claim. This whole defining connection—between law, action-guidingness, reason-giving and normativity—sets the stage for the discussion in the rest of the book, which works out the theoretical consequences of the thesis that the law makes of necessity the normative claim.

2
Generality and Moral Quality

INTRODUCTION

IN THIS AND the next chapter I intend to spell out the essential traits of the normative claim of law, the meaning and status of which were elucidated in chapter one. This goal will be pursued by taking up the treatment the normative claim of law undergoes in the legal theories informed by the basic tenets of analytical legal positivism, in both its inclusive and exclusive versions. The reason for dealing with the two main varieties of contemporary analytical positivism separately is that the champions of inclusive positivism draw a picture of the normative claim of law that is markedly different not only from the picture delineated by the theorists endorsing non-positivism, but also from the picture defended by those who embrace the exclusive version of legal positivism. That is, it is the distinctiveness of the inclusive-positivist account of the normative claim of law that warrants attending specifically to inclusive positivism and keeping its discussion separate from the discussion of other positivist accounts—in particular, Joseph Raz's account, which will be taken up in chapter three.

Whilst the characterisation of the normative claim of law takes shape here by means of a critical examination of the works of a number of legal theorists working within the tradition of inclusive positivism, the greater focus of the chapter is on the normative claim itself, not on inclusive positivism. Hence, the effort to introduce the basics of inclusive positivism and the view of normativity stemming from its fundamental tenets is carried out with an eye to elucidating the traits of the normative claim of law, which is the key concern of the overall argument deployed in the chapter as well as in the book. In other words, by introducing and taking issue with the way in which the theorists endorsing inclusive positivism deal with the normative dimension of the law, I intend to proceed further in my exploration of the essential features of the normative claim of law. Thus, the argument carried out here will be instrumental primarily and predominantly as leading to an improved understanding not of inclusive positivism itself, but of the normative claim of law.

The argument deployed here proceeds as follows. Its first step consists in introducing the fundamental theses of inclusive positivism, with a specific emphasis on the core views concerning the normative claim of law put forward by the theorists who give analytical legal positivism an inclusive twist, such as Herbert Hart, Jules Coleman and Matthew Kramer. In this part, I will show that the torchbearers of inclusive positivism converge on the stance, defended in the preceding chapter, that the normative claim of law is practically oriented, has directive force and is reason-related. To this extent, the champions of inclusive positivism are likely interlocutors of this study. However, the picture of the normative claim of law that can be gleaned from a comparative analysis of the works of Hart, Coleman and Kramer also presents other, more disputable, features. In particular, for all the differences of detail displayed in the approaches of Hart, Coleman and Kramer, those advocates of inclusive positivism deny the necessity of the normative claim of law, its moral quality, and its generality—features that I argue to be fundamental characteristics of the normative claim of law. A critical discussion of the theses concerning the normative dimension of the law formulated by the champions of inclusive positivism is therefore required before the necessity of the normative claim of law can be further consolidated.

More specifically, the nub of the argument deployed in this chapter is that the inclusive-positivist account of the normative claim of law is insightful but not entirely satisfactory, and this for no fewer than three reasons. To begin with, inclusive positivists describe as merely optional and possible a claim that is instead necessary and so distinctive of the law. Furthermore, the advocates of inclusive positivism misrepresent the object of the normative claim of law in so far as, following Hart's insight, they look for a peculiarly legal normativity instead of granting that the normativity of law is a particular instantiation of the normativity of practical reason and is not insulated from moral normativity. Finally, inclusive positivists arbitrarily delimit the scope of the normative claim of law, which is treated as a claim limited to just those legal actors who are committed to a legal system, that is, typically legal officials, instead of as a contention directed at the universality of citizens. By taking issue with the picture emerging from the inclusive-positivist camp, I will argue, first, that denying the necessity of the normative claim of law leads to a misunderstanding of the relationships between law and normativity. Secondly, I shall argue that the object of the normative claim of law is misrepresented in so far as it is conceived of as a peculiar or unique kind of normativity, which, though irreducible to any of the classes of practical normativity we are familiar with in non-legal contexts, shares with non-legal practical normativity the ability to mould practical deliberation in an all-encompassing way. Finally, I shall be arguing that to delimit the scope of the normative claim of law, to the effect that it is seen as a claim made only on those committed to a legal system, is at the origin of both a defective understanding of the legal enterprise and a mistaken picture of the relations obtaining between officials and citizens. These flaws compel us to move beyond the horizons of inclusive positivism in our search for the defining traits of the normative claim of law. Therefore, this chapter overall records a (partial) failure, but one that teaches us something important about the status, object and compass of the normative claim of law. It is precisely because there is so much to learn from a discussion of inclusive positivism, notwithstanding the fact that inclusive positivists are wrong, that a critical presentation of the inclusive-positivist treatment of the normative claim of law is an insightful starting point for a comprehensive study of that claim.

INCLUSIVE POSITIVISM AND THE NORMATIVE CLAIM OF LAW

Inclusive positivism, a thinly veiled form of legal positivism, has been introduced in the Anglo-American tradition of analytical legal philosophy in response to the criticism that Ronald Dworkin made of Hart's theory of law. Dworkin had claimed that the legality of norms does not necessarily depend on their having a social source: there are occasions when legal validity depends solely on morality. The concept of law, then, ought to be explained in terms of a combination of social facts and moral values. In reply to Dworkin, some positivists have argued that the core commitments of legal positivism are not in the end inconsistent with an acknowledgement that morality is numbered among the criteria of legal validity.[1] The legal validity of a norm can be determined by using tests based on content, rather than on procedure alone, without thereby undermining legal positivism.[2] This reply is based on the distinction between the *criteria* of legal validity and the *grounds* of such criteria. In so far as we understand legal positivism as making a specific claim about the conditions for something to exist as a criterion of legal validity (grounds) rather than about its content, the criteria of legal validity can be acknowledged as picking up moral content—and this without our having to abandon legal positivism or its explanatory force, so long as the grounds of those criteria can be argued to be independent of morality. This approach has been taken up by Hart himself, who in the postscript to his *The Concept of Law*, states that inclusive positivism counts as the best interpretation of his theory.[3] Hart's endorsement of inclusive positivism has lent new impetus to research that had begun a few years earlier with Coleman and Will Waluchow, as well as prompting new studies, carried out by Kramer among others.[4]

Coleman describes inclusive positivism in succinct terms when he says that it espouses a view of law as a social practice in which the criteria of legality are established conventionally. Morality, he continues (2001: 173), 'may, but need not, be a criterion of legality', and 'the content of law is generated by a function that operates on the content of those authoritative pronouncements that satisfy the relevant criteria of legality'. By allowing the legality of normative statements to depend on their substantive moral merits, not just on their social sources, inclusive positivism is able to explain in the straightforward sense the 'surface syntax' of contemporary legal practice, which 'includes instances in which morality appears to be a sufficient condition of legality, and sometimes to be a necessary condition', without abdicating the positivist framework of thought (Coleman 2000: 176). That the inclusive approach finds proponents within the positivist camp is warranted by the

---

[1] This defensive strategy has informed to a certain extent the work of David Lyons and Philip Soper. See Lyons (1977) and Soper (1977).
[2] See Lyons (1977: 423–6).
[3] See Hart (1994: 250–4).
[4] The chief contributions to inclusive positivism include Coleman (1982), Waluchow (1994), Coleman (1998), Kramer (1999), Coleman (2001) and Kramer (2004).

statement, endorsed by both inclusive positivism and positivism in general, that the asserted dependence of law on morality has nothing to do with the nature of law but is a contingent feature.[5] Typically, the incorporation of morality into the law depends on the content of the rule of recognition—the convention lying at the foundation of the law and directing the officials of a given system to treat certain standards as criteria of legality.[6] In the inclusive-positivist view, it is not required that the rule of recognition specify social facts only; it may also carry, and often does carry, moral values.[7] So long as the standards of legality are recognised as being established by the practice of officials, then, from the positivist point of view, there is no problem in acknowledging that legality will sometimes end up depending on morality:[8] since this dependence is not dictated by the nature of law, the truth of legal positivism is untouched also in the face of the apparent fact that moral standards contribute to identify the valid legal norms, for the connection between the law and morality, thus stated, is merely contingent—not necessary—and the law is therefore ultimately a matter of convention, just as legal positivism argues.[9]

Inclusive positivism, then, takes up the logical space separating the claim, advocated by various forms of non-positivism, that the standards of critical morality are properly seen as defining components of the law, from the exclusive-positivist claim that 'all law is source based, and anything which is not source based is not law' (Marmor 2002: 104). These two extreme positions seem to allow for a third way, a middle ground where the inclusion of morality within the law can be argued to be neither necessary (as the non-positivist view would have it) nor impossible (the exclusive-positivist view) but merely possible.[10] The latter proposition makes this

[5] Cf Coleman (2001: 107–9) and Kramer (2004: 2).

[6] Importantly, the contingent incorporation of morality into law can also take different routes: the appeal to the features of the rule of recognition is just one explanation of such incorporation open to inclusive positivism, as opposed to the explanation required by it. On this aspect, see Coleman (2000: 175 n 8).

[7] As Coleman (1982: 141–2) puts it, 'a particular rule of recognition may specify truth as a moral principle as a truth condition for some or all propositions of law without violating the separability thesis, since it does not follow from the fact that in one community in order to be law a norm must be a principle of morality that being a true principle of morality is a necessary condition of legality in all possible legal systems'. See also Lyons (1977: 425) and Hart (1994: 250).

[8] In other terms, legal positivism is vindicated if 'the relevance of morality is determined in any legal system by the contingent content of that society's rule of recognition' (Marmor 2002: 105). See also Lyons (1977: 425) and Coleman (1998: 406–7).

[9] This statement makes it apparent that the core commitment of inclusive positivism is no more than a commitment to the conventionality of the grounds of the criteria of legality: what can count as grounds of legality is established by social facts alone and so depends on some convention rather than on moral arguments. On the significance of the link obtaining between legal positivism and conventionalism, see Coleman (2001: 74–102), who constructs legal positivism as the attempt to explain the possibility of the existence and authority of the law by appealing exclusively to the notion of social convention. Whilst Coleman's suggestion is ungrounded if it is taken to be an interpretation of the whole positivist tradition (Kelsen's legal positivism and so much of contemporary continental positivism that sees in Kelsen's view an essential reference can in no way be reduced to the enterprise of explaining the existence of the law in social terms), it can aptly summarise a large part of contemporary analytical legal positivism.

[10] Thus, inclusive positivism can be interpreted as 'a theory of possible sources of legality', to wit, a theory that '*allows* or *permits* substantive or moral tests of legality' (Coleman 2001: 108).

form of positivism an inclusive one since it 'allows that moral precepts can figure among the criteria that guide officials' ascertainment of the law' and so rejects 'the view that every criterion for law-ascertainment in every credibly possible legal system is focused on nonnormative matters of provenance' (Kramer 2004: 2).

The inclusive-positivist acknowledgement that legal validity may depend on substantive moral merits takes a radical form and a moderate one, each yielding a different version of inclusive positivism.[11] In the radical version, such as the one found in Coleman, morality can enter as both a necessary and a sufficient condition of legality. Thus, we may have legal systems where a normative statement cannot qualify as law unless it also meets certain moral standards (and this is a necessary condition), but then we might also have legal systems where a statement becomes law simply by virtue of its meeting a moral standard (morality as a sufficient condition). This implies that there are no constraints on the criteria of legality. Other inclusive positivists reject the thesis that morality can be a sufficient condition of legality. Kramer, for one, is adamant in rejecting the view that, in ordinary cases, consistency with a moral principle could be a sufficient condition of legality for, as he argues, given the existence of widespread disagreement over the content of morality, this position would transmit to the day-to-day life of a legal system a degree of uncertainty and irregularity that puts at risk not only its functionality but, more dramatically, its very existence.[12] Contrary to Coleman's too far-reaching proposition that legal positivism does not presuppose any limit on the substance of the criteria of legality, then, Kramer (2004: 26) claims that:

> there are in fact some constraints on the sorts of criteria that can form a Rule of Recognition. No such rule can consist solely of the criteria that fail to secure the minimum of regularity which is prerequisite to the existence of a legal system.[13]

---

[11] The two differing version of inclusive positivism are discussed at some length by Coleman (2001: 126–33) and Kramer (2004: 24–44).

[12] See Kramer (2004: 26–34). Further criticism of this version of inclusive positivism is presented in Kramer (2004: 97–102).

[13] See also Kramer (2004: 44). Because the two positions are distinct, Kramer (2004: 2–3) suggests that we should call them by different names: incorporationism and inclusive positivism. So, whereas the majority view, which will be followed here, treats incorporationism as synonymous with inclusive positivism, Kramer defines incorporationism as the specific view that it may be the case that moral soundness is *sufficient* to make a standard a legal standard, whereas inclusive positivism, argued to be 'the position with the firmest grounding in Hart's own work,' is taken by Kramer (2004: 2) to be the more general view that 'it can be the case, though it need not be the case, that a norm's consistency with some or all the requirements of morality is a precondition for the norm's status as a law in this or that jurisdiction'. Inclusive positivism and incorporationism are distinct but not inconsistent. Kramer, for instance, adheres to both inclusive positivism and (a moderate version of) incorporationism. More specifically, for Kramer, incorporationism holds true in hard cases but cannot apply to easy cases, where morality can be at most a necessary condition, not a sufficient one. As Kramer (2004: 53) phrases it, 'a norm's correctness as a moral principle can be a sufficient condition for its status as a legal norm in this or that system of law' but 'in credible legal systems where moral correctness does amount to a sufficient condition for legal validity, it does not amount to such a condition in most cases'. For, only in hard cases 'are moral precepts incorporated into a legal regime as some of its norms. If a scheme of governance were instead to treat moral correctness as a sufficient condition for legal validity in all circumstances (rather than only in the circumstances that breed hard cases), it would lack the regularity and coordination that are essential features of anything rightly classifiable as a regime of law'.

72 Generality and Moral Quality

Proceeding on these premises, inclusive positivism endeavours to explain the nature of law by elaborating on the view that the issues surrounding the existence and authority of the law constitute the two central problems of jurisprudence.[14] The study of the normative claim of law is part and parcel of the analysis of the authority of the law: in so far as we accept the idea that the law is authoritative (a source of guidance), we should also acknowledge the existence of a normative dimension to the law. This acknowledgement makes the question of the normative claim of law highly significant.

The inclusive-positivist view of the normative claim of law is shaped by the belief that the normative dimension of the law can be characterised in terms of the practical reasons the law is taken to provide. As Coleman (2001: 71) puts it, 'law purports to govern conduct as a *practical authority*. The distinctive feature of law's governance on this view is that it purports to govern by *creating reasons for action*'. Accordingly, the normative claim is made whenever the law asserts to be able to provide at least some people with practical reasons. Crucially, the reasons for action that the law purports to create are not reasons of any kind whatever, but rather content-independent, peremptory and genuine reasons.[15] They are *content-independent* in that they derive their status *qua* practical reasons from their provenance in formal sources, not by virtue of their substantive dimension, and, hence, are reasons to act independently of the merits of the prescribed conduct. They are *peremptory*, for they cut off any independent deliberation or argument on the part of the addressees as to the value of doing the required act. Finally, they are *genuine*, for (notwithstanding the fact that they are specifically legal reasons, and so are irreducible to moral reasons) they enter into competition with moral reasons. This last feature—genuineness—neatly distinguishes the reasons attached to the law from the reasons supplied by the standards governing games, in that legal reasons (Coleman 2001: 143):

> are not tied to the institution [of law] in the way, for example, many of rights and duties created by the rules of a game are . . . Legal duties arise in law, but they are duties that figure in our determination of what we ought to do generally and not just in our deliberations about what we ought to do in playing the game 'law'.

The content of the normative claim of law can be further specified by taking into account the inclusive-positivist theory of normativity. The key position that the account of normativity occupies in the legal framework laid out by inclusive positivism has been apparent since Hart's seminal version. In Hart's work, the appeal to the normative dimension of the law is essential to criticising the command theories of law and so to introducing a revised form of legal positivism. For Hart, command theories boil down to inadequate theories of the nature of law, for they are unable to make sense of the normative language used in the legal domain. Because legal language is normative, it cannot be reduced without deformation to

---

[14] The centrality of existence conditions and the authority of the law in legal studies is clearly stated in Coleman (2001: 67–73).

[15] On this point see Hart (1982: 255–61) and Coleman (2001: 120–1).

an array of statements expressing the condition of being obliged, or forced, to do something, as command theories have it. Legal language, in other words, consists of statements conveying the state of having an obligation, or being obligated, to do what the law prescribes. Statements of obligation presuppose that one adopt a specific attitude towards the law, the internal point of view, which can be characterised as the standpoint of one who accepts, and so is committed to, the legal enterprise. Since the internal point of view is thought to account for the normativity of *legal language*, in Hart's work we do not find a comprehensive theory of the normativity of *law*, but rather a segment of it. More ambitious accounts of legal normativity are instead formulated by contemporary advocates of inclusive positivism. The most developed of them is put forward by Coleman, who building on Hart's account of the internal point of view and taking us a step further, specifies the conditions making it possible for the law to impose obligations.

Coleman (2001: 88) characterises the internal point of view as 'a basic and important psychological capacity of human beings', the capacity to 'adopt a practice or pattern of behaviour as a norm'. When it is understood as the disposition to endorse given standards, rather than as a belief or credence, the internal point of view can explain how a certain regularity of behaviour can provide practical reasons. The key notion here is that of endorsement. Embracing the internal point of view in respect to regular patterns of behaviour means to endorse those patterns and the practice resulting therefrom. Endorsed patterns are not mere facts, as such constitutively unable to create reasons to act; they do generate reasons to act in accordance with the prescriptions emanating from those practices. The reasons created by an endorsed practice will, in addition, be public, or social, as opposed to personal, in so far as the endorsed practice is not private, but rather shared by, and common to, a multitude of subjects. Thus, to the extent that we define the law in terms of some social practice, we have also an explanation of its normativity.[16] And in the inclusive-positivist view there is indeed a social practice that lies at the foundations of the law: the rule of recognition, which presents the structure of a social convention obtaining among the officials who enact and apply the law. Coleman's strategy, then, consists in explaining the normativity of the rule of

---

[16] The view that at the very core of normativity we find a formalised social practice, the nature of which is conventional, is a recurring trait of analytical legal positivism today. Remarkably, another influential contemporary theory of law, the institutional theory of law introduced and consistently defended by Neil MacCormick since the 1980s, upholds this view. In a nutshell, on MacCormick's (2007a: 11) view, the normative character of the law depends on the existence of a shared legal practice, which in its 'totality' is 'rationally intelligible'. Building on an analysis of the practice of queuing, MacCormick argues that the normative dimension is made possible by the concomitant presence within a social setting of such factors as a minimum threshold of compliance with a given pattern of behaviour, a widely held belief that that pattern is the right thing to do, a mutual awareness of the existence of that shared belief, and some reciprocal expectations towards the conduct the other members of the social group will undertake. In other terms, normativity emerges 'whenever people conduct themselves in relation to others on the basis of an opinion concerning the right thing to do which they suppose to be a mutual opinion, provided that there turns out to be sufficient community (not perfect identity) of opinions held and acted on. I act as I think it right to do, subject to thinking you also think it right and act reciprocally on your opinion, and so on' (MacCormick 2007a: 18). A similar explanatory strategy is explored at length in Lagerspetz (1995).

recognition by relying on the obligatory force of endorsed social conventional practices, and he thereby indirectly derives the normative force of all the other legal provisions—which, then, are taken to borrow their normativity from the normativity of the rule validating them.[17]

Apparently, the nature of the rule of recognition is key to this explanation. Whereas some legal positivists characterise it by appealing to the notion of coordination convention in the game-theoretical sense, Coleman objects to this interpretation, which forces upon its proponents too narrow a conception of the rule of recognition,[18] and opts for an explanatory strategy relying on Michael Bratman's notion of 'shared cooperative activity'.[19] A shared cooperative activity is a convention among parties who share three basic characteristics: they are mutually responsive (each participant in a shared cooperative activity chooses to behave in a way that takes into account the behaviour of fellow participants); they are mutually supportive (each is inclined to help and support fellow participants); and they are committed to the activity that joins them (each is committed to the activity that everyone carries out). A shared cooperative activity is capable of producing obligations to act as prescribed owing to the commitment inherent therein: the participants' mutual commitment fosters mutual reliance and gives rise to legitimate expectations, which in turn provide each person with obligations to act in accordance with the expectations of others. A shared cooperative activity may be said to replicate in this sense the structure of pacts and promises. Like a pact or promise, a shared cooperative activity carries a binding force based on the mutual expectations brought about by reciprocal commitments. Because conventional practices, when they come in the shape of a shared cooperative activity, can clarify the ability to provide obligations, Coleman (2001: 97) concludes that once we understand the rule of recognition as a shared cooperative activity we have a 'plausible and attractive' account of the 'practices of officials necessary to create and sustain law'. The normativity of law is so explained by appealing to the existence of a conventional social practice among the legal officials: to the extent that they adhere to the rule of recognition, it imposes on them an obligation to enforce the provisions validated by them.[20]

Two key points should be emphasised in this explanation of the normativity of law, and, accordingly, of the content of the normative claim of law. First, Coleman's approach makes it possible for inclusive positivism to characterise the normativity of law as a distinctive and specific kind of normativity (call it social

---

[17] This strategy is set out in Coleman (2001: 95), for instance.

[18] The conventional route is explored by Postema (1982) and Green (1985). For Coleman (2001: 94) that route is problematic; for, 'coordination conventions are solutions to games in which the participants' *ex ante* preferences have a specific structure, or are ordered in certain specific ways—ways that constitute what we call "partial conflict" or "battles of sexes" games'. Hence, to represent the rule of recognition as a coordination convention 'would place an arbitrary and baseless constraint in our concept of law'.

[19] See Coleman (2001: 92–4). Although Coleman has since withdrawn his support to this view, it remains the most developed and comprehensive explanation of the normativity of law provided by the champions of inclusive positivism and, for this reason, will be carefully discussed in this chapter.

[20] For this explanation, see Coleman (2001: 77).

normativity), which presents a nature that cannot be reduced without misrepresentation to the nature of moral normativity. In contrast to the normativity of morality, which originates in a critical practice, the (social) normativity of law derives from a conventional practice. Secondly, Coleman's theory of legal normativity remains substantially faithful to the non-cognitivist, expressivist position originally defended by Hart. For Coleman, as for Hart, legal obligations are ultimately grounded on acceptance, namely, the law is authoritative for those who commit themselves to the social convention grounding legal practices. In the absence of acceptance, the rule of recognition is unable to create obligations and the normativity of law collapses. Even in recent developments, then, inclusive positivism remains anchored to Hart's view (1982: 160) that in law obligations do not compel action in a categorical way but, 'as the etymology of "duty" and indeed "ought" suggests', refer to 'actions which are due from or owed by the subjects having the duty, in the sense that they may be properly demanded or exacted from them'.[21]

In sum, the normative claim of law is presented by the advocates of inclusive positivism as the contention that legal institutions can guide action by providing legal officials with practical reasons of a distinctively legal kind, which can be characterised as reasons that enter into competition with moral reasons, but are not reducible to moral reasons, which hold independently of their content, and which preclude further deliberation as to how we ought to act.

This claim has not been consistently treated as a necessary claim of law within inclusive positivism. In fact, the question whether such a claim is necessarily associated with the law is not one that the champions of inclusive positivism take up directly. Therefore, we do not have a common established view of the matter within the inclusive-positivist camp. Instead, it can be argued that some inclusive positivists, such as Hart and Coleman, might be more amenable to acknowledge the necessary status of the normative claim of law, whereas others, such as Kramer, defend a theoretical framework decidedly hostile to it.

Support for the necessary character of the normative claim of law can be extracted from Hart's acknowledgement that the essential function of the law is guidance. After noting that a functionalist definition of the law is more misleading than illuminating, Hart adds that at least one general function ought invariably to be associated with the existence of the law, the function to guide conduct.[22] The qualification of this function as necessary to the law leads to the proposition that the contention to guide action, made at least implicitly by the law, should likewise be considered necessary. Since the normative claim is a specific instantiation of law's avowed purpose of channelling conduct, the necessary character of the

---

[21] This position entails the rejection of any cognitive analysis of obligation, analysis that would link the existence of an obligation to the existence of objective reasons to act in the prescribed way. Therefore, whereas inclusive positivists claim that legal theorists should refrain from engaging in meta-ethical debates (cf eg Hart 1994: 253–4 and Coleman 2002: 172) their views of the normative dimension of the law are grounded on, and vindicated by, certain meta-ethical assumptions.

[22] See Hart (1994: 249).

latter passes on to the former. Thus, the acknowledgement of the guidance function of the law brings with itself the view that the law makes of necessity the normative claim. In this version of inclusive positivism, then, the main question relative to the normative claim is not one related to its necessary existence but rather one concerning its extension. Coleman's treatment is exemplary in that respect. In his reply to Shapiro's defence of exclusive positivism, which is grounded on the assertion of the practical difference thesis,[23] Coleman distinguishes between the claim to make a difference in the way we ought to behave that needs to be associated with the existence of a legal system, and the same claim that needs to be linked with individual legal provisions. In its systemic dimension, the law 'necessarily claims a normative power to create genuine rights and obligations' (Coleman 2001: 144). Thus, for Coleman it is a conceptual truth about the law that legal systems make the normative claim. In contrast, individual laws can, but need not, claim authority. The general normative claim of law, which is conceptually true, 'does not entail any claims about what must be true of any particular law,' since 'what is or must be true of *the law* need not be true of *a law*': between 'what must be true about law' and 'what must be true about *each* law' there remains a logical gap (Coleman 2001: 144). In sum, Coleman embarks on a circumstantiated defence of the necessary status of the normative claim of law, which is conceptually attached to legal systems but not to legal provisions.

This view finds no support in Kramer's version of inclusive positivism. Without considering directly the issue relative to the status of the normative claim of law, Kramer, in his discussion of the Hart-Raz debate on the nature of the obligations created by the law, defends an imperative-based theory that sits uncomfortably with the acknowledgement of the necessity of the normative claim of law. For Kramer rejects, at least in part, the reason-based analysis of legal norms carried out by Raz on the ground that legal norms are not perforce prescriptions and so do not necessarily express practical reasons.[24] Raz's confidence in the relationship obtaining between law and reasons disregards the fact that legal norms can be stark imperatives as well as prescriptions.[25] The notion of imperative is categorically distinct from that of prescription: whereas prescriptions create reasons to act and so inhabit the realm of 'ought', Kramer (1999: 84) conceives of imperatives as instances of 'must', which in isolation from the penalties attached to them 'do not necessarily lay down or presuppose reasons-for-action for their addressees'. In so far as the law is constituted by imperatives, its connection with practical reasons is merely contingent rather than intrinsic. This conclusion calls into question, indirectly at any rate, the necessary status of the normative claim of law: being detached from reasons and from 'ought', imperatives carry no normative claim;

---

[23] 'Practical difference thesis' refers to the claim that 'legal rules must in principle be capable of securing conformity by making a difference to an agent's practical reasoning' (Shapiro 2000: 129). The argument for exclusive positivism, based on the practical difference thesis, is laid out in Shapiro (2000) and Shapiro (2001).

[24] This argument is adduced in Kramer (1999: 83–9).

[25] Cf Kramer (1999: 87), who denies that 'legal norms are always actually or putatively prescriptive' and argues that though they 'can indeed be prescriptions, they can likewise be stark imperatives'.

accordingly, a legal system consisting solely of imperatives will make no normative claim. In such a system, citizens would be given no reasons, be they moral or prudential, to follow legal provisions, provisions that instead reflect exclusively the interests of the officials enacting them. This construction of a legal system blocks the very possibility of associating law and any claim to guide conduct by creating practical reasons. To rephrase the point, in so far as the law consists of stark imperatives, the legal realm belongs to the sphere of 'must', not to the sphere of 'ought'. This erodes the very normative character of the law, for normativity is an 'ought'-related dimension. Accordingly, the normative claim is not conceptually linked with the law. Far from being a necessary, and so distinctive, character of the law, then, in Kramer's version of inclusive positivism the normative claim may be altogether absent in legal systems.

This sceptical attitude towards the necessity of the normative claim of law is given expression, too, in Kramer's criticism of the 'authority thesis'—to wit, the view introduced by Raz that a legal system adopts a normative posture and requires all those to whom it applies to acknowledge its authority as legitimate.[26] In discussing the issue, Kramer denies that the claim to legitimate authority is essential to the law: thus, its elision ends up conflating legal systems and non-legal structures of governance. To this effect Kramer sets out to confute all the major argumentative strategies Raz appeals to in support of the authority thesis.[27] First, Kramer rejects Raz's view that the normative posture of the law is attested by the fact that the statements made by the officials acting on behalf of the law to support their decisions and the mechanisms of enforcement implementing those decisions have a justificatory tenor. In Raz's view, official legal statements are not purely informative and explanatory statements but also serve to vindicate the relevant decisions as legitimate. For Kramer, by contrast, it might well be the case, notably in evil legal regimes, that legal officials confine themselves to statements that serve merely to reinforce the incentives for compliance with the legal requirements by pointing out that violations of applicable legal dictates will give rise to punishments and penalties. Hence, far from incorporating a justificatory tenor, the statements of legal officials may simply be a means of highlighting the correlation between disobedience to law and subjection to punishment. Secondly, Kramer disagrees with Raz on the thesis that unless the normative attitude of the law is acknowledged, the distinction between law and purely coercive systems evaporates. In Kramer's view, purely coercive regimes and legal systems are distinguishable not on the basis of the fact that only legal systems make the claim to legitimate authority but rather on the basis of formal, or structural, elements having to do with the sway of legal requirements. Legal systems present a structure different from purely coercive regimes, for they impose requirements that 'typically apply to indefinitely numerous people for long periods of time' and 'cover a far, far wider range of behaviour than the usual instructions of a gunman' (Kramer 1999: 95). The criteria distinctive of legal

---

[26] This thesis, introduced in Raz (1979: 28–33 and 1994: 199), will be discussed in detail in the next chapter.
[27] See in particular Kramer (1999: 89–101).

systems, then, reside in the generality and durability of legal provisions, as well as in the regularity with which those provisions are applied. We have a fully-fledged legal system whenever those structural criteria are fulfilled and this independently of whether or not some legitimate authority is claimed. Finally, Kramer contests Raz's strategy to ground the authority thesis in certain legal officials' belief, especially the belief of judges, in the legitimate authority of the law. In this context, Kramer notices that such belief is inessential to the law as it is shown by the absence of that belief in monstrous legal regimes, where legal officials, among them judges, simply apply the legal provisions in force without professing confidence in, or committing themselves to, the legitimacy of those provisions.

Kramer's criticism of Raz's authority thesis is also relevant to the discussion of the normative claim of law: if the justificatory tenor may be totally absent from legal statements, form is taken to be enough to distinguish law from non-law, and no belief in the justification of legal provisions is present among judges, not only the claim to legitimate authority that Raz acknowledges to be conceptually associated with the law but also any other justificatory and non-form-related claim, such as the normative claim, fails to be distinctive of, and so necessary to, the law. Otherwise stated: since general, durable and regular systems of governance incorporate of necessity no justificatory attitude and by themselves create no practical reasons, moral or otherwise, the status of the normative posture of the law is far from necessary to legal governance.

FAILURE OF THE INCLUSIVE-POSITIVIST ACCOUNT

The preceding remarks show that inclusive positivism has constructed an illuminating account of the normative claim of law. There is much to praise in, and learn from, a theory describing the normative claim of law as the contention that legal systems possibly provide legal officials with peremptory and content-independent reasons to act, which are peculiarly legal and grounded on the endorsement, if only implicit, of the concerned individuals. This conception constitutes a solid starting point for the comprehensive treatment of the normative claim of law. However, there are at least three reasons to doubt that the inclusive-positivist account provides a satisfactory characterisation of the normative claim of law: inclusive positivists (i) fail convincingly to establish on firm grounds the necessary *status* of the normative claim of law, (ii) wrongly characterise its *object*, normativity, and (iii) construe too narrowly its *scope*. Each of these reasons of dissatisfaction will be considered in turn in the following three sections.

Non-contingent Status of the Normative Claim of Law

Whereas inclusive positivists do not argue explicitly against the necessary status of the normative claim of law, at least when this claim is attributed to legal systems, in some cases they defend a conceptual framework that is blatantly at odds with the recognition of the necessity of that claim. The qualification of the normative claim of law as merely contingent, as found in the works of some inclusive positivists, stands in sharp contrast to the conclusion I drew in the previous chapter, where I argued instead for the necessary status of the normative claim of law. In my argument, I used two basic views as premises of that conclusion. The first premise: by its very nature, the law is an institution aiming to provide some guidance in the practical sphere. The second premise: the essential guiding function of the law is carried out by supplying people with reasons to act, as opposed to prodding or coercing them. Building on these premises, I represented the law as the outcome, direct (legal systems) or indirect (individual legal provisions), of sequences of coordinated directive illocutionary acts. This representation makes it possible for us to ascribe a necessary normative claim to the law, drawing on the argument that some counterparts to the normative claim figure among the constitutive conditions of directive illocutionary acts. Hence, in order to vindicate the view that the normative claim of law is optional, as opposed to necessary, inclusive positivism should proceed by rejecting at least one of the two main premises of the argument for the necessity of that claim.

The first premise states that the law by its very constitution performs a guiding function. This view has been expressly defended by Hart. Notwithstanding his reluctance to make room for function-related traits in the definition of the law, Hart does not call into question the view that the law of necessity purports to direct conduct. Acknowledging such a function not only coheres with the fundamental tenets of legal positivism but is also an element that sets legal positivism apart from non-positivism, which displays a more ambitious functionalism amounting to the view that the law is in no way limited to providing practical guidance, but instead incorporates an aspiration to govern conduct *legitimately*. For these reasons, the truth of my first premise can hardly be challenged from the standpoint of a coherent inclusive positivism.

My second premise—the view that the law in its ordinary work affects of necessity our deliberations as to how we ought to behave—is less firmly connected with legal positivism and will, then, be the nub of the discussion. Coming from the positivist camp we can identify two sorts of challenge to this thesis, one moderate and the other radical. The *moderate challenge* is brought in by Coleman's partial rejection of the practical difference thesis, a rejection which entails that there may be legal provisions that have no impact on our practical deliberation. The moderate challenge is correct, but it cuts no ice where the issue at stake is concerned. Individual legal provisions can have no impact on our practical deliberation, and so fail to work directly in the fashion I take to be distinctive of the functioning of the law, without threatening the necessity of their normative claim as long as they do participate in the specific mode of the directive function of the law indirectly, that is, by virtue of their sharing in, and having an impact on, a system that is devised overall to shape our practical reasoning. The necessary status of the normative claim attached to single legal provisions can therefore be supported indirectly:

individual legal provisions do not of necessity advance the normative claim but this claim is to be acknowledged as one of theirs by virtue of contributing to a system that is normative and so raises that claim.[28] Because a necessary *indirect* claim is no less necessary than a necessary *direct* claim, Coleman's thesis that laws, as opposed to the law, do not of necessity make a practical difference in our practical deliberation, does not call into question the necessity of the normative claim of law.

The *radical objection* to the premise leading to the conclusion that the normative claim of law is necessary comes from Kramer's thesis that the law can channel conduct not by affecting our practical reasoning but rather by issuing stark imperatives.[29] The implications of this thesis for the argument deployed in chapter one in support of the necessary status of the normative claim of law are apparent: the second premise of that argument is directly called into question by the correctness of Kramer's having conceptualised the law as a set of standards that are not necessarily qualified as prescriptions, or sources of reasons, but that can be presented as imperatives, that is, dictates 'only contingently promotive of the addressees' objectives and projects' and produced by some overwhelming superiority, actual or presumed, of a class of legal agents (Kramer 1999: 86). Here, I intend to take up directly Kramer's view of the law as a device that governs behaviour through the issuance of stark imperatives and, by showing that such a view is untenable, to rescue one of the basic premises of the argument for the necessary status of the normative claim of law. In a nutshell, I will argue in what follows that Kramer's position cannot be maintained, for it sacrifices too much of our understanding of the law, and, what is of greater concern from the inclusive-positivist point of view, proves ultimately incompatible with some insights lying at the core of Hart's theory.

The two problems have a common origin: Kramer's characterisation of imperatives. In Kramer's view, imperatives owe their capacity to channel action to the superiority those issuing them have over the addressees. Because the paradigmatic case of superiority in legal contexts is provided by a disproportion in the parties' 'coercive might' or 'strength', the superiority entailed by the possibility of legal imperatives is well captured by the notion of power relation.[30] This type of relation applies to the situation where an agent has power and is prepared to inflict unwanted harm on another subject without running the risk of a comparable retaliation, so that the latter subject is ready to do what she is required to do, this in order to avoid the harm the former agent is in a position to inflict. In so far as the

---

[28] In chapter one (above), this argument is deployed in detail.

[29] This thesis is closely linked with, though conceptually independent of, Kramer's threefold argument against the authority thesis. For, on the one hand, only monstrous legal systems channel action by issuing imperatives, instead of engaging with the practical reasoning of the subjects called upon to abide by legal directives, and so refrain from occupying the sphere of practical deliberation. On the other hand, Kramer's assertions that there may be legal regimes where officials make no statement of justificatory tenor, legal provisions differ in no substantive respect from the directives enacted in purely coercive systems, and judges have no belief in the moral worth of the directives they apply, describe a heinous regime. The notion of a wicked legal system, thus, provides the link between Kramer's claim that the law can be made of just stark imperatives and his argument against the authority thesis.

[30] See Kramer (1999: 85–6) on this point.

existence of this disproportion in strength is known by the concerned parties, it allows for a situation where a party will act in accordance with directives she has no interest in conforming to, apart from the wish to avoid the sanction. Imperatives, then, do not govern behaviour by shaping citizens' own interests and so creating for them some reasons, moral or prudential, to act, but rather direct citizens to act on the interests of legal officials.

The problem with Kramer's account of imperatives is that it cannot vindicate the distinctive sort of guidance that is associated with the law, namely, that a system of stark imperatives is not a legal system but counts, at most, as a system of governance presenting some similarities with such non-legal models as organised coercion, behavioural conditioning and managerial administration. The non-legal character of a system consisting solely of imperatives can be made apparent by taking a closer look at the ideal-type of such a system that Kramer brings in, Despotia. Despotia is an order where 'the governmental officials sustain their own lavish lifestyle by imposing legal obligations on the citizens to pay crushingly heavy taxes' (Kramer 1999: 88). Since the payment of such heavy taxes 'is neither morally obligatory nor promotive of any citizen's interest', Despotia is a system unable to generate practical reasons for citizens 'apart from considerations of staving off the infliction of penalties' (Kramer 1999: 88). In reaction to that one could notice that Despotia has some structural traits (generality, systematicity, regularity and durability) in common with legal systems; but, *pace* Kramer, Despotia cannot be considered a legal system, for no list composed exclusively of structural elements exhausts the requirements sufficient to qualify a system of governance as a legal system. Essential to, and distinctive of, the notion of a legal system are not only certain structural traits but also a characteristic mode of working and deploying its basic function of directing conduct. Despotia lacks that distinctive mode.

Before elaborating on this statement, I wish to emphasise that the reply is not grounded on non-positivist assumptions. One can certainly argue that in his reliance on a paradigmatic example of a despotic system of governance, Kramer, in order to make his case for the possibility of imperative-made systems of the law, begs one of the main questions at stake in the debate between positivism and non-positivism: the question as to whether wicked orders can be qualified as legal. I will not pursue this argumentative line here. Instead, I will grant, albeit only for the sake of argument, the truth of the positivist claim that iniquitous systems of governance, such as Nazi Germany, Fascist Italy and Apartheid South Africa, can be classified as legal systems despite their extreme injustice. The acceptance of the positivist thesis (namely, of defending the possibility of regarding monstrous systems of governance as law) does not, however, force upon us the distinct view that no operative element ought to be included in the definition of the law to the effect that any credible concept of law had better give up any non-structural criterion of distinction between law and non-law. Legal positivism is coherent with a definition of the law based not only on structural elements but also on a typical *modus operandi*.

The strand of legal positivism that insists on the conceptual distinction between law and coercive mechanisms provides a sound example of such an account of the law. The link, established by positivist scholars such as Hart and Neil MacCormick, between law and reasons for action that are distinct from, and irreducible to, those deriving from the sanctions ordinarily attached to legal provisions, can be interpreted as a well-developed attempt to pursue this route.[31] Crucially, in the work of Hart and MacCormick, the recognition of this link is an essential step towards an explanation of the normativity of law: unless we take the law to be a system of governance operating through the creation of practical reasons, and not just through the issuance of commands, we cannot make sense of the normative character of legal practices. This point is argued convincingly by MacCormick in his treatment of the imperative fallacy. By 'imperative fallacy' MacCormick (1973b: 100) means the persisting 'confusion between the imperative and the normative', leading legal scholars to think that '"ought" is derivable from "shall" or "shall" from "ought" ' to the effect that imperative utterances either imply or mean the same propositions as connected with an 'ought'. The argument proceeds from a net demarcation of the normative, or 'ought'-related dimension, and the imperative, which relates to 'shall', not to 'ought'. The imperative fallacy, then, amounts to the conflation of two distinct categories, 'ought' and 'shall', which are, instead, distinct and mutually not derivable.[32] On the basis of this conflation, it is sometimes maintained that commands and statements about what one ought to do form a homogeneous class. This view, however, is misleading, for as MacCormick (1973b: 102) emphasises, 'it is wrong to assert that commands and other "acts of will" mean "oughts" ' and is, likewise, 'wrong to assert that all norms are necessarily derived from acts of, or acts akin to, commanding'. The distinction between imperatives and normative statements can be appreciated by considering that determining the conduct one ought to pursue does not involve of necessity a command: 'a quite normal use of sentences about what people ought to do' is not to command but 'to *state* the principles or rules which are taken to be guides to conduct and standards against which to criticize it, or to *appeal* to such rules and principles' (MacCormick 1973b: 110). In this framework, claiming that the law is made solely of commands and imperatives is tantamount to asserting that the law is a 'shall'-related discourse and so a non-normative practice. In sum, an imperative-based conception of law cannot assist us to understand the normative operation of the law: when the legal domain is conceived as an arrangement of imperatives, *qua* 'shall'-statements, it is completely detached from the normative dimension.

Whereas Kramer does not fall prey to the imperative fallacy (he is indeed well aware of the distinction between 'ought' and 'shall', and, building on that awareness, claims that the law, which may well result simply from stark imperatives, does not of necessity participate in the normative dimension), MacCormick's discussion of the fallacy is pertinent here, for it clarifies the import of the imperative-centred theory of law, such as the one put forward by Kramer. Because no 'ought' can be

---

[31] See MacCormick (1973b) and Hart (1982: 243–68).
[32] In MacCormick's words (1973b: 112), 'commands are one thing and statements about what ought to be are quite another thing. "Ought" is no more derivable from "shall" than from "is" '.

derived from a 'shall', an imperative-centred account prevents us from connecting law and normativity, with the result that not only may laws occasionally fail to amount to normative standards but also the law, in so far as it is made of a 'substance' (imperatives) that is drastically discontinuous with the sphere of 'ought', is structurally incapable of advancing any claim to possess normative force. So, Kramer's explanation of the law in terms of imperatives generates a thorough separation between law and 'ought'. This is a problem, for such a conception of the law, which treats Despotia-like situations as instances of a legal system, runs against the tradition of mature legal positivism and reduces the law to a social practice that does not participate in the normative experience. This configures Kramer's version of inclusive positivism as a kind of pre-Hartian positivism, one that, by disposing of the thesis of the centrality of the normative dimension in the law, ends up very far removed from the roots of inclusive positivism.

To rephrase the point, far from reflecting a non-positivist stipulation about the necessarily benign character of legal systems, the reason-centred conceptualisation of the legal domain is, indeed, a most valuable achievement of contemporary legal positivism. It makes sense, from a positivist point of view, to define the law in terms of morally neutral elements, possibly drawing here on the argument that the law can serve a vast variety of purposes and ideals, some of which are morally commendable while others are morally indifferent or even morally indefensible, which is to say that no definition that cannot make room for the morally indifferent and reprehensible uses of the law could be correct. But the vast number of uses we can make of the law cannot stretch to the point of denying the existence of a distinctive mode where the pursuit of the guidance function of the law is concerned. Defining the concept of law in morally neutral terms is not the same as defining it by appealing to exclusively structural elements. A morally-neutral definition of the law allows in a perfectly straightforward way for some reference to the essential mode of operating of the law. In addition, a reason-centred account is not only compatible with the positivist enterprise but indeed necessary to the acknowledgement of the normative dimension of the law. Kramer's merely structural characterisation of the law regards the core of the law as coercive and so equates the essence of the law to a sanction-dispensing device. This move makes Kramer's theory accountable of the typical defects we impute to command theories of law: if the law were indeed just a system of imperatives, the laws would guide conduct by means of the threat of sanction, which is tantamount to regarding the law as a sphere that might well not participate in the normative dimension at all. In sum, Kramer's view is untenable, for it allows for the possibility of separating legal discourse altogether from normative discourse.

One might respond at this point that my interpretation of Kramer's theory is not charitable. Nowhere in his work does Kramer state that legal systems can be *entirely* made up of imperatives; his contention is rather that some people (legal officials) can address subjects with respect to whom they have such an overwhelming superiority that they need not give any attention to the addressees' needs and interests. This means that even in evil legal systems, only the relationships between officials and ordinary citizens are governed by imperatives; by contrast, the mutual relationships among officials are governed by prescriptive utterances rather than simply imperatives. Therefore, Kramer's account does not expunge normativity from the legal domain; it merely confines the normative dimension of the law to the territory inhabited by the relationships between officials.

These remarks, however, are of no real help to Kramer, for in the view informed by this reply, the essential normative component of the law is rescued only partially and marginally. In the picture provided by this interpretation of Kramer's work, we can construct legal systems in such a way that ordinary citizens do not participate in the normative component of the law at all; this can consist of a dimension that is experienced by legal officials alone. Far from rescuing the normative dimension of the law, this picture makes a mockery of it by treating normativity as a secondary element of the legal domain. The importance of normativity as a category of legal thought is, as a result, radically diminished. This marginalisation clashes dramatically with the centrality that theorists from different traditions attribute to the normativity of law.[33] Furthermore, this questionable result comes at a high price. Kramer's providing for a necessary normative component found at the margins of the law ends up jeopardising the internal coherence of his formal definition of a legal system, for such a provision gives rise to an asymmetry between prescriptions and imperatives in law. There are conceivable legal systems in which no imperatives are found, that is, systems made up exclusively of prescriptions, but the opposite cannot be the case: a legal system in which all the relationships are governed by imperatives is unimaginable—at least some officials must behave in accordance with prescriptions, not stark imperatives, for a system of laws to be possible at all. If even in a disenchanted view of the law, reason-creating provisions find their way into the system, and necessarily so, then it is hardly deniable that the reason-creating capacity constitutes an essential trait of legality. Accordingly, that capacity should be taken as a defining element of the law—no possible law can completely dispose of it—and so, a characteristic that shapes our concept of law to the same extent as do the structural features of generality, systematicity, regularity and durability. And, once the reason-creating capacity is acknowledged to be a defining characteristic of the law, there is no way to deny the necessary status of the normative claim of law, which is conceptually related to that capacity.

To sum up, Kramer's assertion that the law can simply rely on imperatives to channel the conduct of the individuals concerned is mistaken. Prescriptions are a necessary component of the legal enterprise, which generates reasons to act and so is a means to guide behaviour, as opposed to being a device merely aimed at directing conduct with no impact on the practical reasoning of the individuals concerned. Once the idea of a system made up exclusively of imperatives is set aside,

---

[33] Inclusive positivists, like Hart and Coleman, exclusive positivists, like Joseph Raz, and non-positivists, such as Stephen Perry, all agree on this point, which finds a clear statement, for example, in Perry's (2001: 330) claim that 'the provision of an account of the normativity of law is a central task of jurisprudence, if not the central task'.

not only is the very possibility of cataloguing a monstrous regime as a legal system rendered problematic but also, and more importantly in this context, the necessary connection between law and practical reasons is rescued: in so far as it is made up of prescriptions, the law impinges on the practical reasoning of the individuals it applies to by so partaking of the normative dimension. Thus, no instance of law can refrain from at least making a normative claim, directly or indirectly. The upshot of this argument is that the second premise of the argument leading to the necessary status of the normative claim of law has not been successfully challenged by any proponent of inclusive positivism. Since legal positivists are bound also to accept the other basic premise of the argument, as I have argued above, it can be concluded that the advocates of inclusive positivism are mistaken when they assert that the normative claim of law is inessential and contingent.

Moral Nature of the Normativity of Law

Inclusive positivism is not only mistaken in its definition of the status of the normative claim of law but also in its account of the object of that claim, normativity. Inclusive positivists understand the normativity of law as an atypical sort of practical normativity: a social kind that is distinct from, and cannot be reduced to, the normativity of morality, yet shares with the normativity of morality the ability to mould our practical deliberation in an all-encompassing way. This combination is critical, for it forces one to explain both the distinctiveness and the convergence of the normativity of law and the normativity of morality, which are understood to be utterly heterogeneous kinds that, all the same, compete against one another. Here, I intend to show that this combination is not exhaustively explained by inclusive positivists.

Before I can proceed with the argument, however, a clarification is required. The peculiar combination of distinctiveness and convergence that characterises the conception of the normativity of law endorsed by inclusive positivism is not imposed upon this view by the nature of its legal outlook. Inclusive positivism would be far from incoherent with the view of keeping the normativity of law radically separate from the normativity of morality and modelling the normativity of law on the normativity of games. It is a theoretical option open to legal positivism to shape the notion of legal duty on the concept of obligation derived from the analysis of games. The rejection of a game-modelled view of legal normativity is, then, a precise choice made by the contemporary champions of inclusive positivism. This choice is appropriate and problematic at the same time. It is *appropriate* because game-modelled normativity hardly does justice to the claims the law makes on us. It is common sense to regard the law as impinging on our lives in a deeper, more decisive, and more encompassing fashion than a game. The game model implies that citizens are bound to follow the prescriptions of the law only to the extent that they are willing to play the law-game. This picture departs radically from the common perception that we have of the law. The obligations the law claims to create for us, *qua* ordinary citizens, are distinctively different from the ones generated by games. Whereas the normativity of the standards governing games is conditioned upon our participation in the game, such that as soon as we take leave of the game we are not bound to account for its standards in our deliberation as to how we ought to behave, no such easy escape from legal obligations is available. The law is perceived as binding whether we like it or not. However, the inclusive positivist choice is also *problematic* as it introduces a kind of normativity that is irreducible to any of the species of normativity we are familiar with and so requires specific explanation and support from inclusive positivists. Unfortunately, even the most developed explanation of the peculiar normativity of law that inclusive positivism provides (the one given by Coleman and consisting in the appeal to the notion of shared cooperative activity and the mutual obligations deriving thereof) fails for at least two reasons.

First, how much of a role can the notion of a shared cooperative activity actually play in the law? Not so much of a role. This point has been convincingly argued by Matthew Noah Smith, who shows that a shared cooperative activity is a special case of hypercommittal activity, a kind of activity requiring the involved parties to seek agreement and remain committed to sustaining it.[34] The kind of agreement to which the parties in a shared cooperative activity are committed is twofold, conceptual and epistemic. Conceptual agreement entails that the parties agree both intensionally and extensionally on the concept of the activity they are engaged in. Epistemic agreement requires that the subjects involved in a shared cooperative activity have accurate beliefs about the moves others intend to make in deploying the shared activity. These forms of agreement are paralleled by similar sorts of commitment. Accordingly, we have two basic varieties of commitment to a shared cooperative activity, conceptual commitment and epistemic commitment. To those, a further kind of commitment is to be added, practical commitment, which indicates the commitment by each party to engage in the activity with the other parties and to act in mutually supportive forms. Smith's analytic treatment of the notion of shared cooperative activity makes it apparent that such class of activities is grounded on the possibility of close-knit relations among participants, who in addition to being sensitive to the behaviour and agenda of the others will also have to commit themselves to the social practice in hand.

Achieving such a deep participation in a collective enterprise and such a strong commitment to an institution is going to be a tall order even if, following Coleman, we take it that the participants in question are just the officials, to the exclusion of everyone else in the population subjected to the legal system. The kind of participation and commitment required by the model of shared cooperative activity may possibly obtain in legal systems that govern small, homogeneous communities. But it is hard to see how it can obtain in the legal systems of national states and supra-national entities, where the functionaries are not likely to share by default common aims or to be necessarily devoted to a common

---

[34] See Smith (2006: 278–85).

cause. The likelihood of disagreement, in legal contexts, at both a conceptual level and an epistemic level, is reinforced by the consideration that in legal systems officials need not form a homogenous group. As Smith notes (2006: 285), in modern legal institutions legal officials are not just legislators and judges; they also include functionaries working in 'many administrative agencies that have the authority to issue regulations that we have no reason not to take to be law'. The upshot of this manifold composition is that within the class of legal officials we will find people with the most diverse education, background and political commitment to, as well as some degree of identification in, the legal system. This diversity makes highly implausible the existence of conceptual agreement over the shared activity of legal officials. In addition, the disparate composition of the class of legal officials makes it most unlikely that fellow bureaucrats will be acquainted with whatever mutual intentions and plans may exist. This stands in the way of epistemic agreement among legal officials. The combination of conceptual disagreement and epistemic disagreement is bound also to jeopardise the possibility of commitment, conceptual, epistemic and practical. This lack of agreement and commitment emerges not only when we consider the workings of remote departments within a legal system, but also the functioning of specific segments of the same department: even functionaries performing similar institutional roles and tasks need not have shared beliefs about, or any commitment to, their mutual agendas. The effect is that, besides being merely possible and not necessary, no commonality of objectives extends of necessity to all the officials, especially not where they occupy different hierarchical levels and have diverse roles within the same institutional body. The degree of agreement and commitment holding in a legal system is, then, severely limited and falls short of what would be needed to have a shared cooperative activity. The conclusion to be drawn from these remarks is that the model of shared cooperative activity can hardly be said to apply to such a large-scale and temporarily extended social practice as the law.

Secondly, Coleman's appeal to the notion of shared cooperative activity fails to explain what it sets out to do. Coleman appeals to that notion in order to clarify the idea of social normativity.[35] Coleman argues, in short, that the rule of recognition is normative on the ground that it can be equated to a shared cooperative activity, the normativity of which works just like that of pacts and promises. As a result, the law should be recognised as 'a special case of a familiar class of reason- or duty-creating human activities', among which pacts and promises figure prominently (Coleman 2001: 160). The problem remains, however, as to how it is possible to explain the normativity of practices like pacts and promises. The standard explanation of the normativity of such a class of practices is not social in nature but moral: pacts and promises get their binding force through the moral values underlying the practice of keeping promises and pacts, values of wide appeal such as those of fidelity, fair play, mutuality, reciprocity, reliance and justified expectations. But to base the normativity of law on those values is to turn morality into a

---

[35] See Coleman (2001: 96–102).

necessary component of the normativity of law, and so to turn the normativity of law into a variant of moral normativity. From this it follows that inclusive positivism can hardly rely on the standard explanation if it elects to keep faith with its basic insight concerning the social nature of the normativity of law. So, granted that shared cooperative activities do create obligations, inclusive positivism will be at pains to puzzle out how they can bind us without acknowledging that there is no distinction between the grounds of the normativity of law and the source of moral normativity.

Let me rephrase the point from a different angle. Claiming that the obligation-creating capacity of the law resides in the character it exhibits of a shared cooperative activity is, at first glance, a move that coheres with the positivist assumption of the conventionality of the law. The notion of a shared cooperative activity was originally formulated in the context of the philosophical analysis of social conventions. This literature strikes one as the most appropriate place to look where the concern is a theory, legal positivism, that insists on the conventional character of the law and defines it as a social practice with certain defining traits. On closer inspection, however, the reliance on the notion of a cooperative practice poses far greater danger for legal positivism than one might initially suspect. The reason why legal positivism should be wary of the model of shared cooperative activity to explain the normativity of law is that that model does not exempt us from an appeal to morality to ground the capacity cooperative practices have to create obligations. The obligations that cooperative activities can generate are warranted by some values that are distinctively moral and are, in addition, conditioned on the possession of certain moral characteristics vis-à-vis the relevant activities carried out together.

Otherwise put: the duties deriving from cooperative schemes are not owed simply because a cooperative practice is in place in a group of people. The leading literature concerning the obligations emerging from cooperative schemes makes it apparent that other conditions need to hold if the cooperative activity is going to yield binding obligations. Consider Rawls's (1999b) contribution with respect to the emergence of political obligation out of fair-play based considerations, for example. The mere qualification of the political enterprise as a cooperative scheme that is generally accepted is hardly sufficient to create obligations that are imposed on officials and citizens. On Rawls's view, the cooperative scheme needs, in addition to being endorsed, to be mutually beneficial, just, not exploitative and productive of advantages for all participants.[36] Similar conditions apply to make it possible for pacts and promises (the devices to which Coleman appeals to ground his explanation of the normativity of law) to generate obligations. Promissory practices are taken to create obligations in so far as, among other things, appropriate background conditions of choice obtain when a pact or promise is made and consent to the object of the pact or promise can reasonably be given. These conditions making possible the obligatory force of pacts and promises are far from morally

---

[36] See Rawls (1999b: 121–3).

neutral.[37] Moral considerations, thus, are not extraneous to the normativity attached to shared cooperative activities. Indeed, the normative force of shared cooperative activities is made possible by morality itself, for only shared cooperative activities that abide by certain moral conditions succeed in binding and no obligation can arise from immoral enterprises, quite apart from whether they are shared and cooperative. The upshot of this construction is that the normativity generated by the model of a shared cooperative activity is a moral species, not a social species, of normativity.

In sum, Coleman's social account of the normativity of law fails in relying on a resource not suitable to the purport of constructing normativity as a social concept. Coleman's strategy—locating normativity in the structure of the cooperative practices constitutive of the law—does not warrant any distinction between the normativity of law and the normativity of morality: since the species of normativity generated by the model of shared cooperative activity is far from being merely social, inclusive positivism cannot embrace that model and keep faithful to its aim of explaining the normativity of law as a kind of social, not moral, normativity.

Beyond being internally incoherent, it can be argued that the route chosen by Coleman lacks the potential to explain exhaustively the normativity of law, for at least one element of normativity, the justificatory component, cannot be elucidated from within a conventional standpoint. Thus far, the main focus of the discussion has been with the directive dimension of normative standards, but normativity presents not only an action-guiding component but also a justificatory one.[38] Normative standards have this double function: that of guiding behaviour and that of providing a framework for publicly justifying conduct. Accordingly, a comprehensive explanation of the normativity of law should be able to clarify not only the action-guiding propensity but also the justificatory power of legal standards. The framework devised by inclusive positivism is poorly equipped to provide such a twofold explanation, for we cannot account for the justificatory role unless some appeal to critical morality is made. Here are the reasons therefor.

It is inherent in the very idea of justification that we must somehow invoke values. Justifying something means to show that it 'does not merely exist but has value, that it serves some interest or purpose or enforces some principle—in short that it has some point' (Dworkin 1986: 47). It also means to show that this something 'is sensitive to its point' and so 'must be understood or applied or modified or qualified or limited by that point'.[39] Hence, so long as legal standards are

---

[37] Take, eg, the last of the conditions mentioned, the one relative to the object of a promise. It entails that it is far from the case that anything can be promised: if the content of the promise is an illicit act or a morally reprehensible one, the promise is not treated as valid and so generates no practical obligation.

[38] This twofold dimension of normativity was introduced and discussed in chapter one. For further remarks on the justificatory facet incorporated in the normative standards of the law, see Postema (1998: 164–8). Incidentally, acknowledging this justificatory component implicit in legal norms is not a question-begging move: the idea of justification (in the form of justified criticism) is well present in Hart's (1994: 82–91) notion of a social rule from which inclusive legal positivism takes its initial steps.

[39] Dworkin (1986: 47). See also Stavropoulos (1996: 59–61).

understood as normative and incorporate a justificatory dimension, they will carry evaluative considerations among their defining elements. These evaluative considerations can be shown to be moral in nature. Once we accept the thesis that not just any sort of value is suitable in providing a justification, we can, then, see how this happens: how morality, and indeed critical morality, enters the domain of the normativity of law by virtue of the existence of a justificatory component within the normative sphere.

Because the law is a system for regulating and justifying action, as opposed to a system for regulating and justifying belief, the law provides practical reasons, as against theoretical reasons. Practical reasons can be either instrumental or final. Instrumental reasons apply to means, justifying conduct on the basis of its being a necessary means to a certain end. But they say nothing about the worthiness of the ends sought, which we identify *before* any instrumental reason intervenes, and so independently of any such reason.[40] Thus, the justifications that come by way of instrumental reasons can only be partial, derivative and subordinate: these reasons cannot justify the underlying goals of action; they can justify conduct only on the assumption that the goals are in fact justified.

For more comprehensive, conclusive and exhaustive justifications we must invoke final reasons. Final reasons come into play in our practical deliberation on ends. Because they apply not only to the means of acting but also to its ends, final reasons can in principle serve as exhaustive justifications. There are two sorts of final reasons in the practical realm, prudential and moral. Prudential reasons are self-regarding: they appeal to the first-person interests of an agent and disregard other subjects and their needs. But an appeal to reasons exclusively concerned with private and personal gain cannot constitute a valid justification in the public sphere. Public institutions cannot be equated to individuals in the first instance. They are not beings endowed with separate cognitive and volitional capacities, and they do not have private lives. Instead, they borrow whatever kind of intelligence, will or existence is attributed to them from the internal states and biographies of the people who act on their behalf. Public institutions can then be said to be impersonal; likewise depersonalised are their acts as well as the reasons for which they are justified in acting. In addition, public institutions are expressly designed to serve the interests of a collective body rather than to cater to the wishes of the people, groups or classes acting on behalf of those institutions. On these grounds, it is reasonable to endorse the thesis of the discontinuity between public realm and private sphere.[41]

The thesis of discontinuity is associated with the view that the peculiar status, means and powers of public institutions warrant their having both special entitlements and particular restrictions. In discharging their official tasks, those individuals acting on behalf of public institutions are released from some of the

---

[40] This makes instrumental reasons akin to technical rules prescribing a given behaviour as a necessary condition for attaining a given result, rules which typically come in the form, 'If you wish to achieve A, then you ought to do B'.

[41] This thesis is convincingly argued in Nagel (1979: 75–90), among others.

constraints that hold for private individuals, but their conduct is at the same time subjected to ad hoc impositions and limits. There are obligations that are specifically attached to public offices and do not extend to individuals acting in their private capacities. Among those obligations, the requirement that one act in the interests of the concerned community figures prominently. The ensuing limitation in the sorts of reasons that can be advanced to justify the activity of public institutions is another prominent feature. Public offices are shielded from the personal interests of those who fill them in that officials are obligated to the social group concerned with their activities and are responsive to the interests of that group. A failure to act in accordance with those interests, which are other-regarding as opposed to self-regarding, results in an act that is irremediably unjustified: in the public sphere, there is no room for the personal attachments and inclinations that (appropriately) may shape the lives of private individuals. Because the very rationale for attributing special prerogatives and lifting common restrictions would disappear if official functions were not performed in the interests of those governed, the personal interests of public officials do not constitute acceptable reasons that one might advance in order to justify the use of public powers and resources.[42] This bestows on public offices a requirement of impartiality or detachment that does not affect the conduct of individual subjects to the same extent: public institutions are under a special obligation to take into account, and to be equally concerned with, the interests of all the affected individuals.[43] The upshot of these remarks is that prudential reasons, which by definition fail to address the concerns of all the affected individuals, cannot discharge a justificatory function in the legal realm.

Lest this position be accused of uncompromising idealism, it is worthwhile to stress that I am not denying here that public officials may in fact use public powers to further their own personal goals, also when those goals are sharply contrasted with the interests of vast sectors of the population concerned. Rather, I am committed to the view that such uses cannot be justified by appealing directly to the personal interests of those holding office—namely, to prudential reasons. Rather, it needs to be shown that they are capable of serving some more general interests, and this implies an appeal to other-regarding reasons that exceed the boundaries of mere prudence. In other words, the hardly deniable fact that from time to time public officials act according to their own personal interests scarcely settles the issue of how those self-interested acts can be justified: unless officials ground their acts on non-prudential considerations those acts are still in need of justification. On the view defended here, then, allowing for a prudence-based justification of the law is to mistake reasons for motives by mixing up the *psychosociological question* of how officials make use of their powers with the *justificatory question* of how such a use can be defended. No matter how self-interested they may

---

[42] In Nagel's words (1979: 81), 'the added power conferred by an institutional role should be used primarily for the benefit of that institution and its constituents'.

[43] Cf Nagel (1979: 82–6). This point is taken up and framed in terms of the distinction between agent-relative reasons and agent-neutral reasons in Michelon (2006: 51–74).

in fact be, public officials need to appeal to other-regarding reasons to justify their acts. In sum, we cannot base an effort to justify public institutions on self-concern and personal reasons: a public institution remains unjustified unless and until we can show that it promises benefit to an appropriately large section of the population to which it applies.[44]

Because prudential reasons cannot adequately justify practical requirements addressed to others than the subjects whose interests are served by those reasons, we must, in our effort to explain how the normative standards of the law perform their justificatory task, invoke moral considerations. Not only are moral considerations final reasons, but they are also other-regarding reasons: by contrast with instrumental reasons they have the virtue of taking into account not just the means but also the ends of action, and, by contrast with prudential reasons, they have the virtue of taking into account both self-regarding and other-regarding considerations.[45] From the moral point of view, everyone's interests and concerns count equally. We use moral considerations to measure the needs of each citizen impartially, to give full weight to each need, and to make each count in practical deliberation. Thus, moral reasons can provide for the normative standards of the law the necessary justificatory power that instrumental and prudential reasons are lacking.

But not all moral reasons stand on the same footing. There is a long tradition of distinguishing between positive, or conventional, morality and critical, or transcendent, morality. Positive morality is morality as reflected, in that the values are in fact endorsed by the majority of a population at any rate, or by a dominant minority. It mirrors a social practice and so has a conventional status. Conventional practices can explain how something receives widespread acceptance or has social efficacy, but they cannot elucidate the idea of acceptability. And it is acceptability, not plain acceptance, that justification requires: something is justified when it is proved to be acceptable, not when it is accepted, because acceptance corresponds to factual consensus and reaching a factual consensus on

---

[44] This point can be expressed also in the following way. It is acceptable for someone acting as a private individual to guide her action by the sole measure of personal gain and self-interest, because it can reasonably be assumed that the burden of these actions falls primarily and directly on the agent herself. But when it comes to the legal system, and to the people acting on its behalf, this is no longer an option: legal systems are structured in such a way that they directly affect the behaviour of many. Hence, legal officials cannot validly adduce their personal concerns and preferences in justifying the norms they enact. They must instead take into account the interests of all those affected, because in the law, like in any other public context, everyone is equally entitled to pursue their interests and have them protected. For similar considerations, see Raz (1986b: 92–3). A converging supplementary argument for this conclusion is provided in Goldsworthy (1990: 456–7), where it is claimed that only moral standards can fulfil the role of justifying public officials' conduct because immoral or amoral standards would not suffice to justify conduct to the actor as well as to others.

[45] Here, I proceed on the assumption that other-regarding considerations do not account for the whole of morality. The moral point of view factors in the needs of others as well as first-person needs of the self-interested subject, so that self-regarding reasons, too, play a role in moral reasoning, alongside other-regarding reasons. For a convincing defence of this view of morality, see Stroud (1998: 179–81).

something is not to be confused with its justification.[46] Because justification requires us to go beyond the consensus associated with the existence of conventional practices and to take up a critical standpoint, any conclusive justification of public standards, such as the normative standards of the law, will ultimately have to rest on critical morality. This kind of morality makes possible a standpoint without which no exhaustive justification is possible and hence bestows normative standards with the resources necessary to perform their justificatory task.

In addition to being critical, the morality that is relevant to the justification of legal demands, and so secures the partaking of the normative dimension on the part of the law, is rational, for at least in pluralistic societies where various belief systems compete with each other, practical choices cannot be exhaustively justified simply by appealing to the critical stance endorsed by a subject or a social group. What one person regards as correct in the light of her personal values, commitments and attitudes can be found by others to be pure ideology or downright prejudice. Therefore, not all kinds of critical morality can justify. Critical morality can play a justificatory role only if its standards are regarded as acceptable, or at least not reasonably refutable, by individuals with distinct outlooks and evaluative conceptions. And such standards can be provided only by incorporating a rational element. Rationality enables us to analyse, discuss and compare the vast array of critical moralities that different individuals and social groups may endorse. Thus, rationality makes possible the necessary framework within which different worldviews can enter into mutual communication. This way, the exercise of reason bridges the gap between distinct critical moral visions and turns the subjective critical endorsement of a moral system into an inter-subjective practice. Accordingly, moral requirements that pass rational scrutiny can in principle be acknowledged to have justificatory force by individuals with different faiths and value systems, and so can aspire to achieve universal recognition. From which it follows that the morality able to secure the justificatory function of normative requirements is not just critical but also rational.

The conclusion that the justificatory element of normativity rests unexplained unless some appeal is made to critical rational morality reinforces the view that the notion of social normativity is conceptually unable to ground a comprehensive account of the normativity of law. To the extent that normativity is associated with both action-guiding capacity and justificatory power, the normativity of law will bring into operation not just any kind of morality, but critical rational morality. And this runs counter to the inclusive-positivist assertion that the normativity of law is completely independent of the normativity of morality.

---

[46] This point is given a convincing argument by Dworkin, who in criticising Hart's account of legal norms as social rules introduces the example of a vegetarian (Dworkin 1978: 49–58): a vegetarian finds the prohibition against eating meat to be a justified claim—a position that makes sense and is fully understandable and yet, as is plain to see, does not count as a convergent social practice in today's society. This suggests that the justification of a practice is conceptually independent of any convergence of behaviour and attitude that may obtain in society. On this aspect, see also Stavropoulos (2003: 5), among many others.

General Scope of the Normative Claim of Law

The final reason to remain unconvinced by the inclusive-positivist account of the normative claim of law rests on the argument that inclusive positivism arbitrarily narrows the scope of the claim. More specifically, Coleman's proposition (2001: 95) that the question of the normativity of law amounts to the issue as to how the rule of recognition happens to be normative for legal officials entails a double limitation in scope. First, Coleman focuses his attention on the normative claim implied by the social practice lying at the foundations of the law: clarifying the normative claim made by the foundations of the law, then, rather than the normative claim raised by the law is the explanatory task Coleman sets for himself. Secondly, Coleman aims at elucidating the claims the law makes on legal officials rather than on citizens at large. In the inclusive-positivist view, in short, the normative concerns of the law are addressed exclusively to legal officials and, accordingly, do not extend to the rest of the population.[47]

The first limitation may be regarded as benign. There is nothing in principle unacceptable in the statement that 'the capacity of almost all legal rules to *govern* conduct depends on their bearing a certain relationship to another rule—the rule of recognition' to the effect that 'a philosophical account of the very possibility of governance by law ... rests on the possibility of a philosophical account of how the rule of recognition can be a reason for action' (Coleman 2001: 95). In this view, the normative claim that most legal standards make is borrowed from the normative claim associated with the practice asserting the validity of those standards. Hence, the normativity of legal standards is a case of indirect, or systemic, normativity, where the normativity of legal rules is a function of, and is derived from, their membership in a system that is normative. There is nothing amiss in this strategy.

In contrast, the second limitation is problematic. It amounts to the requirement that the law generates practical reasons for only a minority of the individuals concerned—legal officials—whereas the law makes no claims at all on the rest of the population. Since ordinary citizens are involved in no shared cooperative activity, and so have no reason to follow the dictates of either the rule of recognition or other legal standards, there is no way to extend to other citizens the normative claim the law makes on legal officials. Any claim the law makes on citizens remains, then, unexplained by inclusive positivism.

The upshot of this explanatory deficit is that inclusive positivism supplies a radically lacunose and significantly incomplete picture of the normative claim the law makes. The gap affecting the explanation provided by inclusive positivism could be filled in different ways. One could, for example, imagine a situation where the obligatory force the law claims to have on ordinary citizens derives from non-legal sources, say, the coercive potential of what is issued by a legal authority bestowed with the monopoly of force or the occasional coincidence in content of legal requirements and moral requirements. But neither of these options is without

---

[47] This limitation is clarified and discussed in detail in Himma (2005).

problems for inclusive positivism. On the one hand, coercion is by its nature unable to create obligations, as opposed to compelling action. The first option, thus, has the unpalatable implication that the law is made normatively empty for citizens: citizens would be not obligated, but rather just obliged, to act as prescribed by the law. As a result, citizens would regard the law as a source of information on the imminence, or likelihood, that certain behaviour is sanctioned. On the other hand, the normativity that laws can derive from their stating moral duties cannot be classified as a case of social normativity. In so far as inclusive positivism sticks to its characterisation of the law as socially normative, therefore, the solution does not cohere with its basic assumptions.

The incompleteness of the theory produced by inclusive positivism is a problem in itself. But the difficulties with the inclusive-positivist account of the scope of the normative claim of law do not stop with this explanatory deficit; they invest also the consequences of such incompleteness. The main problematic consequence of the inclusive-positivist incomplete treatment can be elicited by building on Sylvie Delacroix's remark that the attitude ordinary citizens maintain in respect to the law ought to be considered an integral part of the legal enterprise rather than something external to it.[48] The conceptual connection linking the law and the attitude citizens have toward it is due to the fact that 'law's overall success in giving rise to reasons for action that are deemed "conclusive" by the non-official part of the population does matter' to legal officials (Delacroix 2006: 174). The shared cooperative activity on which legal officials embark cannot be reduced without deformation to a form of rule-worshipping. Legal officials do not set up the legal enterprise for its own sake; officials rather set up the legal enterprise because they see in it the opportunity to reach further objectives they regard as valuable. This remark discloses the truth that the legal domain, even when it is understood minimally as a cooperative activity shared by politicians and bureaucrats, is shaped by a bulk of purposes, namely, those purposes that provide the explanation of why officials commit themselves to create and apply laws. Hence, these purposes should be acknowledged as elements essential to the legal enterprise. Their essential character depends chiefly on the fact that in their absence, the commitment of some people to the legal enterprise would not only remain unexplained but would also be completely lacking, and so no legal system could emerge. For, if the law were not perceived as a suitable means to chosen ends, officials would not bother to initiate and sustain a legal system. And the law is capable of serving the objectives in the pursuit of which legal officials commit themselves to the legal system only if citizens at large treat the standards issued by the officials as reasons for action and so conform to them. Therefore, no official would take any interest in a legal system that is not widely treated as normative by ordinary citizens, which is to say that if such a legal system ever arose, it would soon collapse. In conclusion, if we want to make sense of the legal enterprise performed by legal officials and so, ultimately, of the existence of the law, the scope of the normative claim that the

---

[48] See Delacroix (2006: 174–83) for the argument supporting this view.

law makes has to be acknowledged as directed to citizens, rather than being limited to legal officials. From this it follows that the inclusive-positivist explanation of the scope of the normative claim of law is not only lacunose but also incapable of grasping the role that normativity plays in the legal enterprise.

CONCLUSION

In the present chapter I have introduced and critically discussed the account of the normative claim of law defended by inclusive positivism in order to spell out the essential traits of that claim. Inclusive positivism makes a serious and insightful attempt to construe the normative claim of law as the contention that legal systems may make in order to provide legal officials with peremptory and content-independent reasons to act, which concur with the demands of morality to determine how one ought to behave. The practical reasons legal systems claim to provide are peculiarly legal, that is, they can be reduced neither to moral reasons nor to the kind of reasons created by games, and they are grounded by appeal to their endorsement, if only implicit, by the officials.

Throughout the chapter, I argued that there is much to praise in this characterisation of the normative claim of law, which discloses some fundamental characteristics of that claim, such as its reason-based feature and practical orientation. At the same time, I showed that other components of the characterisation are questionable and not convincingly supported by argument. In particular, I took issue with the theses that the status of the normative claim of law is optional, instead of necessary; that the object of that claim is distinguishable from moral normativity; and that the normative claim is addressed exclusively to legal officials and not to the generality of people concerned by the existence of a legal practice. In addition, once the normative claim of law is proved to be necessary, moral and general in scope, it cannot be validly grounded on some kind of endorsement or commitment in the inclusive-positivist fashion: it is far from true that most citizens endorse either the requirements of a legal system or the point of the legal enterprise. True, in well-functioning legal systems we can reasonably expect to find a significant number of people favourably disposed to the system, not only among legal officials but also among citizens. But, this feature is far from necessary for a legal system to obtain as a normative social practice. What is more, even in the most successful legal systems, the support can hardly be said to extend to all citizens: even in perfectly functioning legal systems, sectors of the population are likely to disagree with certain legal requirements or, indeed, with the very idea of having the law. To link the normativity of law to its endorsement would mean to rule out the possibility of making sense of the obligation to behave in accordance with the prescriptions of the law that even dissidents, far from committed to the legal system, are claimed to have. This leads to the conclusion that the appeal to the notion of endorsement or commitment is not a sound foundation of the normative claim that the law makes.

In sum, the treatment of the normative claim of law discussed in this chapter provides insight into that claim but it also leaves a number of problems unsolved. Before we can arrive at an adequate comprehensive characterisation of the normative claim of law, we need to establish this claim as a moral contention addressed to the community at large and to provide some ground for it. Inclusive positivism is not in a position to take us that far. But there is nothing in principle that forces us to look outside the positivist camp to find such a comprehensive characterisation. Building on Raz's writings concerning the concept of law and legal authority, we can ascribe to him a rigorous positivist theory of the normative claim of law that shares none of the shortcomings of the approach of the inclusive positivists. Whether Raz's treatment of the normative claim of law is able to further advance our understanding of the normative dimension of the law is the subject matter of the next chapter.

3

Content-dependence and Discursive Character

INTRODUCTION

IN CHAPTER TWO, the discussion of inclusive positivism was used to shed light on some of the fundamental traits of the normative claim of law. Here, the critical confrontation with exclusive legal positivism, and more specifically with Joseph Raz's account of the nature of law, will contribute to promoting our understanding of that claim, as well as to spelling out other essential aspects of the claim. As with much of most contemporary analytical legal positivism, exclusive positivism is a form of conventionalism. The advocates of exclusive positivism (Marmor 2002: 104):

> share the view that there are conventional rules of recognition, namely, conventions which determine certain facts or events that are taken to yield established ways for the creation, modification, and annulment of legal standards.

Once we give the name of 'sources of law' to the facts establishing the law, exclusive positivism can be defined, albeit crudely, as the theory holding that 'legal validity is exhausted by reference to the conventional sources of law: all law is source based, and anything which is not source based is not law' (Marmor 2002: 104). In this picture, morality enters into the definition of the law in no way and so is not part of the concept of law: the law is a realm independent of, and insulated from, morals. From this, it follows that moral considerations have no effect on legal validity and are at most relevant to the characterisation of legal reasoning.

Building on these premises, the proponents of exclusive positivism consider normativity not as a legal concept but as a moral concept. Legal prescriptions are not necessarily morally binding, although they can bind morally, namely, to the extent that they happen to conform to moral standards. Accordingly, normativity is not a property essential to the law, for legal directives may well fail to establish obligations. The upshot of this construction is that the obligations possibly created by the law are moral obligations that arise from the legal system. Nonetheless, the law is far from being normatively inert, for the law does of necessity *claim* for itself normative force. Whilst an instance of the law may in fact not possess normative force, no system counts as a legal system unless it incorporates a claim to guide action by impinging on the practical reasoning of the concerned individuals. Hence, the thesis arises that a normative claim of some nature or other is a defining element of the concept of law and that normativity is therefore a legally relevant notion.

This summary shows that the exclusive-positivist account contributes significantly to our understanding of the essential traits of the normative claim of law by acknowledging the non-contingent status and moral quality of the claim. The account of the normative claim put forward by exclusive positivism is, therefore, worthy of some discussion with an eye to assessing how and to what extent it can help clarify the fundamental components of the normative claim of law.

In this chapter, I will focus exclusively on a paradigmatic example of exclusive positivism: Raz's theory. However, before getting under way with a discussion of Raz's work, a caveat should be introduced. Raz frames his thesis respecting the claim of law to guide action by shaping the practical reasons one has in terms of authority. From the common assumption that 'necessarily law, every legal system which is in force anywhere, has *de facto* authority' (Raz 1994: 199), he argues that the law, for reasons conceptual in nature, claims legitimate authority (a notion in terms of which effective authority can be explained) and goes on to conclude that 'though a legal system may not have legitimate authority, or though its legitimate authority may not be as extensive as it claims, every legal system claims that it possesses legitimate authority'. In Raz's framework, claiming legitimate authority is tantamount to contending that people are being provided with protected reasons for action. Thus, the claim to legitimate authority that Raz ascribes to the law is to be regarded as the exclusive-positivist equivalent of the normative claim. A discussion of Raz's account of legitimate authority and his ascription to the law of a necessary claim to legitimate authority are, therefore, themes that are germane to the study of the normative claim of law.

Raz's appeal to authority in order to define and to characterise the normative claim of law forces us to confront the debate on the nature and limits of authority, especially legal authority. The concept of authority, albeit central to both political theory and jurisprudence, is elusive. Even if we circumscribe our survey to the analytic tradition in contemporary jurisprudential studies, we will find neither a settled definition nor a widely shared characterisation of authority. This concept has given rise to controversy right from the start, and even in the recent literature one fails to find a consistent specification.[1] In the existing literature, authority is largely regarded not as a monolithic, undifferentiated concept, but as a generic notion that can be broken down into different species. So, we usually find a distinction between theoretical and practical authority, and another between de facto (or effective) and de jure (or legitimate) authority.[2] In the first pair, theoretical authority is a heuristic guide that provides its addressees with reasons to believe in certain propositions and facts, whereas practical authority is directly concerned with the realm of action and gives reasons to act in accordance with its instructions. In the second pair, effective authority is the ability to bring about compliance, a sort of effectual power that claims legitimacy, or is believed to be legitimate, and

---

[1] See, in this regard, Raz (1986a), Regan (1987; 1989), Green (1988; 1989), Moore (1989), Alexander (1990), Soper (1989), Friedman (1990), Hart (1990), Ladenson (1980), and Shapiro (2002).

[2] For a clear account of these distinctions, see Raz (1979: 3–11), Friedman (1990: 59–63) and Hurd (1991: 1615–20), among others.

therefore brings forth allegiance, whereas legitimate authority is a justifiable power that validly creates obligations binding upon a group of people.

These widely shared distinctions provide a basic vocabulary and a preliminary conceptual framework that can be used to understand the model of authority Raz has consistently defended in a number of works since the late 1970s.[3] I therefore take them as the starting point of my discussion, the aim of which is twofold. First, I intend to explore Raz's treatment of legal authority and claim to legitimate authority in order to specify further the fundamental characteristics of the normative claim of law and to establish its necessary status as well as its moral nature. Secondly, I will adopt a critical stance and argue that Raz's characterisation of the reasons claimed to be supplied by the law is hardly tenable. In particular, I will contest his thesis that authority can be explained by way of content-independent reasons that have exclusionary force: authoritative provisions are not such that they necessarily replace and pre-empt the substantive reasons they depend on. The relationship between authoritative directives and moral reasons is not governed by an 'exclusionary logic' that purports completely to isolate an authoritative provision from the underlying moral arguments that justify it. This means that if we are to make sense of the law, conceived of as a framework for the exercise of authority, we will have to take a discursive, or inclusionary, approach rather than an exclusionary approach.[4] In a discursive approach, authoritative provisions and moral reasons are distinct but ultimately connected: they form distinct classes, but their separation is only temporary and limited, not absolute. It will be shown that this position is rich in implications for the characterisation of the normative claim of law, which, accordingly, is to be equated with the claim to guide action by providing reinforced—as opposed to protected—reasons holding to the extent that their content is not irremediably unfair or morally tainted to a great extent.

RECONSTRUCTING RAZ'S ACCOUNT OF THE NORMATIVE CLAIM OF LAW

Raz's account of the normative claim of law is part of a coherent framework connecting together practical reasoning, authority and the law. *Practical reasoning*

---

[3] The places where Raz expounds and defends this view of authority, which has proved significant for legal and political philosophy alike, are mainly Raz (1975: 49–84; 1979: 3–33; 1986a: 23–105; 1989: 1179–200; and 1994: 194–221).

[4] By discursive, or inclusionary, approach I mean an account whereby the different elements of a whole are regarded as mutually transparent and so as capable of communicating with one another. Accordingly, an inclusionary relationship, as opposed to an exclusionary one, consists in a two-way linkage between the parts of a whole. The inclusionary model is fundamentally based on discourse: it is grounded on a communicative model of rationality shaped by the ideal of (rational) dialogue, in that it operates on a principle of openness to criticism under which nothing is exempt from discussion and everything can be questioned, since there is no component of the whole that falls beyond the reach of critical scrutiny. Among the contemporary works that can be considered part of the discursive tradition so described, we have Perelman and Olbrechts-Tyteca (1969), Aarnio, Alexy and Peczenik (1981), van Eemeren and Grootendorst (1984), Habermas (1984; 1987; 1996) and Alexy (1989a).

provides the basis for an explanation of both authority and legal systems; at the same time an understanding of *authority*, which is essential to the characterisation of the normative claim of law, is essential, inter alia, to a correct grasp of the concept of *law*.[5] Given the close connection by means of which Raz is able to bind practical reasoning, authority and the law, it is useful to provide a short introduction to each of these concepts as Raz explains them.

The account that Raz gives of *practical reasoning* begins with a detailed analysis of the notion of a reason. On this approach, a reason is a fact that justifies either an action or a belief. Reasons for belief delimit the theoretical sphere; reasons for action, which are reasons 'for a person to perform an action when certain conditions obtain' (Raz 1975: 19), mark instead the practical realm. Reasons for action exist in many varieties. Raz provides a detailed taxonomy and draws there a distinction of particular relevance for legal authority: that between first-order and second-order reasons.[6] There are inhabiting the practical sphere, not only reasons for action or first-order reasons, but also reasons to act for a reason or second-order reasons.[7] Practical reasoning, then, is structured at two different levels: a basic level where we reason about action, and a higher level wherever reasoning is directed to reasoning itself, or rather, where practical reasoning becomes an action in regard to which reasons are adduced. Second-order reasons can be positive (that is, reasons to act for some reason), or they can be negative (reasons not to act for some reason), and in this latter case we have 'exclusionary reasons'.

Two features of this scheme ought to be pointed out. First, the two levels on which practical reasoning is articulated are completely insulated from each other. In general, a reason can override conflicting reasons, or be overridden by them, depending on the comparative strength of the reasons in question.[8] But this criterion (comparative strength in the balance of reasons) proves ineffectual when it comes to solving conflicts between reasons belonging to different levels: first-order reasons stand on a footing different from second-order reasons, so their relative strength cannot be compared. Second-order reasons always prevail over conflicting first-order reasons, owing not to their greater strength but to their higher status in the hierarchy of reasons. Hence, there can be no real competition between first-order and second-order reasons: the relation between them is one of replacement and exclusion.[9] And this is actually the second feature of this multi-layered and hierarchical structure of practical reasoning: the balance of reasons does not always determine what ought to be done in any particular situation.[10] If a second-order reason comes to bear on the matter in question, it will determine the correct course of action by displacing and trumping all others reasons. The overall balance of reasons thereby loses its force as a criterion of action.

---

[5] On this connection between practical reasoning, authority and the law, see Raz (1989: 1154).
[6] See Raz (1975: 15–35).
[7] Cf Raz (1975: 39–40).
[8] On this feature of reasons, see Raz (1975: 25–8).
[9] This exclusionary trait of rules is dealt with in some detail in Raz (1975: 39–48).
[10] See Raz (1975: 45–8).

This account of practical reasoning serves as the premise in Raz's definition of a rule, explained as a reason for action of a particular type, namely, a protected reason to act. A protected reason is a first-order reason combined with an exclusionary reason: it is a directive instructing us both to behave in a certain way and to disregard other reasons to act.[11] The exclusionary component built into a rule means that rules enjoy 'a relative independence from the reasons which justify them' and can be regarded as 'complete reasons in their own right' (Raz 1975: 79). This definition of a rule as a protected reason for action can be justified functionally. Rules function as time- and labour-saving devices that also reduce the possibility, when deciding what to do, of mistakes in calculation.[12] No standard can play this role, however, unless it guides behaviour in an exclusionary fashion. If rules are to function as time- and labour-saving devices, they must be able not only to justify a selected course of action but also to exclude from the final count other reasons that might otherwise come to bear on the matter. This exclusionary force makes it possible for rules to simplify our practical reasoning: rules crystallise a given balance between practical reasons and apply the balance directly whenever the relevant conditions arise, this without requiring any thought about the matter.

Raz uses this account of practical reasoning and rules as his premise in characterising an *authority*, which he defines as the ability to issue directives of a certain kind.[13] This certain kind means, first, that authoritative directives are independent of content (they are formal provisions that ought to be obeyed no matter what they recommend) and, secondly, they are exclusionary or pre-emptive instructions in that their underlying substantive justification (or dependent reasons) are removed from the reach of practical reasoning.[14] This renders authoritative directives autonomous vis-à-vis their substantive justifications: the way an authority guides the action of its subjects is by direct reference to its authoritative instructions rather than by reference to what are claimed to be its ultimate justifications. The reason why authoritative directives take effect independently of their underlying substantive reasons is that they reflect and replace these reasons rather than add to them. This is the premise for the 'dependence thesis', which claims that (Raz 1986a: 47):

> all authoritative directives should be based on reasons which already independently apply to the subjects of the directives and are relevant to their action in the circumstances covered by the directive.

There are a couple of important implications that flow from authority thus understood. First, the view that the idea of authority should be associated with the

---

[11] In Raz's words (1975: 73), 'the rule is taken not merely as a reason for performing its norm act but also as resolving practical conflicts by excluding conflicting reasons'. This feature of rules is further elaborated on in Raz (1975: 190–4).
[12] See Raz (1975: 58–73).
[13] Cf Raz (1979: 16–25) and Raz (1975: 63–5).
[14] Raz (1986a: 46) puts forward on this basis what he calls the 'pre-emption thesis' according to which 'the fact that an authority requires performance of an action is a reason for its performance which is not to be added to all other relevant reasons when assessing what to do, but should exclude and take the place of some of them'.

notion of exclusionary and content-independent directives fits in a coherent way with the thesis that authority claims to be binding (within the limits of its competence) even if it is mistaken. An authoritative directive purports to exact compliance whether or not the balance of reasons proves it right, compliance that is claimed to be due simply by virtue of the fact that the directive comes from a competent institution.[15] Secondly, an authority so conceived (as a body setting forth reasons with exclusionary force) plays a mediating role: in replacing dependent substantive reasons with formal directives, an authority mediates between such substantive reasons and the people to whom they apply. This mediating function provides insights as well on the nature and justification of authority. For one thing, the *nature* of authority is such that an authority exacts compliance in so far as its directives are followed as such, without recourse to their underlying reasons, simply by virtue of the mediation of the authority. For another thing, the mediating role of an authority is key to its *justification*: normally, authority is justified if those subjected to it are likely better to comply with the relevant practical reasons if they accept the authoritative directives than if they were to follow those practical reasons directly (normal justification thesis). An authority thus makes a difference in our practical reasoning: while it brings into play no practical reasons beyond those we already have, it enhances the likelihood that we will act on the right reason.

These features of authority in general are reproduced within legal authority. The *law* is a structure of effective authority that 'claims binding force to the exclusion of certain contrary considerations'.[16] What makes legal institutions instances of de facto authority is, first, their raising an authoritative claim that people believe to be legitimate and that is by and large effective, and, secondly, their possibly failing the test of normal justification, a possible failure in consequence of which they cannot be considered legitimate authorities.[17] The link holding between the law and authority is further specified by the 'authority thesis', which amounts to the view that legal systems can be understood as sets of authoritative standards reflecting a normative posture, namely, requiring all those to whom they apply to acknowledge their action-guidance.[18] In other words, the authority thesis asserts

---

[15] In the words of Shapiro (2002: 383), authorities 'appear to place themselves above the truth—their right does not seem to depend on their being right'.

[16] Raz (1989: 1169). This statement entails the idea that 'the notion of authority is inextricability tied up with that of law' (Raz 1979: 29). More specifically, Raz establishes a strict link between the law and effective authority. Furthermore, effective authority is associated with, but does not collapse into, the notion of legitimate authority, since 'the explanation of effective authority presupposes that of legitimate authority' (Raz 1979: 29).

[17] The reason why legal institutions fail this test is that abiding by legal directives as such, independently of the underlying substantive reasons that apply to us, does not necessarily make us more likely to better comply with these reasons than if we judge the same reasons directly on their own merits. In fact, quite the opposite may happen: some people are more likely to better comply with dependent reasons precisely upon refusing to acknowledge the authority of the law. So the claim to authority made by the law is justified only in part. On the conception of law as de facto authority, see Raz (1979: 28–33).

[18] This means that inherent in legal systems is a claim to legitimate authority: legal systems, even if morally defective, cannot abstain from claiming authority. This point is made clear in Raz (1979: 28–33 and 1994: 199).

that although legal systems can hardly be said to vindicate any universal authority, they do assert themselves as comprehensive structures providing content-independent reasons to act in the prescribed way.

The idea of exclusion plays a prominent role in the picture drawn by the authority thesis. Legal systems, understood as structures for the exercise of authority, claim to issue provisions of a certain kind, that is, provisions capable of excluding and pre-empting all those reasons that do not emanate from them. Laws are accordingly regarded as directives purporting to provide content-independent protected reasons for action, namely, as directives that, independently of their content, carry both a prescription to behave in a certain way and an instruction excluding courses of conduct based on dependent reasons.[19] Thus, the appeal to the notion of authority enables Raz to specify the distinctive features and nature of the normative claim of law: in so far as it is a claim to legitimate authority, the normative claim of law can be equated to the assertion that the law purports to create reasons of a special sort, to wit, content-independent reasons to act that are moral in nature and that follow an exclusionary logic.

Both the fundamental features and the nature of the practical reasons that the law claims to create depend on Raz's characterisation of legal authority. As authoritative reasons (that is, reasons deriving from some authority), the reasons claimed to be established by the law are second-order reasons precluding one from acting on some first-order, non-legal reasons and holding independently of their substantive contents—indeed, acquiring their distinctive character not through their being something valuable or desirable, but through their emergence from given sources and thus binding, irrespective of their merits. Likewise, their authoritative character shapes the nature of the reasons the law claims to create: the notion of legitimate authority is a moral notion and so are the reasons stemming from that notion.

The moral nature of the reasons the law claims to create emerges most clearly when one considers that the law guides not only the conduct of the people issuing legal directives but also the conduct of citizens at large. The behaviour of a social group cannot be guided unless the legal provisions serve the interests of everyone, that is, the general interest of the concerned social group, as opposed to the convenience of those who issue the practical directives, for no one can be legitimately bound to behave in a way that corresponds to an interest that has not been endorsed. To put it in Raz's (1986b: 92–3) own words:

> while one can accept the law as a guide for one's own behaviour for reasons of one's own personal preferences or of self-interest one cannot adduce one's preferences or one's self-interest by themselves as a *justification* for holding that other people must, or have a duty to, act in a certain way.[20]

---

[19] For a clear statement of this point, see Raz (1979: 141–6).
[20] This point is restated in Raz (1984: 130): 'my self-interest cannot explain why [others] ought to do one thing or another'. See also Raz (2004: 4–6).

The requirement to act on other subjects' preferences or interests does not hold, for it makes a person live his or her life for the convenience of others and so turns the person into a means to others' lives. In so doing, it fails to acknowledge one's personhood as an independent end and undermines the dignity distinctively associated with human subjectivity. This means that the law needs to attempt to create reasons that comport with the convenience of all the addressees, that is, the general interest. Because the appeal to general interest turns prudential reasons into moral reasons, the outcome of this argument is that the reasons the law claims to generate have a moral nature. The only explanation of the normative posture of the law (that is, its contention also to create obligations in people other than those constituting the ruling class) is provided by the assumption that legal provisions are meant to constitute moral reasons; not, however, just any moral reason whatever but rather the specific and peculiar moral reasons emerging from, and attached to, the existence of legal institutions, namely, the moral reasons that are legally recognised.[21] In summary, 'the law claims for itself moral force' and 'legal obligations are real (moral) obligations arising out of the law' (Raz 1984: 131). The notion of obligation is the same in both legal and moral contexts, notwithstanding the fact that the contents of moral obligations arising from the law can diverge from the contents of obligations arising from non-legal practices.

In his more recent work, Raz elaborates further on the authoritative dimension of the law and deploys a specific argument that links this dimension with the nature of law. Raz calls it the 'argument from authority', and designs it to show that certain basic features of the concept of law are determined by the authoritative disposition of the law. The argument from authority runs as follows. First, Raz notes that for as long as the law claims authority, it must be capable of having authority, meaning that it must be an institution of a sort that in principle possesses the fundamental properties of an authority (instantiation thesis).[22] This does not amount to asserting that the law will always command authority without fail. To be sure, any claim may turn out to be false, meaning that the law may fail to exert its authority. But the failure of the law in this respect is a contingent possibility rather than a necessary feature. For if the claim to authority made by the law failed of necessity, then, the very point of invoking this claim would be lost: the claim would be not merely false but meaningless as well.[23] There are, in particular, two

[21] See Raz (1979: 33).

[22] As Raz (1994: 200) puts it, 'in order to be able to claim authority, the law must at the very least come close to the target . . . it must have some of the characteristics of an authority'.

[23] This point—that the failure of the law to be authoritative is only contingent—is something that Raz (1994: 199–204) elaborates on by bringing a counter-example, namely, the clearly non-contingent failure of statements about volcanoes. Both kinds of statements (about volcanoes and about the law) can ultimately fail of authority, to be sure, but the two failures have to be kept distinct. Statements about volcanoes have none of the features distinctive to authoritative instructions, so their inability to be authoritative is such in principle: their lack of authority is necessary and their claim to authority unintelligible. By contrast, the failure of a legal statement to be authoritative is only contingent and occasional: there is in principle nothing to prevent it from being authoritative. Therefore, the law provides the basic features for something to be authoritative even though this something may occasionally find itself lacking the requirements necessary for it to be a *legitimate* authority.

fundamental features of authority that Raz underscores as relevant to the discussion. First, an institution can be authoritative only if it presents us with directives about the way we ought to behave. Secondly, we must find it possible to identify a statement of an authority without having to rely on the underlying justification: the existence and content of an authority must be distinguishable 'in ways which do not depend on raising the very same issues which the authority is there to settle' (Raz 1994: 203). This second requirement is the key to Raz's argument from authority, for it implies that the law is a kind of institution that can exert authority only if its directives are independent of the moral reasons that justify them and that they are to replace: we need to be able to identify the law without resorting to substantive considerations (identification thesis). Raz concludes on this basis that the concept of law is ultimately a matter of social fact, not of moral values.[24] By the same token, the idea that the law purports to bind us by exercising authority over us will have to be regarded as an essential element of the concept of law. On this view, the claim to legitimate authority is an essential feature of the law: of necessity the law contends that legal provisions provide reasons incorporating an exclusionary dimension.[25] Thus, 'the claim to authority is part of the nature of law' (Raz 1994: 199), that is, it is essential to any explanation of the concept of law.

ENGAGING WITH RAZ'S ACCOUNT

In a nutshell, Raz's account of the normative claim made by the law consists of five key theses. Raz argues that the normative claim of law (i) is *essential* to the definition, and so to the concept, of law, (ii) takes the shape of a claim to *legitimate authority* and, hence, (iii) amounts to the contention to generate *content-independent* reasons to act that (iv) incorporate an *exclusionary component* and (v) have *moral nature*. Framed in these terms, Raz's account contributes significantly to advancing our understanding of the normative claim made by the law along with its fundamental traits. By establishing a connection between the normative claim and authority of the law, Raz is able to specify the content (which coincides with the content of legitimate authority), features (that is, content-independence and exclusionary force),

---

[24] The conclusion that the law, *qua* authoritative structure, is a matter of social fact falls in line with exclusive legal positivism and correspondingly disqualifies a number of other theories on the nature of law, such as inclusive positivism, interpretivism and natural law theory, just to name the most comprehensive alternatives. In Raz's (1994: 209) view, all these alternative theories are 'inconsistent with the authoritative nature of law' (as exclusive positivism is not) because they do 'not allow for the fact that the law necessarily claims authority'. It follows from this inconsistency that, unless we are prepared to reject the idea of the law and authority as conceptually intermingled, we should acknowledge exclusive positivism as the most adequate theory of the nature of law. In conclusion, then, Raz's reflection on the notion of authority provides, among other important things, an allegedly conclusive argument for a specific view of the concept of law. The claim to authority, once drawn into the concept of law, yields the positivist thesis that the law is a matter of social fact and, correspondingly, that moral considerations have no decisive role in identifying the law. Raz's treatment of authority is therefore essential to his theory of the nature of law.

[25] See also Raz (1979: 30).

the status (which is necessary) and the quality (which is moral) of that claim. Equally important, Raz's characterisation of the normative claim of law is to a large extent correct. Indeed, in so far as it amounts to the assertion to guide action by affecting one's practical reasons, the normative claim of law is conceptually related to the notion of legitimate practical authority, is essential to the definition of the law (for no system failing to make the claim to guide conduct by shaping practical reasons can be said to be legal) and presents a moral quality. The problem with Raz's account of the normative claim of law rests not with the treatment of the content, status and nature of that claim, but with its assertion of the content-independence and exclusionary dimension of the normative requirement that the law claims to provide. That the normative claim of law is content-independent and follows an exclusionary logic remain, ultimately, as unsupported assertions, or so I will argue here, defending the view that the reasons the law claims to create are neither exclusionary nor content-independent. This is criticism of a specific, albeit central point of Raz's account without suggesting, however, that the general theoretical framework set up by Raz fails to contribute significantly to a correct understanding of several aspects of the normative claim made by the law.

Main Argument

Taking issue with Raz's view that the practical reasons generated by the law are content-independent and present an exclusionary dimension requires one to challenge his conception of authority, for the latter is the essential premise from which the characterisation of legal reasons derives. In Raz's framework, authoritative directives are completely separate from dependent substantive reasons and so can exclude them. The conceptual independence of these two kinds of normative standard—authoritative directives and substantive reasons—is justified instrumentally. What makes necessary the insulation of authority (its preventing the substantive sphere from invading) is its function in practical reasoning.[26] No authority could make any practical difference if it allowed us, in the course of using its directives, to appeal to substantive considerations.

---

[26] It is important to note here that this functional argument is not the only argument Raz uses to support his view of authority centred on the notion of exclusionary reasons. Another argument, the phenomenological argument, is provided to the same effect. The phenomenological argument is grounded on the consideration that in the ordinary understanding, appealing to the exclusionary logic explains better than any other strategy (eg the one depicting practical reasoning as a procedure of weighing and balancing reasons) the reasoning that takes place in the presence of an authority. Raz is aware that this further argument, which is inconclusive unless it is combined with functional considerations, can at most play an auxiliary role in vindicating the exclusionary dimension of authority. The fact that an authority is experienced to be compelling can indeed be satisfactorily explained not only by recurring to the notion of protected reasons, with their in-built exclusionary dimension, but also by appealing to the idea of weighty reasons (cf Raz 1989). The recourse to phenomenological considerations, in other words, does not settle the issue of the nature—exclusionary or discursive—of authority. For this reason, the phenomenological argument will receive no attention in what follows.

This instrumentalist justification is rooted deeply in, and coheres with, Raz's general attitude to the law. His contribution belongs to a tradition in the philosophy of law that, in virtue of being 'realist and unromantic in outlook', embarks on 'the enterprise of demythologizing the law' and resists any 'moralizing myths' (Raz 1994: 194). This tradition does not attribute special value to the law, which is not regarded as an intrinsically worthwhile institution. So there is no point in seeking the law, so to speak, for its own sake. The law is conceived of as an instrument rather than an ideal: it is a tool functional to other, more fundamental and intrinsically valuable results, a structure that allows us to achieve ends that are worthy in themselves.[27] Any value the law has is thus something it owes to factors external to it.

Here, I will focus specifically on the way the insulation thesis (that is, the statement of the complete insulation that authoritative directives preserve from substantive justificatory reasons) combines with the instrumentalist attitude toward the law. I contend that this combination gives rise to a fundamental tension. Instruments owe their rationale and justification to the goals with respect to which they function: unlike goals, which are significant in themselves and therefore do not depend on anything else, instruments are closely dependent on the ends they serve. Their being functional vis-à-vis something else implies that instruments are merely intermediate goods, the autonomy of which is only limited, depending as it does on things more fundamental and intrinsically valuable. To be sure, instruments have an identity distinct from the ends to which they function. But their separation from these ends is only relative: they would have no *raison d'être* were it not for these ultimate goals and would make no sense but for their service in enabling us to reach these goals. Instruments, then, do not enjoy a status of complete independence and absolute autonomy.

The same goes for the law. If we understand the law as a means rather than as an end in itself, we have to acknowledge it as having only a limited autonomy from that which can lend to its ultimate value. Legal discourse cannot be taken to operate in complete independence but should rather be acknowledged as remaining receptive to substantive arguments stemming from other sources. Thus, as a non-intrinsically valuable institution, the law is only partially independent, autonomous and separate from its conclusive justifications. Just as with any other means, which can always be checked against the justificatory ends upon which it constitutively depends, the law remains constantly amenable to clarification, revision and fine-tuning in the light of the goals that make sense of it. The instrumental nature of law, then, ultimately delimits its autonomy as well and renders it constitutively open to influences coming from the intrinsically worthy standards that justify it. Hence, on a coherent instrumental approach, legal directives, as well as the practical reasons stemming from them, can never gain complete independence from

---

[27] This view is expressed eg in Raz (1979: 223–6). In fact, the thesis that 'law . . . is a tool in the hands of men differing from many others in being versatile and capable of being used for a large variety of proper purposes' (Raz 1979: 226) can be considered to lie at the core of Raz's general account of the law.

their underlying justifications. Having no *raison d'être* in themselves, legal directives enjoy only *relative* independence vis-à-vis the substantive ends they serve and cannot but retain some link to the values by which they are ultimately justified.

Stated otherwise, for as long as legal directives cannot claim any intrinsic value, they will not be able to exclude the substantive reasons justifying them—at least not entirely and definitively—but will only be able to sum them up provisionally and temporarily. Just as with any means vis-à-vis its ends, legal directives (authoritative provisions) retain, at a deep and essential level, an intimate connection with their underlying substantive reasons. By the same token, justificatory substantive reasons are such that, because of their intrinsic value, they can at any time be resurrected and used in support of, or against, the authoritative directives that summarise them. In conclusion, there is no way that we can take authoritative provisions and completely divorce them, according to an exclusionary logic and in a content-independent fashion, from the underlying justifications that give them point and substance.

This means that we cannot, taking an instrumental approach, support the thesis that makes the authoritative provisions of the law and their underlying justifications radically independent from one another. This thesis requires an argument showing that authoritative directives are ends in themselves. In other words, it cannot be argued that authoritative directives retain in any conclusive manner an absolute insulation from substantive reasons justifying them unless they can be shown to have an original value neither derived from such reasons nor dependent on them. But given the instrumental status of the law, the authoritative directives emanating from legal systems *are* instrumental. Since no independent status can be derived solely from instrumental considerations, there is no conclusive argument that Raz can adduce to show the intrinsic significance, and so the fundamental independence, of authoritative provisions. Instrumental and functional considerations, such as those employed by Raz, can only establish something as a means: they can only ground the *relative* and *functional* independence of the law, not an *absolute* and *intrinsic* one. Accordingly, Raz cannot coherently deny that the authoritative provisions emanating from the law remain open to revision in the light of substantive reasons. He can at best show the relative and temporary insulation of the authoritative provisions of the law from the substantive reasons they are meant to sum up.

The thesis that the authoritative provisions of the law exclude underlying justifications from practical reasoning therefore remains unexplained. The limited and instrumental separation that Raz's approach can guarantee does not by itself support the thesis that authoritative directives provide content-independent reasons with exclusionary force. The logic of exclusion presupposes a radical distinction between form and substance. As long as authoritative provisions and substantive reasons continue to exhibit no more than a partial separation, the relationships between these two types of standards cannot be exclusionary: it will be discursive, or inclusionary. Discursive relationships are such as obtain between entities that are distinct but intermingled, meaning that they can be neither fully equated nor radically insulated. A discursive relationship presupposes a mutual permeability of standards, that is, the possibility of an interchange among mutually irreducible standards. The relationship between the authoritative provisions of the law and substantive reasons is precisely one of permeability and interchange. So an appeal to the logic of exclusion is ill-placed in such contexts and should yield to a reliance on the logic of discourse.[28]

In sum, defining the law as an instrument, thus relying from the outset on arguments based on the functional role of authority, will make it impossible to show that the authoritative directives stemming from the law enjoy the fundamental status required of them if they are to function with full autonomy from their underlying justification. Raz proceeds on just such an instrumental premise, so his attempt to rescue authoritative directives from justification—such that they will never need any justification for as long as they exist—amounts to a switching of priorities: authoritative considerations (introduced as a means) gain priority over substantive reasons (introduced as ends). The natural relationship between means and ends is thereby turned upside down: the essential is made subordinate to the accidental, the accessory is hypostatised, the secondary and unnecessary is made to prevail over the primary and fundamental.

The exclusionary quality of authoritative provisions is not made less problematic by the limitations that Raz introduces respecting the insulation of those provisions from their justifying reasons. For one thing, Raz acknowledges that the exclusionary force of authoritative directives in the law can have a limited scope to the effect that only some kinds of conflicting reasons, not all of them, are excluded.[29] Authoritative legal directives, in other words, may simply exclude only a few substantive reasons and allow one to decide what to do on the balance of all the non-excluded substantive reasons and the authoritative directives. Furthermore, provisions bestowed with exclusionary force should be understood not as reasons against *deliberating*, or against including certain reasons in one's *deliberation*, but rather as reasons against *acting* on the results of the deliberation based on the excluded reasons. The existence of directives displaying an exclusionary component prevents us from acting on the balance of reasons, but nothing will bar us from calculating that balance provided that we do not act on such a calculation. The existence of authoritative directives, thus, implies no surrender of judgement,

---

[28] This conclusion should not be taken to mean that the use of authoritative directives *requires* making reference to substantive reasons. In fact quite the opposite is true: authoritative directives can be used *without* having to adduce dependent reasons. But then this possibility (of using authoritative directives without invoking any underlying substantive justification) should not be taken to mean that the two standards are fully cut off from each other—they are not. What it does mean is that the formal standard is relatively opaque to substantive reasons, as well as relatively independent of them and autonomous. But communication does happen between the two standards, which is exactly what the discursive approach counts on and what marks it apart from the exclusionary approach: while discursive logic has no need to deny that the different standards of practical reasoning enjoy some autonomy, the exclusionary logic turns this possibility into a requirement, not simply *allowing* a use of authoritative directives that is independent of substantive reasons, but *requiring* such a use.
[29] See Raz (1979: 19–25).

for those subjected to authoritative directives are free to form their own personal judgements on the matters covered by the authority.[30]

However, this double limitation is of little help either to rebut or to weaken the critical argument presented in the foregoing, for it has no effect on the quality of the insulation setting substantive reasons apart from authoritative provisions by blocking that insulation. The first limitation merely confines the scope of the problem. It is true that in Raz's framework not all the reasons shaped by one's goals are excluded by the relevant instrumental authoritative directives of the law; thus, in relation to the non-excluded reasons the priority of ends over means is not called into question. But this leaves the problem in place for the remaining reasons, namely, all those reasons that are, instead, excluded. Therefore, the appeal to the scope-limitation introduced by Raz can at most circumscribe the problem; it cannot resolve the problem. The second limitation is of even less help. It amounts to the view that the domain of deliberation taking place in the presence of authoritative directives is unaffected by the exclusionary component of those directives, for nothing prevents the people subjected to authority from exercising their independent judgement, provided that, no matter what their assessment of the situation may be, their conduct does not depart from what the authoritative directives prescribe. This strategy succeeds in rescuing the possibility of deliberation in a very narrow sense. The practice of deliberating, especially in practical affairs, is valuable for the most part owing to its susceptibility to inform action and to its function in facilitating the choice of the right conduct. Whilst the practice of deliberating can be regarded as having some worth for its own sake, the chief value of deliberation lies in the fact that it can contribute to determining what the best conduct in a given context is. Hence, although strictly speaking, a device barring the behaviour following on deliberation does not call deliberation directly into question, deliberation, especially in practical matters, is simply being paid lip service in a system that requires that one not act on its results, to the effect that one should be content with checking whether the assessment of the reasons summed up by an authority is sound and, then, follow the instructions of the authority, no matter whether that assessment is shown to be correct or not. Taking deliberation seriously is a more significant matter than simply to deliberate with no view to being able to act on it, and it requires, too, the guarantee that those subjected to authority be allowed to take action following their deliberation.

Finally, the criticism presented in this section stands even if we acknowledge the significance of Raz's distinction between the deliberative stage and the executive stage in the law. This distinction can hardly be taken to hamper the view that applying the exclusionary logic to the law serves to invert the natural relationship between ends and means. In Raz's work, the distinction between the deliberative stage and the executive stage takes the following form.[31] It reflects common experience that before an act is performed, one typically passes through two stages—

---

[30] Cf Raz (1986a: 38–42).
[31] In what follows I will refer mainly to Raz (1994: 187–92).

deliberative and executive—which for analytical purposes can be neatly distinguished, although they are often closely knit in practice. The deliberative stage is that in which the merits of alternative courses of conduct are taken into consideration and a choice among them is made; the executive stage consists of implementing the decision reached in the deliberative stage when the appropriate circumstances are at hand. This distinction might be thought to support the exclusionary dimension of authoritative demands in legal settings, especially when it is coupled with Raz's statement that the authoritative provisions of the law belong to the executive stage.[32] If diverse reasons for and against alternative courses of conduct are used to decide what is to be done in the deliberative stage, which is not the stage to which the law belongs, the reasons supporting a decision previously deliberated cannot be reconsidered again in the executive stage, and thus in the legal context (at least in so far as we remain within the executive legal stage), and will operate as an exclusionary instruction to be acted on, or executed, as opposed to being deliberated further. The classification of authoritative legal provisions as executive considerations, then, leads to the conclusion that authoritative legal provisions follow an exclusionary logic.

Raz's distinction between the deliberative and executive stages can be given either a weak or a strong interpretation, but in neither case can it provide support to the thesis that authority conforms to an exclusionary pattern. Let me explain why.

If we take the distinction of stages as a rigid distinction and so conceive of the two stages as absolutely separated and mutually impenetrable, the distinction simply serves to instantiate the inversion of priority between ends and means that characterises the exclusionary logic when applied to the law. For if, in the executive stage, one simply acts on the results of the deliberative stage without ever being given a chance to reconsider these results, the authoritative provisions of the law, the nature of which is instrumental, gain priority over the substantive reasons, which are ends underlying these provisions. The outcome of this construction is that we should keep to the results of our deliberation even when, in the executive stage, it becomes apparent that the decision reached in the deliberative stage is unable to support the goals that we had originally set out to pursue. The rigid interpretation of the distinction between stages, then, reinforces the problematic insulation of the means from the ends that these means are supposed to serve, and concretises the priority, here argued to be questionable, of means over ends.

If, instead, we understand the distinction between the deliberative stage and the executive stage in a weak sense, as indeed Raz himself seems to do, the distinctiveness of exclusionary reasons becomes lost. To interpret the difference in a weak sense amounts to seeing the deliberative stage and the executive stage as distinct but not insulated, to the effect that it is always possible to move from one stage to another and back again, to wit, to re-open the deliberative stage during

---

[32] As Raz (1994: 191) puts it, 'the law consists of the authoritative positivist considerations binding on the courts and belongs essentially to the executive stage of the political institution (the state, the church, etc.) of which it is a part'.

the executive stage whenever the decision concluding the deliberative stage ceases to hold its appeal for us. This is tantamount to depicting the exclusion of the substantive reasons underlying an authoritative statement as merely tentative: in so far as the two stages are permeable and the merits of one's decision can be assessed again, even after the executive stage has once been reached, the instructions resulting from deliberation are always revisable and any conclusion of the deliberative process is only presumptive. There is nothing amiss with this picture, but it differs not at all from the one shaped by a discursive notion of authority. In both views—weakly exclusionary and discursive—authoritative dispositions are only relatively detached from the underlying substantive considerations. Qualifying the exclusionary character of authoritative considerations as revisable, then, implies the denial of the conception of authority as a device creating protected reasons for action and leads to its depiction instead as a device producing reasons that, being revisable and so permeable to non-authoritative considerations, concur in the final decision on a par with substantive reasons. Therefore, in a weak interpretation of the distinction between deliberation and execution (Mian 2002: 118):

> there can be no such thing as absolute exclusionary force. There has to be the initial deliberation stage, in which nothing is excluded. More critically, there has to remain the possibility of exclusionary force being revoked throughout even the execution stage . . . [which] means that the calculation has to be checked from time to time. And so exclusionary reasons can always be outweighed. Hence the distinctiveness of the exclusionary account is lost.

To rephrase this point, the mutual openness of the deliberative stage and the executive stage should be taken by those coherently endorsing an exclusionary conception of authority in order to deny the authoritative character of the instructions resulting from the deliberative stage and so of legal directives. The consequence of a weak interpretation of the distinction between stages is that the authority of the law collapses, at least in so far as one accepts the exclusionary conception of authority: once the exclusion is acknowledged to be merely tentative, to the effect that the reasons considered in the deliberative stage can be recalled and appealed anew, there is no consistent way to explain how those reasons might be considered authoritative without thereby denying that authority follows an exclusionary logic.

Objections and Counter-objections

Someone wishing to defend Raz might want to deny a discursive relationship between authoritative provisions and substantive reasons in the law by taking up the distinction between clear mistakes and great mistakes. This distinction is actually Raz's own: he introduces it himself and uses it to rescue the exclusionary dimension of authority. Having set out an exclusionary account of authority, Raz (1986a: 61) considers the objection that an authority cannot be genuinely exclusionary on the ground that 'authoritative directives can be overridden or disregarded if they deviate too much from the reasons which they are meant to reflect'. Whenever the contents of a directive stray too far from their underlying justification, the authority that issued that directive will no longer be able to enforce it as binding. So it becomes apparent, on the rationale of this objection, that the power of an authority depends on, and is ultimately limited by, the substantive reasons that justify its existence. It makes sense that Raz should reject this claim, whereby authoritative directives are binding only on the condition of not deviating too much from the right reason, for what inspires it is the discursive conception of the relationship between authoritative directives and substantive reasons. The assumption behind this claim is that everyone has the option of weighing every time 'the merits of the case before he can decide to accept an authoritative instruction' (Raz 1986a: 61). This in turn means that (1986a: 61–2):

> we always have to go back to fundamentals. We have to examine the reasons for and against the directive and judge whether it is justified in order to decide whether its mistake, if it is not justified, is large or small.

This claim is wrong, Raz argues, for it fails to show any appreciation of the distinction between great mistakes and clear ones. A clear mistake is one that can easily be spotted, not requiring us to retrace the process of substantive reasoning that produced it, not requiring us to go back and think harder: a quick look will be enough for us to become aware of it. Whenever an authoritative directive diverges too far from its underlying justification, the mistake will become immediately apparent. So, even though authoritative directives can be disregarded if they deviate too far from their underlying justification, this does not mean that a discursive relationship has been established between the two standards. Directives retain their imperviousness to substantive reasons, and authority its exclusionary character, because no substantive reasoning, or weighing of the merits, is involved in appreciating a gross discrepancy.

Yet this is precisely the point that needs to be demonstrated. Raz's counter-objection looks unconvincing, proceeding as it does on the aprioristic and unsupported assumption that if an authoritative directive departs too far from its underlying substantive justification, the mistake will necessarily be clear to us and transparent. It is not obvious that this is always going to be the case, for authoritative directives are normally grounded on *more* than one justificatory argument and can in fact be regarded as the upshot of different substantive reasons combined. This event makes proportionally less apparent any divergence a directive may exhibit from its underlying substantive justifications. As a result, even a gross deviation will not necessarily be self-evident.

Consider, by way of an example, the authoritative directive requiring tobacco products to carry health-warning labels, and assume, for the sake of simplicity, that this directive strikes a balance solely between two values: health concerns (prevention of smoking sought by encouraging smokers to quit smoking and by discouraging non-smokers from picking up this bad habit in the first place) against market concerns (preserving free trade by keeping external interference at a minimum).

Since this directive by hypothesis makes a compromise between two competing values, a paradigmatic case of gross deviation from its underlying justification would be that in which one of the two values were completely neglected for the sake of the other. Suppose now that at one point the competent authority accepted a construal of this directive that make it possible to use fine print for the warning label, in fact, print so fine that it practically takes a magnifying glass to read it. On this construal, the directive becomes inefficacious, no longer in a position to curb the habit of smoking, and in so doing brings about a gross deviation by having failed to maintain the compromise, sacrificing one of the two original justificatory values to the other. Raz would have this seen as a clear mistake. But is it really so? It would not be hard to imagine someone arguing that the fine print, far from undermining the compromise, is actually required by it, this stemming from the argument that large print would ruin the look and feel of the tobacco product being sold. And since packaging and branding play a role in at least some people's decision to smoke or not to smoke, a directive requiring large print for the warning label (thereby affecting in a direct way the aesthetics of the package) would amount to an undue interference in free trade. Thus, it can be argued that it would be altogether reasonable to construe the directive as allowing fine print for the health warnings, for this would protect the free-market enterprise while making it possible that meticulous and wary smokers be informed about the caveat respecting the risks of smoking. The point here, of course, is not to assess this hypothetical argument on the merits, but to illustrate a scenario in which someone might present it. For this possibility shows that establishing whether or not a directive deviates dramatically from its underlying justification may well require argumentation.

In sum, being grossly mistaken is not the same as being clearly mistaken: while a clear mistake is necessarily self-evident by definition, a gross mistake is not. That is, to establish whether or not a directive deviates too far from its ultimate justification may require weighing opposed and competing substantive reasons, a structured technical procedure that is subject to specific standards and that requires, for its part, specific skills and expertise.[33] The outcome of this process of weighing and balancing cannot, as a rule, be predicted, much less taken for granted. So on at least some occasions a gross deviation from the substantive justification will be far from immediately apparent and in fact may take some work to identify. Raz bases his defence of the exclusionary nature of authority on the distinction between great mistakes and clear ones, but in fact this defence amounts to a *petitio principii*: it begs the question as to why gross deviations are clear to see in the first place. The impact that gross deviations may have on the binding force of authoritative provisions remains a serious objection to the thesis of radical insulation between form and substance.

A more promising attempt at setting out the autonomy of authoritative discourse from substantive reasoning in law stems from Emilios Christodoulidis, who in a paper on the question of the relationship between universality and par-

---

[33] To appreciate the structure and scope of this process of balancing, see the seminal contribution of Alexy (2002a: 44–110); for further insights, see Alexy (2003).

ticularity takes up and further develops Raz's theory of exclusionary reasons. In his essay, Christodoulidis argues that formal legal provisions cannot be revised in a discursive fashion when they cease to reflect their underlying substantive justification. The reason here speaks to the very nature of law. Substantive considerations, such as appropriateness, ought not to enter the legal domain, for this is a place where 'particularity is abstracted, more-or-less fixed and reduced to role and rule' (Christodoulidis 1999: 224). To allow substantive considerations into the law would be to:

> stretch the plasticity of law to a point beyond recognition . . . a point where law would be too poorly selective to perform even elementary functions in society—notably its function of providing some certainty of expectations.

Christodoulidis supports this claim by bringing Luhmann's systems theory to bear on the matter, turning to it for help in addressing the question of the revisability of exclusionary reasons in the light of dependent substantive justifications. In particular, we can use this theory in order better to understand the division of roles that permeate our lives and in order to appreciate the complete autonomy that different social roles enjoy. On this account, roles are exclusionary in the sense that when a person takes up a role, he or she will no longer be in a position to appreciate the reasons underlying and justifying the code attached to this role.

Christodoulidis illustrates the point with the example of marriage. A marriage arises out of love and is justified by it. But when we marry, we take up a role *qua* spouse that is different from the role of a lover. A spouse sacrifices the spontaneity of love on the altar of a formal code that regulates marriage, a code aimed at providing for the couple a stable and lasting relationship. This role code guides the spouse by means of an exclusionary rationale: spouses who follow the code will not only refrain from asking themselves what love (one of the reasons underlying and justifying the institution of marriage and its code) would require; they will also lose their ability to acknowledge and endorse the reasons lying behind love. From the separation of roles brought about by following the code, the lovers' point of view becomes impenetrable to spouses. There is a conceptual impossibility involved. It is not as if spouses did not *want* to return to love, enveloping it. They simply *cannot*, for that would compel them to put their role as spouses on hold, and this suspension, even if temporary, would come at the cost of permanently destroying the role being suspended. Social roles cannot be suspended, for 'they are aspects of a reduction that makes it no longer possible for them to remain open to the substantive' (Christodoulidis 1999: 232). Roles, which then follow an exclusionary logic, also form the basis of legal authority, which depends for its very possibility on a reduction to roles, as understood in systems theory. And just as social roles are exclusionary, so are the authoritative directives of the law: here, too, reverting to the substantive reasons that justify an authoritative directive would amount to dissolving its authoritative status.[34]

---

[34] See Christodoulidis (1999: 233–6).

This argument certainly does have an advantage: it grounds Raz's thesis concerning the exclusionary dimension of an authority on a sophisticated theory of society—Luhmann's theory. But this theory is mistaken in so far as it radicalises the distinction of roles to the point of making exchanges between roles and their justifying reason inconceivable. There is no doubt at all that we take up distinct social roles in our lives, and that these roles—not only the reason supporting them—directly influence to a large extent our perception of the world. However, by claiming that no discursive relationship can obtain between roles and their justifying reasons, we thereby commit ourselves to a view of roles as separate entities having no unifying element in common at all. This carries too far the insulation and exclusionary nature of roles. The distinction that roles maintain from one another and from their own justifying reasons does not prevent them from having a common ground: this is something they indeed do have, and it makes it possible for them to enter into communication.

We can see this if we set aside for a moment the notion of a role as a discrete entity and conceive of it instead as a particular aspect of human lives, that is, as a specific attribute that adds to the framework of our existence and basic identity as human agents. There is no denying the importance of social roles as constitutive of our overall personality, but in this capacity they are supervening on, derivative from and conditional upon our being human. It is as human agents that we can assume this or that social role: our identity as bearers of social roles is built upon a substratum that is generically human and, as such, can be filled with this or that role according to the varying circumstances and contexts. Our participation in human agency thus constitutes the preliminary, essential condition of our being able to take up a role.[35] In this sense, human agency makes up the common source of all roles. This priority of human agency over specific roles, as well as its non-derivative, non-contingent status, is corroborated by the fact that presupposing a notion of agency not already socially encumbered is necessary for us if we are to make sense of the possibility of choosing this or that role, among the many that are available, to engage in. The very possibility of taking up a specific role is made possible by our being human agents, for unless we can acknowledge ourselves as distinctively human, we cannot even begin to appreciate the manifold options set out by more specific roles in society. To better grasp that we are not reducible to an assemblage of social roles, and so that social requirements ought not to be regarded as exhaustive of our identity, consider a contrast introduced by Christine Korsgaard (1996b: 120): 'you may cease to think of yourself as a mother or a citizen or a Quaker', because these identities are contingent and so 'may be shed', but you can never cease to think of yourself as a human agent. The necessity of human

---

[35] The notion of human agency, which is key to this counter-objection, is left somewhat vague here but will be made clearer later on in the book (see chapter five). The reason to postpone the introduction of a more accurate definition of human agency is, first, that the good sense of the counter-objection presented here can be understood, I believe, by relying on an intuitive notion of human agency; and secondly, that the exact characterisation of human agency requires a number of argumentative steps, the introduction of which at this stage would require an excessively long detour.

agency, which is imposed upon us, can be contrasted with the optional nature of any particular social role, which instead can be more or less easily discharged. The contrast makes it apparent that our identity as human agents is non-contingent and that human agency is not only an indispensable element of our nature but also the source and unifying trait of all the other identities we take up, socially conditioned identities whose status is derived from human agency and subordinate to it.

The priority of human agency explains as well why social roles cannot be understood as radically separate and autonomous: they take human agency as their ultimate unifying element, and this enables communication among them by providing a common ground for interaction, a deeper level of discursive exchange. People occupying different roles in society are likely to have different preferences and standpoints, and the values they espouse may even be radically divergent. But as human agents they can and do enter into a dialogue aimed at reaching a mutual understanding, this without thereby dissolving their social roles. So it is far from accurate to describe these roles as severed by any radical, exclusionary insulation. Roles are better described as specific articulations of a wider, all-embracing mode of existence—our existence as human agents—that forms a common identity within which these roles can interact and be transparent vis-à-vis one another, as well as the reasons justifying them, without thereby disintegrating. Thus, in Christodoulidis's example, the roles of lover and of spouse will certainly produce different outlooks on the world, but neither of them is necessarily opaque to the other. Spouses and lovers have enough in common to acknowledge and understand each other. Furthermore, we will not be able to honour our role as spouses if we are completely blind to love, one of the main reasons justifying our taking up the role of spouse in the first place. The contrary claim—whereby love is so impenetrable to us as spouses that we cannot even fathom what the reasons of a lover might be—would commit us to denying any common denominator between lovers and spouses. This, however, is a mistake, a failure to appreciate that spouses and lovers are in the first place human agents, and it comes at the cost of dehumanising both spouses and lovers.

In summary, the division of roles in society is not a basis on which the argument shaped by systems theory can conclusively demonstrate the complete insulation of form and substance that is needed to rescue Raz's understanding of legal provisions as content-independent reasons presenting an exclusionary dimension. Because systems theory cannot demonstrate that distinct roles stand in any relation of radical diversity, it can rescue a *partial* independence of authoritative directives from substantive reasons but not the absolute separation required by the exclusionary logic. Just as role-holders cannot completely neglect their common source (their being human), so authoritative directives cannot completely free themselves of their underlying substantive justification. As a consequence, Raz is right to claim that practical reasoning is multilayered:[36] the standards that we

---

[36] The multi-layered model is criticised by Michael Moore (1989: 872–3), who claims that such model contradicts the truth that when we are faced with a practical dilemma, 'morality never gives us reasons that exclude morally compelling considerations from counting'. Moore is right to describe

balance in the presence of an authority when deciding what ought to be done are not all of a single kind; we do have a division of labour and roles between authoritative directives and substantive reasons.[37] But it does not follow from this (correct) thesis about the structure of practical reasoning that the authoritative directives of the law are exclusionary reasons having the power to pre-empt their underlying substantive justifications. Practical reasoning does work on different layers, but this does not make it rigidly hierarchical or exclusionary. The different layers are discursive in their engagement. The discursive relationship existing between authoritative directives and background substantive justifications makes it possible for certain directives or reasons to acquire special strength in virtue of their source. And even though authoritative standards may enjoy a prima facie priority over substantive reasons, the priorities so established are relative, not absolute.

The point can be restated by appealing to, and radicalising, Stephen Perry's theory of reweighing reasons. Perry criticises Raz for giving too narrow an account of second-order practical reasons, an account in which these reasons can only operate in an all-or-nothing fashion, and this is a mistake. Properly understood, a second-order reason can affect the relative weight of applicable first-order reasons and so modify in some cases the balance of reasons for action, this without necessarily making the balance exclusionary. Hence, a second-order reason will generally operate as a reweighing reason, that is, as (Perry 1989: 932):

> a reason to treat a [first-order] reason as having greater or lesser weight than the agent would otherwise judge it to possess in his or her subjective determination of what the objective balance of reasons requires.

On this view, exclusionary reasons constitute a special case of second-order reweighing reasons, in the sense that they are reasons to treat another reason as having zero weight.[38] Perry uses the notion of reweighing reasons to revise and generalise Raz's case for the privileged status of authoritative directives in practical

morality as comprehensive (in the sense that we have no special reason to rule out any sphere of practical reasoning), but this fact does not necessarily support the simple non-multi-layered model. The view of morality as comprehensive does rule out exclusionary reasoning, to be sure, but not discursive multi-layered reasoning. In fact, there is no exclusion of reasons required by this model, but rather, and less demanding, a ranking of them is allowed: instead of being required to exclude substantive moral reasons when working out the overall balance of pros and cons in a course of action, we are allowed to rank authoritative directives and substantive reasons and assign to each a different prima facie strength. And there is nothing in the view of morality as comprehensive that forces us to rank all relevant considerations equally; rather, what this view does is to allow an all-embracing interaction between different kinds of reasons, thus allowing a division of labour among them. Hence, so long as it is only in a relative way, as opposed to an absolute one, that authoritative reasons condense and entrench a given balance of substantive considerations, this outcome will be coherent with the comprehensive view of morality.

[37] So the model of practical reasoning adopted here differs from the simple model put forward in Moore (1989: 859–72), Alexander (1990) and Hurd (1991: 1667–77), which describes a linear process in which we weigh and balance reasons that all stand on the same footing with none of them enjoying any prima facie priority over any other, in that no sphere can be excluded from moral deliberation when reasoning all things considered.

[38] Cf Perry (1987: 221–3).

deliberation. But at a deeper level, it seems that Perry's view cannot be squared with Raz's. The notion of reweighing reasons is consistent with acknowledging only a limited separation of form and substance.[39] Therefore, it makes sense only within a discursive conception of practical reasoning, not within an exclusionary one. Exclusionary reasons cannot be understood as a special case of reweighing reasons: these two standards—exclusionary reasons and reweighing reasons—are governed by a different logic—an exclusionary logic as against a discursive one—and each of these two are ultimately incompatible and mutually exclusive, relying as they do on radically different theoretical rationales. Once practical reasoning is acknowledged as being not only multi-layered but also discursive, there is no way to render it exclusionary: by hypothesis, second-order reasons remain (at least to some extent) transparent to first-order reasons.

The discussion conducted so far shows that different standards of practical reasoning are permeable to one another, with authoritative discourse being always transparent to, and dependent on, the substantive reasoning underlying it. This counts against Raz's thesis of a radical separation between legal directives and their underlying moral justification. In legal contexts, the relationship between form and substance is inclusionary, not exclusionary, and this means that justifications need to be recognised as essential elements of the legal directives grounded on them.

THE NORMATIVE CLAIM OF LAW AND ITS AUTHORITY

Criticising Raz's characterisation of the normative claim of law involved the rejection of his conception of authority. This rejection is not meant to sever the connection Raz establishes between normative claim and authority of the law. However, for this connection to hold without contradiction in the new framework, where the practical reasons the law claims to generate do not include an exclusionary component, it is necessary to show that a discursive model of authority is workable. In this section I intend to frame a view of legal authority that counts as an alternative to Raz's by gathering together the occasional constructive remarks I have so far injected in my critique and setting out a discursive account of the authority of the law. This will not be an exhaustive statement, of course, for the effort to work out a comprehensive conception of authority would require an essay in its own right and, apart from being beyond the scope of this chapter, would constitute more a detour than an advancement in the explanation of the normative claim of law. The aim of this section, accordingly, is modest: it consists mainly in showing that a discursive model of legal authority poses no insurmountable theoretical question and is, in principle, in a position to cope with the main issues concerning the authority of the law. The account provided in the remaining pages will, then, represent a preliminary treatment that provides a general framework

---

[39] This point is made clear as well in Perry (1987: 222 and 1989: 944).

within which an adequate concept of legal authority can find its place. This framework revolves around a core set of ideas that have been variously discussed in the contemporary Anglo-American literature on authority, ideas such as that of *reinforced request*, *non-exclusionary force* and *content-dependence*. Therefore, I will present legal authority as a complex and derivative concept that can be defined in terms of other simpler and more fundamental elements.

Let us consider, first, the idea of a request. The dominant approach, which is positivist in character, has been dismissive of this idea, arguing that the concept of request cannot be used to account for authority because authorities do not make requests but prescribe conduct. As Raz (1979: 15) puts it, 'one requires authority to be entitled to command but one does not need authority to be entitled to request'. Whenever we are subject to a legal authority, in other words, we are not being *requested* but are rather *required* to act according to the law; so it is the command, not the request, that best describes what an authoritative issuance does.[40] This account reflects an abandonment of the imperative framework, but only a superficial abandonment.[41] In fact, like the command theory of law, the positivist approach not only constructs legal authority as an institution issuing command-like directives, but also, and consequently, depicts legal relationships as vertical relationships between subjects within a hierarchical arrangement. At the cost of some oversimplification, brought about by stripping off several technicalities, this view would have us understanding the law as a conventional institution that, as the result of an unconstrained, arbitrary process of creation, can take any content whatsoever.[42] Correspondingly, laws are the product of the will of the ruling class, a will that everyone else is required to abide by under the law.

This view of authority may seem appealing, but it is nevertheless partial. A legal system cannot be depicted as a fundamentally vertical structure without distortion, nor does the division of labour and roles between law-making institutions and citizens mean that the former have the absolute upper hand when it comes to determining the contents of the law. This is so because the law, even when understood

---

[40] This sort of distinction is commonplace in the positivist tradition. Thus, requests are described in Raz (1979: 14–5) as providing reasons for action that come on top of substantive reasons and contribute to the determination of the final balance on which to act; not so a command: rather that *adding* 'to the balance by which the addressee will determine what to do' (Raz 1979: 14), a command will supply reasons 'on which to act *regardless* of whatever other conflicting reasons exist' (Raz 1979: 14–5, emphasis added). Inherent in the idea of a command, then, is the idea of an exclusionary reason having the power to replace all the first-order reasons it is intended to sum up.

[41] We can appreciate what this means if we consider Hart on the authority of the law. The idea of a legal directive, Hart states, cannot without oversimplification be equated with that of a command (a legal authority, in other words, is not simply an institution devoted to issuing commands): unlike commands, legal directives provide reasons for taking the prescribed course of action. These reasons, however, are not reasons in any ordinary sense: they are sufficient reasons (peremptory and content-independent), which is to say that the legal directives from which they stem ultimately retain an imperative character. More generally, Hart finds that 'buried in the idea of command there are . . . elements which are crucial to the understanding of law' (Hart 1990: 113). And this view is revealing of the link connecting the positivist approach to the imperative framework.

[42] See Kelsen (1967: 198) for a concise statement of this conception of the law. Kramer (1999: 78–112) further elaborates this understanding of the law.

as nothing more than a set of normative requirements,[43] functions so as to channel and direct behaviour by giving subjects reasons why they ought to act as prescribed. This mode of operation carries a specific significance, namely, ultimately recognising legal subjects as autonomous individuals, to wit, people who are able to understand the directives issued by officials and are capable of directing their own behaviour accordingly.[44] The burden of this construction is that, as much as ordinary citizens will have no formal role in law-making, they nevertheless influence the outcome of the process. The variety of contents that laws can take is shaped and bound to a considerable extent by the conception of subjectivity underlying and inherent in the very idea of the law. No law that exceeds limits will in fact count as law, for its addressees would have no way of making any sense of it without renouncing their status as autonomous subjects with cognitive and deliberating capacities—the status associated with the typical mode of operandi of the law. Thus, the people formally entrusted with creating the law are not free to give it simply any content at will. Certain contents are quite literally out of bounds and could not possibly make their way into the law, even if law-makers wished they could, for that would imply a situation in which enacted laws no longer existed as specifically *legal* requirements. Law-makers need to take into account the defining characteristics of those to whom legal provisions are addressed, *qua* subjects of the law, for otherwise we would end up with provisions that do not count as law in the first place: we would have ultra vires directives, that is, directives that are illegal, or at best non-legal, as a result of going beyond the constraints implicit in legal practice and constitutive of it. This, in turn, suggests that legal systems should be conceived not as vertical structures of command but as the outcome of a discursive interaction between law-makers and those to whom the laws apply.

This point may be further clarified by considering Fuller's criticism of the 'vertical' picture of legal institutions. The criticism proceeds on the distinction between two forms of social ordering: managerial direction and the law.[45] Some general features are shared, to be sure. Thus, both managerial direction and the legal system 'involve the direction and control of human activity', and both 'imply

---

[43] This characterisation of the law as a set of normative requirements is far from exhaustive. We cannot account comprehensively for the law without looking beyond authoritative directives; that is, without at least also bringing into the picture the defining features specific to a community regulated by a legal system—its form of life and its shared self-understanding. But for the sake of argument I am proceeding here from the most basic account of the legal phenomenon currently available; and because this account is so basic, it will also, I hope, be the least controversial, and it will help us show the positivist view to be inadequate even granting only the thinnest and most minimalist set of assumptions about the nature of law.

[44] For similar considerations, see Postema, (1987: 91–3).This may seem to be a strong conjecture. But a nearly identical statement has consistently been defended even by the advocates of the command theory of law (the tradition from which the different versions of contemporary legal positivism stem). Hence, my claim cannot be said to be in any way arbitrary or controversial. For an account of how this thesis has been accepted into modern positivism, see Postema (2001: 475–80).

[45] As Fuller himself points out, the distinction is somewhat artificial, since 'the two forms of social ordering present themselves in actual life in many mixed, ambiguous, and distorted forms' (1969: 208). Still, a distinction does exist, as can be appreciated from certain essential features embodying which a given ordering can be said to belong to one or the other of the two forms.

subordination to authority' (Fuller 1969: 207). But the differences carry more weight than the similarities. Managerial direction implies a subordination of a certain type: 'the directives issued in managerial contexts are *applied* by the subordinate in order to serve a purpose set by his superior' (Fuller 1969: 207). Not so in the case of a legal system, for if citizens behave lawfully in their dealings, they do so on the understanding that the laws serve the interests of society generally, not the specific interests of the law-giver. This is clearly an important difference, for it defines the diverse structures the two kinds of social ordering exhibit: managerial systems are constitutively vertical, being designed primarily to regulate relations between subordinates and superiors, and only secondarily relations among people standing on the same footing; conversely, legal systems are horizontal, in that they (Fuller 1969: 207–8):

> normally serve the primary purpose of setting the citizen's relations with other citizens and only in a collateral manner his relations with the seat of authority from which the rules proceed.

As one might expect, the underlying principles are different, too. In contrast to a managerial system, which results from an effective chain of command ('a one-way projection of authority, originating with government and imposing itself upon citizens'), a legal system stems from 'an interplay of purposive orientations between the citizen and his government', and so cannot function unless these two groups—citizens and officials—can relate through a harmonic interaction (Fuller 1969: 204). So it is not just partial and simplistic to regard the law as exclusively the product of those in power—it is plainly wrong, a serious mistake that warps the nature of law, turning it into a scheme of managerial direction. The law does set up managerial relations, to be sure, but these are only one of its many components; a component that, more importantly, lies at the periphery of the law, not at its core. The core of the law consists not in subjecting a social group to the plans of another social group, as the command theory maintains, but rather in the ability of the law to secure a reasonably stable framework ultimately functional to enabling social interactions between equal and autonomous beings. Reciprocity of interactions, not managerial direction, makes up the foundation of the law.

So, the doubts cast on the idea of request, in so far as its ability to explain authority is concerned, spring from an imperative preconception. As soon as we set aside the command theory and conceive of the law as the condition as well as the product of interaction among different subjects, we see that we have to change the concept of legal authority accordingly, construing it no longer as akin to that of command (for this would amount to rendering the law as a vertical structure primarily designed for managerial direction) but to that of the request, since in this way we can better account for the discursive dimension of the law as a primarily horizontal, non-managerial system.

Further considerations strengthen the link between authority and request. It is common to connect authority and command as opposed to request, this on the assumption that requests are bits of directive language that allow for the possibility of refusing to carry out the required conduct, which would scarcely be taken as an adequate response to the dictates of an authority. Consequently, requests should be considered tokens of politeness that do not apply to the relationships between authority holders and authority subjects. This account is misleading, however, for requesting is not just a polite move in the pursuit of something. The full quality of the request can be grasped by bringing William Alston's treatment of directive speech acts to bear on the issue.[46] In Alston's view, we ought to resist the temptation to represent a request as a directive illocutionary act that has no connection with obligation. Requesting is not the same as expressing an interest in the conduct that constitutes the propositional content of a request. Instead, it amounts to altering the normative status of the addressees by putting them in a position in which they ought to make a practical decision that they would not otherwise have to make. Faced with a request, one is compelled to react to it either by complying with it or by providing reasons for non-compliance. This account reveals that requests have a normative potential. The existence of such potential enables us to construe a request as an act of speech that is distinguished by degree, not by kind, from those typically affecting a normative status. In other words, the difference between a command and a request cannot be presented as a categorical difference, to the effect that whereas commands can change one's normative status by introducing requirements that one would not otherwise have, requests can only convey the interest that some considerations are being taken into account. Both commands and requests, in this construction, introduce additional requirements and so affect the normative position of the subjects addressed. Vindicating the relation of continuity that holds between commands and requests contributes to dispelling the sense of oddity possibly associated with the thesis that authoritative instructions are to be understood in terms of a sort of request. In so far as requests are acknowledged as participating in the normative dimension, nothing prevents us from concluding that requests, under certain conditions, can engender obligations, which constitute the paradigmatic case of a normative requirement. More specifically, the genre of obligation created by authoritative statements *qua* requests consists in a disjunctive duty either to act on the relevant authoritative provision or to put forward acceptable reasons for not doing so.

This conclusion shows that a request-centred account of authority does not rule out the possibility of looking at authority as an obligation-creating device. Crucially, such an account of authority is not only possible but also adequately takes account of the fact that a conceptual connection arguably obtains between authority and disjunctive obligation. Accordingly, the obligations generated by an authority are not to be seen as categorical duties. The disjunctive character of obligations generated by an authority finds support in the picture of the relations between authority and reasons drawn by John Cunliffe and Andrew Reeve. In their treatment of authority, they discuss at length the compatibility of authority

---

[46] See Alston (2000: 97–103).

and autonomy, which is understood in terms of taking responsibility.[47] According to an influential strand of contemporary political philosophy, exemplified in Robert Wolff's (1970) work, authority and autonomy are at odds, for acting on authoritative demands is tantamount to surrendering one's judgement and deferring to an external source, as opposed to relying on one's capacity to assess the situation and acting on that independent assessment. The anti-authoritarian argument is convincing in so far as it is applied to an authority conceived as a virtually unlimited power; the scenario changes completely, however, if we are justified in understanding authority in more limited terms. The nub of the counter-objection to the autonomy-based anti-authoritarian argument, then, resides in the capacity to show that authority can accommodate the exercise of critical reflection as well as the performance of the conduct stemming from, and consequent to, that reflection, which are vital ingredients of autonomy on the part of those subjected to authority. No such accommodation is possible, however, unless a non-deferential model of authority can be devised.

A non-deferential model of authority takes autonomy seriously while at the same time acknowledging that autonomy does not compel one to deal personally with every matter and so allows for delegation of power. In order to be compatible with one's autonomy, however, the handing over of one's prerogatives needs to be associated with accountability. Typically, accountability takes the form of checking the reasons for what is done by the authority, that is, asking questions and expecting answers in relation to authoritative directives and their relation to the original objectives, whose pursuance is sought. Accordingly, the sort of authority compatible with autonomy is one in which reliance is made on someone else's judgement, but such reliance is accompanied by the capacity and willingness to evaluate the reasons supporting that judgement, as well as to question them whenever appropriate. In other words, to be compatible with autonomy, authority needs to imply a merely conditional acceptance of another's judgement and does not require a once-and-for-all authorisation to act in one's name. In the non-deferential model, the presence of an authority does not force us to abdicate our judgement but simply implies a temporary suspension of our exercise of judgement and acceptance of the assessment of someone else. In so doing, we remain in a position to monitor those exercising authority, who at any stage of the exercise of authority are accountable for their directives.[48] Because accountability is associated with the discursive practice of asking for and being given the reasons underlying a directive, specifying the reasons that ought to be acted upon is a requirement for those holding authority. The exercise of authority, then, is not impermeable to reasoning. By contrast, the discursive practice of exchanging reasons is, indeed, constitutive of the relationships involving authority.

---

[47] I refer especially to Cunliffe and Reeve (1999).

[48] In this model, in accepting your authority I 'let you get on with the job, or use your discretion', and yet 'I also wait to see whether the outcomes are delivered, whether you do achieve the objectives that led me to accept your authority in the first place' to the effect that your conduct is accountable (Cunliffe and Reeve 1999: 461).

In sum, by seeing 'the recognition of authority as a process involving the continuing reflection and judgement of the authority subject' (Cunliffe and Reeve 1999: 459), the non-deferential model establishes a connection between authority and reason-giving.[49] The upshot of this construction is that in order to secure autonomy, the functioning of authority needs to be understood in terms of a discursive relationship between authority holders and authority subjects to the effect that 'authority is recognized as the result of dialogue or even negotiation' (Cunliffe and Reeve 1999: 459). The non-deferential model of authority, with its insistence on the reason-giving component, supports the picture of authoritative directives as requests demanding either that one comply with their propositional content or provide reasons to depart therefrom that are acceptable from the point of view of the authority. Hence, conceiving of authority as a non-deferential structure implies the acknowledgement of a request, not a command, as the chief interpretative category of authoritative systems and directives.

It will not suffice at this point, however, simply to equate legal authority with requests as such. The institutional nature of law, the division of competences within the law, and the function of the law are such that we need to work out a particular kind of request to account for authority: a reinforced or particularly compelling demand that holds special strength. This idea of a reinforced request enables us, on the one hand, to steer clear of the mistaken command theory of law and, on the other, to account for the privileged role that legal directives play in our decisions about how we ought to behave. A reinforced request affects our practical reasoning in a distinctive way. In contrast to commands, which expel other reasons by exclusion, reinforced requests at most present us with certain particularly weighty reasons for action, reasons that have a specific source-based strength built into them. So the point is to present compelling reasons for action without thereby issuing an exclusionary command. An authoritative directive issued by a legal institution does not force such exclusion: rather, its operation is closer to that of a reinforced request in that both enjoy a prima facie priority over non-authoritative requirements, but a priority that is not so entrenched as necessarily to force a replacement of the substantive reasons applicable to the case at hand. This is so, for a legal directive differs from these substantive reasons not in kind, but only in force. An instruction coming from an authority affects our practical deliberation not by barring substantive reasoning, but rather by competing with it from a position of advantage. There is a systematic bias at play: the reinforced reasons that come with authoritative standards will generally outweigh, by virtue of their source, any other reasons that would otherwise apply. So an authoritative standard will as a matter of fact prevail over conflicting substantive reasons most of the time, but not always. There will be cases in which the extra strength built into an authoritative issuance will not enable it to outweigh conflicting substantive reasons, this even within its own sphere of competence. In these cases, we have to

---

[49] This connection is made apparent also by the analogy that Cunliffe and Reeve establish between authority and bargaining process.

act contrary to the demands of an authority, but the departure will only be possible under very special circumstances, which is to say that a really strong case will have to present itself in order to rebut the directives of an authority.[50]

These remarks also show that questions of merit can affect the scope of legal authority. Authoritative directives doubtless owe their special force to their source, not to their content: their special binding force comes from the fact that they are issued by a competent law-making body. So, too, for the reason that since authoritative directives are only relatively transparent to their underlying justifications, the merits of each directive will be immaterial most of the time in the ordinary functioning of authority. But none of this should suggest that substantive considerations are entirely displaced by authority: they merely get pushed into the background. As an institution empowered to issue reinforced requests, legal authority does not follow exclusionary logic but rather a discursive logic. There is always a relation that authority retains with its underlying justificatory substantive moral reasons, so that these are never ruled out a priori, frozen, so to speak, in an exclusionary fashion. They are always there in the background and can at any time be reintroduced and brought to bear directly on authoritative discourse. So we can easily allow that they remain in the background, but we can never cut them off, for that would deprive all authoritative directive of its substantive moral justification. And authoritative directives *need* this moral justification, for without it they would run the risk of losing their binding force or, in the extreme, they might well end up denying their very existence, in that they would have no reason to exist if they no longer reflected the underlying justification on which they are ultimately dependent.

This content-dependence of legal authority can be made more perspicuous by means of a reference to some of the literature on the validity of legal provisions. In particular, here we can fruitfully appeal to Radbruch's formula, which states that the validity of formal law will be independent of its content only for as long as this content does not reach the point of extreme injustice, a point beyond which any authoritative directive will cease to exist as law.[51] This formula has recently been recast by Robert Alexy into the more perspicuous and analytically sophisticated claim that single norms duly issued by an authority can, from the participant's point of view, shed their legal character if they should become iniquitous or unjust in the extreme.[52] But even in this restatement, the formula cannot fully grasp the content-dependence of legal authority, for it recognises that authoritative provisions cease to exist only in the case of *extreme* injustice. This leaves out of account those authoritative directives that, while not unjust in the extreme, are flawed nonetheless because they effect *serious* departures from their underlying justifications. This construction of the requirement is too strict. To be sure, the formula

---

[50] On the defeasibility of authoritative directives, and the exceptional circumstances in which they may fail to exert their authority, see Waluchow (2000: 56–61).

[51] See Radbruch (2006: 6–8).

[52] See Alexy (2002b: 40–62). The following remarks have benefited enormously from some conversations I had with Robert Alexy. The usual disclaimers apply here.

devised by Radbruch and further specified by Alexy does cover the typical instantiations where the content of an authoritative directive becomes so significant as to affect its authority. But these cases do not exhaust the entire spectrum of situations where substantive considerations can or should affect the deliberations of an authority. A discursive account of legal authority will therefore have to go beyond the strict requirement stated in the formula. We do not have to wait for *extreme* injustice in order to bring substantive considerations into play; we ought also to be able to invoke such considerations whenever an authoritative directive violates in *significant* ways principles of justice that have rational support on their side. In other words, although legal authority can, by virtue of its existence, lend *some* support to actions that would otherwise be considered unreasonable or unjustified, it must not push too far in this direction: there is a point beyond which the patterns of justification cannot be breached, a point beyond which the substance of a legal requirement matters. In fact, legal directives are supposed to specify and contextualise their underlying justifications, not defeat them, so these justifications take precedence, and there is nothing in the idea of authority that would legitimate an effort to undermine this priority.

But, while legal authority is non-exclusionary and content-dependent, it can all the same carry out the typical functions of authority as Raz and others understand them. To begin with, even on this non-exclusionary and content-dependent conception, authority provides us with settled, acceptably clear directives that we can count on to achieve cooperation. We can follow legal authority, trusting that our fellow citizens will do likewise (blatant injustice being the exception, for when we see it, we can and in fact ought to refuse to follow the authority from which it stems). So, even though formal reasoning is permeable to substantive discourse, we ought not to conclude from this permeability that authoritative directives become any less certain or reliable than those of the exclusionary sort. Legal authority can accommodate substantive standards in its formal framework without thereby jeopardising the certainty of the law. It is only in the case of severe injustice that the scheme breaks apart and directives lose their ability to impose obligations. Even here, however, it is difficult to reject the model on grounds of uncertainty or instability, for 'the more extreme the injustice, the more certain the knowledge of it' (Alexy 2002b: 52); furthermore, disagreement in qualifying something as a case of severe injustice is just as likely as disagreement and uncertainty in determining the contents of the law while leaving substantive considerations to one side.

A second function served by legal authority understood on the model of a reinforced request is that of simplifying practical reasoning: the special force of legal directives enables us to proceed, for as long as we deem fit, on the assumption that these directives continue to embody a correct balance between and among all relevant reasons. So we can follow these directives as the most practical means of choosing the right course of action, without having to go through the whole process of reassessing the balance of reasons with each new case. This balance has already been worked out and condensed in the directive itself, so we can save time and reduce the risk of error in practical deliberation, safely relying on the directive as a predetermined solution to most of the practical problems we have to deal with. Nor do we have to reassess the balance of reasons from scratch every time an occasion arises in which a directive might be called into question. All that is needed here is a critical attitude and a readiness to act contrary to the demands of an authority whenever this is morally required.

There is also a further function that authority can serve when understood as permeable to substantive reasons, a function that Raz's conception cannot serve: it can create new reasons for action. Thus, on the one hand, the source of a request—its coming from an authoritative provision—can sometimes in itself count as an extra reason for acting as requested, a reason that comes on top of the substantive considerations we may already have made, and which may tip the scale in favour of compliance. On the other hand, an authoritative request can create a reason for action where none existed before, or it can create an additional *independent* reason that may change a pre-existent balance of practical reasons.[53] In so doing, a legal authority serves the peculiar function of setting up new frameworks providing the necessary conditions for the normative existence of certain acts. And these in turn acquire in this way a new status, that of reasonable, intelligible and justifiable acts: for it is owing to the existence of a legal authority that it becomes intelligible and reasonable to behave in ways that would otherwise not be conceivable, understandable or legitimate. An authority, then, expands the range of intelligible and meaningful acts that are available to us, rendering these normatively possible simply through its existence and action.[54]

A final advantage gained by the discursive conceptual framework over the Razian account is that we can just as easily explain the role of authority in practical reasoning, but without giving way to some of the baffling implications we would otherwise have, most notably the paradoxical conclusion that legal authority cannot really have any general or comprehensive justification. For Raz's normal justification of authority fails in this respect (even when buttressed with possible further arguments, such as those from respect and consent)[55] on the ground that it leads to the view that whether a legal directive is authoritative 'depends on the person over whom authority is supposed to be exercised: his knowledge, strength of will, his reliability in various aspects of life, and on the government in question' (Raz 1986a: 73). The problem here is not only that 'the government may have only some of the authority it claims' but also, and more seriously, that 'it may have more authority over one person than over another' (Raz 1986a: 74). There is something amiss in the view that the law exerts its authority in different degrees in accordance with different matters and different people *qua* object of authority. True, it is theoretically interesting, albeit contrary to common

---

[53] On this function an authority can perform, see Hurd (1991: 1616–17).

[54] This ability of the law to transform behaviours, by endowing them with a new, legitimate status, ultimately ends up reshaping as well its own nature as an institution: in setting up and securing the conditions that make new forms of behaviour conceivable and intelligible, legal authorities abandon their former selves as merely constraining institutions and take up as well a role in quite the opposite direction, by (also) expanding, not (only) limiting, our freedom of action.

[55] See Raz (1986a: 70–105) for a discussion of the comprehensive justification of legal authority.

sense, to present the law as less authoritative than it appears to be, but the wider and stronger conclusion that authority cannot be justified as such, not in any general terms, is self-defeating in the end: it comes at the cost of giving effect to a *reductio ad absurdum* of sorts, on the ground that the law is a comprehensive institution and so issues (also) general and abstract directives, those not specific to the instant case. So, while it makes sense to describe the law as having less authority than it seems to have, it makes no sense to challenge the validity of its claim to authority as being particular and subject-related. The failure to set out a general justification for legal authority is a serious fault, and it is a failure to which the discursive conception is responding. The law can be recognised *on principle* as legitimately authoritative, so long as it continues to provide reasons for action that are claimed to be non-exclusionary and are, at least to some extent, content-dependent. Clearly, the question whether a given legal system is generally justified cannot be answered without submitting to scrutiny the specific features and content of the legal system in question. But the possibility that legal authority may be generally legitimate is not, in the discursive framework, precluded from the outset. So the question of the justification of the law in general makes sense. This is an advantage over Raz's account. Rather than making the general claim that authority is necessarily unjustified all the time, we ought to find it possible to have a non-subject-specific justification that does not thereby commit us to vindicating the authority of the law no matter what its requirements might be. This is precisely what the non-exclusionary conception is designed to make possible: it enables us to make sense of the general justificatory question, all the while encouraging a critical approach to the claims of legal institutions.

In summary, different functions may be ascribed to an authority understood as an institution that makes reinforced requests to act in some specified way. These functions are such that authority can in fact make a practical difference in our reasoning about what we ought to do: its issuances (modelled after the ideas of reinforced request, non-exclusionary force and content-dependence) can change our practical deliberation by intervening in the balance of substantive reasons. Thus, they serve as powerful, albeit not necessarily conclusive, devices with which to channel action.[56]

CONCLUSION

In this chapter I critically examined Raz's treatment of authority, which, it was contended, is supposed to make a significant contribution to our understanding of the normative claim of law and grasping of its essential features. In particular, I

---

[56] The way a legal authority so conceived can make a practical difference is understandably different from the way in which a legal authority can when understood in Raz's terms. But there is nothing in the concept of authority itself that compels us to take up Raz's version of the practical difference thesis. So there are *different* ways, not a single one, in which authority can make a difference in our practical reasoning, different ways in which it can modify the panorama of our practical reasons.

argued here that we ought to retain Raz's view that the normative claim of law is conceptually related to the notion of practical authority and thus implies a purport to guide conduct by impinging on practical reasoning; that the nature of this claim is moral since normativity itself is a moral notion; and that the normative claim is essential to the legal enterprise and so defining of the domain of the law. But Raz's account of the normative claim of law can also be misleading, especially in so far as it implies the thesis that the reasons the law claims to generate are content-independent and have exclusionary force. This conclusion derives directly from Raz's conception of authority in combination with the assertion that the normative claim of law is the contention that it possess legitimate authority. The defects of Raz's view of the normative claim of law turn on the picture of authority that Raz introduces. The bulk of this chapter was accordingly devoted to a criticism of Raz's exclusionary model of authority and to the suggestion that it be replaced with an alternative framework. I argued that Raz cannot convincingly show that authoritative requirements are radically insulated from their underlying justifications. Christodoulidis integrates Raz's account with a sophisticated theory of society, namely Luhmann's systems theory; but this attempt, too, fails to make a case for the drastic separation of form and substance. Hence, a satisfactory view of legal authority ought to be built around a core set of ideas—reinforced request, non-exclusionary reason and content-dependence—the common element of which is constituted by their implying the permeability of authoritative directives and justificatory moral reasons. On this view, authority is not separated from justification: authoritative directives merge with the moral reasons underlying and justifying them. Crucially, the connection so established between authoritative directives and moral reasons is necessary and conceptual, even though this is not always apparent in the ordinary functioning of the legal system. These characters are transmitted to the normative claim of law by virtue of the conceptual connection holding between the claim to authority and the claim to normativity in law. Therefore, the normative claim of law is to be understood as the claim to make reinforced requests that follow a discursive logic and function as content-dependent reasons to act.

Part II

Grounds

In chapters one to three, I defined and characterised the normative claim of law. In doing so I considered the treatment the normative claim has received within analytical legal positivism, proceeding on the assumption that analytical legal positivism can supply valuable insights into the normative claim of law even if it does not put forward an entirely satisfactory account and, indeed, requires revision at several fundamental points if it is to prove adequate. This critical approach did not lead to a radically anti-positivist view, as my characterisation of the normative claim of law owes much to the positivist treatment. Yet it cannot be reduced to the picture defended by any proponent of legal positivism and it is, in certain important respects, not in tune with the basic tenets underlying the positivist theory of law. Hence, it is fair to regard it as amounting to a non-positivist stance.

The results of the argument deployed in Part I can be summarised as follows: the normative claim of law should be seen as the claim that legal systems and legal provisions alike necessarily make in order to generate, in officials and citizens alike, moral reasons that compete with other practical reasons to shape conduct, but enjoy a position of advantage over these in having a certain strength built into them simply by virtue of their legal status, provided that their requirements do not severely depart from critical rational morality. The practical reasons that the law claims to create, it was also argued, possess a strength comparable to the strength of reinforced requests coming from an authority, but they remain transparent to the underlying justifications, that is, to the principles that justify authority to issue requests in the first instance.

I also noted, in passing, that a claim so constructed cannot be grounded on some kind of endorsement, acceptance or act of will, in the inclusive-positivist fashion. No claim having the features mentioned above will find its source in a non-cognitive element, for no pure voluntary trait can be shared by the universe of subjects addressed by legal institutions. The occasional and incidental remarks relative to the grounds of the normative claim of law made in Part I, however, do not amount to a comprehensive foundation of that claim (nor indeed to the beginning of it), if for no other reasons than this: their negative quality, which implies that they can, at most, tell us how that claim *cannot* be grounded, as distinct from telling us how it *can* be grounded. At the end of Part I, thus, a question remains open: the grounding question, namely, the question of what makes the law normative and, hence, warrants the normative claim that the law makes.

Part II addresses the 'grounding question'. Answering it amounts to providing a *theoretical justification*, or deep explanation, of the normative claim of law by elucidating why the law should be taken to be normative and how normativity finds its way into legal practice. 'Theoretically justifying', as understood here, means explaining the grounds for, or clarifying the basis for lending a certain status to, something (in this case, the normative claim of law). Thus, in this context the idea of justification should not be taken as having moral or practical import; that is, justifying is regarded as a theoretical undertaking not as a practical one. A theoretical justification is similar in this sense to a description, or plain explanation, except that a description would merely account for the appearance of a phenomenon stating *what* this phenomenon is or consists in, whereas a theoretical justification goes deeper and explains *why* the phenomenon so accounted for takes such a form. Where we are concerned, this involves showing how the law comes to contend to guide conduct, or showing what this action-guiding claim rests on, or again where it comes from. For this reason, I will be using 'justification' interchangeably with 'foundation', 'grounds', 'origin' and 'source'.

The attempt to provide the normative dimension of law with a foundation is taken here to be a reflection of the conviction that no study of the normative claim of law can be regarded as complete unless it incorporates an account of how that claim can be grounded, or theoretically justified.[1] However, the significance of the grounding question has hardly found general recognition among legal theorists. A number of them deny the importance of the grounding question and argue that normativity is best regarded as 'groundless'. This statement can be understood in several ways. We can distinguish a moderate version and a radical one. The moderate variant of the thesis that the grounding question ought not to concern us takes in turn two distinct forms. These can be summarised in the view that legal theorists are entitled to disregard the grounding question, for such a question either (a) lies outside the concerns of jurisprudence (subvariant 1), or (b) is hardly a general question and is of concern exclusively to those who endorse a determinate philosophical framework, that is, practical constructivism (subvariant 2). Subvariant 1 is paradigmatically expressed by Jules Coleman, subvariant 2 finds an exemplary statement in Joseph Raz's recent work.

Coleman (2002: 172) argues that, following the example of Herbert Hart, legal theorists ought not to be concerned with 'the question of how normativity gets into our practices'. We are not only entitled to presuppose, or assume, the existence of the normative dimension of law but, indeed, we had better do so. Far from being arbitrary, this presupposition is required, because normativity is what allows us to make sense of our practices and renders them recognisable. As a result, setting out to elucidate the normative dimension of our practices would be to reverse the priority of explanation and 'illicitly supposes that we can so much as make sense of "our practices" without already assuming our answerability to norms as an

---

[1] The significance of the grounding question for the study of normativity is stated by a number of scholars. Compare Copp (2005: 194–7), among others, who reacts to Hubin's (2001: 462–8) Humean argument against the need for determining the source of normativity.

explanans' (Coleman 2002: 172). In so far as legal theory is aimed at making sense of legal practice, the grounding question is, hence, 'a theoretical unpromising question, akin to "How did this carburettor emerge from these molecules?" or "How did consciousness emerge from primordial ooze?"' (Coleman 2002: 172). The chief implication to be drawn from this view is that legal theorists ought to resist the question of how normativity enters legal practice and concentrate instead on different normative questions, such as 'the problem of explaining the possibility of legal authority' or the attempt to characterise 'the distinctive features of the normativity of our practices' (Coleman 2002: 172–3). Coleman's remarks can be regarded as a moderate instance of the thesis that we need not ground the normativity of law. Coleman does not deny the theoretical significance of the grounding question as such; rather he advances the more limited thesis that from the point of view of a discipline interested in explaining legal practice, as is the case with jurisprudence, the question of what makes the law normative is irrelevant, for the normativity of law is not something we need to justify; rather it is something to be assumed, a datum in the absence of which a practice would not be recognisable as a legal one at all.

The moderately sceptical attitude about the relevance of the grounding question finds a different sort of claim in Raz's work. In a debate with Christine Korsgaard on the notion of value, Raz notes that the question of the source of normativity is not a general philosophical question that one ought to be interested in; rather it is a question that makes sense only within a given metaethical approach. Raz specifies this claim by arguing that the worries about the source of normativity make little, if any, sense unless one accepts the truth of practical constructivism.[2] Therefore, as long as the truth of the constructivist picture of normativity is not established, one is perfectly entitled to be less than concerned with the theoretical justification of normativity. This way, Raz narrows down the significance of the grounding question, which, he argues, not only lies outside the boundaries of jurisprudence (as Coleman believes) but, indeed, has no relevance for practical philosophy in general, at least in so far as practical constructivism cannot be shown to possess a privileged philosophical status. Like Coleman, however, Raz does not intend to deny the relevance of a correct understanding of normativity for the study of law, nor does he claim that the grounding question is idle. To the extent that Raz acknowledges the significance of the search for normative grounds, limited as this significance might ultimately be, his position can be interpreted as a moderate statement of the groundlessness of normativity.

A more radical challenge to the significance of the grounding question comes from those theorists who regard the theoretical justification of normativity as a totally irrelevant exercise, arguing that what is normative has no independent standing and can be reduced to the factual: call it the reductive thesis. In a nutshell, the reductive thesis is the view that normativity does not designate any part of human experience as having its own autonomous stance and is fully co-extensive

---

[2] See especially Raz (2003: 138–50).

with the factual: normative concepts, properties and statements not only correspond but are reducible to factual concepts, properties and statements. This thesis entails the radical irrelevance of the grounding question, for facts are generally regarded as something about the way the world works and so in need of no theoretical justification. That is, most philosophers would agree that there is nothing making facts exist: facts just exist and are there to be grasped (as opposed to being grounded). As a consequence, there can be no illuminating explanation of the sources of facts—facts are, so to speak, self-grounded. In sum, reducing norms to facts is tantamount to eliminating the foundational concerns once and for all: here the question of what gives something a guiding capacity is not merely argued to be irrelevant from the point of view of legal theory or from the point of view of non-constructivism-oriented practical philosophy; it is held, indeed, to depend on a mistaken understanding of the nature of normativity. Being an arrangement of facts, what is normative need not be grounded, since talking about the sources of facts is little more than fanciful nonsense. In a word, on the view shaped by the reductive thesis, the search for the origin of normativity, here conceived as nothing but a matter of fact, is both pointless and misleading.

These distinct positions denying the relevance of the grounding question, as introduced thus far, have different theoretical implications and present different features. Their comprehensive treatment would, then, require an analytic discussion of each diverse stance that is sceptical about the need for normative grounds, along with distinct arguments against them. Given the purpose of this book, however, such a comprehensive treatment is not necessary; for the moderate statements do not call into question the significance of the grounding question per se. Their truth, accordingly, does not condemn a discussion of the grounding question to absolute irrelevance; rather it either excludes the significance of that question from a certain disciplinary ambit or confines that significance to certain philosophical horizons. The limited import of the moderate thesis should, therefore, not worry us all that much in this context. Partial as it might be for legal theory, or for non-constructivist practical philosophy, the importance of establishing the foundation of normativity is still warranted for the purposes of this book, which, for one thing, is mainly concerned with issues raised in the contemporary debate among legal theorists, but is not limited to those issues. For another thing, as will emerge more clearly later, especially in chapter five, it sets out a positive argument owing much to, and indeed accepting the basics of, Kantian practical constructivism, the endorsement of which, it will be contended, enables one to elucidate key dimensions of the normative claim of law. For these reasons, once the purposes and the theoretical framework of this essay are taken into account, the views defended by Coleman and Raz fall short of the mark where rendering the grounding question insignificant is concerned. Therefore, I will confine myself to discussing, in chapter four, the radically sceptical stance concerning the grounding question; that is, the position shaped by the reductive thesis, the truth of which would be lethal to the project undertaken in the remaining part of this book, where the grounding question is explored at some length.

Exploring the grounding question requires a number of changes in the focus of the discussion. These changes reflect my concern in the following chapters not with meaning and traits of the normative claim of law but with its theoretical justification, and the point of the discussion carried out in the rest of the book is not confined to the normative claim; rather it includes, too, the normativity of law. Thus, from now on the chief problem is no longer that of grasping the *meaning*, *status* and *essential features* of the *normative claim* of law but rather that of providing *grounds* for the *normativity* of law. The relevance of normativity in this context turns on the fact that normativity is the notion shaping the meaning of the normative claim of law. Accordingly, in order to justify theoretically the normative claim of law, we need to turn our attention to the concept defining the contents of the normative claim and to make sure that that concept is not groundless. In other words, the normative claim of law remains ungrounded unless one can provide an undergirding for the dimension from which that claim originates and of which it is a specific instantiation. Hence, the relevance of the discussion of the normativity of law carried out in chapters five and six. More specifically, in chapter five I will establish the grounds of the normativity of practical reason, whilst in chapter six I will show how the discussion of the grounds of the normativity of practical reason bears on the grounds of the normativity of law and normative claim and contributes, too, to a determination of some elements of the normative dimension of law. In their combination, then, chapters five and six will present an argument leading from the exploration of the grounds of the normativity of practical reason to the elucidation of the grounds of the normativity of law and of the normative claim of law.

4
Why Grounds are Needed

INTRODUCTION

IN THIS CHAPTER, I will introduce and discuss the stance that gives rise to the most radical challenge to the significance of the grounding question. This position, which has the greatest potential for rendering insignificant the discussion undertaken in the following two chapters, is built on what I call the reductive thesis. In the second section of the chapter, I introduce the basics of the reductive thesis before adducing arguments to the effect that the legal view shaped by this thesis is ultimately untenable. In doing so, I will draw on two sets of considerations: the first set appeals to the remarks concerning the categories of 'is' and 'ought' as set out by Hans Kelsen; the second refers to the kind of guidance associated with legal standards, guidance that does not depart substantially from the guidance offered by moral requirements. The argument deployed in this chapter is, therefore, two-tiered.

The first strand of the argument is based on the statement of a categorial divide between 'is' and 'ought'—a thesis commonly defended by those working in the Kantian tradition of practical philosophy. This argumentative strand elaborates, too, on the different predicates that apply, respectively, to facts (here understood as paradigmatic inhabitants of the 'is'-dimension, or what is the case) and norms (that are regarded as typical instances of the 'ought'-dimension, or what ought to be the case). The attributes defining what the normative is are efficacy (the actual correspondence between issued norms and social behaviour) and validity (the actual existence of norms). These two attributes are interlinked but not identical, so they should be kept separate. Neither efficacy nor validity is a predicate that can be applied to facts: strictly speaking, facts are not either efficacious or inefficacious, and they are not either valid or invalid. Instead, facts are defined by means of a different predicate, social acknowledgement. This attribute can be regarded, roughly, as the factual equivalent of normative efficacy. The approximate equivalence of those attributes suggests that factuality and normativity do not form completely distinct, hermetically sealed, or incommunicable categories. However, the absence of a factual equivalent of normative validity, especially when this is combined with the impossibility of equating efficacy and validity, brings to light a discontinuity between what is factual and what is normative. Because normativity is characterised by a predicate, validity, that has no equivalent in the realm of facts, normativity and factuality can hardly be regarded as identical and so reducible the one to the other.

In the second strand of the argument showing the existence of a normative core that is not reducible to what is factual, I focus on the specific kind of guidance—unqualified and categorical—that normative legal standards are taken to provide. By criticising the specific variant of the reductive approach defended by David Copp, I will show that no standard reducible to an arrangement of facts can guide conduct in an unqualified and categorical form. Facts can guide only in combination with some subjective states and dispositions: unless they are subjectively acknowledged, or endorsed, facts cannot guide conduct. The requirement of subjective endorsement, which can even be merely implicit, means that the sort of guidance facts provide is subject-dependent and contingent, as opposed to categorical. Fact-based standards, then, are constitutively incapable of explaining the unqualified guidance the law purports to supply. Denying the existence of standards other than factual standards is, therefore, tantamount to leaving out of account the sort of claim-guidance made by the law. This poses a dilemma: either we take seriously the claim the law makes to guide its addressees categorically, which compels us to abandon the reductive thesis; or we accept the reductive thesis, but in so doing we are forced to reformulate the kind of action-guidance associated with the law in a fashion that departs substantially from the common interpretation given to legal guidance.

The two strands of the argument converge in showing that the reductive thesis is untenable and should be abandoned for failing to explain, first, how categories (normativity and factuality) can be regarded as identical when different predicates (validity and efficacy, on the one hand, and social acknowledgement, on the other) are applied to them; and secondly, how the law can happen to have the categorical kind of action-guidance that it in fact has.

THE REDUCTIVE THESIS

The most radical form of scepticism about normativity is based on the *reductive thesis*, that is, the view that normativity designates no segment of human experience as having its own independent existence. The reductive thesis makes the normative co-extensive with the factual: every normative phenomenon is at bottom an arrangement of facts; accordingly, normative statements mean the same as statements about facts. In this view, the ontological, epistemological and semantic status of norms are identical, respectively, to the ontological, epistemological and semantic status of facts; which has the consequence that norms belong to the 'is' rather than to the 'ought'. This means, among other things, that there is no difference in kind between what is normative and what is not normative. The reductive thesis, in other words, marks an attempt to explain the entire domain of human experience and understanding in terms of one category—the category of factuality—which, then, is taken to be the only fundamental and elementary category of human thought and so the category from which any other category derives, to which any other category can be ultimately reduced, and in terms of which any other category can be unpacked. To put it concisely, far from being an irreducible and basic category, normativity is a subset of factuality to the effect that 'the concepts of *normative, recommend,* and *matter* are here conflated with, or reduced to, psychological appeal' and normativity is seen as a kind of motivating power (Parfit 2006: 338).

A reduction so framed does involve a sceptical element, but it does not render the reductive thesis eliminativist with respect to the normative. That is, the thesis does not deny the existence of normative concepts and properties; indeed, it recognises them as part of human experience. It does not, however, regard them as having distinctive features in need of special justification. The normative, on this conception, does exist, not however as a primitive category but as a derivative one, namely, as the effect of this or that constellation of facts. Normativity, therefore, does not make up its own dimension and does not bring any further complexity to a world already known to exist—the world of facts—which normativity does not enrich in any distinctive way, for it does not form a class apart or any separate genre. In sum, the reductive thesis denies the specificity but not the existence of the normative, for which reason its reduction should not be understood as designed to *eliminate* the normative.

This makes it possible for us to view the position shaped by the reductive thesis as a component of a wider metaethical approach: *practical naturalism* (also known under the name of ethical, or moral, naturalism), a view pertaining to the genus of practical (ethical or moral) realism, which constructs normative items as subkinds of natural or social facts. This is to say that normative properties are equivalent to factual properties (natural or social properties) and normative statements are synonymous with statements descriptive of states of affairs. In this view, something exemplifies a normative instance in virtue of its possessing certain factual features and the normative status of any situation is made up entirely of the factual properties of that situation. As a result, norms are discoverable and analysable in the ordinary ways in which natural or social facts are discoverable and analysable. In a word, for the champions of practical naturalism, the factual entirely controls and also exhausts the normative.

Practical naturalism has some attractions: as a form of realism, it can make robust sense of the objectivity of normative standards, allowing that those standards be truth-apt; as a form of naturalism, it offers to reduce normativity to a domain of experience (factuality) that we are familiar with and by doing so bridges the gulf between 'is' and 'ought'.[1] Hence, in so far as practical naturalism argues that there is no genuine feature of human experience that remains forever outside the purview of the domain of facts, it should be interpreted as a position concerned with holding categorial complexity to a minimum and sharing a wariness of any attempt to transcend the realm of facts. For an advocate of practical realism, anything irreducible to facts takes on a numinous aura of mystery and should consequently be demystified: we should 'ask no more of the world than we already know

---

[1] Compare Lenman (2006: 2).

is there'.[2] The idea underlying practical naturalism is to secure normativity safely within the disenchanted world of facts, finding a place for it within this world as described by the hard sciences, the sciences, that is to say, whose theories are based and tested on hard facts and which never argue from fact to anything beyond what experience can determine.[3] In this sense, the scepticism shaped by the reductive thesis can be regarded as part of a broader commitment to demystify the world around us, under a strategy designed to help us find a way out of the philosophical conundrums we are apt to concoct through a tendency to try to arrive at a new categorial dimension for each set of phenomena we find unfamiliar and for which we lack an account. If, instead, we stay grounded in the factual, and fashion normativity exclusively out of social facts, taking a sceptical approach to anything that departs from the factual, we will find that we can dispel much of the mystery surrounding normativity and break down any remaining puzzles into familiar questions.[4]

These metaethical views can be translated into a *legal theory* reducing the normativity of law to an arrangement of facts. Generally, on this view, the facts forming the co-extensive basis of the normativity of law are the phenomena of force and power. The normativity of law ought accordingly to be explained by reduction to the arrangements of the social facts connected with the emergence of force and power. The normativity, force and power of the law all lie in the same conceptual space and cannot exist other than through this interconnection. This position corresponds to a comprehensive, or general, theory of law that has been extensively explored by, and discussed at length among, legal scholars. Conceptually, that theory can be regarded as an anti-idealist legal approach; historically, it was first put forward by scholars working in the tradition of legal positivism. Not surprisingly, then, a concise summary of the legal theory shaped by the reductive thesis can be found in Kelsen's restatement of the empirico-positivist stance. Whilst Kelsen interprets his 'pure theory of law' as a contribution to the positivist tradition, he departs from the empirical strand of legal positivism, which dissolves the

---

[2] This statement is Blackburn's (1984: 182). Blackburn uses it to describe the view of practical realism, and the reason why it can also be made to describe the view of normativity shaped by the reductive thesis is the safe, conservative attitude the two views share with respect to ontologies: the fewer there are, the less likely we are to depart from the factual and paint fantastic worlds of supernatural flavour.

[3] Another connection that can be established here is between practical naturalism and physicalism, the latter of which combines an ontological claim about properties of the world with a semantic claim about predicates, holding that properties are real only so long as they are governed by natural laws, and that predicates are valid only so long as they can be analysed in observational terms, or terms susceptible of empirical enquiry. On physicalism, see Leiter (2002: 1–3).

[4] Here I would like to add, incidentally, that whilst a connection undeniably exists between the position shaped by the reductive thesis and the scientific worldview, rejecting the reductive thesis does not condemn one to adopt a pre-scientific worldview. Likewise compatible with the latter is the non-reductive thesis that normativity is rooted in, and so connected with, factuality, yet is not completely reducible to factuality. In this alternative view, facts and norms form distinct and mutually non-derivable categories to the effect that the distinction between 'is' and 'ought' can be preserved (at categorial level, as opposed to ontological level) without making reality more complex and without denying some kind of connection (different from identity) between 'is' and 'ought'.

'ought' into the 'is' by denying the autonomy of what is normative. In Kelsen's reconstruction (1967: 102), empirical positivism regards the law as a 'means of bringing about certain [forms of] behaviour' and so as something standing in relation with the prescribed conduct as cause to effect. In this view, in which 'the meaning of an "ought" different from one of "is" cannot be assumed', legal acts are to be regarded as attempts 'to create in men certain ideas whose motivating power causes them to behave in a certain way' (Kelsen 1967: 102). The outcome of this construction is that (Kelsen 1967: 102):

> the law—in its relation between law-creating and law-obeying men—is viewed as an enterprise comparable to, say, that of a hunter who places a bait to catch game.

This means that the normative has no existence autonomous from the factual and, consequently, the 'ought' has no meaning separate from the 'is'. Hence (Kelsen 1967: 103):

> from this point of view, merely the natural, causally connected, events and the legal acts merely in their actuality, but not their specific meaning, are taken into consideration.

In sum, in Kelsen's interpretation the legal theory shaped by the reductive thesis equates 'what ought to be' to arrangements of facts, such as the chance that one's action has some legal consequence, or the likelihood of a sanction following conduct in breach of legal directives. This theory is therefore also a view about what it means to fall within a normative legal standard: it ultimately means being compelled to behave as that standard requires, regardless of what such compliance implies. This statement involves some simplification, to be sure, but it captures the basic point that viewing the normativity of law as co-extensive with the facts of force and power (that is, as the product of coercive systems) ultimately makes normativity inseparable from these forces. Accordingly, the core of the reductive thesis in law consists in reinterpreting the legal connections as causal links inhabiting the sphere of 'is', instead of as relationships informed by the principle of imputation—the principle attending to the domain of 'ought'. The defining trait of the reductive thesis in law, thus, is the elision of the legal 'ought' and its reinterpretation in factual terms. On this view, normativity is denied any specificity (that is, any distinctive feature not justifiable by reference to sheer power alone) and we are thereby relieved of the need to find a specific foundation for the normative claim of law.

So described, the reductive thesis encompasses a number of juridical-theoretical options. A familiar, historically important example of a legal theorist who argued in defence of the reductive thesis in law is Jeremy Bentham. The reductive thesis can be found, in particular, in Bentham's general account of obligation, a concept that Bentham understands as roughly equivalent to duty, and through which he filters the main issues in the debate on normativity of his day. A brief survey of Bentham's concept of obligation will make it possible to underscore the historical link between legal positivism and the reductive thesis. For Bentham, the concept of obligation is central to the law and should accordingly figure prominently in legal analysis, especially when it comes to investigating the nature of law, a question that in turn is found at the core of descriptive jurisprudence. Bentham understands obligation as a broad concept, encompassing legal practices and moral practices alike. While legal obligation shares a common denominator with moral obligation, it also takes a specific form distinctive to it. An obligation is legal in so far as it singles out an act with respect to which a penalty, or sanction, in a given system of laws follows, or is likely to follow, non-compliance. Similarly, laws are normative in so far as penalties attach to them for non-compliance, penalties carried out by officials in keeping with the substantive and procedural rules established in the legal system itself. This way, Bentham establishes a conceptual connection between the normativity of law and the penalties administered by officials charged with enforcing the law. There is normativity in the law, then, in proportion to likelihood that those who disobey the law will bear the consequences of their disobedience. This is in essence a probabilistic, sanction-based view of normativity, and it paradigmatically exemplifies the non-eliminative sort of legal theory informed by the reductive thesis.[5] The reason why this does not amount to a form of eliminativism is that Bentham does not propose to rid the law of the idea of obligation. In fact, he points up just how central a place normativity occupies in the law by stating that 'whatever business the law may be conversant about, may be reduced to one sort of operation viz. that of creating duties' (Bentham 1970: 249). And since 'duty is a common measure for every article of law' (Bentham 1970: 294), the law itself would prove to be unintelligible to us if we eliminated the idea of normativity from its study. Yet, having said this, there is a certain way in which normativity should be approached on a demystifying view of the law, as Bentham's is;[6] that is, normativity should be reduced to some known factual phenomenon that can be given a clear account. It is for this reason that Bentham establishes a conceptual connection in law between obligation and fact, and the fact of sanctions in particular, to the effect that a legal obligation becomes such only by virtue of a sanction, or the likelihood of it, understood as a consequence for failure to act as the obligation requires. This amounts to denying that the normative has any *specific* existence in the law, and to that extent it renders Bentham's conception of normativity a conception that is shaped by the reductive thesis.

The legal reductionism inspiring Bentham's account of obligation no longer forms a part of the legal positivist view. In particular, Hart's critique of it drove

[5] Bentham was not alone in upholding this view. His most famous disciple, John Austin, likewise understood the study of law as aimed at demystifying the workings of the law, and likewise defended a probabilistic theory of the normativity of law. See Austin (1954: 14–8). The same goes for Oliver Wendell Holmes (1897: 458), who claimed that key normative concepts, such as those of legal right and duty, do not exist 'apart from and independent of the consequences of [the] breach [of law], to which certain sanctions are added afterward'. Normativity should thus be 'washed in cynical acid', so that nothing remains for us to observe and work with except the operations of the law, at which point we can recognise legal obligation to be 'nothing but a prediction that if a man does or omits certain things he will be made to suffer in this or that way by judgement of the court' (Holmes 1897: 458). See also Holmes (1897: 461–2).

[6] For a discussion in which Bentham's approach to normativity is so described, as demystifying yet non-eliminative, see Hart (1982: 1–20).

legal positivists to reject Bentham's account of normativity by drawing a clear line of distinction between the concept of normativity and that of sanction, thereby appreciating that there is nothing amiss in the idea of something's being normative without an attendant sanction, be it certain or likely.[7] Thus, unlike legal positivism in its original form, as paradigmatically blocked out by Bentham and his best-known disciple, John Austin, contemporary legal positivism makes no attempt to reduce the legal 'ought' to the fact of power. This is not to say, however, that the reductive programme has disappeared: Bentham's epigones may have departed, to be sure, but some non-positivists have revived it, and the result has been that while there is no longer a significant form of legal positivism representing the reductive effort, an approach to normativity shaped by the reductive thesis does survive among non-positivists.

The contemporary, non-positivist legal theory based on the reductive thesis can be summarised, not without embarking in a reconstructive effort, in terms of three basic stances, which can all be found in the major works of the legal theorists embracing the reductive thesis: (a) the critique of foundationalism; (b) the equation of normativity, the law and obligation with, respectively, factuality, power and sanction; and (c) the demystification of the idea of authority.

(a) From the point of view of the defendants of the reductive thesis, the very question of a grounding is regarded as a paradigmatic instantiation of an approach informed (and indeed misled) by foundationalist concerns. In the account of Stanley Fish, a contemporary champion of the reductive thesis, *foundationalism*, or essentialism, is a programme consisting in an 'attempt to ground inquiry and communication in something more firm and stable than mere belief or unexamined practice' (Fish 1989: 342). Foundationalism, regarded as a natural outcome of the logocentric tradition in Western philosophy, seeks to transcend individual experience and discover universal truths, or truths potentially valid for any object in a given class; if successful, this transcendence attains objective knowledge. It does so by finding a *ground* understood as 'a reference point or checkpoint against which claims to knowledge and success can be measured and adjudicated' (Fish 1989: 343). The foundationalist programme, then, consists in finding independent reference points that remain constant regardless of context, culture, interests and concerns—all influences to which they remain immune, securing for them a changeless fixedness that has come to be recognised as the hallmark of objectivity. These objective, practice-independent points represent safe grounds within which to develop models and methods incrementing our knowledge and awareness of the existent; and what makes the process safe (that is, objective) is that the guidelines have been worked out in advance, independently of the circumstances of their use.

Despite widespread support for the foundationalist project in contemporary legal theory, Fish finds the project deeply flawed. Especially problematic for him is the idea of seeking context-independent, supra-historical grounds within which

---

[7] This view is extensively defended by MacCormick (1982: 232–46), among others.

to carry out research. There is in fact a conceptual impossibility involved that makes this a futile attempt (Fish 1989: 344):

> questions of fact, truth, correctness, validity, and clarity can neither be posed nor answered in reference to some extracontextual, ahistorical, nonsituational reality, or rule, or law, or value; rather ... these matters are intelligible and debatable only within the precincts of the contexts or situations or paradigms or communities that give them their local and changeable shape.

This proposition is set squarely against the foundationalist idea, for it reclaims all that is contextual, historical and situated. There is no way to transcend the local experience and perspective, because everything is local, contingent and changeable. We would therefore be subject to a delusion if we committed ourselves to fashioning objective, independent knowledge out of what is context-specific and what necessarily carries a perspective, that of people and practices in process. And it is this perspective, rather than an abstract or allegedly neutral one, that we should value as the fertile standpoint within which to work.[8] The deep flaw that Fish attributes to foundationalism, then, consists in its striving for a transcendent objectivity, that is, in assuming that objective knowledge makes it necessary to transcend the situatedness and circumstantial character of human experience, and in pretending actually to be able to accomplish as much.

(b) This criticism of foundationalism with its search for grounds bears directly on the question of *normativity*. Like anything else, normative standards, according to Fish, are embedded in a community, as extensions of existing contexts and practices. It follows that what is normative *is* embedded; so closely are the two predicates intertwined that each presupposes the other: if something is normative, it is thereby embedded in a practice (where a practice is conceived as an array of social facts). That basically gives us Fish's statement of normativity-as-practice (Fish 1989: 13):

> it is simply not possible even to conceive of a constraint (or rule or law or principle) without already having assumed a context of practice in relation to which it is intelligible.

Subscribing to this theory, then, means rejecting as illusory the intuitive and widely accepted distinction between 'what is' and 'what ought to be'.

Fish's endorsement of the reductive thesis is clearly of wide scope, and it therefore easily applies to legal theory as well, coming to bear in particular on the question of the *normativity of law*, which on this conception is understood as reducible to the force, or power, by means of which a legal system is established and preserved. This is a thesis that Fish defends paradigmatically in his discussion of those sections of *The Concept of Law* in which Hart criticises the reduction effected by legal positivism in its early stages.[9] Hart (1994: 78) finds the reductive thesis unhelpful, for unless we can explain what is special about a rule—what makes it different from any plain habit or other pattern of behaviour—'we cannot hope to elucidate even

---

[8] See Fish (1989: 436–41).
[9] This position is defended in Fish (1989: 503–24).

the most elementary forms of law'. Thus, in one of the early statements of the positivist mode of legal theory, Austin elucidated these forms by subsuming them under the broad category of command and coercive power (that is, all are forms derivable from the use of commands and coercive power). Even granting, however, that this reduction clarifies and makes manageable an otherwise complex phenomenon, it does so by excluding from it or ignoring as irrelevant anything that cannot be made to fit within the broad category of power. Thus, we have here a strategy that consists in identifying a single aspect of the law (the use of commands backed by the threat of force) and magnifying it to bring under its purview the *whole* of what the law is. This is the law construed as the gunman situation writ large. The problem with this reduction leads Hart to represent the law through an element more central to it, which he detects in the concept of a rule. It is not force but rules that form the authentic basis of the law. This is the point at which Fish intervenes, arguing that Hart's rule model does not really make a clean break with Austin's earlier gunman model: the idea of a rule adds nothing to that of force, merely masking it instead 'by attenuating it, by placing it behind a screen or a series of screens' (Fish 1989: 504). If Hart's attempt to account for the nature of law by substituting rules for coercive power achieves anything, it is not to remove but to relocate force. The force envisioned in the gunman model is the force needed to *create* the legal system; the kind envisioned in the rule model is instead the force needed to *interpret* and *apply* the rules of law established under such a system. Force therefore remains within the system and continues centrally to inform the definition of the normativity of law.

There is, then, a continuity between the gunman model and the rule model, in that both rely crucially on the idea of coercion. This continuity is owing for the most part to the nature of rules as standards rooted in practices. In Fish's account, rules do not function as self-enclosed entities pertaining to the dimension of 'ought'; rather they draw their content from the very practice, which is seen as inhabiting the sphere of 'is', that they are meant to govern. Even more importantly, the meaning of practices is pliant in that what a practice means, and so what social arrangements make the most sense in view of that meaning, is a matter of interpretation. This basic idea, forming the core of the interpretive turn that Fish has tried to bring about in jurisprudence, clearly also applies without a change in the rules. A rule, just like the practice in whose fold it develops, finds its ultimate determinant in interpretation, and just as rules and practices are embedded in context, so is the activity by means of which they are interpreted.[10] Interpretation, then, on Fish's theory, does not proceed by its own strictures or independent standards of correctness, since the activity is itself set deep in context.[11] So, instead of the independent standard guiding us to the correct meaning of a rule, we have the dominant interpretive view, the one that establishes itself *in context*, here and now, as the de facto prevailing standard of interpretation; and it does so by means of its

---

[10] On the centrality of interpretation in legal practices, see Fish (1989: 120–40).
[11] Stated otherwise, no guideline of interpretation exists apart from the interpretation itself. Cf Fish (1989: 150–4 and 300–3).

ability to displace alternative views rather than by virtue of its own internal logic. But clearly, such an ability to achieve broad mainstream consensus by capturing the public mind depends on the cultural mood of the moment. This makes interpretation a rhetorical exercise in persuasion, a manipulative activity designed to sway opinion in one's favour.[12] The activity is in this sense political and, as with anything political, involves power and the use of force. With force, therefore, we have 'the bottom-line category of interpretive and deliberative activity' (Fish 1989: 10). So, if we think of rules as essentially *interpreted*, that is, as the outcome of an interpretive activity, we will have to understand them as ultimately based on power relations and force. And the same will have to be said of normativity, by reason of its inherent connection with rules. Just as rules cannot transcend existing practices, neither can normativity. It is not the 'ought' but rather practices (and so 'is') that serve as the benchmark in this relation, for normativity acts as a context-dependent variable, its content filled by those who prevail in the power struggle of politics and the law. Only apparently, then, do rules, and hence normativity, give us much of an advance over power and coercion as the core elements around which to build a concept of law. Hart's rule model constructs power as only a secondary element, rather than as the primary element as per the gunman model. But the two models really come to the same thing, since, in so far as it is based on interpretation and so is deeply political in the sense of its making a rhetorical appeal involving persuasion, normativity is ultimately no different from power. Normativity may *look* different from power, for it slips in a layer of discourse (or symbol) between the law and force, but it can never be authentically severed from force. The same applies to the law itself, which is described by Fish (1989: 523) as 'inseparable from force'. Of course, this is a *principled* use of force (what makes it so is the mediation of discourse) but principle is itself a construction, the outcome of an interpretive activity that unfolds in the whole context of power. So we have here a clear statement of the reductive thesis: normativity does not carve out its own space, defined by an ingrown set of standards, but develops instead according to the logic of power; it is in effect a coercive instrument appearing to be principled for being filtered through discourse, or through any kind of idealising process or story line through which power takes on the quality of something that coerces by virtue of its own inherent good.

An account of the normativity of law, likewise shaped by the reductive thesis, can be found in the deconstructionist theory of law defended by Drucilla Cornell. Like Fish's interpretive-based theory, Cornell's deconstructionism not only understands normativity as being grounded in fact but also argues that the facticity of the law persists in the face of any attempt to dematerialise the law and conceptualise it in an

---

[12] Fish actually gives rhetoric a caustic meaning, by defining it as the 'forceful presentation of an interested argument'—hence his understanding of it as 'another word for force' (Fish 1989: 517). Compare Fish (1989: 87–102), criticising Dworkin's account of interpretation, which involves a radically different understanding of deliberation and rhetoric.

idealist fashion.[13] For, on the deconstructionist account found in Cornell's work, the way to understand normativity is by pinning it down to its factual sources; specifically, normativity is reducible to power. This reduction is made by distinguishing different forms of power or force, and two forms in particular. There is the force needed to *establish* a legal system and the kind needed to *maintain* and preserve the law under such a system, the former called 'foundational violence' and the latter 'law-conserving or jurispathetic violence' (Cornell 1992: 163). But in any event, there is no doubt in Cornell's mind that force, be it foundational or law-conserving, bears a connection with normativity. The normativity of law comes into being precisely by means of an act of imposition, enforcement and violence: force comes *essentially* into play in the establishment or conservation of normativity. If the fact goes largely unnoticed, it is because such a use of force and violence does not usually work itself out openly but is rather masked by rhetorical devices.

So, while deconstructionism does not take kindly to the idea of violence as the foundation of the law—its point being precisely to lay bare this truth—it ends up *reinforcing* that same reduction, the very one it sets out to pick apart. For, taking an ideological stance against violence, looking somehow to replace the current state of affairs with a non-violent arrangement, will not suffice to disengage the deconstructionist account of normativity from its factual setting and place it within a different theoretical horizon. And until that is accomplished, it will not be possible to tell deconstructionism conceptually apart from any other legal theory deriving the normativity of law entirely from social facts. In sum, in its commitment to spell out the relation between the law and power, deconstructionism winds up having to take the view that the law depends entirely on power for its bindingness and, this being the case, the normativity of law is reducible to its ability to force those under its purview to behave as required by the law itself.

Cornell's version of deconstructionism, then, gives us a view of the normativity of law as closely linked to power, indeed, as exhausted within it. That is because any account of normativity appealing to the 'ought' (a non-factual dimension) will be deconstructed as an attempt to conceal the true nature of law behind a facade of ideality.[14] Deconstructionism thus ends up embedding normativity in an

---

[13] The core of Cornell's approach to the normativity of law is laid out in *The Violence of the Masquerade: Law Dressed up as Justice*, in which Cornell responds to Dominick La Capra's (1990) criticism of an essay by Jacques Derrida (1990) on the relation between authority and force. The matter in controversy is how properly to interpret the deconstructionist account of this relation. That is, does deconstruction simply expose the 'nakedness of power struggles and . . . violence masquerading as the rule of law', leaving 'in its stead only the "right" of force', or can it look closely at force and draw the 'all-too-real distinctions between different kinds of violent acts' (Cornell 1992: 155)? For La Capra, deconstruction gives a monotone account in the former sense; Cornell responds by defending instead the latter interpretation, arguing that deconstruction is a discriminating philosophy whose ability to demystify the relation between law and power hinges precisely on an ability to qualify different manifestations of power under the law. And this is where the issue of normativity comes in.

[14] This suspicion toward any attempt to overlay the 'is' with the 'ought', or otherwise to work the two together, emerges most clearly in Cornell (1992: 124–8). It also emerges in the deconstructionist account of Cover (1986: 1628), for whom any interpretation of the law achieves, wittingly or not, the result of masking the violence inherent in the administration of justice and the judge's imposition of a sentence.

earthwork of factual reality. It does so precisely by denying the law any ideality, and especially the ideality of the law as an essentially argumentative practice; but it also does this by recognising the foundational role that power relations play in shaping legal forms.

(c) This picture of normativity leads straightaway to the critique of *authority* regarded as a myth—the third fundamental thesis argued for by the defendants of the reductive thesis in law. Cornell's treatment is again exemplar. Cornell views authority as one of the many myths that, from the deconstructionist standpoint, populate the law. The myth of legal authority is that the power wielded through the law can exist in any form that transcends brute force. It is, in other words, the myth of legitimate power, in a form distinct from and irreducible to plain power, understood as simply the ability to exercise control over others. What makes the idea a myth is that 'violence cannot be fully rationalized and therefore justified in advance' (Cornell 1992: 157). This point is more formally stated in the proposition that 'there can be no metalanguage in which to establish the "external" norms by which to legitimate the legal system' (Cornell 1992: 157). Cornell cautions us against mistaking this for the view that 'might makes right', since deconstructionism, at least in its more sophisticated varieties, rejects any scheme equating force with legitimacy.[15] What the myth means, rather, is that when we seek out the source, or origin, of the authority of the law, and so of its normativity, we will find not ideas but force. Yet force alone—sheer power unconstrained and unguided—cannot give rise to authority: nothing springs from force except force itself. Something is needed if we are to legitimise such use of force, power, violence, and that something involves some mystification—that is, it involves developing and maintaining the myth of authority. So, while on the one hand, brute force cannot breed authority, the two do not exist in complete separation, and the liaison between them is effected through the myth of legitimate power. Stated differently, power is unlikely to stand on its own and needs a patina of legitimacy in order to be exercised effectively. That legitimacy is offered by a justificatory discourse giving power (the use of it under the law) a foundation in the myth of authority. This is a mutually reinforcing scheme whereby power resorts to myth to stand up as law and be legitimately exercised, and the law in turn resorts to power for its efficacy; in fact, the justificatory claim of law 'can never be fully actualized' in a discourse that 'grounds itself' (Cornell 1992: 163) and is therefore severed from power. There is a justificatory gap in the law whereby it, too weak to hold its own, finds its mainstay in force, power, violence, which in turn can be exercised precisely because they appear not to be such. A mystifying conceit makes them come aglow with authority, whence the deconstructionist view of the law as force made to look like authority, or of authority as the special cachet that force is lent in the process of justification. Again, this is not a celebration of violence but simply an appreciation of the way the law actually works. It is posited, period, for it serves nothing but interests and power, and any argumentative practice by which the law seems to

---

[15] See Cornell (1992: 157–61).

unfold is not a foundational but an instrumental component of the law; it is instrumental to power, the true foundation of the law. The law therefore comes into being through an act of foundational violence and achieves permanence through a continued practice of 'jurispathetic' violence.

This conclusion is reinforced by Fish's remarks on authority.[16] Fish demystifies authority through a critique of the widely accepted distinction between authority and power, by long tradition considered normative and factual phenomena, respectively. Power is commonly understood as the *naked* exercise of will on the part of the state's officials, by contrast with authority, understood as a *principled* use of such power: power does not by itself command authority, but power sensibly or virtuously exercised does. As Fish argues, however, it is wrong to assume that we are faced here with two alternatives, that there is no sharing of space between normativity as an institutional virtue and power as an institutional fact. Indeed, the two meld together into the single phenomenon called power, which never unfolds as brute factuality but rather comes into being with governing standards already built into it. The melding does not mean that authority dissolves and becomes nullified as power; for, on this conception of power, the use of power is always driven by a standard and can never be equated with brute force, 'even when its instruments are "rifles, clubs, and tear gas" '.[17] What makes power invariably principled is its being a practice, for practices always embody standards. This is precisely the device through which the distinction between 'is' and 'ought' fades away. It does so through the embeddedness of power, on the reasoning that although power is always rooted in a practice, and so is always governed by standards (standards by virtue of which power merges with authority), no other kind of standard is available by means of which power is constrained. Just as there is no standard transcending its own situatedness (overcoming the contextuality of human experience, with its forms of community and the practices these engender), so power and authority cannot apply any standards originating in any source outside these same practices. If there is any distinction between power and authority, it cannot be made to rest on their respective use of different standards, for in either case the standards are embedded. There is no such thing as a practice-independent norm. The two phenomena therefore cannot be told apart: power gains principle to yield authority, but principle grows in the context of practices, community and factuality, meaning that authority retreats back into power. We can see, then, the perfect synthesis that takes place between power and authority, and hence, more generally, between facts and norms. The two coalesce into a single concretion so well that no categorial distinction between 'is' and 'ought' can be made at all, since a kind of reduction is effected whereby what is normative is contiguous with, for arising in, an existing practice: it is proximate to social reality and so to what is factual.

---

[16] See in particular Fish (1989: 132–40).

[17] Fish (1989: 134). This is because the use of billy clubs and suchlike always originates in a *practice*. So even when power is wielded as brute force, there is a guiding practice that sets the standard by which such force is used. On the point that power is principled *ab ovo* because rooted in practice, see Fish (1989: 521–2).

THE IRREDUCIBLE CORE OF THE NORMATIVITY OF LAW

In this section I will argue against the view that normativity can remain groundless. The argumentative strategy I set out here consists in challenging the core tenet underlying that view (the reductive thesis) through an argument showing that *normativity* cannot be adequately explained by appealing solely to social facts. Importantly, once normativity is acknowledged not to be exhausted by factuality, the thesis should also be abandoned that the *normative force* and *normative claim of law* can be fully accounted for without having to explain its foundation. For this conclusion—rejection of the reductive thesis and restatement of the need to ground normativity—I will provide two distinct sources of support, which will be presented separately and discussed below. Overall, the argument deployed in this part aims to show that the question concerning the grounds of the normative claim of law is an issue of genuine theoretical significance and one that is still awaiting satisfactory treatment.

Legal-theoretical Considerations

The reductive thesis can be shown to be untenable by building on Kelsen's remarks concerning the distinction between the efficacy and validity of the law, a distinction that ultimately traces back to the more comprehensive statement of the categorial divide between 'is' and 'ought'. While the considerations that follow rely on (the neo-Kantian component of) Kelsen's legal theory,[18] and more specifically on his treatment of the normative dimension of law, they are not meant to provide an authentic interpretation of the historical Kelsen nor to contribute innovatively to Kelsenian scholarship. In this context, my use of Kelsen's legal theory is instrumental and selective: I have no intention to subscribe to the legal theory championed by Kelsen and his epigones; rather, I will make use of remarks originally made by Kelsen himself and by scholars working within the legal tradition stemming from Kelsen's writings (let us call this legal tradition 'continental normativism' for lack of a better phrase) in order to counteract a specific thesis about normativity: the reductive thesis. In a nutshell, I build in this subsection on Kelsen's distinction between the efficacy and validity of the law in order to argue that the predicates applicable to, and defining of, normativity differ from those applicable to, and defining of, factuality. This observation flies in the face of the reductive thesis, for identical categories are expected to bear identical attributes; conversely, different predicates apply categories that are distinct and not equivalent. Therefore, in so far as the predicates applied to norms differ from the attributes associated with the existence of (social) facts, one can reasonably conclude

---

[18] On the neo-Kantian component of Kelsen's legal thought see the lucid reconstruction and highly original discussion that can be found in Paulson (1992). Also of interest in this context is Paulson (1998).

that normativity and factuality differ too, and are not reducible, one to the other, without a good deal of strain and oversimplification. An analytic discussion of the predicates linked to normative requirements and facts respectively will provide support for this conclusion.

Following the tradition of continental normativism, the standard attributes linked to the existence of norms are efficacy and validity. First, a norm is typically said to exist on the condition of its being efficacious, which means that the people it applies to recognise that norm as being in force—they follow the norm habitually when the conditions for its application obtain, and do so with a regularity of behaviour that is sufficient to warrant the assessment that the norm operates as a widely practised and accepted standard. The efficacy of a norm might otherwise be described in this sense as its 'having been established': a norm becomes efficacious to the extent that it establishes itself in a given community, gaining firm footing in that context or coming into the mainstream as a generally and consistently followed standard of behaviour. Efficacy, then, amounts to actual and constant application of, as well as obedience to, a directive; a directive is efficacious if it is regularly and consistently applied and obeyed such that a relation of correspondence can be established between the behaviour of the subjects addressed by the directive and the content of that directive. Crucially, so long as efficacy can be defined as the conformity between normative requirement and actual conduct, whether a norm is efficacious is largely a matter of empirical and sociological observation. An observer sufficiently familiar with a system of norms, and who knows what the norm provides for, can determine the efficacy of the norm simply by examining its use, or rather, the outward behaviour of those who have to use it, the people entrusted with its enforcement as well as its addressees. For example, an observer of traffic laws in Britain could establish the contrast between the legal provision against jay-walking and that against running a red light. The former is largely inefficacious, since most British pedestrians seem oblivious to it, whereas the latter is efficacious, since most British drivers predictably follow it.

The other attribute used to point out that a norm exists is validity. By validity is meant the meaning content of a normative standard. Beyond factual existence, that is, an external and sensible existence, norms and systems of norms exist as meanings, to wit, they exist as interpretative frameworks giving determinate sense to events. This specific existence, which is distinct from the psycho-physical and social mode of existence, requires us to conceive of standards (also) as meaning contents, which extend further and beyond the specific acts and processes involved in their enactment. When understood not as an act but as a meaning content, a normative standard does not merely exist as a piece of the sensible universe unfolding in time and space, but also exists in a significatory sense, that is, as a meaning of the portion of the universe to which that normative standard applies and thus as something inhabiting the realm of concepts (where time- and space-related considerations are only indirectly relevant). It is the meaning-related dimension of normative standards and systems of normative standards, then, that enables us to regard them not only as efficacious or inefficacious, but also as valid or invalid.

Validity differs from efficacy by its being primarily meaning-related, as opposed to primarily nature-related or society-related, and, accordingly, describes norms not as natural or social facts, that is, external happenings, but as meanings or interpretative frameworks. Within the legal tradition of continental normativism, validity is to be regarded as the 'specific' existence of the norm, that is, an existence separated from the psycho-physical existence of the norm.

Notably, when applied to single norms, the idea of validity can be further specified and taken to designate system-membership. A directive forming part of a larger framework by virtue of fulfilling the criteria for membership in such a framework is thereby regarded as valid and so is taken to exist in a peculiar and distinctive way. This restatement of the validity of a norm as system-membership allows us to appreciate that validity is an intra-systemic relation, a relation making no direct reference to the community regulated by the relevant norm or system of norms, but rather referring exclusively to the system of norms addressing a given group. Also, this restatement makes it clear that systems of norms are to be understood here as frameworks of meanings, as opposed to sets of acts and arrangements of natural or social realities. This further characterisation of validity enables us to restate the difference between validity and efficacy: efficacy describes a relation between a norm and a community; validity describes the relation between a norm, on the one hand, and other norms and clusters of meanings, on the other. Crucially, in the latter case no necessary reference is made to the community or its members, only to norms as components of a system. It follows that the validity of a norm, unlike its efficacy, depends on whether the criteria for the membership of the norm in a system are met. And even though this assumption is performed by the relevant community of users, it cannot be established by sociological observation about what the majority does with respect to the norm in question. Empirical enquiry of this sort, however successful it may be at assessing the efficacy of a directive, will not offer great insight into its validity. To understand validity, one has to endorse at least up to a point an internal point of view.[19]

Stating the differences between efficacy and validity is not to claim that validity stands completely apart from efficacy, to be sure. For both single norms and systems of norms, a connection exists between validity and efficacy. Single norms as well as systems of norms will in the long run lose their validity if they consistently fail to regulate behaviour, such that there is no conformity between normative requirement and social conduct. In this respect, efficacy not only figures among the conditions of validity but can indeed be conceived as the main condition, or *conditio sine qua non*, of the validity of systems of norms and, though to a different extent, norms. Ultimately, no system of norms or individual norm can be taken to be valid unless the behaviour of the individuals concerned with that system or norm corresponds by and large to the requirements set by that system or norm. But the relation thus said to obtain between efficacy and validity is one of dependence, not one of identity: validity *depends* on the main condition enabling

---

[19] The point is amplified in MacCormick (1981: 29–44).

it—efficacy—as opposed to *being identical* to efficacy. Stated differently, in the picture drawn here, efficacy figures as the existence *condition* (that which sets the prerequisites that should obtain for something to be valid), whereas validity figures as what is *conditioned*. By definition, a condition is not identical to what is conditioned, for it is a condition only if it is kept apart from what is conditioned, such that it makes sense to construct a conditioning relation between them. In a word, what is conditioned cannot exist without presupposing its existence condition, yet it does not coincide with its existence condition.[20]

To summarise, two pairs of properties—efficacy vs inefficacy and validity vs invalidity—define the existence of, and are to be applied to, norms. Typically, a standard will be said to exist if it can be qualified as efficacious and valid: the former predicate designates the recognition of a standard by a certain community, the latter, its meaning content. The two properties are related but distinct, and their distinction can be made most apparent once one considers that only in one case, where efficacy is concerned, can we rely on empirical enquiry alone to make the relevant assessment. In contrast, validity cannot be investigated in this way, for it takes meaning into account, which in turn makes it necessary to explore the non-factual side of the equation, for meaning is not entirely, or even primarily, based on fact.

Now, if something were to become normative simply by virtue of its being efficacious, we could indeed equate norms to social facts and make a good case for the reductive thesis. Indeed, just as norms can be said to exist if efficacious, so can social facts be said to exist in much the same way, by appeal to a criterion equivalent to efficacy; that is, we have a social fact only if people in a community, or a relevant subgroup, widely and habitually acknowledge its existence (conversely, the same social fact will cease to exist if enough people in the community fail to see it as such for a long enough period). Since the equivalent attribute for norms, namely, efficacy, is established in the same way—by habitual acknowledgment of the norm as existent—a connection can be set out between normativity and factuality in that respect. But then norms are typically also described as valid, and it is with this second property that the reductive thesis begins to run into trouble, because no property that is equivalent to validity can be ascribed to social facts. Social facts are simply not referred to as valid or invalid; they are rather acknowledged or not acknowledged by the relevant community. Nor is the existence of a single fact predicated on its membership in a given system. Of course, social facts can be grouped together as belonging to this or that system, but that will only help us in *classifying* them and figuring out their relationships—it will not call question into their *existence*. And therein lies one important distinction between social facts and norms, for the membership of a norm in a system *does* establish its existence. The distinction loosens up the connection between norms and facts and presents a problem for the proponent of the reductive thesis, who will have to work through the matter in order consistently to argue for an identity between normativity and

---

[20] Compare Kelsen (1992: 59–61).

facticity. Indeed, the identity of any two catagories, whatever that be, implies that what can be predicated of one can also be predicated of the other, and this is precisely what cannot be done here: norms can be valid, facts cannot, and membership in a system is a necessary condition for the existence of a norm, but has no bearing on the existence of a social fact. In both cases, habitual recognition does help us to settle questions of fact, namely, the efficacy of social facts and norms alike, but it does not account for the whole of normativity. Hence, the irreducibility of normativity to facticity.

The argument for the view that normativity cannot be reduced to facticity can be restated in slightly different terms by pointing out this basic contrast: while it makes no sense to speak of a social fact that is not observed to exist and so lacks social recognition, the same idea makes perfectly good sense with respect to norms. That is, there is nothing unusual about an existing standard being temporarily or partially inefficacious. Indeed, this is an ordinary event, and the reason, as was pointed out above, is that the existence of a norm is predicated not only on its efficacy (on its being socially recognised) but also on its validity, that is, on its inclusion as a part of a framework of norms. In fact, validity is a distinct criterion for determining the existence of a standard, for a temporary or partial inefficacious standard can still be said to exist. Stated in still another way, efficacy, or social recognition, acts as the sole criterion of facticity but not as the sole criterion of normativity: facticity is therefore exhausted in efficacy, or social recognition, as normativity is not.

Let us go back to the rule against jay-walking as compared with that against running a red light. On the account based on the reductive thesis, only one of these standards can properly be said to exist: the rule against running red lights exists in Britain because the relevant community complies with the rule on a regular basis. By contrast, on the same account the rule against jay-walking, which British pedestrians make a practice of disregarding, has therefore, in the same context, lapsed into inexistence or is no longer recognisable as anything like a rule. Whilst consistent with the reductive thesis constructing normativity as an exclusively factual phenomenon, this conclusion does not square with the way in which we ordinarily conceptualise the existence of norms. *Both* rules, not just the one against running a red light, can properly be said to exist in the legal system in force in Britain, regardless of their degree of efficacy. Stated more bluntly, nobody familiar with the existing legal practice would say that in Britain there is no rule against jay-walking since most people out in the street ignore the rule whenever and wherever they can, or when they think it safe to do so. The reason why *both* rules exist, and why they are considered that way, has little to do with their efficacy and everything to do with their validity: they exist because both have been duly issued and so meet in full the criteria for significance and membership in the system of norms in place in Britain. In summary, efficacy does not *exhaust* the existence of norms but only *contributes to* it, as but one of two factors counting toward a judgement of existence, the other factor being validity. This contrast, with validity and efficacy being taken both to affect the existence of a norm, thus allowing for such a thing as a valid yet inefficacious norm that will still be recognised as such, that is, as an existing *norm*, shows that efficacy cannot fully account for the existence of norms. This consequently shows that the two roles of validity and efficacy cannot be equated, nor can the former be reduced to the latter—which is precisely what the advocates of the reductive thesis would need to establish, namely, a reduction, in order to make a compelling case for the view that normativity does not exist in any genuine or distinctive sense.

A defendant of the reductive thesis might concede at this point that the terms *validity* and *efficacy* do refer to different features of the existence of a norm, but add that, duly analysed, they end up designating the *same* property, only they do so in highlighting different aspects of it. Hence, normativity *can* be reduced to facticity, for the two properties, that is, validity and efficacy ultimately describe the same phenomenon or reality and can in this sense be equated. But this reply fails. If an identity did hold between efficacy and validity, we would then have to show that standards cannot meaningfully be described as 'valid yet inefficacious', since that would involve a fundamental contradiction. Yet, it makes perfect sense to describe standards in this way. Not only can actual standards in the world be described as valid yet inefficacious (the jay-walking example is certainly only one of many that can readily be called up), but no conceptual error is involved, either. This is because we have here two different notions, and the difference between them runs deep; that is, we have before us not just different shades of one notion but notions that cannot ultimately be traced to the same property. On the one hand, with validity, we are saying that something is or is not invested with meaning content, namely, is or is not an interpretive category; on the other hand, with efficacy, we are saying that something does or does not have the recognition and support of a community or of the bulk of it. Clearly, meaning content is one thing, community acceptance quite another. Once we establish a norm *qua* meaning content, it will be another, and quite different, question when it is asked whether that norm also has the backing of a community of addressees, that is, whether the norm is also *efficacious*. The answer to this latter question does not follow from the answer to the former, whence the very real possibility, far from absurd or illogical, of a norm that is valid yet inefficacious. Efficacy is not defined by validity, and so is not exhausted in it, any more than validity is defined by efficacy and so is not exhausted in it. The difference between the two notions is such that validity cannot in any way be equated with efficacy.

In summary, defining normativity as factuality is tantamount to neglecting a property typically counted as essential in determining whether something exists as a norm, this property being the existence of the norm *qua* meaning content. Clearly, such neglect amounts, in turn, to an exercise in predicate-cutting, and hence to an impoverishment of the normative dimension. Reduction counts here as simplification. That much can be established on the basis of the irreducible difference that exists between the two key properties involved, validity and efficacy. If the difference is irreducible, as I have argued it must be, then the reductive thesis on normativity is bound to at least be partially false, for it accounts for the use of only some, but not all, of the properties ordinarily associated with normativity. To be sure, the champions of the reductive thesis are right to find a connection between normativity and facticity. What establishes the connection is that both facts and norms can be placed in a relation to the community of users and accounted in terms of the efficacy, or social recognition, that they gain within the community. But then the reductive thesis pushes this connection too far, in effect turning it into a relation of identity. The problem with such an identity, between normativity and facticity, is that it cannot be set up without also setting up an identity between the two accompanying properties, that is, between validity and efficacy. But this would amount to equating the habitual acceptance of a norm with the norm *qua* meaning content, and this cannot be accomplished without considerable strain. This leaves us with only two options where the reductive thesis is concerned. We can accept this thesis as a *partial* account of normativity, one that leaves certain core properties of normativity out of the picture. As the alternative, we can accept it as a *comprehensive* account, but one that achieves its comprehensiveness at the cost of distorting the properties that it equates, thus distorting the concept of normativity itself, which is what happens when merely connected or overlapping phenomena are fused into a single thing. Therefore, while a connection does undeniably obtain between normativity and social facts, this does not mean that normativity can be equated with either of these qualifying facts or be reduced to them.

Especially crude in that respect is the reduction of normativity to the facts of force and coercion. As discussed above, norms are qualified not only by the means used to enforce them, but also by their validity, and validity can certainly be accounted for in a number of different ways (we can view it as the formal inclusion of a norm into a system, for example), but none of these ways involves reducing validity to force. For, we will eventually run against the hard fact that force is inherently factual and validity inherently non-factual. Inclusion into a system of norms may be a fact, to be sure, but not in the same way as the use of force is a fact. This shows that the non-factual component of normativity cannot entirely be reduced to facticity, at least not without a good deal of strain. Similarly problematic is the reduction of normativity to the chance, or probability, that some sanction will follow a conduct in breach of legal requirements.[21] The probabilistic

---

[21] This interpretation of normativity is theoretically important and not just historically so, since it can be found not only in the version of the reductive thesis held by the advocates of the now out-of-fashion sanction-based theory of law but also in the contemporary variants of that thesis endorsed by the advocates of the law-and-economics movement. In brief, the law-and-economics movement holds that the law cannot be considered in isolation from the economic interests the laws are themselves designed to protect. Though normativity in the economic analysis of the law is accounted for in many different ways by use of diverse economic tools and concepts, these accounts all share the view that the influence the law has on behaviour is largely a matter of prudential calculus. This view, as Lewis Kornhauser argues, is only natural in an economic analysis of the law, for it comports with the economist's understanding of motivation as grounded in self-interest. The main assumption here is 'that the agent has a well-defined preference relation over the set of actions available to her that permit a representation of these preferences as a preference over outcomes and a set of beliefs that conform to the axioms of probability theory' (Kornhauser 1999: 7). This set of preferences and beliefs becomes a de

reading is untenable, for the likelihood of suffering a sanction is neither a sufficient nor a necessary condition for the emergence of normativity. As it is put by Peter Hacker (1973: 142) (who here expands upon points originally made by Henry Sidgwick and brought, especially by Hart, to the attention of legal theorists), 'we can conjoin a statement of the likelihood of sanctions for non-performance with a statement that the act in question is obligatory, without any sense of redundancy or tautologousness'.[22] This means that normativity is not exhausted by, and so cannot be reduced to, the existence of the chance that disobeying certain requirements is going to be sanctioned. Any coincidence between what is normative and what is likely to be sanctioned is purely secondary, subsidiary and contingent, as opposed to primary, analytic and necessary: that something will probably be sanctioned does not entail that it is a normative requirement and so ought to be done (not even prima facie). Reducing what is normative to the likelihood of suffering a sanction for non-compliance is, thus, misleading and prevents us from getting at the core of normativity. Although a connection does exist between normativity and the imposition of sanctions, normativity is not determined by, or reducible to, the probability of suffering penalties. Therefore, the probabilistic theory of normativity, one species of the reductive thesis, can at most take in a constituent of what is normative (the nexus obtaining between non-performance of the conduct required by a norm, or system of norms, and the (presumptive) justification of the sanction, or censure, for the omission), but fails to account fully for normativity. When understood as a comprehensive account of normativity, the position shaped by the reductive thesis is, hence, not just limited but, indeed, deceptive.

---

facto decision-making standard, in that the agent 'chooses the action that maximizes her expected utility' (Kornhauser 1999: 7). Legal obligations do play a role in this context, but only because they have a basis in the calculus of interests; they can influence 'behaviour in one of four ways: by altering payoffs, beliefs, preferences, or the choice set' (Kornhauser 1999: 7). So, when the various prudential accounts of the normativity of law offered by the law-and-economics movement are stripped of their technicalities, they reveal a basic resemblance to the sanction-based approach, for they proceed on the assumption that the 'individual obeys the law in order to avoid a sanction: obedience is her self-interest' (Kornhauser 1999: 6). What is different here, with respect to the classic understanding of obligation and normativity as grounded in a corresponding sanction, is that the sanction itself is framed in economic terms: someone mulling over a decision to break the law will view the sanction as simply an economic cost, a liability acting as disincentive to disobeying the rules of the law. Legal rules are thus conceived of as first-order reasons to act in the manner prescribed by the law; failure to do so carries an economic cost, a disadvantage weighing against a decision to break the law, a counterpoise to disobedience: obedience is accordingly understood as an act capable of reducing such costs, other things being equal, and it is on this basis, through an informal cost-benefit analysis, that the law commands obedience (cf Cooter 1984 on this point). So conceived, then, the normativity of law comes down to a social fact: the ultimate ground of normativity is a state of affairs whereby 'non-compliance imposes an internal "utility" cost on the agent' (Kornhauser 1999: 11), and normativity can therefore be understood simply in terms of economic incentives, disincentives and costs, all of which are social facts.

[22] Compare Sidgwick (1967: 23–38). See also Hart (1982: 143–7) and Hart (1994: 82–91).

Metaethical Considerations

There is also another way in which the reductive thesis falls short. It fails adequately to account not only for the validity of normative legal standards, but also for their action-guiding capacity. The idea of action-guidance is inherent in the very *concept* of normativity, the essential point of which is to provide people with reasons for action, that is, with reasons that should be taken into account in practical deliberation, and that consequently play a role and carry weight in the process by means of which a decision is made about what course of action to take in any given circumstance.[23] The degree of deliberative weight that a normative standard can exert (its action-guiding capacity) depends largely on context; that is, it does not entirely depend *in vacuo* on the sheer weight of the reasons proffered, since reasons are themselves liable to be received in different ways in different contexts. In any case, however, the law is one context in which the weight of normative standards is invariably significant. This is in two ways. For one thing, legal directives come with a certain degree of embedded force built into them from the outset on account of their source;[24] for another, they apply to their addressees within the legal system, regardless of whether these people acknowledge or endorse these prescriptions. So we have here a second trait of legal standards—their applicability independently of acquiescence, that is, their categorical, compulsory or unqualified status—and this, too, must be accounted for as a component of the normativity of law along with the action-guiding purport of the law. The practical guidance of a legal directive applies across the board, namely, to all those in the class specified by the directive itself, whether or not they agree on what the directive calls for or requires of them. We have to do, then, with a form of guidance that does not admit of any option as to whether it will be accepted or rejected, and this gives legal standards a 'blanket purview' that the account shaped by the reductive thesis fails to explain.

Unlike the first failure described, that is, the inability adequately to elucidate the validity of norms, this second failure stems not so much from the legal theory at work in the reductive account as from its metaethics, that is, from its exclusive reliance on empirical considerations in striving to explicate normativity in law. As discussed, in the reductive account, normativity is ultimately resolved into a factual phenomenon and so normative properties are explained away as empirical properties. This way, the action guidance of normative standards is set on an empirical foundation. This is good as far as it goes, but a problem comes up in this connection whose solution, it seems, cannot be found by proceeding on an empirical basis alone: that is, we have to account *empirically* for the specific way in which the action-guiding capacity of the law is exercised. In other words, we need to explain not just the capacity of the law to guide action but the categorical and

---

[23] The idea that inherent in normativity is an action-guiding principle, or that norms seek to *guide* action by giving *reasons* for action, is introduced and discussed in chapter one.

[24] The argument for this claim is stated in chapter three.

unqualified demands corresponding to the practical guidance provided by the law. The demands of the law will be able to achieve such categorical guidance only to the extent that they embody some broad, non-contingent trait, that is, something that everyone involved (all the people subject to the claim) will recognise as inherently valuable quite apart from whatever other subjective states, beliefs, interests or affiliations they may have. There will have to be some common ground universally recognised as not subject to bargaining, to the give-and-take of life between and among people interacting from different material and ideological positions in society. Anything short of this standard will be something that anyone can choose without contradiction to follow or not follow for any number of reasons.[25] But this is clearly not the way of the law. The law deals not in contingency but in necessity, which is not the epistemic necessity of universal laws of nature, but the deontic necessity of what everyone subject to the law ought to conform to, independently of personal likes and dislikes. No empirical account of the normativity of law can satisfy these criteria: empirical investigations deal in facts; they can work out theories and principles by which to understand these facts and even predict what will necessarily have to happen. But this kind of necessity (along with the theories and principles addressed to it) pertains entirely to the world as it is and has next to nothing to say about the world as it ought to be. Then, too, the facts making up the raw material of an empirical investigation need not fit any definite or necessary pattern. This is especially true of the sorts of facts we are concerned with here in an investigation of normativity, these being the facts of social life. Social facts are awash in contingency. This contingency, in a world that might at every turn have very possibly been different from what is it, carries over to any empirical study and definition of normativity. Any normativity constructed out of facts alone will therefore serve to guide action, but in the contingent way appropriate to the collection of facts serving as its building material. It cannot, therefore, be the normativity associated with the law, regarded as capable of guiding action in a way that necessarily applies to all those concerned.

The way in which the law guides action is thus non-contingent, unqualified and categorical, and its normativity will have to be accounted for accordingly. That is, it will have to be set on a foundation grounded not in fact but in concept, its core element being not an empirical truth (a theory of the world) but a conceptual proposition. What does it mean, though, to invoke a conceptual proposition as distinguished from an empirical truth? To begin with, it does not mean calling for an account of the normativity of law independent of the evidence at hand that might support or contradict the account itself. In other words, the conceptual propositions referred to are not a contemporary equivalent of analytic propositions, regarded with suspicion in post-Quineian philosophy, but rather exist *in connection* with facts and empirical truths. An account of normativity grounded in concept is therefore very much amenable to revision in light of any relevant facts that may

---

[25] Here, 'without contradiction' means that at least some of these reasons will be fully legitimate grounds with respect to the standard at hand.

come to bear. This should not suggest, however, that facts are co-extensive with concepts. The relation between them is clearly not one of identity but one of abstraction from one to the other, from fact to concept. We can think of facts in this sense as the material basis of concepts, and concepts as that which we come at by abstraction from facts. Concepts are the tools, ideas and principles we develop in the effort to organise and understand facts or make sense of them, an ongoing activity by which we keep shaping and reshaping our concepts to retain the sense of the fit we have made with the corresponding facts. This involves a process of abstraction from the particular, a process whose upshot is an abstract product. The difference can be described in both ontological terms and methodological ones. Ontologically, in answer to the question of what there is, facts can be said to exist as empirical entities or as entities occurring in space and time, and concepts as immaterial abstractions. Methodologically, in answer to the question of what we know, facts can be described as entities that we come to know through a process of observation, and concepts through a process of abstraction from what is observed. Any attempt to reduce concepts to facts will therefore involve not one but two reductions, requiring not only that we somehow turn concepts into empirical entities but also that we collapse abstraction and explanation into observation and description.[26]

The categorical character of the normativity of law thus needs to be set on a non-empirical, conceptual foundation, a foundation grounded in concept yet responsive to fact. Indeed, although not established by facts and not accountable solely on empirical terms, no such foundation can be constructed independently of facts, a fortiori in that the facts being dealt with here are the facts and forces of social, economic, political and cultural life, in which the material element proceeds in conjunction with the conceptual in a relation of mutual feedback. It follows that the specific form of practical guidance provided by the law (its categorical reach and unqualified force) should correspondingly be explained on the basis of empirical and conceptual considerations combined. The account shaped by the reductive thesis is set up in such a way that it cannot attempt any such combination, for in seeking to reduce normativity to facticity, it excludes from the normative all things conceptual, in line with an empirical approach that ends up crippling one's ability to explain (a) what is distinctly normative about normativity, and (b) even more importantly, what is distinctive about legal normativity. An empirical approach, in other words, makes it difficult for us to explain (a) the 'ought' involved in action guidance, and (b) the specific form of guidance in which we are all compelled to act under such a rule quite apart from whether we like what is being prescribed or not. We would have to show, on this approach, how normativity can guide action in a

---

[26] This latter distinction must of course be taken with a grain of salt, considering that observation, and indeed sensory perception, is itself a process of abstraction. But it should nonetheless be intuitively clear that it is one thing to observe and another to abstract, which requires us to impart a form to the facts we observe and bring out their interconnections, thus explaining them or making them predictable or otherwise interpreting them in a way that fits what we observe. All such activity is conceptual, and concepts I accordingly understand as covering a broad range of abstractions so long as they are not immediately or exclusively sensory.

necessary, unqualified and categorical way, but we would have to do so *empirically*. The basic obstacle and constraint here consists in the effort to focus exclusively on facts and to dismiss anything non-factual as imaginary, unreal or fantastical. This effort is misleading, for it ultimately amounts to indulging in what might be called fact-worship, that is, being overzealous about facts, clinging too tenaciously to the factual, with the consequence that the normative is searched for in what is anything but normative. Indeed, as was observed earlier, an empirical investigation is an investigation into the factual, into the world that *is*, not into the world that *ought to be*, and any necessary element coming out of such an investigation is consequently bound to be an empirical necessity about what *will* happen, not a normative necessity about what *ought* to happen. So, even assuming that the account informed by the reductive thesis can promote our understanding of the normativity of law by uncovering and bringing to light its necessary element, it will have given us the wrong kind of necessity, the sort that comes out when 'what necessarily *is*' becomes a blueprint for 'that which necessarily *ought to be*'. But we are not concerned with this natural kind of necessity. Natural necessity may play a role in shaping the law and its operation (it may come into a mutual relation with the normativity of law), but it is plainly not the *core* element of such normativity. The way to find the right kind of necessity is by forging a connection between the factual and the conceptual. Yet the empirical investigation mandated by the reductive thesis cannot make this connection and so fails to show action-guidance to be normative in the non-contingent way that is peculiar to the law.

The reader will not have failed to notice that the argument against an empirical definition of normativity has been supplemented by certain metaethical considerations relative to the ontological and epistemological status of normative standards. These questions are of central concern to the contemporary debate in metaethics, whose inquiry into the status of normativity focuses, in particular, on the normativity of morality. This metaethical focus gives us a vantage point that makes it possible to see where the discussion of normativity in legal theory overlaps with the corresponding discussion in moral theory, and this also suggests a strategy, namely, looking at the reductive account of the normativity of law through the lens of the corresponding metaethical view of normativity, a view that shares with that account certain fundamental assumptions. This will enable us to appreciate better the shortcomings of an empirical definition of normativity.

The metaethical view closest to the legal theory shaped by the reductive thesis is practical naturalism. Particularly relevant to us here is a recent contribution to practical naturalism offered by David Copp, 'Moral Naturalism and Three Grades of Normativity'. In his contribution, Copp considers the question of whether, once we accept the idea that morality is normative, we ought thereby to reject practical naturalism. At first sight, this question may appear only loosely connected to that of whether the normativity of law can be accounted for by way of a theory shaped by the reductive thesis. A second look suggests, however, that the connection is real. Two points show that this is the case. The first of these pertains to the way practical naturalism itself is defined, namely, as the view that moral properties 'are ordinary garden-variety natural properties', and so, properties having the same basic ontological and epistemological status as the properties characterising facts (Copp 2004: 7). This brings the naturalist account of *moral* normativity into line with the account of the normativity of law shaped by the reductive thesis, for in either case the attempt is to take an object (the normativity of morality, on the one hand, that of the law on the other) and resolve it into elements whose status is empirical. Secondly, these two kinds of normativity (that of morality and that of law) enter into a specific connection that can be established from within the reductive account itself. The contemporary champions of this account hold that the law is deeply permeated with elements of non-law, and a parallel permeability can therefore be acknowledged on this basis between the normativity of law and that of non-legal standards. This is significant, for it shows that, within the framework set by the reductive thesis, the way the *normativity of morality* is approached bears directly on the study of the *normativity of law*. This connection, between the normativity of morality and normativity of law, can be made apparent by noticing that the attitude morality takes to its addressees can be analogised to the attitude the law takes to the subjects of legal prescriptions. This is to say that we have, here, two action-guiding practices, the law and morality, in which (a) the subject being addressed is understood as autonomous, and (b) the model being proposed entails a commitment from which one cannot simply withdraw on the basis of personal gain, however this may be construed. Thus, morality turns to individuals as moral beings, that is, as beings who can understand and follow a moral conception, and the law turns to them as citizens, that is, as individuals who can comply with the prescriptions of the law on the basis of reasons given for such compliance. This feature converges in the law and morality alike, imposing on both practices the form of necessity. The law and morality are alike in setting out principles that are intended to apply categorically to the subjects concerned regardless of whatever else they may happen to find convenient at the time. This is in contrast to other action-guiding practices, such as etiquette, which are discretionary. An etiquette of gentlemanly conduct, for example, may apply to those who consider themselves gentlemen or wish to become gentlemen, but it does not imply any deep or binding commitment to that standard in the sense just discussed, whereby subjective states are made irrelevant.

The main point made here, therefore, is the similarity that can be observed between practical naturalism and the legal theory informed by the reductive thesis, from which we can acquire a vantage point on the question of normativity. Copp's discussion of moral normativity can then provide insight into the discussion of the reductive thesis in the law, and I will use his discussion to explore further the strengths and weaknesses of the legal account shaped by the reductive thesis.

Copp begins in his essay by laying out the basic problem from which his entire discussion proceeds: namely, if we accept, as most people do, that morality is normative, should not this undermine practical naturalism from the start? In fact, practical naturalism understands moral properties as amenable to empirical description, so the question arises as to how empirical properties, and so the moral discourse based on them, can play any role in guiding action and directing choices. The problem becomes quite explicit in identity-naturalism (for which moral properties *are* empirical properties: the two are identical), but it also comes up in connection with constitution naturalism, a version of practical naturalism in which moral properties are said to be *constituted* by empirical ones and are in this sense regarded not as identical with them but as supervenient on them.[27]

Copp contends that practical naturalism is well equipped to account for the normativity of morality, and he sets up his argument by distinguishing three grades or modes of normativity: generic, motivational and authoritative. Generic normativity is ascribed to anything not primarily descriptive, that is, to anything that contains an evaluative ingredient strong enough to act as a source of evaluation, and which thus carries prescriptive or recommendatory force. Motivational normativity gets ascribed to anything capable of weighing on the motives we may have for doing or not doing something: it pulls on the levers of motive, thus acting as a source of motivation, without yet spelling out any reasons for acting on such motivations. That further layer is achieved by authoritative normativity, at which level a normative standard provides reasons for action and in this sense not only bids us to act as the standard itself specifies, but also establishes the reason why we ought so to act. Authoritative normativity thus contains its own justification, and in this sense it can be said to act as a source of self-sufficient practical reasons.

This analytical treatment, breaking normativity down into three grades or modes of operation, enables Copp to recast his initial question accordingly: the broad question of whether morality naturalistically construed can still be normative becomes, analytically, whether, when construed, it can be (a) evaluative, (b) motivating, and (c) reason-creating. This threefold question is further clarified in light of the distinctive way in which morality is said to be normative, which is to say that the normativity claimed for morality is not simply conditional but unqualified or categorical, that is, independent of psychological and subjective states of moral agents. We should therefore seek to explain how morality naturalistically construed can exhibit the following capacities: (a) as a source of evaluation, a capacity for essential prescriptivity, this being the ability of a moral standard to prescribe by virtue of what it says rather than by virtue of the circumstances in

---

[27] We can appreciate here the plastic nature of practical naturalism, which can coherently be shaped into either of two views about moral facts, understood on the one hand as identical to natural facts (identity naturalism) and on the other as constituted by, and so supervenient on, them (constitution naturalism). Aside from their specific difference, both types count as varieties of practical naturalism, since both claim that moral facts and properties are a genus of natural facts and properties, as opposed to *sui generis* facts and properties, namely, facts and properties different in kind from any other fact and property. This implies a view of morality as continuous with science: 'moral truths are discoverable in just the way scientific truths are; moral facts, being nothing other than a species of natural scientific facts, import nothing mysterious into our picture of what the world includes' (Shafer-Landau 2003: 3). This claimed continuity between science and morality is constructed as being both epistemic and ontological: epistemically, the processes by which we come to understand moral facts are the same as those by which we gain scientific knowledge; and the reason is that, ontologically, moral facts do not amount to anything over and above natural facts.

which the standard was formulated or to which it applies; (b) as a source of motivation, a capacity to motivate reasonable agents, namely, subjects capable of acting on rational motives and so motives that others, too, can acknowledge and accept; and (c) as a source of authority, a capacity to offer reasons, reasons of broad appeal whose force is owed not to contingency but to principle. If we assume, thus, that morality exhibits all three grades of normativity,[28] then we have to see how each of these grades or capacities can be explained naturalistically.

Copp proceeds at this point by offering a naturalistic definition of morality as 'a system of standards the currency of which in the relevant society would contribute better than that of any other such system to enabling the society to meet its needs' (Copp: 2004: 26). According, to this view, moral standards are measured against the problems and needs of a society to the effect that a standard is morally good in so far as, if it had currency within a society, it would do well in enabling that society to attend to its problems and basic needs.[29] This view, which is named the 'need thesis', asks us to assess a moral code 'on the basis of how well it does or would contribute to the relevant society's being able to cope, to meet its needs'.[30] The moral theory resulting from the need thesis is a kind of practical naturalism of the reductive sort. The reductive component of that theory boils down to the fact that in it normative standards are explained by invoking notions (societal problems and needs) that are empirical. For it is no less 'an empirical matter to determine whether a given moral code is such that its currency in a society would best serve the society's needs' than 'to determine whether I need a drink of water' (Copp 2001: 227). In sum, in the framework devised by Copp, moral facts, propositions and properties are natural, or empirical, facts, propositions and properties.[31]

Morality, so defined, is argued by Copp to exhibit all three grades of normativity: generic normativity, on the basis that whatever helps a society to meet its needs is thereby inherently valuable; motivational normativity, owing to the motivational force of the reasons offered at the level of authoritative normativity, a motivational force recognised for reasons on the assumption that 'a rational person is disposed to be moved by reasons', at least under favourable circumstances (Copp 2004: 27); and authoritative normativity, as will be explained shortly. In this last sense, normativity clearly plays a pivotal role. Indeed, for one thing, normativity cannot be considered complete until it achieves authoritativeness, importantly understood as the ability to proffer reasons from which moral agents can be expected to act; for another thing, it is this ability that hinges the motivational

---

[28] As Copp (2004: 30–4) does, at least for the sake of argument and not without caveats.

[29] By basic, or fundamental, needs, which are opposed to merely derivative needs, Copp (2001: 191) means 'the things that are required in all likelihood by any society in order to avoid impairment of the capacity to have a system of values or stable and endorsed preferences over societal options'. The distinction between kinds of societal needs—basic and derivative—is dealt with in detail by Copp (2001: 172–7). Among the basic needs, Copp explicitly ranks and discusses the need to ensure the continued existence of the population that constitutes the society, the need for cooperative integrity, and the need for peaceful and cooperative relationships with neighbouring societies.

[30] Copp (1997a: 196–7). For a detailed account and defence of these theses, see Copp (2001: 103–24 and 190–217).

[31] Compare Copp (2001: 229).

power of morality, or at least this is the dependency set up in Copp's framework. It thus becomes essential for Copp to explain *naturalistically* how morality can make its way to the higher ground of authoritative normativity.

By Copp's own definition, a moral standard or conception becomes authoritatively normative by way of its ability to offer reasons that any agent will act on (or will recognise as proper reasons to act on) if he or she is thinking *rationally*. And what it means for an agent to be rational is to follow, or be able to follow, the dictates of practical rationality. Thus, on this view it is essential that practical rationality be tied down to a naturalistic account, that is, that it be treated not as a concept but as an empirical phenomenon. Copp aims at this result by connecting rationality and the capacity efficiently to serve one's own values. Since these values are among those we choose ourselves, to serve them is to act as self-governing agents, and the corresponding standard (of practical rationality) is therefore termed by Copp (2004: 34) a standard of 'self-grounded reason'.[32] In his recent work, Copp further elaborates on the idea of a value and a standard of self-grounded reason and gives to the theory a Kantian twist by connecting the values setting standards of self-grounded reason to the identity of persons, here conceived as autonomous agents, that is to say, agents who can exercise systematic control over their actions on the basis of policies and plans they have devised by, and for, themselves.[33] In Copp's construction, personal values are said to be deep psychological features that not only inform our long-term intentions, plans and policies, by so enabling us to live a self-governing life, but also contribute decisively to determining our self-esteem. As 'grounds of our self-esteem' values are 'embedded in our identities' and should be regarded as 'aspects of our self-conception' that function as a 'compass in our lives' (Copp 2005: 194). So understood, the standards of self-grounded reason stemming from, and generated by, personal values are authoritative. What makes them so is that what they require (acting to serve our own values) not only comes with a reason for doing so but also specifies this reason in such a way that we cannot see ourselves rejecting it; that is, the standard is so framed that embracing it makes us self-governing agents, and presumably no rational agent could conceivably dismiss this idea. For, no one could properly say, 'I am rational but do not conceive of myself as self-governed'.

The argument showing that it is a real impossibility coherently to conceive of ourselves as being at the same time rational and yet not governed by our own selves in turn rests on the so-called 'self-conception strategy'. Originally developed within the Kantian tradition of philosophy, this strategy consists in specifying a conception of the self and then arguing that is something we must necessarily embrace as the sole basis from which to proceed in all matters of theoretical and practical relevance alike. Owing to its foundational role as the bedrock of all moral

---

[32] In a nutshell, self-grounded reasons are reasons rooted in a person's own standpoint and nature. As such they make room for both self-regarding concerns and other-regarding concerns, which distinguishes self-grounded reasons from purely self-interested reasons. On this issue compare Copp (2001: 168–9) to Copp (1997b: 88–93).

[33] See especially Copp (2005).

thinking and guidance, a self-conception so specified is going to transfer its weight to the practical standards worked out on its basis. So, to the extent that the self-conception is understood as necessary, its standards are likewise bound to carry the same sense of necessity. In other words, we will have reason to act on those standards and this reason will be perceived by us as absolutely compelling, as something we cannot choose to reject as a matter of discretion, since doing so would amount to rejecting a necessary conception of the self (if that were at all possible) and so a necessary part of who we are.[34] Not only does this make a standard of self-grounded reason authoritative, but it also explains how morality itself gains authoritative normativity. It does so by virtue of its special connection with practical rationality, this being the naturalistic standard of self-grounded reason.

It all evidently comes together in a tight circle, but the central point is to understand that Copp is offering a naturalistic explanation of the authoritative powers of normativity. For such a naturalistic account, if it holds up, promises to provide for the legal theory shaped by the reductive thesis a ready empirical explanation of how normativity can guide action. True, Copp's account applies to *moral* normativity (it empirically explains *moral* normativity as a source of authority); but the extension to the normativity of law can easily be made in light of the analogies existing between the two forms of normativity, that of morality and that of law.

The problem here is that Copp's account is naturalistic in name only. In fact, on closer scrutiny we can see that his definition of morality as practical rationality does not restrict its scope to the empirical but spills over into the conceptual. This is particularly evident in Copp's argument for the authority of standards of self-grounded reason. Self-grounded reason is, on this argument, the reason of rational moral agents. Its standards are accordingly universal (valid for all agents) and categorical, or unexceptionable (not subject to any single agent's power of exception or discretion), and they gain this authority by way of the constitutive role they play in forging rational agency itself, a role that consists in describing a conception of the self and showing it to be necessary, in that there is no other way that rational agents could possibly conceive of themselves in thought or action. But this necessary, constitutive role of self-grounded reason cannot be established on empirical grounds alone. Indeed, Copp uses to this end a strategy (the self-conception strategy) whose empirical component is only marginal. As much as it may invoke the factual, such as the fact that certain means serve certain ends or are very likely to achieve certain results, the core of it is nevertheless conceptual. There is nothing inherently empirical about the idea that rationality consists in efficiently serving our values and that efficiently doing so instantiates or enhances our self-government, as the self-conception strategy has it. This idea cannot be derived empirically, as observing existing practices or societies would be. It is not a factual truth but a conceptual proposition that standards whose currency contributes better than that of any other standard to enabling us to serve our values can also instantiate or enhance our self-government. The conceptual nature of the

---

[34] On this point, see Copp (2004: 35–9).

argument used in the self-conception strategy informs, too, the related idea of rationality. This is not an empirical idea but a conceptual one. The tight bond between rationality and normativity (as established by Copp, who makes rationality the very linchpin of normativity) makes it so that normativity itself is to be cast in a conceptual mould. Only on condition of defining normativity in such conceptual terms (by bringing an idea of rationality into the definition) can Copp claim morality to be normative at any level of normativity, authoritative or otherwise. Since concepts differ from facts in kind, rather than in degree, they cannot be reduced to facts without distortion. The same applies to normativity. A conceptual definition of it (as Copp's definition undeniably is) cannot without distortion be called empirical or be used as a basic component of any theory attempting any kind of naturalism.

In summary, the weight that Copp places on rationality throughout his account of normativity shows that normativity (in this construction) is conceived in concept and stays that way. It cannot be turned into anything essentially empirical or fact-like, for that would transform his theory and would also deprive it of its power to explain normative practices as having authoritative force in any of the relevant senses ordinarily associated with morality, that is, morality understood as a principle or standard that applies across the board, in such a way that any calculating, by any of us, as to whether we ought really to be committed to or bound by such a guide would make that guide *ipso facto* non-moral (or meaningful as a rational standard but meaningless as a moral one). And without an authentically naturalistic account of morality, the legal theory informed by the reductive thesis is left without any device by which to reduce normativity to the 'is' and yet still be able to account for its authoritative force, to wit, for its capacity to guide unconditionally the action of everyone within a given jurisdiction.

CONCLUSION

This chapter was devoted to the shaping of a reductive thesis, what I interpreted as a sceptical approach to the grounding question, an account described as an attempt at explaining the normativity of law without invoking any ground whatever. It was argued that this attempt commits us to an untenable view. In the reductive thesis we find the basic claim that normativity does not single out a peculiar category of human experience and understanding and can be explained instead as the result of certain combinations of social facts. In other words, there is no specificity to the 'ought', and what appears to be unique about this sphere—its inherent ability to command authority and guide action—can ultimately be made co-extensive with what goes on in the sphere of the 'is'. I argued that this reduction involves a good deal of strain, for it comes packaged with two glaring yet unaddressed problems that we have to solve on our own.

First, since we are being asked to equate the normative with the factual, we have to figure out how an identity can be established between two things (norms and social facts) that are described by different sets of predicates. Norms, unlike facts, can be described not only as efficacious or inefficacious but also as valid or invalid. Yet validity (by which standards are described) cannot be reduced to efficacy, and this leaves us with only two options. We might give up on the reduction, accepting that only norms can be valid or invalid, and not, then, social facts; or we might still try to show how validity can be reduced to efficacy, but until such a feat is accomplished we would have to take the reduction as an arbitrary exclusion from normativity of a property regarded as essential to it (this property being, of course, validity), and we would therefore have to accept, in this case, that norms *cannot* properly be described as valid.

Secondly, I argued that even if we assume, for the sake of argument, that this problem can be overcome—that one day we will figure out how to explain validity as a form of efficacy, thus reducing normativity to facticity—we will still have given effect to the wrong sort of reduction. We will not have explained normativity in the relevant sense that matters to us, whereby a rule, standard, principle or paradigm becomes normative in virtue of an ability to guide action unqualifiedly, meaning that the rule in question stands on the basis of reasons acceptable to everyone in the group and does not admit of any 'opting out' once the rule has been set down. The legal account shaped by the reductive thesis cannot account for it, since it cannot invoke any source of normativity other than social facts (or an arrangement thereof). It can therefore explain some forms of action guidance but not all of them, and especially not the forms peculiar to the law (and morality); it can show how the law can compel action, but not how it can do so in the categorical way just described, independently of anyone's willingness to accept the guidance of the law.

In summary, the view shaped by the reductive thesis is asking us to accept a distorted view of normativity, one that fails in two important respects. And the more important point is that in either case the distorted view is owed to the reductionism by which the account proceeds, namely, is owed to the insistence of the account on reducing all things normative to social facticity. To conclude, the critique presented in this chapter was selective, because it was confined to rejecting exclusively the reductive component of the account regarding normativity as groundless, while leaving open the possibility of a number of other theories, whose common trait consists in their non-reductionism and their recognition of the significance of the grounding question. It is one of these non-reductive strategies that I intend specifically to look in the next two chapters, this in my search for an answer to the question we are left with once we abandon the reductive thesis and eliminate the distortions that give rise to it. I mean, of course, the question of what can make the law normative and so can ground the normative claim of law.

5

Grounding the Normativity of Practical Reason

INTRODUCTION

Having argued in the last chapter that the grounding question is meaningful and still awaits for a satisfactory answer, I devote the remainder of the book to explaining how a foundation can be provided for the normative claim of law. Thus far, Part II has been cast largely in the negative, with an argument *against* radical scepticism about the source of the normativity of law, but from now on the discussion will be positive in nature, with an argument directed not against the critique of foundationalism about normativity but *for* a foundation of the normative claim of law. This I will do by embracing a broadly Kantian perspective and arguing that if we are to explain adequately the normative claim of law, we will have to turn to some contemporary discussions of Kant's conception of humanity *qua* source of the normativity of practical reason.

Two views explain this appeal to the Kantian tradition of philosophy. The first of these is that if we are to provide an adequate foundation for the *normative claim* of law, we will first have to determine the grounds of the *normativity* of law. In other words, we cannot understand the source of the normative claim of law unless we first consider the source of normativity. And the second view is that the law and the normativity of law enter into a special relationship with practical reason and with the normativity of practical reason, respectively, the law and the normativity of law being a special case of practical reason and the normativity of practical reason, meaning that the law is constructed as a species of the genus consisting in practical reason (and the same therefore holds for the normativity of law with respect to the normativity of practical reason). Of these two views, it is the second that has the greater potential for controversy, and this introduction will therefore focus on the second view, clarifying its meaning and scope.

Practical reason is reason as it applies to action: it delimits the point of view from which rational reflection resolves the question of what ought to be done. Accordingly, to view the law as a special case or subset of practical reason is to claim that the law is centrally concerned with rationally determining what ought to be done, an idea that can be analytically broken down into the tripartite view of the law as (a) practical, that is, an activity essentially concerned with action; (b) rational, that is, an activity conceived in and guided by reason; and (c) deliberative, namely, a reflective activity, an activity concerned with deliberating what one ought to do. While none of these more specific theses has gone unchallenged in jurisprudence, the overall idea presented by them has won wide support in the contemporary debate. Indeed, there is little disagreement, even among scholars otherwise deeply divided over various theoretical and philosophical issues in the law, that (a) the law is a practical rather than a theoretical activity; (b) the law is a system designed to influence our reasons in choosing to act in one way or another rather than simply our conduct, meaning that the law speaks the language of reason rather than that solely of will; and (c) the law is at its core an argumentative exercise of (rational) deliberation rather than an entirely rule-bound and mechanical process.

The first thesis characterises the *law as a praxis*, and so as an activity within a domain mainly concerned with finding answers to practical questions. As a praxis, the law is an institutional mechanism through which a social group determines what its members ought to do and forbear from doing. The mechanism thus comes into play when one is deciding on a course of action: different alternatives are compared by weighing the reasons for and against each of them, and once the process has been carried through, a general standard emerges, establishing the way in which one ought to conduct oneself with respect to the matter at hand. In this sense, the law works primarily as a system of rules, principles and policies by which to regulate not belief but action.

The second thesis lays emphasis on the connection between the law and the *reasons* for acting as the law requires: in as much as the law may be primarily concerned with governing action, it does so, in the first place, not by drawing the boundaries of conduct or defining an environment within which to constrain conduct, but by pointing to the reasons for acting in the designed way. The law, in other words, acts directly on our deliberation and only indirectly on our conduct: while there is no denying that subjection to the law leads ultimately to a resolution in terms of coercion—into our being forced to act in compliance with the law—it is also true that this pressure is essentially exerted by way of the reasons for such action, and so by setting up a framework within which to reason about action by spelling out the reasons for or against a certain course of action. The language of the law is thus a language of reasons, or at least it can be so translated without loss of meaning. So, on this conception, the law presents two faces, for on the one hand, there can be no law without power and force, which remain at least to some extent opaque and irreducible to reasons, but, on the other, the law also bears an essential connection to reasons. This is not to say that the law is entirely determined by rational considerations, let alone that it is necessarily so determined. Still, the connection is there (between the law and reasons), and to fail to see this would be to fail to appreciate the specificity of the law and its central and distinguishing features.

The third thesis presents the law as a *deliberative* rational activity aimed at both establishing principles of conduct and resolving specific disputes. This thesis connects with the second, for the law so construed (as a deliberative activity) cannot be set apart from reasoning. Reasoning occupies a central place in legal practice and consequently shapes it from the inside. And it is not reasoning *in general* that lies at the foundation of the law but reasoning of a special sort: it is a form of *practical* reasoning informed by rationality. This argument, known in the literature as the special case thesis, has been developed in particular by Robert Alexy,[1] but it forms part of discourse theory broadly. It presents legal discourse as a special case of general rational discourse and regards both as inhabiting the practical domain.[2] This thesis, then, introduces a distinction between legal and rational discourse in practical matters (between legal reasoning and rational deliberation) but denies that this distinction (and partial coincidence) implies a conceptual discontinuity. True, the law is an argumentative activity subject to constraints that set it apart from other types of practical reasoning[3]; but the two are alike in two fundamental respects, in that both activities (the reasoning at the foundation of the law, on the one hand; rational deliberation at large, on the other) are concerned with the basic question of what ought to be done, and they both find in rational correctness their regulative ideal.[4] These shared features are such that legal and practical reasoning are not fully independent of each other: they are to some extent interdependent. Discourse theory expresses this interdependence by bringing out the two sides of legal deliberation: its discursive side, governed by principles of reason and rationality, and its decision-making side, which is authoritative and institutional. It is the discursive component that provides the common ground between the law and practical reason, thus dispelling the myth of a conceptual separation between them.

The three main theses making up the conception of the law as a form of practical reason (as a species of this genus) yield in combination what may be called a moderate legal rationalism. What makes it rational is its emphasis on the role of reason in the shaping of the law, accordingly conceived as an intrinsically rational enterprise, except that the rational element (to whatever extent it may be intrinsic, acting as it does from the inside) cannot account for the whole of the law, whose rationalism must therefore be qualified. This rationalist conception of the law, in other words, does not suppose that power relations play no role in the law: it

---

[1] See Alexy (1989a: 212–20; 1999b).

[2] Others legal theorists who do not subscribe to discourse theory yet support the same thesis, which amounts to acknowledge the dependence of legal reasoning on practical reasoning, are MacCormick (2005: 139–41) and Dworkin (2006: 1–35). MacCormick describes legal interpretation as 'a particular form of practical argumentation in law, in which one argues for a particular understanding of authoritative texts or materials as a special kind of (justifying) reasons for legal decision. Hence legal interpretation should be understood within the framework of an account of argumentation, in particular, of practical argumentation' (MacCormick 1993: 16).

[3] Among the most significant features of deliberation in the law that account for its distinction from practical reasoning are that roles in legal discourse may be unequally distributed, participation is not necessarily voluntary, the duty of sincerity is not without exceptions, the reasoning is bound by procedural constraints (including time limits), and not all participants are required to be impartial.

[4] It should be noted, in this second respect, that rational correctness in law is not the same as rational correctness in other species of practical rationality, such as morality, prudence and political instrumentality, for in each of these areas there is a form of correctness (or justification) distinctive to it. *Legal* justification is bounded by conditions that distinguish it as a statute-bound activity that is subject to precedent and procedures, requiring that statements be justified within the framework of a given system rather than unconditionally or absolutely.

recognises that the law is shaped by a variety of factors, including interests and power, and so is not entirely governed by public reason. The moderate or qualified rationalist conception of the law just described, with its three main constituents, can be presented as one in which the law, along with other kindred realms, reflects the overarching realm of practical reason, along the lines of what is otherwise known as the thesis of the unity of practical reason.[5]

To uphold the unity of practical reason is not to view practical reason as a monolith. In fact, it is called unity precisely because it ranges over different sorts of reason, and what accounts for their unity, despite the specificities that render each unique, is their action-governing purpose. Practical reason thus covers a number of subtypes of reason, among which are moral, prudential and instrumental reason, with the last of these to be broken down further according to its shaping by aesthetic, economic, political or legal principles and values, or by any other sort of standard, not excluding plain considerations of efficiency. Practical reason, then, is both unified and ramified: it is unified in the sense that practical reason itself lies at the core of all its subtypes; but this unity only constitutes a thin level of discourse, beyond which practical reason ramifies into its different forms, into a vast array of practical activities, each having its own specificity, each distinguished by its scope and subject matter as well as by its governing principles and its peculiar notions. So, on the one hand, we find the shared vocabulary of practical reason and, on the other, the specific vocabularies of its many forms; and while the latter vocabularies account for the variety of practical reason, it is the former that imparts cohesiveness to the whole and acts as the essential condition that makes possible the relating and interacting of the different forms of practical reason.[6]

Just as this construction does not turn practical reason into a monolith—just as it does not entail for its different departments the same content, the same context of application, the same sphere of validity, without any possibility of conflict—so likewise it does not imply that these different departments or segments of practical reason are compartmentalised as so many separate activities, existing in complete isolation, each sealed off from the others without any sort of interaction between them. The unity of practical reason thus presents these two faces: on the one hand, it means that the different segments of practical reason cannot be reduced to a single substance without depriving them of their individuality and transforming them beyond recognition; on the other hand, it means that, precisely because they develop out of practical reason, relations among them obtain, enabling them to connect. Their sharing in the general features of practical reason, in other words, is such that their distinction does not amount to any separation but rather makes for a partial overlap and reciprocal influence. This relationship between the different segments of practical reason can be described

---

[5] This thesis finds an explicit recent restatement in Pavlakos (2006: 141–51).
[6] This view of the relations between the general principles of practical reason and their different instantiations is part of discourse theory, and it is Robert Alexy in particular who has made the argument with respect to the law, with his conception of legal discourse as a complement to and specification of general discourse (Alexy 1989a: 287–95).

as one of genus-continuity and species-difference. The different instantiations of practical reason are specific *cases* of practical reason, in the sense that they take contents, forms and principles that concretise, add to and specify in different ways the contents, forms and principles of practical reason generally understood.[7] The relationship is thus one of difference and continuity, combined in such a way that practical reason can be conceived as an 'integrated continuum' proceeding 'from the prudential, to the moral, to the complexity of the political, and from political authority to the "autonomy" of legality' (Palmer Olsen and Toddington 1999: 298).

There are at least three features of the law that account for its membership in the conceptual family of practical reason. First, the basic vocabulary and fundamental ideas of the law are forged by practical reason itself: in the law, as well as in most of the other practices shaped by practical reason, the basic terms and concepts either consist in or are developed out of a core set of ideas proper to practical reason, ideas such as obligation, permission, empowerment and right. Secondly, several legal practices are concerned with finding rational ways to cope with practical issues and set standards of required conduct. And thirdly, rationality plays as crucial a role in the law as it does in other areas of practical reason: legal standards must satisfy rational principles if they are to make sense, and rationality can accordingly be said to act as a regulative idea of the law.

The conceptual continuity between the law and practical reason makes it possible to regard the normativity of law and that of practical reason as having the same foundation. To conceive of the law as a subset of practical reason is to conceive of it as an enterprise with its own substance, sphere of application and structure—but an enterprise having its source in practical reason nonetheless, of which the law is an instantiation. This means that if we are to find the *foundation* of the normativity of law, we must look for it in the normativity of practical reason. The law may differ from the other branches of practical reason in a number of important ways, but it nevertheless belongs to the same genus as the other branches and so shares with them a common foundation. There is ultimately no distinction, then, that can be made between the source of practical reason and the source of law. Hence, an account of the foundation of the normativity of law must in the first instance be an account of the foundation of practical reason.

That gives the essential rationale for the discussion that follows, for I explore in this chapter a strategy for establishing the foundation of the normativity of practical reason. This is a strategy devised within an extraordinarily influential philosophical tradition, the Kantian tradition, which I have drawn from precisely because it has paid special attention to this question. The argument deployed in this chapter proceeds thus. First, I introduce the basics of Kant's account of

---

[7] This picture of the relation between the general idea of practical reason and its specific segments is something I developed over time in a series of conversations with George Pavlakos. I am most grateful to him for the valuable help he has given me in clarifying my position. Needless to say, responsibility for the views expressed herein, as well as for any errors of form or content, rests solely with me.

normativity and show that, for Kant, the source of the normativity of practical reason is located within a concept of humanity. I then discuss a preliminary objection to this account, thus clearing the way for a more detailed discussion. The objection is that Kant's account is irrelevant to the study of the normativity of law, this for the reason that Kant focuses on a different kind of normativity, namely, moral normativity. This objection is discussed in the third section, where I show that Kant understands not only the categorical imperative—the fundamental moral law—but also the hypothetical imperative as grounded in the idea of humanity. This implies that Kant's account has application to the normativity of practical reason in general, and hence to the normativity of law, and for this reason: to the extent that the law can be considered a (highly institutionalised) case of practical reason, the normativity of law can be considered an instance of the normativity of practical reason. In this section, I also observe that while Kant's proposal is solid in its main features, it is not uncontroversial, for it comes with a peculiar metaphysics establishing the connection between normativity and humanity. This metaphysics needs to be spelled out and supported by an analytical argument. But rather than completing Kant's account, by defending the metaphysical view on the basis of which the connection is established, I instead follow, in the fourth section, the lead of a handful of contemporary scholars who provide a pragmatic, or action-related, reinterpretation of Kant's main ideas. This refashioned view of the grounds of normativity, which I am putting forward, I chose to call the modified Kantian account: Kantian, for it preserves the main features of Kant's concept of normativity; modified, for it recasts in terms of human agency the concept of humanity that Kant posits as the foundation of normativity. Thus, we no longer have a metaphysical attempt to define the essence of humanity, but a pragmatic effort to single out the conceptual features of human agency. These distinctive features—reflectivity, rationality and autonomy—frame human agency as the basis without which specific subjects could not give content to any conception of themselves. We can therefore understand those features as representing together the minimum condition for the construction of a self-conception of human agents, or as an enabling condition for our process of identity-making as human agents. Because this self-conception is itself a non-contingent element of human agency, it is going to carry normative weight: each of us needs identity in order to structure a life, so the structure imparted to an identity (whatever it may be) is going to function as a model. Hence, the idea of human agency as the source for the normative force of practical reason.

KANT'S ACCOUNT OF THE SOURCE OF THE NORMATIVITY OF PRACTICAL REASON

Kant devotes large sections of his writings on practical philosophy to a systematic study of obligation, for he sees an explanation of the obligation-creating power of practical reason as the core of any moral project.[8] In the notion of obligation,

Kant couples the normative demands of practical reason with the motivational power of such demands. In treating of obligation, Kant is in a position to explain why practical reason has force. Thus, he explains the source of normativity, its obligation-creating power, and why he understands such an explanation as laying the very foundation of ethics. Before Kant expounded his practical philosophy, the question as to the grounds of obligation had been approached from two different perspectives, the one rationalist and the other sentimentalist. On the rationalist approach, normativity lies in a real property of deeds, viewed either in isolation or in relation to the context in which the deed is carried out, which amounts to explaining bindingness as a distinctive quality of certain kinds of conduct: certain kinds of conduct are intrinsically correct, and in such cases performance is constitutively obligatory.[9] On the sentimentalist approach, by contrast, normativity lies not in the conduct itself but in a faculty—the moral sense—with which human subjects are endowed: a given conduct will be good, and hence due, in so far as the moral sense ascertains that it is so. This amounts to making affection the source of normativity, affection understood as the sentiment of approval felt by competent observers in the presence of certain courses of conduct.[10]

Kant found inadequate both the rationalist and the sentimentalist way of explaining the normative force of practical reason and he initially explored the possibility of working out an eclectic view, a compromise between the rationalist and the sentimentalist accounts.[11] Then, in his 'critical' period, he arrived at a far more radical solution, which is systematically laid out in his major works on practical philosophy, notably in *Groundwork of the Metaphysics of Morals* and in *Critique of Practical Reason*.[12] These foundational works do not undertake to set out a complete system of ethics (an endeavour taken up in *The Metaphysics of Morals*), but are rather aimed at identifying, justifying and grounding the fundamental principle of morality. And this is what makes them relevant here. *Groundwork of the Metaphysics of Morals* is divided into three chapters. In the first chapter, Kant introduces the basic principle of morality and discusses the main features of the moral common sense; in the second chapter, he subjects the principle to a philosophical critique by means of which he gives it a more accurate and rigorous definition; in the third chapter, he justifies the principle by connecting it with the metaphysics he had previously set out in *Critique of Pure Reason*. This justification continues in *Critique of Practical Reason*, which can accordingly be seen as an integration of, and complement to, the final chapter of *Groundwork of the Metaphysics of Morals*.

---

[8] In fact in his *Enquiry concerning the Clarity of the Principles of Natural Theology and Ethics*, Kant (1968 AK 2:298) defines obligation as 'the primary concept' in ethics, and such it remains so from that point onward.
[9] It was Price (1974) and Clarke (1978) who offered the rationalist position of the day.
[10] This view is paradigmatically defended by Hutcheson (1971).
[11] This synthesis is attempted in *Enquiry concerning the Clarity of the Principles of Natural Theology and Ethics* (Kant 1968).
[12] The source of normativity is discussed as well in *Religion within the Boundaries of Mere Reason* (Kant 1902), *Anthropology from a Pragmatic Point of View* (Kant 1974), and *Metaphysics of Morals* (Kant 1996).

178 *Grounding the Normativity of Practical Reason*

In *Groundwork of the Metaphysics of Morals*, Kant gradually fleshes out his account of the source of the normative force of practical reason as he progresses, by synthesis and analysis, toward the final statement of the fundamental principle of morality. If we are to get a full grasp of Kant's account it will help to follow him in this progression. Nothing, Kant argues, that is not absolutely and unconditionally good, or good in itself independently of its relation to other things, has any moral worth. This requirement renders ineligible for service in any foundational role in morality the 'talents of the mind', such as intelligence, wit and judgement, the 'qualities of temperament', such as courage, resolution and constancy of purpose, and the 'gifts of fortune', such as power, wealth, honour, health, well-being and contentment—all things 'without doubt good and desirable in many respects', but things whose worth is conditional in that they are valuable only under certain conditions (Kant 1959 AK 4: 393). In fact, their worth depends ultimately on there being 'a good will' that 'sets a limit to the esteem in which [the same gifts and qualities] are rightly held and does not permit us to regard them as absolutely good' (Kant 1959 AK 4: 394). Whence the conclusion that only the 'mere' will—the pure power of choice—can be unconditionally good and can 'shine like a jewel for its own sake as something that has its full value in itself' (Kant 1959 AK 4: 394). So, for Kant, moral worth is non-contingently linked with the will, and in the will (in some trait inherent in the will or constitutive of it) the basic requirement of morality must be found.

But we are not bound to do good every time we exercise the power to choose: if the will is to be unconditionally good, it must be well-directed. So, it becomes essential to find the standard by which to govern the will and orient it to the good. We could easily do this by observing the pure will in operation if only this were possible. But the will as such is not amenable to any sort of direct observation in its pure form, for we are inevitably going to find it admixed with whatever purposes may happen to be guiding us when we decide on a course of action. This suggests to Kant (1959 AK 4: 397) the need to focus instead on another idea, that of duty, which can more easily be probed in its pure form, and which 'contains [the concept] of good will, though under certain subjective limitations and hindrances'. So we can investigate the pure will by proxy, focusing on the thing closest to it, our sense of duty. In other words, the pure will can be approximated by looking at what makes it good, and since this ability pertains to duty, we can investigate the idea of duty as a means through which ultimately to arrive at the foundation of morality.

This examination of duty and the practice of acting from duty prompts Kant to argue that moral worth does not derive from the results achieved through the exercise of willpower, or from any of the variety of ends that may guide the will, or from the inclinations that accompany the will in choosing how to act: these things are all contingent, for they all *add* to the will rather than constituting it. The will can neither be equated to the results it produces nor is it constituted by the results achieved, ends chosen, or inclinations heeded. Rather, constitutive of the will are principles of volition. In fact, the power of choice (at least in rational beings, and human beings among them) is governed of necessity by principles: a rational will cannot be unprincipled, or lawless, for otherwise, in the absence of some guiding principle, it may turn into an arbitrary power and fall prey to contradiction, thus casting off its rationality. So the basis of moral worth has to reside in the principle by which we guide our power of choice (Kant 1959 AK 4: 400).

The principles of volition, Kant argues, are principles that we choose freely for ourselves rather than finding them imposed on us by natural necessity or causation. This stance is grounded in Kant's metaphysics. Among many other things, Kant in his metaphysics addresses certain basic antinomies that had engaged the debate in his day. One of those antinomies is determined by the uneasy relation between the free will and determinism. The party of free will asserts that we are not causally determined and can act by means of our own decision; the determinists, instead, argue that freedom is an illusion, this on the ground that everything happens causally in accordance with the laws of nature. Free will and determinism have traditionally been cast as an antinomy, for they cannot both be true: our action cannot be both freely chosen and causally determined. Yet in the second book of the 'Transcendental Dialectic', a key section of *Critique of Pure Reason*, Kant presents the two views as compatible: freedom and natural causality are consistent as the ruling principles of two distinct spheres, with causality governing the phenomenal world of 'appearances' (of things sensible) and freedom the noumenal, intelligible world of 'things in themselves' (Kant 1965: A537/B565). Kant's solution to the antinomy originating in free will and determinism, then, appeals to the distinction between the phenomenal, or sensible, world and the noumenal, or intelligible, world.[13]

The appearances inhabiting the phenomenal world of the senses are 'mere representations connected in accordance with empirical laws', having a spatio-temporal existence, and knowable by humans through the subjective forms of intuition (Kant 1965: A537/B565). Everything in the phenomenal world takes place through a prior cause: 'among the causes in appearance there can surely be nothing that could begin a series absolutely and from itself . . . All actions of natural causes are themselves in turn effects' (Kant 1965: A544/B572). This causal connection, having no end or beginning, means that freedom has no place in the phenomenal world: everything is subject to the laws of nature, every movement is driven by necessary causation; all is predetermined, nothing is freely chosen. And in this all-encompassing causal sphere we have the meaning of determinism. But causal explanations cannot account for the whole of existence: in fact they do not shed light on the prime cause, the origin of all the other chains of cause and effect making up the phenomenal world. In other words, causal explanations give rise to an infinite regress: every occurrence is explained by pointing to its cause, a prior occurrence is produced in turn by another occurrence, and so on *ad infinitum*, and

---

[13] These two worlds can be interpreted as forming either an epistemological distinction or an ontological one. On the epistemological interpretation, phenomenon and noumenon are two standpoints from which to approach the same reality; on the ontological interpretation, they count as distinct realities, or distinct worlds. I am taking this distinction to be ontological, despite a lack of textual evidence in favour of either interpretation, and am taking into account that the whole argument which follows can easily be reframed in epistemological terms with only minor tweaks. On the two interpretations of Kant's distinction, see Prauss (1974), among many others.

there is no way to prevent the regress by causal explanation alone. If the sensible world itself comes into existence by causation, we can only explain this existence by postulating a special kind of cause undetermined by prior causes. So the noumenal world comes into play, an intelligible world of a different order that Kant posits as the prime cause, a world inhabited by things not as they appear to be but as they are in themselves.[14] By hypothesis, things-in-themselves need no cause to originate, for otherwise the regress would begin anew. They are causes of a special kind: uncaused, spontaneous causes governed by a different law, the law of freedom, shaped by reason.[15] By positing this separate, but connected, existence of radically different causalities—the appearances vis-à-vis things-in-themselves—Kant can account for freedom and the possibility of a free will. The freedom of choice, namely, practical freedom, or independence from causal necessitation, enabling the will to choose for itself the laws on which to act, is made possible by transcendental freedom, consisting in the independence that things-in-themselves enjoy from natural causes.[16]

This conclusion carries an important implication for us as human beings: that we cannot be reduced to appearances alone, in that we participate instead in a scheme that exhibits a dual nature. On the one hand, we are cast in a sensible existence subject to the constant laws of nature, our action driven by inclinations and causally determined in a necessary way—and in this respect we are empirical beings amenable to naturalistic explanation.[17] But at the same time we exist as intelligences, as noumenal entities, endowed not only with sensible perception but also with apperception, a faculty not amenable to empirical explanation, and we also possess spontaneity, a faculty by which the will can 'start to act from itself, without needing to be preceded by any other cause'.[18] Our acts in this sphere, then, proceed not by the causal determination of some inclination or other force that compels them in any necessary direction, but by a free power of choice, meaning: our acts are ultimately chosen.

In summary, a human being has (Kant 1959 AK 4: 452):

> two points of view from which he can regard himself and from which he can know laws governing the employment of his powers and consequently governing all his actions. He can consider himself first—so far as he belongs to the sensible world—to be under the laws of nature (heteronomy); and secondly—so far as he belongs to the intelligible world—to be under laws which, being independent of nature, are not empirical but have their ground in reason alone.

---

[14] Things-in-themselves exist outside space and time. They therefore elude intuition and cannot be known but only presupposed. Still, this does not make the presupposition arbitrary, for it is instead necessitated by the nature of the things we do know.

[15] On the idea of spontaneity, understood as the ability of certain things to originate a state from themselves, or be their own cause, see Kant (1965: A533/B561).

[16] See Kant (1956 AK 5: 28–30).

[17] Kant (1965: A539/B567). From this perspective, 'the human being is one of the appearances in the world of sense, and to this extent also one of the natural causes whose causality must stand under empirical laws' (Kant: 1965: A546/B574).

[18] Kant (1965: A533/B561). On the faculty of apperception, see Kant (1965: A546/B574).

Kant's Account of the Normativity of Practical Reason   181

So it is by virtue of our rational capacity that we can exercise a free will, as intelligences inhabiting the noumenal world, a realm of freedom in which we can escape the grip of natural necessity.[19] Importantly, too, our dual nature (as beings subject to the senses but governed by the intellect) carries the implication that in the sphere of action we ought to conceive of ourselves as free, as intelligent beings endowed with reason, capable of acting under an idea of freedom, and so on a principle of our own choosing.[20]

This construction explains Kant's assumption that the principles of volition constitutive of the will are not imposed on the will from the outside but are freely endorsed, self-determined. This understanding of the will as constituted by freely chosen principles is framed within a metaphysical conception of the human being. And, as constitutive of the will (which alone can achieve unconditional goodness), these principles of volition can qualify as building blocks making up the foundation of morality. Yet not all principles of volition stand on the same footing: no will that proceeds by principles responding to the demands of subjective inclination can be described as well-directed; for if we choose by inclination, we are thereby acting by the dictates of sensible determination and are therefore inhabiting the realm of natural necessity, not that of freedom. This renders us blind to morality, which can only make sense against a background of free choice informed by reason. Morality will not make any sense in a context of causal determination.[21] Further, if morality were grounded in a principle receptive to inclination, it could not make the claim to objectivity ordinarily associated with it: unlike reason, inclinations dwell by and large in subjectivity. Only a rational principle can impart objectivity to morality and make it universally compelling. Therefore, no sound connection can be established between morality and the will unless the will (the power of choice) is exercised according to reason. Only in this way, when the will operates by the guidance of rational principles, can it participate in the noumenal dimension and be authentically free, thus aspiring to unconditional and objective goodness. This leads Kant to conclude that the good will is 'a power to choose only that which reason independently of inclination recognizes to be practically necessary'.[22]

This concludes Kant's discussion of what he calls the common moral cognition, the everyday unreflective awareness of the requirements of morality. So he gives us a *preliminary* statement of the fundamental principle of morality. But no such statement can be complete unless we subject it to the scrutiny provided by critical philosophy, which directs us to look for an a priori moral standard, one independent of any conditions of intuition, and whose content is neither learned nor

---

[19] Kant (1965: A541/B569). So, while we do stand affected by external stimuli, their action does not run so deep as to silence our power to choose. In this sense, Kant describes the human will as an '*arbitrium sensitivum*, yet not *brutum* but *liberum*' (Kant 1965: A534/B562).

[20] This implication is spelled out in Kant (1959 AK 4: 448).

[21] On the relation between freedom and morality in Kant, see Hill (1998) and Guyer (2000: 29–171).

[22] Kant (1959 AK 4: 412); stated otherwise, the only well-directed power of choice is that 'in itself completely in accord with reason' (Kant 1959 AK 4: 413).

derived from empirical evidence.[23] Critical philosophy gives us both the form and the content of the fundamental moral principle.

Its *form* is that of the imperative.[24] Imperatives can generally direct in either of two ways, hypothetically or categorically. Hypothetical imperatives 'declare a possible action to be practically necessary as a means to the attainment of something else that one wills (or that one may will)'. Depending on the kind of end the hypothetical imperatives require, they will be either problematic or pragmatic.[25] A problematic imperative is a technical imperative of skill, prescribing the means necessary to achieve the ends sought, but it will not tell us whether those ends should be sought in the first place: rather, it gives us the instrumental rationality by means of which an end can be achieved, regardless of what that end might be. The pragmatic imperative is a prudential directive instructing us to do what is necessary to achieve the end that we ought all to want to pursue as rational subjects, namely, happiness understood as a basic interest in our own well-being. The two kinds of hypothetical imperative, then, are guided by two different kinds of rationality—the one instrumental and the other prudential—but despite this difference, both are conditional, that is, both depend on and serve an end, thus neither qualifies as an absolute principle of necessary action. Unless we aim at the specific ends they are designed to achieve, we can disregard these imperatives without thereby acting irrationally. Their being conditional on a purpose makes hypothetical imperatives ultimately unfit to function as grounding principles of moral obligation. By contrast, the categorical imperative 'declares an action to be objectively necessary in itself without reference to some purpose—that is, even without any further end' (Kant 1959 AK 4: 415). This feature of the categorical imperative—its holding unconditionally, and hence its being absolute and objective, or apodeictic—makes it fit to give form to the fundamental principle of morality.[26] This form needs to be law-like and must apply universally rather than conditionally; that is, it must apply for all rational beings, and it is rendered specific in the prescription to 'act only on that maxim through which you can at the same time will that it should become a universal law' (Kant 1959 AK 4: 421). That describes the form of the fundamental principle of morality: the form of a universal law.

The *content* of the fundamental principle of morality is provided by Kant in different formulations, all of them presented as equivalent but each emphasising a different aspect of the principle. Two of these formulations prove particularly useful in studying the grounds of the normativity of practical reason, these being the formula of humanity as an end in itself and the formula of autonomy. The formula of humanity as end in itself reads (Kant 1959 AK 4: 429):

---

[23] This means that in order to identify and justify the basic principle of morality 'we have to progress by natural stages, not merely from ordinarily moral judgement . . . to philosophical judgement . . . but from popular philosophy, which goes no further than it can get by fumbling with the aid of examples, to metaphysics' (Kant 1959 AK 4: 412).

[24] See Kant (1959 AK 4: 413–14).

[25] Kant (1959 AK 4: 414). See also Kant (1956 AK 5: 17–19).

[26] See Kant (1956 AK 5: 32–3).

act in such a way that you always treat humanity, whether in your own person or in the person of any other, never simply as a means, but always at the same time as an end.

This emphasises the subject of the fundamental principle, humanity, which Kant understands to be one of three fundamental capacities, or 'original predispositions', of agents, the others being animality and personality.[27] Animality is the name for the instincts and impulses by which animate beings preserve their existence, and personality consists in the ability to give oneself over to the moral law. Humanity corresponds instead to the set of rational capacities: as such it bears no specific connection with morality, for its function consists rather in enabling us to represent an end to ourselves fully consciously and to deliberate on how to achieve this end. In humanity, we have the ability to select not only the proper means to a given end but also the end itself, by comparing and systematising different ends, thus forming an overall idea of our well-being.[28] Humanity can thus be described as an all-purpose ability (a condition necessary to the pursuit of any purpose regardless of what that may be), and this is the feature that makes it an end in itself, not subordinate to other ends, and a capacity that cannot be given up without impairing our very possibility to act.[29] The formula of humanity is complemented and specified by the formula of autonomy, which emphasises the legislative power connected with the rational capacities constitutive of humanity. The formula of autonomy depicts 'the will of every rational being as a will which makes universal law' (Kant 1959 AK 4: 431), and it accordingly prescribes that we ought to will and choose to live by universal principles, meaning principles that every rational being can recognise as appropriate principles on which to act (Kant 1959 AK 4: 440). In the formula of autonomy, the rational will emerges as the ultimate giver of universal laws; which means that human beings act in two roles, not only as recipients of moral laws (as capable of understanding and following moral laws) but also as the makers and authors of such laws, and hence as legislators. And by virtue of this legislative power, humanity gains dignity, understood as 'unconditional, incomparable worth' over against 'relative value—that is, a price' (Kant 1959 AK 4: 435–6).

These two formulas, autonomy and humanity as an end in itself, not only contribute to a specification of the fundamental principle of morality but also make clear that Kant understands the normative claims advanced by morality as having their source in humanity, presented accordingly as 'the ground of [the categorical] imperative', as 'the supreme practical ground' on which basis to 'derive all laws for the will' (Kant 1959 AK 4: 428). This conclusion—humanity as 'the ground for every enactment of practical law' (Kant 1959 AK 4: 431), and so also as the

---

[27] These three fundamental capacities are defined in Kant (1902 AK 6: 26–8). Further discussion is provided in Wood (1999: 118–22).

[28] See Kant (1974 AK 7: 183–6). We should not let the term *humanity* lead us astray into thinking of it as exclusive to the human species: it is not—as can clearly be appreciated from Kant's definition of it—for it rather describes a general capacity of rational subjects as such; that is, anyone is said to have humanity who can choose an end by a process of reasoning. In this sense, Kant cannot be accused of any 'speciesism', the fallacy of placing special value on a species or its members simply by virtue of belonging to that species. On this point, see Wood (1999: 119–20), and compare Aune (1980: 112–3).

[29] See Kant (1959 AK 4: 428–9).

foundation of the normativity of morality—is justified by ascribing to humanity a status as 'something whose existence has in itself an absolute value' and hence the status of 'an end in itself' (Kant 1959 AK 4: 428). It is as such, as the 'ultimate end or value'—as an unconditional end, universal and objective, which makes possible all other ends, all contingent ends—that humanity can be said to ground morality. This attribution of an absolute unconditional value to humanity is in turn justified by pointing out that rational agents ultimately depend on this value as a necessary condition of their existence: a rational agent 'necessarily conceives his own existence' as an 'objective value' (Kant 1959 AK 4: 429). So as Kant wraps up his moral theory, he has set out not only the supreme principle of morality but also its source, explaining why the demands of morality can exert normative force: the normativity of morality is grounded not in some real property of conduct (as rationalism would have it) or in any special sentiment (as it would be on the sentimentalist view) but in humanity: in our ability to establish for ourselves ends that we have arrived at by our own devices through a process of reasoning.[30]

RELEVANCE AND SHORTCOMINGS OF KANT'S ACCOUNT

Kant treats the source of obligation in the context of a study aimed at establishing the fundamental principle of morality. But while Kant focuses on *moral* obligation, finding its grounds to lie in humanity, he also points out that humanity grounds as well the normativity of the *hypothetical* imperative. Kant's focus on the normativity of the categorical imperative is mostly owed to the robust normative claim of morality, whose demands purport to bind universally, unconditionally, absolutely and objectively. This claim is nothing short of formidable, requiring, therefore, a strong argument in support. But if the argument works here, establishing for the grounds of moral obligation a compelling account and a solid principle, then a fortiori the same argument will prove effective in grounding the less exacting demands of other forms of practical reason. Hypothetical imperatives count as one instance where we can see Kant applying this logic. In a cursory discussion of the hypothetical imperative, Kant (1959 AK 4: 417) poses the question of 'how we can conceive the necessitation of the will expressed by the imperative in setting us a task'. He starts out by noting that this question (the question about the grounds of hypothetical imperatives) 'requires no special discussion' (Kant 1959 AK 4: 417), the reason lying in the analytic link that obtains between content and grounds of a hypothetical imperative. In analytic relations, each term contains the other, so either term can be endorsed without the other having to be separately endorsed: by mere analysis, the appropriateness of each term can be made to follow from the appropriateness of the other. So long as it is an analytic relation that holds between the components of a hypothetical imperative—between its content

---

[30] As Korsgaard (1996a: 65) would summarise it, 'nothing except my own will can make a law normative ... only those maxims ... to which my own will commits me—are intrinsically normative'.

and grounds—we can proceed by mere analysis to make the grounds of the imperative explicit. This suggests to Kant that hypothetical imperatives carry normative force simply because no will can fail to use the means necessary to the pursuit of the ends it sets freely for itself. This statement can hold true to the extent that we base it on Kant's definition of will, which is something altogether different from a wish, want or desire: a will that fails to treat as binding the means necessary to achieve a chosen end fails by this very test to qualify as a will in the first place.[31] So it is by Kant's own definition of the will that the necessary means to an end sought by the will acquire their normative force, which force in turn transfers to the hypothetical imperative.

This explanation holds true for both the problematic imperative, which is constitutive of instrumental rationality, and the pragmatic imperative, in which prudential reason consists.[32] Problematic imperatives find expression in analytical propositions, in that (Kant 1959 AK 4: 417):

> in my willing of an object as an effect there is already conceived the causality of myself as an acting cause—that is the use of means; and from the concept of willing an end the imperative merely extracts the concept of actions necessary to this end.

The imperative of prudence likewise finds expression in an analytical proposition but, unlike the problematic imperative, it sets an end—happiness—that does not reflect any determinate concept:[33] 'although every man wants to attain happiness, he can never say definitely and in unison with himself what it really is that he wants and wills' (Kant 1959 AK 4: 418). Because of this indeterminateness (whereby we cannot accurately specify the end dictated by prudence, and to that extent cannot work out the means necessary to the attainment of this end) we may not see the imperative of prudence for what it is, namely, an analytical proposition. But the indeterminateness that suggests otherwise affects the *content* of this imperative, not its *source*. Where source is concerned, the imperative of prudence behaves no differently from the technical imperative,[34] in that the normative force of both imperatives can be established in the same way, analytically: 'since both command solely the means to something assumed to be willed as end, the imperative which commands him who wills the end to will the means is in both cases analytic' (Kant 1959 AK 4: 419). So, in conclusion, Kant does not see the hypothetical imperative, in any of its forms, as needing any detailed justification.

This cursory treatment of hypothetical imperatives should not obscure what Kant takes to be the source of their normative force: he locates this source in the

---

[31] See Kant (1959 AK 4: 417).

[32] See Kant (1959 AK 4: 419).

[33] Happiness and its role in moral thought do receive specific discussion in Kant, but the idea itself is left deliberately vague, on the basic premise that different people can specify its content in different ways without thereby acting irrationally, which means that any attempt to specify such content in any definite manner would be vain.

[34] 'If it were only as easy to find a determinate concept of happiness, the imperative of prudence would agree entirely with those of skill and would be equally analytic. For here as there it could alike be said "Who wills the end, wills also (necessarily if he accords with reason) the sole means which are in his power"' (Kant 1959 AK 4: 417).

idea of a free will, in the faculty of establishing by reason the principles on which to act. This faculty forms as well the basis of humanity (as Kant understands this idea), which by this connection comes to ground the normativity of non-categorical imperatives, too. So, in Kant, *all* imperatives (regardless of their kind) ultimately find in humanity the source of their normative force: different arguments and methods establish such force, but its source remains the same. This is to say that Kant offers a unified theory of the normativity of practical reason, for categorical imperatives and hypothetical imperatives account jointly for the whole of practical reason, with the categorical imperative covering all ends whose validity holds unconditionally (which makes this the imperative of all moral reason) and the hypothetical imperative governing all contingent ends. Within this latter rubric falls the whole range of conditionally valid ends: not only those that Kant discusses directly (the ends involved in technical, or instrumental, reasoning and those associated with prudence, or self-interest), but also the ends framed under aesthetic evaluations and economic considerations, to name but two examples.[35] So, in Kant's framework, the whole of practical reason (moral, instrumental, prudential and so on) ultimately depends on the same grounds for its normativity, meaning that practical reason carries normative force by virtue of its linkage with humanity understood as the rational power to decide for oneself the ends worthy of pursuit.

But, as much as Kant may have offered deep insights into the normative force of practical reason in general, and not only of morality, suggesting that we consider *humanity* to be the source of such normativity, his account still falls short in important respects, most notably in the robust metaphysics on which it is based and in the cryptic argument by which humanity is posited as the source of normativity. First, the metaphysics: Kant bases on the distinction between noumenon and phenomenon the view of humanity as not reducible to sensible existence, consisting instead in an ability to act on freely chosen rational principles. This power of choice, Kant argues, is something that comes to us by way of our participation in the noumenal world, where we can achieve transcendental freedom, meaning independence from sensible determinations; and from this source comes our practical freedom, the freedom to choose our actions without having to adhere to any laws of strict causality. This ability to choose freely and unconditionally the principles on which to act makes up the core of this view of humanity, a most distinctive view, and one that can withstand scrutiny only on the condition that we take it on board along with its underlying metaphysical distinction between phenomenon (appearances) and noumenon (things-in-themselves). Failing that condition the special view of humanity would collapse—it could scarcely be conceived of any longer as the only unconditional end, nor, for that reason, could it

---

[35] This idea is expressed most clearly by Korsgaard (2009: 46–7), who claims that 'the hypothetical imperative may be extended tocover any case of action in which the agent is selfconsciously guided by a conception of the state of affairs he is trying to realize in the world. In this guise, the hypothetical imperative appears to be the general normative principle of practical application.'

make normative the demands of practical reason. Therefore, a given metaphysical view comes as a condition for accepting the Kantian idea of humanity and his related conception of humanity as the source of the normativity of practical reason: Kant sets up his argument so that we cannot subscribe to the idea of humanity unless we also subscribe to its underlying metaphysical view. So if we are to accept this idea on Kant's terms, we have to be prepared to defend the underlying metaphysical view, and that by making this view compatible with a scientific worldview.

This seems too heavy a burden to place on an account of humanity, and hence on an account explaining why practical reason, having its source in humanity, carries any normative force. We should not want to make the validity of such an account dependent on the validity of a disputable metaphysical view.[36] This point is further supported by the consideration that even if it were granted that we could set Kant's metaphysical view on a sound theoretical footing, we would still have to look carefully at its practical implications, especially in connection with its distinction between noumenon and phenomenon. In particular, on a rationalistic interpretation of this distinction, these implications are far from alluring. For, on this interpretation we would find that the distinction between noumenon and phenomenon spells the undoing of our practical existence. To wit, so long as we participate in an existence of reason, we are rational—necessarily so, by virtue of that fact—and we cannot but answer to the call of reason, which is to say that we have fulfilled our true human nature as beings who live by the dictates of reason. But at the same time, any act we commit contrary to reason will mark our failure in that respect (our failure as human beings), with each such act attesting to our inability to overcome the sensible imperfections that keep us tethered to the phenomenal world. Any lapse will mean that we cannot free ourselves from this world, an inability that amounts to giving up our noumenal, or rational, existence, thus accepting an imperfect, and hence inferior, life—the life of sensible existence. The rationalistic view thus posits a Manichean distinction between the realm of reason, wherein lies the excellence of humanity, and the realm of the inclinations, which pulls in all the faults and shortcomings that come with human existence. Furthermore, this same distinction between spheres raises as well the question of whether the free will is free after all. In fact, we cannot really deem ourselves to be free in acting according to reason unless we can equally choose to do otherwise, acting *contrary* to reason. On the rationalistic interpretation of Kant's metaphysics, however, we are not free to *that* extent, for the moment we act contrary to reason, we have forsaken our noumenal status and embraced an existence subject to the senses. Yet in this existence—in the phenomenal world—we are bound by natural necessity and have no freedom, for freedom pertains exclusively to the noumenal world. Thus, if we disregard reason, allowing desires and inclinations to determine our conduct, we have also, and dramatically, renounced freedom. The resulting

---

[36] For a critical discussion of Kant's metaphysics see, among others, Velkley (1989), Ameriks (1992), Hudson (1994), Adams (1997), Watkins (1998), and Allison (2004).

picture is one in which we are never free, for whichever way we go, we will fall subject to either of two forces—rationality on the one side, nature on the other—that each compels us to act in certain ways, since both are forms of necessity, leaving no latitude for freedom of action. In sum, Kant's metaphysics represents a questionable theory and proves unattractive in the practical sphere, too. Thus, it would not serve as a good basis on which to explain the grounds of the normativity of practical reason.

The other major issue in Kant's account of the normativity of practical reason is not the metaphysical view per se or its practical consequences, but rather the argument showing the source of such normativity to lie in humanity. In short, the reason why humanity, rather than some other capacity, ought to be considered the ultimate foundation of the unconditional good (that is, the source of the unconditional demands of morality) is stated in *Groundwork of the Metaphysics of Morals* to be that 'a man necessarily conceives his own existence' as having unconditional value (Kant 1959 AK 4: 429). Now, if we leave out of consideration the metaphysical assumptions at work in *Groundwork of the Metaphysics of Morals*, we find that Kant is essentially arguing something to the effect that because we all necessarily conceive of ourselves as worthy of an unconditional, absolute existence governed by principles that we establish by the rational exercise of our power of choice, then this faculty—humanity—ought to be understood, by virtue of that consideration, as grounding the normativity of the demands of practical reason. So, Kant is deriving the role of humanity as the source of normativity simply from a widespread assumption among us that our own humanity holds unconditional worth. This may well be the case, but it is not yet an argument: it cannot stand alone and requires support and revision.

THE MODIFIED KANTIAN ACCOUNT

Despite the difficulties besetting Kant's account of the normativity of practical reason, just outlined, his account contributes too importantly to the debate to be dismissed altogether. The core of it can be rescued, provided that it goes through revision, and this requires a twofold move. First, the normativity of practical reason will have to be grounded in a conception of humanity that, contrary to Kant's conception, is unencumbered by strong metaphysical assumptions and is yet for all practical purposes nevertheless necessary and universally valuable; secondly, it should be clarified how a metaphysically unburdened conception of humanity can endow practical reason with normative force. The account making these adjustments maintains a strong connection with Kant's original approach, and for this reason I will call it a Kantian account, albeit a modified one that redresses the shortcomings of the original.

Action and Human Agency

The first move in my two-pronged rescue strategy consists in grounding the normativity of practical reason in an idea independent of Kant's metaphysics. This is going to require a pragmatic, or action-centred, reading of Kant's concept of humanity, a concept originally developed as part of a metaphysics. From the pragmatic perspective here adopted, the concept of humanity summarises the properties someone must have in order to be deemed capable of carrying out action and hence be recognised as an acting self.[37] The properties of humanity (on the pragmatic view of this idea being developed here) are thus capacities without which a subject would be incapable of *action* (in the relevant sense of action to be introduced below). They can therefore be considered *defining* properties, for, by hypothesis, no one who lacks or rejects them can properly be said to act: to deny them is to deny one's distinctive status as an acting subject, as a subject having a specific existence in the practical sphere. A member of humanity, then, is defined by the range of necessary capacities making for the possibility of action. These capacities mark out a pragmatic unit (the subject understood as a doer of deeds, or as an agent) rather than a metaphysical entity, a being. The idea that can be constructed out of these capacities accordingly encapsulates a system of action-enabling conditions, a set of requirements in the absence of which no action could take place. This is clearly a practical idea, not a theoretical one, and this characteristic makes it possible for it to be maintained independently of any metaphysical support, and generally to make sense apart from any metaphysics.[38]

From here on, the difference between Kant's own account and the modified Kantian account just introduced will be signalled by calling *humanity* Kant's metaphysical notion of humankind and *human agency* the pragmatic notion by means of which I am proposing to revise Kant's original idea. Like Kant's idea of humanity, human agency singles out a general capacity, but unlike Kant's humanity, which is metaphysically grounded, human agency rests on a purely practical anchorage.[39]

---

[37] The word *action* is being used here as a term of art to designate not just anything done generally but a specific sort of conduct, as explained below.

[38] My treatment of the human agent does not describe the self understood as a metaphysical entity persistent across space and time, nor does it assume the existence of a unitary and continuous consciousness. It is a matter of dispute whether such a subject of experience, explainable in terms of psychological connectedness, can in fact exist, so I will not rely on this notion here. Instead of going for an exhaustive definition of the self, I will construct those features of the human agent that have relevance in the practical sphere. Thus, I will be dealing less with human beings understood as loci of experience and representation and more with human *agents*, that is, with pragmatic notions that can make continuity of action meaningful. On this practical concept of human agency compare Scheffler (1982), Darwall (1982), Gillet (1987), Velleman (1989: 81–211), Honnefelder (1996) and Korsgaard (1996a: 363–97).

[39] What prompted my choice not to concern myself with the metaphysical status of the human subject was not an anti-metaphysical prejudice but an acknowledgment that it is still very much an open question what this status is: sticking to the practical terrain makes it possible to put forward, with regard to human subjectivity, claims that do not depend for their validity on the ongoing metaphysical inquiry into the matter.

The idea of human agency typically describes adult humans with no serious disabilities, impairments or dysfunctions. But the capacities this idea singles out as here discussed are not distinctive to the human species (they may well be found in non-humans, too, to a greater or lesser extent), nor, for that matter, are they necessary for someone to be regarded as a human being. Hence, nothing about this particular idea of human agency should be taken to imply that human beings *alone* are capable of action (in the strict sense of action shortly to be clarified) or that *all* human beings have this capacity. Human agency therefore does not distinguish humans from non-humans: the traits of human agency do have a necessary role, to be sure, but as essential preconditions for action in the practical sphere, rather than for membership in the human species. As much as action may be something that humans *typically* engage in, and this makes it non-arbitrary to describe as human anyone capable of action, or anyone with a capacity to carry out action, it is not by singling out a kind of conduct and a set of capacities peculiar to humans and common to all humans that action and human agency acquire their essential meaning. Indeed, action and human agency would lose much of their point if our basic interest in them lay in the use we could make of them as defining conditions on the basis of which it might be determined what makes someone a human being: human agency is not species-specific (despite what its name may suggest), nor is it an attribute someone comes to have simply by virtue of belonging to a biological class. Rather, human agency is something that someone comes to have by showing a capacity for action. From this species-independent perspective, then, there would be nothing conceptually amiss in considering a non-human being capable of acting, and so an agent, or, vice versa, in finding that a human being is not, after all, capable of acting, and so is not a human agent.[40]

Another way to look at human agency, thus expanding on this concept, is to see it as the outcome of an exercise that begins with an enquiry into action. This is a constructive exercise, to be sure, but it is not arbitrary, since it proceeds under the constraints framed by the overall aim of the study within which it is carried out, this aim being to establish the foundation from which the normative force of the demands of practical reason arises. Because at least some of these demands are acknowledged to bind necessarily and universally (depending on the form of practical reason from which they issue), the defining properties of human agency must analogously be such that no one can be considered an agent who does not possess them, that is: *every* agent must incorporate these properties (that is why they are called *defining* properties) or must otherwise be led to incorporate them by force of rational argument and so, as long as an agent thinks clearly or rationally, must

---

[40] It might be asked at this point whether the idea might not be better served by the simple term *agency* than by *human agency*, since this latter expression carries a definite anthropocentric connotation that may make it misleading. That much is true, but then any such misunderstanding can be dispelled simply by pointing it out, as I have just done. Then, too, there are two reasons that weigh in favour of *human agency:* first, as has also been observed, the capacity for action at the core of human agency is something that can be found paradigmatically embodied precisely in human beings; and secondly, the expression makes it possible to underscore the Kantian roots of my account by staying as close as possible to Kant's own vocabulary.

acknowledge them, albeit implicitly. This in turn makes human agency a transcendental concept: the properties or capacities constitutive of human agency are non-contingent capacities of universal application among all acting selves.[41] In sum, in my construction human agency is defined by a list of *practically necessary capacities* or properties: practical in the sense that they go into an account of *action*, and so of the *acting subject*; and necessary in the sense that no adequate account in this regard would be possible without them. Human agency, in short, is a practical concept summarising the essential capacities, independent of subjective dispositions, personal inclinations and individual peculiarities, without which we would not be able to carry out action, and which are therefore shared by all beings capable of acting.

Action

Action, as we have seen, occupies a central place in the construction of human agency undertaken here, and it therefore suggests itself as a natural starting point for discussion, considering, too, that this is an enquiry into the normativity of practical reason and that practical reason is reason as it applies to action. But what exactly is meant here by *action*? As a generic term, action is used in a variety of different ways and is ordinarily taken to mean anything done (a deed or an act committed) or any behaviour or conduct engaged in. In this generic sense, action is clearly a rather loose term that can be used in reference to any number of different things so long as they involve someone doing something, or even only something being done. But the meaning of action we are interested in is technical and therefore much narrower, referring as it does to a privileged class designating what may be considered deeds and conduct *par excellence*.

So then, how do we go about selecting this special class of deeds and conduct properly so called that deserve the name *action* as paradigm cases of doing? My strategy will be comparative: precisely because action singles out a special class, I will consider different kinds of behaviour or conduct and compare their main features in order to arrive finally at full-fledged action.[42]

We work from basic case to paradigm case, and the most basic form of doing from which to start is what might be called *spontaneous conduct*, neither controlled nor driven by any purpose, examples being blushing, hiccupping and blinking. While such spontaneous acts do count as forms of conduct on the ground that they always involve someone's doing something, they lack two fundamental characteristics of action, these being purpose and control. Indeed, these acts tend simply to 'happen' or to 'come about' in an event-like manner in that the person or subject

---

[41] This comports with the transcendental approach, which consists in singling out features that can be argued to be necessary for thought and action, and in deriving therefrom the truth of other necessary features whose necessity is not immediately apparent. The resulting set, ideally, would capture features both necessary and distinctive, such as apply *invariably* across an entire group and *exclusively* to that group.
[42] As this idea of full-fledged action suggests, the comparative strategy here adopted is not blind but is rather guided by a sort of benchmark, what was just referred to as a paradigmatic case of doing. This manner of proceeding is standard in action theory: see, eg, Velleman (2004: 281–3).

with whom they originate is playing a passive role, certainly aware of what he or she is doing but not in any way *willing* this conduct or engaged in it: much more its outward expression than its source, much more a locus of physiological and kinetic phenomena than a thinking subject. This gives only a pallid idea of what an actor is, and spontaneous conduct therefore falls quite short of the standard I am calling *action*.

For something that will more closely resemble action, then, we have to introduce purpose and control. This yields a teleological kind of conduct, whose two fundamental traits make it more specific and hence less inclusive than what can be found at the base level. More to the point, purpose and control narrow our range to a kind of conduct that might be called *reflexive*, as exemplified by my realising that my glasses are falling, thereupon swinging my arm out in an attempt to catch them before they hit the floor and break. This is both controlled (since my movement follows that of my glasses and is consistent with an attempt to keep them from hitting the floor), and purposive (since there is an aim involved, which is that of protecting my glasses). Hence, we say that whenever someone does something for a purpose and controls it, rather than being controlled by it or passively receiving it, the resulting conduct is at least reflexive. As much as this (reflexive) conduct may be active, however, in the sense of its requiring an active role on the subject's part, it is not yet intentional. This is because events unfold too quickly to give one any opportunity properly to *intend* anything: 'when you extend your hand reflexively, you react before you know it', and only afterwards do 'you observe your reaction' (Velleman 1996: 722). Here, conduct can in a sense be said to precede any acceptance, knowledge or endorsement of what is done: true, the act is one we might end up appreciating post facto (with consequences we might end up welcoming and may even have willed had we only had foreknowledge of them at the time of the act), but at *that* time, neither the act nor its consequences could have been genuinely sought or willed.

Reflexive conduct can thus be described as controlled and purposive yet unintentional, a characterisation that sets the stage for the next level, where we find conduct that is controlled and purposive as well as intended. An example might be someone waking up to a sunny day one Sunday morning and deciding to make the most of it by going out for a long walk instead of doing the usual house-cleaning. In contrast to the kind of conduct just described as reflexive, where there is no time really to *think* about what we are doing, except *after* the fact, this form of conduct does come about as a result of such a reflective, pondered moment of decision and is therefore a case of conduct not only purposely but also knowingly carried out by someone who actually *meant* to do whatever it was that he or she did. Conduct at this level of action I will therefore call *reactive*, since its mechanics are those of an immediate, albeit intentional, response to a certain state of affairs, meaning that this conduct unfolds by means of a combination of mental states and attitudes (such as my realising that this is a beautiful, sunny day and my feeling that it would be a shame not to take advantage of it), coupled with prompting coming from the outside (in the example, a sunny day). Reactive conduct can be considered such only if it is essentially driven by internal forces that might cumulatively be referred to as *inclinations*, a broad term that I take to include any number of pattern-like instinctive impulses and desires, whether primary (such as hunger, greed or the need to sleep), constructed (such as a *sommelier*'s response to the bouquet of a fine wine), or otherwise individual (such as a specific craving for *Sachertorte* or a predisposition for risk-taking). This inclinational component is essential, in that no reaction could be elicited without it. Reactive conduct can thus be understood as any conduct resulting from an interaction between someone's inclinations and the environment. The environment functions as an incentive or a disincentive, as the case may be, and correspondingly engages or disengages the subject's inclinations, with this person behaving in response to the stimuli coming from the environment (a response secured by the interaction of the environment with the inclinations). Reactive conduct thus consists in an adaptive reaction to changing conditions in the world around us, a reaction guided by our inclinational response to our construction, appreciation or awareness of the environment: the environment provides a constant flow of stimuli that may or may not prompt the agent into action, and the agent will fashion in response to these stimuli an inclinational reaction that may consist in active engagement (a drive to intervene in the world), or in a shrinking away from any action, or even in a turning away or recoiling from whatever the stimulus was.[43]

As much as control, purpose and intention may be central to our practical mode of existence, and may account for a large part of it, they do not account for the whole of it nor, for that matter, do they make up the core of what I consider to be action *par excellence*. In order to get there, we need a further, accreting element the incorporation of which yields what I will refer to as *principled conduct*, so called because it consists in conduct that depends essentially on our adoption of rules, general standards, guidelines, criteria, schemes, plans, and the like, which might cumulatively be referred to as principles. The final element thus consists of principles, relying on which we get *action* proper, a form of conduct essentially different from the reactive types of conduct so far considered, for on this higher plane we no longer have the immediacy of response necessitated or essentially driven by instinct and inclination: instead of reacting or adapting to a stimulus, situation or environment that engages a more or less automatic or deep-seated drive, we act in pursuit of a principled end or proceed from a standard or idea that certainly does function as a medium of interaction with the environment but, just as crucially, enables us to behave independently of whatever the situation happens to be, or it enables us to overcome this situation if the relevant standard requires it. Principles are in this sense understood as irreducible to inclinations and as independent of the play of stimulus and response: inclinations are strictly tied to stimuli in a way that makes them contingent; conduct based on principles, by contrast, can chart its own course

---

[43] Korsgaard (2009: 98) has expressed the same thought by noting that conduct 'requires both an intentional movement and a representation or conception of the world'.

and stay true to it and in this sense can be considered non-contingent. Precisely for the same reason, principles can be said to define the kind of individual one wants to be or, once taken up, the kind of individual one is.[44]

This form of conduct can be illustrated by going back to the example of someone with a craving for *Sachertorte* and who cannot resist having a bite or two once the cake is spotted. If this person responds to the occasion by going ahead and having a slice, then he or she can be said to have behaved reactively to a stimulus, consisting in the availability of a food that is experienced as delicious; if, however, on such an occasion we resolved to resist the temptation, then we would be said to have behaved not just with control, purpose and intention (all of which are consistent with an inclinational response to a stimulus) but also on a principled basis. The occasion would not just be 'felt', experienced or perceived, but evaluated, and our response to it would be not just reactive but guided by a principle, meaning that we evaluate the situation as one that is likely to tempt us into a gratifying yet unhealthy form of conduct, and we decide to avoid that risk by conforming to the healthy principle that we had set for ourselves when we decided to have a balanced diet. In summary, if instead of acting contingently on the short-term basis of whatever feeling or desire makes the strongest demand on us when the occasion arises or when a stimulus elicits that feeling or desire, we choose to act in view of the long-term and general consideration of what seems best all-around, in such a way that the extemporary pressure of inclination or impulse can be recognised and overcome, or otherwise taken into account consistently with the principle we are acting from, then we will have principled conduct. Principled conduct should not be mistaken for virtuous conduct (as when resolving to forgo dessert, for this is just one instance of it), but rather describes the broader (yet still specific) category of conduct determined not simply by circumstance but by something (a reasoned principle) that enables us to take into view the larger picture of what lies beyond this or that circumstance: this is conduct by *action* rather than by reaction.[45]

The difference between action and reaction is crucial to this entire discussion and so needs to be articulated a bit further. We have already seen that reactive conduct, though it may be controlled, purposive and intentional, is, owing to two related dependencies that characterise it, really contingent. The first of these is a dependence on the inclinations, which at this level ultimately decide what we end up doing (or at least they function as the weight that tips the scale when we decide to act in one way or another); and the second is a dependence on circumstance, meaning that the situation before us functions as a force in its own right in shaping our conduct. In both of these respects there is a *controlling* influence on our

---

[44] This point is argued with great force in van Willigenburg (2004: 47–8).

[45] The same idea (of principled conduct) has been expressed by Joseph Raz (1999: 38–42) through a distinction between control and guidance: principled conduct is not just controlled but guided, and we are said to *guide* our conduct when, in addition to *controlling* our inclinations (which essentially amounts to a *constraint* on action, however effective it may be), we look beyond and impart a broader sense of *direction* to whatever it is that we decide to do.

conduct, in the sense that we could possibly act otherwise but end up not doing so on account of these two forces, one of them internal (the inclinations) and the other external (circumstance). And the connection between them is given by the previously discussed mechanics of stimulus and response, since the inclinations are especially liable to be engaged when the occasion for them arises, and the interplay tends to be automatic, with little, if anything, going on in between. Not so in the case of *action*, the core component of what I am calling principled conduct, which differs fundamentally from reaction in both of these respects. This is because action is *deliberative* and therefore proceeds in the way it does on the basis of a reasoned assessment of the situation at hand, an assessment that breaks the tight bond between stimulus and response at work in reactive conduct. Thus, in the first place, action breaks the dependency of conduct on the inclinations: it can in this sense be described as *proactive* rather than reactive. In the second place, action breaks our dependence on circumstance: it can in this sense be said to play a *guiding* role, for there is a standard involved in the assessment of the circumstance that we are called upon to respond to, and this standard or principle is independent of what that same circumstance would otherwise suggest or encourage. The principle is independent to the extent that (a) it is followed *despite* what the inclinations impel us to do, or at least it explains why we chose to act as we did; and (b) it has been worked out or endorsed *before* a situation arises that calls those inclinations into play. There is also a third way in which principles can be described as independent; for it may happen that a principle is worked out *in process*, just as a situation comes up or unfolds that we somehow have to deal with, and in this case (a sort of learning experience, in the sense that we figure things out as we go along), we can still be said to be acting independently of extemporary forces precisely because we are dealing with them on the basis of a reasoned discussion, which might be a monological discussion (reasoning on our own) or a dialogical one, carried out in the course of an exchange with someone else.

In all three ways, our acting can be described as that of full-fledged action, its distinguishing feature being the intervening process by which an immediate, inclinationally controlled reaction to a stimulus is turned into a reasoned response decided on the basis of an independent consideration or a general standard. This is not to say that action *bypasses* the inclinations at the root of reactive conduct, for no such thing can take place, short of our becoming automata or humanoid creatures devoid of the passional component of the human way of experiencing life. So, instead of bypassing this reactive component, action takes it into account and incorporates it as a necessary ingredient of human sensibility, but an ingredient which can be fashioned into something other than raw impulse, in such a way as to enable us to act in accord with a standard. And this is exactly what happens in the case of action. Its standards embody a kind of generality that makes them irreducible to inclinations, and in fact their point is often enough to *counter* the forces of inclinations. This brings into the equation a mediating element that loosens the strict connection by means of which an external stimulus prompts in the subject a corresponding reaction by the engagement or disengagement of a certain inclination. Unlike reactive conduct, then, action—its principled counterpart—is adaptive by virtue of being mediating rather than by virtue of mere reaction. And, while subjects performing actions do respond by inclination, this reactive component does not gain control, for it can be outweighed or displaced by general standards, which in this sense function as the driving force, thus making this kind of conduct more volitional than voluntary, more idea-driven than passion-driven or bound by circumstance. So described, principled conduct differs from an inclinational-reactive response by bringing into play a further element, and this further element makes it a form of action. For this reason, besides being attributed to a subject, principled conduct can be said to be *performed* by a subject. Accordingly, it is only when conduct is principled that action in the strict sense is generated. Strictly speaking, we have no action unless some guiding general standard or principle is incorporated into, and orients, conduct.

In summary, we have seen four basic forms of conduct. The first three forms (spontaneous, reflexive and reactive conduct) encompass among them control, purpose and intention, yet none of these traits can make our conduct anything more than a reaction: it is not conduct that we really *choose* to engage in; rather, it 'happens' to us as passive recipients. That means that conduct on this level can at best be *attributed* to someone: it cannot properly be described as conduct that someone *performs*, for this implies on the part of the agent an active, guiding role that can only come about once the connection that brings agents under the controlling influence of inclinations 'switched on or off' by external stimuli is broken. Only at a higher level—that of principled conduct, which breaks the double bind of circumstance-activated impulses and inclinations—can one be described as doing something in actively performing. Central to this form of conduct is what I have called *action* proper, in which an agent acts on the basis of a plan, standard or principle, either worked out in advance or in the process of reasoning about what to do. In either case, an independent element is introduced that mediates between stimulus and response and provides a fuller measure of character, if nothing else because it opens up a space in which we can choose to act differently from the way in which instinct, given the situation at hand, might dictate. We thus have a general sense of doing (conduct at large) and a specific sense (principled conduct) that narrows the range of possible conduct to action proper, in which agents are seen fully as beings capable of responding to the environment in the multifold, proactive way just described. It is only in this stricter sense that the term *action* will be understood as relevant to the discussion that follows, and it has to be understood in this way unless specified otherwise.

Human Agency

A human agent can thus be defined as anyone capable of action: what makes someone a human agent is a capacity not only for reaction (which is wanton and can go any which way) but also for conduct framed in view of one or more principles into which are embedded principles providing guidance.[46] This is called principled conduct, and it is defined by the very set of capacities, those of human agency, by which it is enabled.[47] This is an entire complex of capacities, but they crucially involve an ability to step back and act in ways not dictated by circumstance or inclination, and hence an ability to reason about the practical situation at hand and give ourselves a sense of possibility and direction that would otherwise not be available. An inability to do this would mean that we cannot properly deem ourselves to be human agents.[48]

The capacity for action crucially relies on certain dispositional capacities (dispositional in the sense that, except for any interfering factors, they come into play whenever the relevant occasion arises). These dispositional capacities function as prerequisites or preconditions of action: they are in this sense *constitutive* of human agency, in that no action, and thus no agency, would be possible without them. Let us see, then, how human agency is further characterised by these necessary enabling capacities.

Let us start from the general standards constitutive of principled conduct, and so of action: principles cannot be worked out by relying on perception alone, that is, on an ability to receive inputs (or sensory data) from the environment and identify them as being of one sort or another. If we are to frame practical principles or devise plans of action—indeed, if we are to base our conduct on any sort of principle we set for ourselves—we need to be able to have a representation of the world more richly articulated than that which mere perception makes possible, meaning it will not suffice to identify external stimuli and respond to them accordingly, in a reactive or spontaneous way: it will also be necessary to *reflect* on these stimuli. Hence, the first precondition of action: a capacity for reflection, or *reflectivity*.

Reflectivity is the general capacity to think before we act, or to take a critical standpoint from which to assess a situation and hence not be forced into a certain line of conduct just because this is what the present circumstance or the inclinations engaged by it urge. Reflectivity, in other words, is the mediating element that

---

[46] The notion of wanton I have taken over from Frankfurt (1971: 10–4), and it should be defined only by reference to what is random, without also necessarily bringing into play all the other traits of wantonness, such as malicious or spiteful conduct or licentiousness or sexual promiscuity. As much as wanton conduct may include these traits, they should not be understood as essential to it: they are rather potential consequences that *follow* from the randomness, that is, from the lack of guiding criteria.

[47] It should clearly emerge from this formulation that human agency is a *capacity* for action rather than the action itself, the done deed, a conduct performed. This is consistent with sometimes, and even frequently, acting by mere reaction to whatever stimulus excites an inclination. In fact, human agency should not be confused with *actual* adherence to principle: what is essential to human agency is instead the *ability* to act from a principle or standard, and hence the ability to break the bond between stimulus and reaction that seems to assert itself as the default mode of conduct.

[48] The term *human agent* is being used here to designate an agent in general, and *human agency* to designate agency in general (the two pairs are interchangeable), simply because it is with human beings that we paradigmatically associate the basic capacity at hand: it is humans that we typically think of when we describe a capacity to take a perspective and act on a different basis than that of the inclinations. Neither this remark, however, nor the use I am making of the term *human agent*, should be taken to mean that non-human beings cannot be agents in the strict, technical sense specified. The reason for my usage is explained in greater detail above.

makes it possible for us to step back and take a perspective on the situation before us, in such a way that we are not confined to the blind mechanism of stimulus and reaction. Our reflective capacity enables us to respond to the promptings of the environment not simply by yielding to our likings and desires but by taking into account the principles we endorse.[49] It is these principles that offer the standpoint from which to evaluate all those forces, both internal and external, which make a claim on us in the here and now. So, instead of doing what seems most appealing (because most likely to satisfy an initial desire) or most natural (because the situation makes it seem that way), we can create a situation in which these forces are not necessarily constraining; that is, we can bring to bear on the matter a principle, or a reflective standpoint in light of which other practical possibilities for action become apparent, in such a way that *we* cause our own conduct instead of our impulses causing us (or determining our choices and conduct and hence the kinds of persons we end up being). As an essential and qualifying capacity of human agency, then, reflectivity enables us to respond non-reactively to the promptings of the environment by bringing into play a standard on the basis of which the immediate givens of circumstance and inclination can be critically assessed, thereby opening for ourselves practical options that would otherwise be invisible to us.

But it takes more than reflectivity to account for the whole of what is distinctive about human agency. In fact, reflectivity links up conceptually to other capacities that derive from (some dimensions of) it. This is because reflectivity, in enabling one to reflect on one's conduct, gives one as well the ability to reflect on oneself. In turn, self-reflection gives one *self-consciousness*, a turning inward on oneself and one's inner states. And self-consciousness takes two connected but conceptually independent forms of awareness: on the one hand, the *awareness of one's self as composite*, as made up of mutually irreducible components; on the other hand, the *awareness of this self as an individuality*, existing as such in distinction to the environment and to other subjects. We will therefore want to take a closer look at self-consciousness in both of its components.[50]

To begin with, self-consciousness enables one to see that even though the self functions as a whole, in unity, it does not form a single, undifferentiated substance but is rather a compound, its components being one's different inclinations (the instincts, the impulses, the desires, the drives, and so on). And through this discovery one comes to appreciate that the unity of the self consists not in a state given to one but in a construction, in a composition and synthesis by which one's multiple elements work together.[51] These elements exert forces that drive one's action in different directions not necessarily compatible or coherent with each another— hence the synthesis needed to achieve continuity of action. A subject will not have

---

[49] As Connie Rosati (1995: 61) puts it, a reflecting self 'comes to dissociate herself from some of her desires, motivations, and traits, while identifying with others. This capacity to step back, to engage in self-reflection, gives persons a kind of freedom from identity with their immediate activities or their immediate motivational tendencies'.

[50] Self-consciousness is considered a distinctive element of human agents and dealt with in some detail in Korsgaard (2009: 109–32).

[51] Cf Korsgaard (2002: 125–32).

any coherent conduct unless the subject can reduce to unity (or at least to a working whole) the forces operating within itself,[52] a unity to achieve which one must prioritise; and prioritise *consciously*, establishing among the elements of the self a ranking on which basis to determine what course of action one should take on any particular occasion.[53] This task requires that one choose the principles from which to act,[54] and this choice in turn requires reasoning and deliberation.[55] For in order to prioritise the constituents of the self, subjects must take into account not only their raw instinctual powers but also the role played by logic (their logical force). In other words, human agents must weigh the reasons for and against acting on the claims of this or that component, by considering the resulting course of conduct and what it leads to, the advantages and disadvantages it carries, thereby taking the larger picture into view.

Thus, human agents have a capacity for reasoned conduct—a capacity that would not be possible but for the self-consciousness by which we can reflect on the components of the self. This capacity ultimately originates in reflectivity but moves one step further: under reflectivity we can reflect on the pull of our inclinations, but the capacity for reasoned conduct enables us to transform the pull of our inclinations into *reasons*. This ability to grasp, work with and process reasons I will call *rationality*. Rationality, in a nutshell, describes our responsiveness to reasons: a rational person is understood as one who can understand, respond to and act from reasons. Rationality enables us to work out principles and take them into account as determinants of conduct, by building them into our general framework of action and giving them, accordingly, the proper practical weight. It is therefore by virtue of our rationality that some of the forces bearing on action are lent specific force (or endowed with a distinctive significance) and are prioritised over other forces or influences. Thus, the ability to act for reasons adds another layer of reflection, and though it does not *stay* the forces of instinct, for these still operate within the self and can therefore tilt action this way or that, it does free us from a strict dependence on such forces by giving us the power to *choose* whether or not to be guided by inclinations.[56] The demands of these inhabitants of the self are filtered by rationality and fashioned into principles that synthesise and unify them, and in this way, principles become the ultimate basis of action.[57] This means that not only

---

[52] On this requirement, calling for unity of action, see Korsgaard (2009: 18–26).

[53] On the need to prioritise, see Korsgaard (2009: 107–8).

[54] This is a kind of choice that only human agents have the ability to make. In the words of Korsgaard (2009: 127), 'unlike the other animals, we are conscious of our causality, and it is therefore up to us how we exercise it. We choose the laws or principles of our own causality'.

[55] On this need to reason and deliberate, see Korsgaard (2009: 120–1).

[56] In this function, rationality can be said to achieve what Kant referred to as negative freedom, meaning our independence from determination by desire and inclination: rationality is what enables principled conduct, by which expression I mean precisely the human ability not to be determined by such alien causes as desires and inclinations. In the words of Schneewind (1998: 20), 'desires are among the necessary conditions of human action, but they are not sufficient conditions'. On negative freedom, see Kant (1930: 121–2), and Kant (1956 AK 5: 28–30). For critical remarks, see Allison (1998), Hill (1998) and Guyer (2005: 115–45).

[57] Cf Korsgaard (2009: 117–32).

does self-consciousness force reasons upon the agent, but self-consciousness also makes reasoned conduct the hallmark of action, which is typically the product of a reflective attitude. Reasoned conduct depends on the ability to have reasons for doing or not doing something. This involves weighing such reasons when several come to bear on the matter, as well as working several reasons together into a coherent whole, or into a wider scheme, and considering the consequences of action in choosing between alternative courses of action. Rationality, in short, is what makes it possible for us to have action as distinct from mere reaction. The ability to appreciate reasons and act on this basis therefore specifically and distinctively describes anyone capable of action, and so anyone who is an agent; which in turn makes rationality essential to human agency, an essential element in the definition of human agency.

The second form of self-consciousness is that by means of which we gain an awareness of our individuality, that is, of our separate existence as individuals independently of other subjects. This awareness enables us to distinguish between our own determinants of action and heteronomous determinants of action. Our own determinants are of a kind that derive from our free choice, and following which we are said to act on principle; heteronomous determinants are, by contrast, those that are imposed on us, not only by the environment but also by other agents. Whenever a course of action is imposed on us, we can regard ourselves as the *means* to that conduct rather than its authors; if, by contrast, we can override the heteronomous imposition, we can to that extent deem ourselves to be the authors of our own actions. This is not to say that we must filter out *all* heteronomous determinants *all* of the time (for these are bound to have at least some influence on us at least some of the time). Authoredness requires, rather, that we retain an ability to *choose* whether we ought so to be determined, such that the ultimate responsibility for our action rests with us. Stated in the negative, we *cannot* be described as self-guided (the authors of our own conduct) if we cannot filter out the heteronomous determinants. We *can* be considered the author of an action only if the action is not forced upon us from outside, that is, only to the extent that we put it to use by freely choosing our action independently of heteronomous forces of determination. This capacity for self-determination we can refer to as *autonomy*.[58] Autonomy means self-governance. It turns us into genuine agents, that is, authors of our own conduct and self-legislating subjects capable of establishing a rule over ourselves.

Autonomy presents two interconnected dimensions, one in the negative and one in the positive:[59] we are autonomous in the negative sense in so far as we are not bound by any external authority, and in the positive sense in so far as we can give a law to ourselves, in that we have a capacity to choose or work out standards

---

[58] So understood, as the capacity for self-determination, autonomy is a clearly Kantian concept, on which see Kant (1956 AK 5: 3–35) and Kant (1959 AK 4: 431–6). Cf Allison (1998: 273–302) and Wood (1999: 156–90).

[59] This twofold dimension of autonomy is presented in Reath (2006: 127–31).

by which to govern our action. By autonomy is thus meant, in the negative, our independence from standards imposed from the outside and, in the positive, our capacity to select or devise standards of conduct, standards that count as authoritative either because they are our own making (we are their authors) or because we decide upon reflection to follow their guidance (they exert a certain pull on us, and we endow them with authority by our decision to act on them). And because a standard is a criterion serving as a general guide to action, the positive dimension of autonomy enables not only practical freedom but also self-direction through planning and organisation.[60] In combination, the two dimensions of autonomy (the two ways in which we are said to be autonomous) render the forces exerting pressure on us from the outside as only *influencing* our conduct rather than *determining* it. An autonomous subject is 'someone capable of deciding for herself what to do, and capable of executing these decisions without interference of certain kinds', including coercion and other manipulative and distorting external forces (Copp 2005: 170). As a result, the standards guiding the conduct of autonomous subjects receive their authority from the subjects themselves, to the effect that autonomous subjects are not only 'independent spheres of judgement and choice' but also 'sources of their own actions' and centres of normative guidance, or agents endowed with the power to shape the normative landscape they inhabit (Reath 2006: 207). Autonomy enables agents to set their own ends, rather than having ends imposed on them by others or by circumstances, so these are ends that the acting subject deems worthy of pursuit, and that she accordingly pursues based on her own reasons, on principles of her own choosing. The same attributes therefore apply to the resulting conduct: autonomous conduct is self-directed conduct engaged in for reasons we formulate ourselves.

So conceived, autonomy is a precondition of action: no conduct is principled unless it is on the whole dictated by standards that we choose for ourselves. Any lack of autonomy makes our conduct correspondingly unprincipled: it defeats the idea of principled conduct by turning into extemporary external forces the very principles on account of which our conduct can be described as principled, or as shaped by principles. That is to say that in order for there to be any *action* at all on our part, the principles that account for our conduct must be ones we endorse or interpret as our own, and which we accordingly choose to live by. Our principles, then, can be constitutive of action not just because they are more general and less contingent than the external forces of conduct as determined by the interplay of inclinations and stimuli, but also because we can *identify* with these standards: they define who we are as agents. And the reason why this is possible—why principles can play this role in shaping our identity—is precisely that they have not been imposed on us but have instead been chosen or at least have been willingly adopted. They can be described in this sense as self-governing standards: they define who we are not only by way of their content but also by virtue of their

---

[60] This point is clearly stated in van Willigenburg (2004: 46), among others.

having been autonomously chosen. For these reasons, explaining why there can be no action or any sense of identity without autonomy, I am considering autonomy an essential and defining trait of human agency.[61]

With these points made, we have the groundwork on which to build the case for human agency as a practical concept. The argument so far has been that action is not only controlled, purposeful and intentional but also principled; that principled conduct is made possible by a capacity to reflect; that agents are consequently capable of reflection; that the capacity for reflection—reflectivity—produces self-consciousness; that self-consciousness makes an agent aware of both the internal components of the self (the inclinations) and the heteronomous determinants of action (circumstances and other people), and that this awareness, enabling agents to lead an existence distinct from the forces internal to their selves and from the heteronomous determinants of action, brings with it two further capacities: rationality (stemming from one's independence from the internal components of the self) and autonomy (meaning independence from the heteronomous determinants of action). In brief, reflectivity goes through self-consciousness to accomplish rationality and autonomy, and although both of these originate in reflectivity, they elaborate on it. For rationality and autonomy do not simply function as variants of the capacity to *reflect* on action but also entail the capacity to *act on reasons* and *independently* to *determine* what these reasons should be, or what standards should form *the grounds of action*. Thus, whereas reflectivity, rationality and autonomy all connect conceptually to one another, none is reducible to one of the others, for each encapsulates a different aspect of human agency. This means that rationality and autonomy come into play alongside reflectivity in making up the foundation of human agency: human agency is founded on reflectivity, and therefore on the capacity to guide action by way of autonomously chosen reasons (whence the complementary foundational roles of rationality and autonomy). Reflectivity, rationality and autonomy therefore provide the skeleton of human agency, its most basic content. And human agency can be defined as the capacity to make decisions independent of internal extemporary forces and external interferences, establishing in this way not only what form of conduct to adopt but also the reasons on which to base such conduct. Stated otherwise, human agency is the capacity to act on models established by reflective, rational and autonomous choice; and human agents are subjects capable of acting on self-imposed reasons, reasons they have worked out for themselves exercising their capacity for reflection.

A final clarification is in order before we turn to the implications that this construction has for the normativity of practical reason. What I described as the traits constitutive of human agency (reflectivity, rationality and autonomy) are relevant in the context of this discussion about the normativity of practical reason only by

---

[61] This character of autonomy can be appreciated also by bearing in mind that what gives us autonomy is our awareness of our individuality, separateness and independence. And this awareness in turn we get from our self-consciousness, which figures as a distinguishing feature of agents, what makes agents different from non-agents.

virtue of their role as preconditions of action. As such they have a *conceptual* function. They state the conditions without which there can be no action, and this renders them conceptual as distinct from psycho-physical traits; they are capacities *attributed* to agents rather than characteristics describing their psychological and physical make-up (and in this sense, as attributed capacities, they act more as properties than as traits). My point in this section, in other words, has not been to single out the psychological, much less the physical, characteristics that make it possible for us to engage in action (as previously defined). Rather it has been to single out the conceptual properties on the basis of which someone can be regarded as an acting subject, or someone capable of action: the interest has lain not so much in showing how action is (physically and psychologically) possible as in illustrating what *constitutes* action, and hence what traits are constitutive of human agency. The account of human agency defended here should in this sense be interpreted as a kind of 'creation myth', that is, as a narrative aimed at clarifying the *nature* of human agency rather than about its psychology or biology. The attempt, in this narrative, has been to block out some central features of what I take to be our self-understanding *qua* individuals capable of engaging in action, and this understanding is best elucidated by looking not at the material substratum of action (meaning the psychology and biology describing how human agents actually think and act and how their action can actually be performed) but at the concepts through which action is defined. While the practice in question (the practice understood as action) does certainly involve an acting subject equipped psychologically and biologically, and so amenable to a psycho-physical description (among several others), the description I am interested in is that which brings out the *idea* of action, and this idea is something that can be grasped without taking into account any of the functional elements of action: human action and agency can be appreciated apart from these other elements. The reason for this is precisely that human agency *is* a concept (or, to be more accurate, it is a practice defined through a family of interrelated concepts), and this assures it of independence from all the psycho-physical elements that accompany action and make its performance possible.

The reason for taking a conceptual approach to action and disregarding its psychology and biology is given by the overall concern of this discussion, a discussion devoted to exploring the foundation of normativity. Normativity cannot be brought into any straightforward connection with psycho-physical traits, for these are factual or empirical traits inhabiting the dimension of the 'is', in contrast to normativity, which inhabits the 'ought'. That the two categories of 'is' and 'ought' are separate is an old philosophical saw, albeit not one that has gone altogether unchallenged.[62] The separation between 'is' and 'ought' is argued on the ground that facts differ in kind from norms: norms cannot be reduced to facts, and they retain a conceptual separation from facts, for in the first place having different

---

[62] The *locus classicus* where one can find this thesis is Hume (1888: 469–70). For a sustained attempt to deny the categorial distinction between 'is' and 'ought', see the now classical essay by Searle (1969: 175–98).

properties from facts,[63] and in the second place, owing to the denial of the possibility of deriving one set of properties from the other. The general principle at work here is that no instance of a category defined by a certain set of properties can legitimately be obtained from a set including no instance of that category or displaying none of its properties, and this applies to norms and facts, whose difference is qualitative, making it logically impossible to derive the former from the latter.[64] The logical non-derivability of the 'ought' from the 'is' renders the fields they designate conceptually autonomous, one and the other. And it is this logical divide between 'is' and 'ought' that makes it unjustified to attempt to arrive at normativity by appealing to psychological traits. Such a move would imply a leap in the argumentative process, which in turn would require an appropriate transformation rule for its justification.[65]

In short, normativity belongs with the 'ought' and so cannot be grounded in a system of psycho-physical traits, for these belong with the 'is', and the 'is' will not work as a source for the 'ought': a foundation so conceived would amount to a transition from one category (the 'is') to another (the 'ought') none of whose properties can be derived from any of the properties of the former. The difficulties involved in attempting such a derivation are formidable indeed, and it is for this reason that the source of normativity is being constructed here as a set of conceptual properties rather than as a set of psycho-physical traits.[66] Indeed, while normative predicates and statements cannot be equated with conceptual ones or brought into any straightforward connection with them, the distinction between the two spheres—norms and concepts—is not so rigid and unbridgeable as that between norms and facts, which is more like a dichotomy than a distinction.

Human Agency and Normativity

On the modified Kantian approach, the normativity of practical reason is grounded in a (pragmatic) definition of human agency. In this, the approach shows a great deal of continuity with Kant's own account, in which the normativity of

[63] On the dominant view, the difference between 'is' and 'ought'—between facts and values, description and prescription—lies in the different degrees of objectivity by which statements pertaining to these different spheres can be ascertained: we cannot be as objective about the validity of norms, values, and the like, as we can about the truth or accuracy of descriptive statements. For a critical introduction to this view, see Searle (1969: 182–4). Other properties distinguishing facts from norms are discussed in chapter four.

[64] To derive the 'ought' from the 'is', thus breaching the logical non-derivability of the former from the latter, is to commit what Moore (1903) called the naturalistic fallacy. The same principle also bars a transition from descriptive statements to prescriptive ones. On this point, see Hare (1952: 79–93), Black (1969), Flew (1969), Thomson (1969) and Miller (1981).

[65] On the notion of an argumentative leap or 'jump', and on the related notion of a transformation rule, see Peczenik (1996) and, for a more detailed account, Peczenik (1983).

[66] This makes it clear that my treatment is selective, not intending to establish *all* the features that differentiate human from non-human agents. But as was noted earlier, while this treatment can be supplemented with a biological account of human agency, it retains a conceptual autonomy from such an account.

practical reason is grounded in subjects rather than in the world. Thus, Kant's original account and the modified approach both proceed on the assumption that what makes something normative (what makes it authoritative, binding, valuable) is not an inherent property but its having been so *constituted* by us: a norm is not binding in itself—by virtue of its inherent normativity, a real property of the world. Rather it becomes binding solely by virtue of its relation to human agents. Normativity could not emerge but for a constituting act on the part of human agents, and in this sense the normativity of objects is said to depend on fundamental features of human agents.[67]

The dependence of normativity on human agency can be explained by pointing out the conceptual connection that binds normativity to reasons. Normativity is reason-centred, in the sense that normativity will not arise except through the use of reasons: reasons *for* something and reasons *against* something; reasons why something *ought* to be done and reasons why it *ought not* to be done—reasons that in either case lend special force to the idea that this thing ought to or ought not to be done, for it is only through reasons that human agents can genuinely be engaged and prompted into action as agents properly so called. Indeed, reasons will appeal and make sense only to human agents, who alone, among all living subjects, are responsive to reasons. This point finds a clear statement with Joseph Raz (1999: 67), who observes that 'aspects of the world are normative in as much as they or their existence constitute reasons for persons, that is, grounds which make certain beliefs, moods, emotions, intentions, or actions appropriate or inappropriate'. On this view, it is the capacity to recognise something as a reason and to respond to it in some appropriate manner that endows normativity with a world of practices and events otherwise normatively inert: nothing is innately normative; things draw their normative force from the outside, specifically, from human agents. This capacity to use reasons—to appreciate that something is a reason for someone to act—I have described as a distinguishing feature of human agency, and this is to say that human agency not only enters into a conceptual connection with normativity (in that reasons are central to both) but also imparts normativity to the world, by conferring value on some of its parts and attaching reasons to matters that would otherwise be normatively inert. It is therefore through the essential capacity to offer, appreciate and respond to reasons that human agency can legitimately be viewed as the source of normativity.

Importantly, the connection obtaining between the normativity of practical reason and human agency holds true in general, independently of the specific characteristics and subjective dispositions of single human agents. Stated

---

[67] I should reiterate here that my account is specifically concerned with the normativity of practical reason rather than with normativity at large, by which is meant the 'characteristic common to everything that appears on the "ought" side of the distinction between what is and what ought to be' (Dancy 2000: vii). This is a wide class of things inclusive of deontic statements, evaluative considerations and rules originating out of social practices, such as language and etiquette; and it also includes, alongside the practical oughts, having direct implications for conduct, theoretical oughts such as are established by science. So, instead of taking into account the entire spectrum of what counts as an ought, I am only considering that portion of it delimited by the practical uses of reason.

otherwise, the normativity of practical reason depends on the responsiveness to reasons, and this responsiveness, being rooted in the general capacity for self-reflection, describes *any* human agent. This is to say that the normativity of practical reason lies ultimately in a certain basic, non-contingent property of acting subjects, property distinctive to human agency and so attributable to all human agents indiscriminately. The normativity of practical reason, then, derives from a feature that on a pragmatic and transcendental account can be shown to be constitutive of human agency. Therefore, human agency, articulated in terms of reflectivity, rationality and autonomy, can be seen as standing in a conceptual connection with normativity and working as its ground.

To appreciate what is involved in conceiving of human agency as the source of the normativity of practical reason, we ought specifically to consider the role that human agency plays through its defining features. These features give structure to the broadest and most basic self-conception, the kind of conception that agents of necessity have of themselves. Indeed, agents need to form an account of themselves as acting subjects.[68] Such an account comes by way of self-reflection, which, then, produces not only self-consciousness but also a self-conception. Now, the broadest and most basic self-conception that agents of necessity have, which I will call the *minimally necessary self-conception*, derives directly from, and is framed by, the defining features of human agency.

The self-conception informed by human agency is a *necessary* one, since it shapes a way of understanding ourselves that no human agent can coherently change or abandon. This is to say that any failure on our part to conceive of ourselves in keeping with the minimally necessary self-conception will prevent us from describing ourselves as capable of action (as performers of actions): a contradiction would arise between our conception of ourselves and our status as human agents. The minimally necessary self-conception thus defines a view of ourselves that we are not able to forsake without at the same time ceasing to retain our distinctive status as human agents. This feature of the conception places it in a range beyond that of what is optional, in that no clear-thinking human agent can fail to view herself in this way, as someone having a capacity for reflectivity, rationality and autonomy. The minimally necessary self-conception can be understood as necessary, then, because we could not disavow this conception even if by hypothesis we wanted to, for we would then lose our most basic capacities for thought and action.

---

[68] This point is clearly and most convincingly argued in Korsgaard (1996b: 120–2). Her argument, in summary, is that agents must necessarily commit to and be governed by some conception of their practical identity because they would otherwise lose their grip on themselves and be unable to make reasoned choices between different options. This is a practical necessity (we cannot really choose not to have a conception of ourselves that we live by), but it is also importantly a *general* necessity, in that the conception involved (this sense of identity) is understood as something by which to distinguish ourselves, not from *other* agents but from *non-agents:* it is that on account of which we view ourselves as members of humankind, rather than as unique individuals. If we fail to acknowledge a generic practical identity originating in human agency, then we will not be able to act in conformity to *any* self-conception. Hence, the necessity of having a broad conception of ourselves as human agents.

This is a *practical necessity*. By practical necessity I mean that human agents have to avoid inconsistency with the commitments underlying, and implicit in, their status as agents, or as subjects capable of action. This idea can be restated through the concept of a performative contradiction as originally articulated in speech act theory. Speech act theory describes a performative contradiction as something we commit any time we presuppose, claim or imply something that contradicts the content of the speech act we perform. To be sure, the concept of a performative contradiction was originally understood to apply only to a specific practical context, the context of language and communication, but it can be generalised and extended to other practical domains.[69] Performative contradictions take place not only in word but also in deed; that is, we have a performative contradiction when what is explicitly *said* contradicts what the same utterance presupposes (even if only implicitly) in order to make sense, but we also have a performative contradiction when what is explicitly *done* contradicts what the same act presupposes in order to count as an action. A performative contradiction, then, can be described as an inconsistency in conduct (whether in word or deed) whereby the content of an act contradicts the necessary conditions of its existence. Conduct that does not originate in reflectivity, rationality and autonomy is performatively contradictory: it is inconsistent with our acting as human agents and so with our distinctive practical identity.[70] Any act that we carry out, disregarding or contradicting the standards arising out of reflectivity, rationality and autonomy, can thus be said to contradict, by its content, the distinctive conditions that define us as agents: we contradict our distinctive status as human agents, as performers of action, whenever we fail to act autonomously by going through the reflective process of weighing the reasons for and against the chosen course of conduct and acting on that basis. Anything done that is not in keeping with the principles arrived at by reflectivity, rationality and autonomy will imply a performative contradiction in human agency: it will mean that we are acting as if we were not human agents. A tension thus comes about that can be explained conceptually, and which materialises on the level of action.[71]

As the name suggests, the minimally necessary self-conception of an agent as a reflective, rational and autonomous subject is a *minimal* conception, not a full conception; that is, it does not prevent specific human subjects from developing, on this basis, more specific, richer conceptions. The way different individuals come to

---

[69] One such extension of the concept of a performative contradiction has been its use in legal theory. See, in this connection, Alexy (1996) and Alexy (2002b: 35–9).

[70] By *practical identity* I mean the way we understand our existence as acting selves, as individuals moving about in the practical sphere: it is an organising principle by which we order what we encounter in our lives as practical agents. In forging a practical identity, we express a characteristic mode of being, or living, that defines who we are as practical agents and distinguishes us from other like agents.

[71] This idea that behaviour carried out in contradiction to reflectivity, rationality and autonomy brings with it a performative contradiction reveals a conceptual link connecting the modified Kantian approach to pragmatics; which is to say that the modified Kantian approach, in working out a transcendental concept of action, also incorporates a pragmatic component into this concept. I wish to thank Giorgio Bongiovanni for pointing this out to me.

regard themselves, specifying this or that additional self-conception, is largely a subjective matter dependent on any number of factors. We are subjects with particular histories, ideals, social connections, cultural bonds and religious ties. These factors deeply affect the specific identities and self-conceptions we come to take up throughout our lives. But however a self-conception gets specified, it will have to take as its implicit or explicit foundation the ground layer of reflectivity, rationality and autonomy. These are the foundational generic features of human agency that constitute one's necessary and non-contingent self-conception. All further features are contingent on these basic ones and optional, not in the sense that a fuller conception is optional, but in the sense that *how* an agent specifies one's self-conception is largely a matter of choice, which is also in part determined by social factors, a matter of developing this individual feature rather than that. In conclusion, the variety of agent-specific self-conceptions have their starting point as well as their limit in the minimally necessary self-conception common to all agents—a starting point, for it cuts crosswise to include all these specific conceptions and operate as their substratum, distinguishing human agents as such in the practical sphere, the realm of action and agency; and a limit, for it cannot be circumvented in building the variety of specific conceptions. Hence, we cannot think of ourselves in terms of a specific identity unless we first recognise ourselves as beings bestowed with reflectivity, rationality and autonomy. Living up to any particular self-conception implies being a reflective, rational and autonomous subject to the effect that no one exists as a distinctively human agent unless she works from a minimally necessary self-conception.

In this role as the basis of specific self-conceptions, the minimally necessary self-conception acts at the same time as a precondition and as a product of acting subjects. Thus, a kind of dualism is set up. On the one hand, the minimally necessary self-conception exists *before* and *beyond* the agent as a *deep conception* enjoying a good measure of independence from this or that agent, which is to say that the conception is only marginally dependent on one's inclinations, and it cannot be disposed of without loss of one's practical identity, for its constituent features cannot be given up without thereby giving up one's distinctive existence *qua* human agent. At the same time, however, the minimally necessary self-conception is the outcome of the capacity for self-reflection that enables human agents to move about in the practical sphere in specific ways and makes each individual capable of recognising herself as such.

This weak dualism that the minimally necessary self-conception brings about in the human agent can also be explained by way of the contrast between the constituent capacity for reflectivity and the constituent capacity for autonomy. Autonomy enables agents, among other things, to decide for themselves what forms of conduct they should adopt and what reasons they ought to be acting on in doing so. This means that inclinations and heteronomous determinants can have a grip on agents only to the extent that agents themselves choose to heed such inclinations and determinants. Still, especially when addressed to one's self, reflectivity enables agents to shape individually a practical identity by making it possible for these agents to engage in relationships not only with others but also with themselves, thus giving rise to a self-conception. This gives content to a space that originates *with* the human agent but that the human agent cannot simply modify at will—a space not immediately responsive to the subjective inclinations of individual human agents. Hence, the weak dualism in question:[72] at base there lies the minimally necessary self-conception, a single conception whose form and content, though inherent in the agent, *precedes* individual agents and so cannot be established or changed by them; but then this conception is developed into a working conception specific to each agent, and at this point the constituent forces (autonomy on the one hand, reflectivity on the other) come into play. Their interaction and mutual relation enables the human agent to move about in different spheres of action, the one more staid and independent, the other more subjective and self-directed. Importantly, the restraints on one's autonomy that derive from the minimally necessary self-conception originate not outside human agency but in another feature constitutive of human agency, reflectivity. The dualism in question, then, is not imposed by external factors but is rather ultimately dependent on the ability of the capacities defining human agency, especially autonomy and reflectivity, to interact and enter into a mutual relation.

In this deep role as constitutive of practical identity, the minimally necessary self-conception explains in an important way the normativity of practical reason in the account of it offered by the modified Kantian approach. To elaborate upon this point, the deep level at which the conception operates means that it *describes* how human agents are (describing the minimal, necessary features everyone in the class has), at the same time as it also *prescribes* how human agents ought to behave. In its descriptive role, the conception accounts for the general structure of human agents, defining features that every acting subject has. But the conception also carries normative force, defining a model that no agent can afford to ignore without thereby falling outside the boundaries of human agency and so contravening the organising principle expressive of the subject in the practical sphere. Hence, the minimally necessary self-conception provides a necessary foundation, the indispensable horizon out of which we constitute ourselves as human agents. In other words, by virtue of its very role as an enabling condition, the minimally necessary self-conception also functions as a limiting condition, setting a standard that restricts the range of options available to subjects in the practical sphere, thus constraining their freedom of choice. This freedom cannot expand to the point where it contradicts the elements constitutive of human agency, the defining elements of the minimal conception itself.[73] In the end, the minimally necessary self-conception will compel

---

[72] This form of dualism is weak, for it does not imply an ontological duplication of the human agent as distinguished into two separate selves or substances: from an ontological point of view, the agent may well be seen as a single self and substance. Ontological univocity does not prevent the agent from operating in two distinct spheres: a contingent sphere, whose content depends on each agent's subjective inclinations, and a necessary sphere defining the basic status of the human agent and thereby transcending individual agents and their preferences.

[73] On this aspect, see Wood (1999: 70–5).

certain practical choices, those tending to preserve and advance the basic capacities of human agency, and rule out certain others, those that run in quite the opposite direction, posing an obstacle to our flourishing as human agents or even to our acting in a way consistent with human agency.[74]

It is in this normative function that the minimally necessary self-conception accounts for the normativity of practical reason. The demands of practical reason draw their normative force from the minimally necessary self-conception, which in turn originates in human agency and gives substance to the identity of individual agents. More specifically, practical reason exerts normative force by virtue of its close connection with an element—rationality—constitutive of a self-conception contrary to which no human agent can act. The normative force of practical reason derives from the foundational role that rationality plays in forging the practical identity of human agents, for whom there is no option but to comply with the demands of practical reason, for this compliance is required in order to give effect to the minimally necessary self-conception, which cannot be ignored the way one might ignore some other standard or model concerned only with setting out a contingent ideal. Indeed, unlike such surface-level, goal-setting standards, the minimally necessary self-conception operates at a profoundly deep level, forming the basis of human agency, so anything done contrary to it is likely to undermine the identity endowing each person with a distinctive existence in the practical realm. Thus, a failure to heed the demands of practical reason would amount to giving up on something deeper than this or that end: it would cause us to forsake our distinctive status as human agents proper, for these demands come to us by way of the minimally necessary self-conception, which defines the basic, indispensable traits of human agency.

We therefore have a duty to comply with the demands of practical reason, or at least we have to comply with them unless we are ready to give up our distinctiveness as human agents. To reject the demands of practical reason is to reject the minimally necessary self-conception and, more specifically, its rational side; which in turn has the effect of downgrading our practical existence and assimilating us to non-human agents, that is, to subjects incapable of action. Our abiding by normative standards, then, is tantamount to acting in accordance with a self-conception that, while not exhaustive of ourselves *qua* human agents, cannot be avoided by any human agent either: it is inescapable and not something that we can consider an option. And, as just noted, it is in particular the rational side of human agency that we stand to relinquish by disregarding the demands of practical reason, and any loss of rationality translates into a loss of human agency. What is normatively required is what is expressive of the practical identity framed by human agency, and indeed what is constitutive of such an identity. Human agents

---

[74] In setting such conditions, the minimally necessary self-conception can be said to act rather like a principle; its functioning can be compared to the principle of *modus ponens*, which in the words of Korsgaard (2009: 69) 'describes what you do when you draw the conclusion, but it is also a normative principle', giving instructions for working from a given set of premises to draw not simply conclusions, but *valid* conclusions.

are bound by the normative requirements of practical reason because and to the extent that they are human agents and wish to retain that status.[75] The question 'What ought to be done?' can only be resolved once we have a view about who we are: just as in answering the question of what we ought to do we forge a self-image, gaining insight into our selves, which is to say that this self-image shapes an idea of what we ought to do and, indeed, it proves necessary in developing such an idea.

This account of human agency can explain the normative force of the most robust demands of practical reason, namely, the categorical demands that, on a view shaped by Kant's practical philosophy, issue from morality. Therefore, the account can explain the normative force of *any* demand of practical reason. This point receives a full argument in Korsgaard (1997), where the normativity of instrumental reason is discussed from a Kantian stance. Korsgaard criticises as partial both the Humean and the realist explanation of the normativity of instrumental reason: Humeans fail to explain the capacity of instrumental reason to guide human conduct; practical realists, for their part, fail to explain its motivational capacity. Korsgaard uses this criticism to introduce an approach that grounds the normative force of instrumental reason in a Kantian idea of humanity, arguing that humanity has its basis in autonomy. Autonomy, in its turn, links up with rationality. This it does to the extent that (Korsgaard 1997: 219):

> to be rational just is to be autonomous. That is: to be governed by reason, and to govern yourself, are one and the same thing. The principles of practical reason are constitutive of autonomous action.

Rationality, then, passes through autonomy to form part of the very idea of humanity, thus qualifying as an element constitutive of what gives us a distinctively human identity. Even though we do not *always* have to act rationally, any failure to do so will recoil on our identity, in that any irrational conduct we engage in will detract from our autonomy, thus making our identity that much weaker. Out of this connection between autonomy, rationality and humanity emerges the normative force of practical reason. The demands of practical reason exert normative force to the extent that rationality is constitutive of our identity. This normative force attaches properly to the demands of both moral and instrumental rationality, for it is Korsgaard's (1997: 247) argument that even 'conformity to the instrumental principle is . . . constitutive of having a will', and that the will, in its turn, forms a constitutive part of our practical existence and identity as human agents.[76] This means that instrumental reason owes its normative force to its being a case of reason as such, which is to say that an agent failing to heed the demands of reason, instrumental or otherwise, will face loss of identity as an agent. The government of instrumental reason is something we can reject, to be sure, but only on pain of relinquishing our practical existence: 'a person who does not conform to the instrumental principle' forswears her will and so 'becomes a mere location for

---

[75] In Korsgaard's words (1996b: 102): the claim that practical reason has on us ultimately 'takes the form of a reaction against a threat of a loss of identity'.

[76] See also Korsgaard (1997: 253–4).

the play of desire and impulses, the field of their battle for dominance over body through which they seek satisfaction' (Korsgaard 1997: 254).

Korsgaard's argument applies equally to practical identity as this notion is understood in the present section, that is, as defined by reflectivity, rationality and autonomy. I am in agreement with Korsgaard, in other words, in ascribing to rationality, in all of its forms, a constitutive role in shaping the identity of human agents. We cannot act contrary to the demands of practical reason without thereby sacrificing our practical identity. Instrumental reason is normative because, and to the extent that, rationality is constitutive of our practical identity, no differently than the way non-instrumental reason is. Furthermore, the approach accounts, too, for the normativity of prudential reason, this by virtue of the substantial similarity that ties prudential reason to instrumental reason: both kinds of reason exhibit the form of the hypothetical imperative. In conclusion, then, the minimally necessary self-conception defining human agency serves to ground the normativity of hypothetical and categorical imperatives alike. From which it follows that not only moral directives but also the hypothetical ones (in their various forms) find the source of their normative force in the minimally necessary self-conception of human agents as reflective, rational and autonomous subjects. Hence, the unified explanation the modified Kantian account offers of the grounds of the normativity of practical reason: whatever form practical reason may take, its normative force lies in human agency—in its constitutive reflective, rational and autonomous capacities.

A Reply to an Objection

In the previous section, an account of the normativity of practical reason was defended that grounds such normativity in certain capacities understood as necessarily associated with human agency and so as *constitutive* of such agency. In contemporary philosophy, this has come to be known as a 'constitutivist' strategy:[77] it consists in attempting to determine what is constitutive of agency and locating therein the source of the normativity of the statements of practical reason, be they moral, prudential or otherwise action-guiding.

The constitutivist strategy is open to an objection that, if it stands, would prevent one from successfully grounding the normativity of practical reason. The objection is quite simple. It questions the basic assumption at work in the strategy and can be stated thus: even assuming that some capacities can indeed be neces-

---

[77] This label can be found in Enoch (2006: 72), for instance. The constitutivist strategy is explored in Velleman (1996: 2000), Korsgaard (2009) and Rosati (2003), among others, and it actually designates not one but several strategies, or at least several variants of the same strategy. They differ from one another in many important respects, especially in virtue of the fact that they do not necessarily share the same philosophical assumptions and have been devised with an eye to responding to the most diverse theoretical quandaries. No suggestion, then, is being made here that Velleman's, Korsgaard's or Rosati's theories all belong to the same philosophical tradition or proceed from shared metaethical assumptions.

sarily associated with human agency, and that no one can be considered a human agent who does not think and act on the basis of those capacities, why should that be a reason for being a human agent in the first place? The objection, in other words, charges that the constitutivist view takes practical reason to be specifically binding on human agents simply because the standards and dictates of practical reason are conditional on capacities regarded as essential to human agency. But there is nothing about constitutivism that can show human agency itself to be non-contingent, nothing that can show why we have to be human agents so conceived. This means that we can, in effect, dispense with human agency and choose to live under a different guide, and with that done we can ignore the demands of practical reason, for these demands issue from a dispensable view of agency. It may well be—so the objection goes—that by withdrawing from a commitment to act on a conception of ourselves as reflective, rational and autonomous agents, we thereby no longer qualify as *human* agents. But we are not by any account *forced* to proceed in that way: we might even accept the idea of being regarded and regarding ourselves as *non-human* agents, adhering perhaps to the conception that David Enoch (2006: 179) calls 'shmagency', which makes us human agents in every respect but for the fact that we neither acknowledge nor act on the minimally necessary self-conception and so do not regard ourselves as essentially committed to the whole business of performing action. The problem with the constitutivist strategy, in short, is that it fails to provide a necessary foundation for the normativity of practical reason to rest on: it does so to the extent that it fails to rule out the possibility of subjects who might not concern themselves with the project of being human agents after all, or for whom reflectivity, rationality and autonomy are not constitutive of agency, in that their essential interest lies elsewhere, in living up to the standard not of human agency but of shmagency, in such a way that no fundamental contradiction is involved for these subjects if their mode of existence qualifies as one of non-human agency. It is this possibility—of our being non-human agents without really contradicting ourselves—that exposes the constitutivist strategy to the charge of resting the normativity of practical reason on a less than firm foundation.[78]

Now, the question forming the basis of this objection—'Why be an agent?'—is amenable to at least two interpretations involving altogether different issues. These two interpretations should therefore be taken up separately in replying to the objection.

In the first of these two senses, the question at issue properly means: 'Why should we *care* to be agents? What is in it for us?' This is really a question about motivation, and what prompts it is the observation that, on the constitutivist account, no penalty attaches to a failure on our part to satisfy the demands of practical reason: practical reason may well have its own normative force, and this force may well transfer to its directives, but if we can disregard these directives without

---

[78] This objection has been made, among others, by Skorupski (1998: 345), O'Day (1998: 69–2) and Fitzpatrick (2005: 673–7).

suffering any consequences, then there is no reason for us to comply. The constitutivist strategy is untenable, on this view, for it fails to point out any cost that we must bear for having departed from the requirements of practical reason: we therefore have no incentive to satisfy these requirements, and their normative force thus remains idle. This, in essence, is like asking: 'Where is the normativity in a standard that we can ignore at will without being penalised for it?'

Another statement of this objection is by way of Ken O'Day's critique of Korsgaard's argument for the view that reasons are public, or that they can have normative force only to the extent that they can be shared or be made to concern everyone collectively.[79] O'Day agrees with Korsgaard on this point, but he disagrees with her on the way to go about explaining and justifying this public character of reasons: this cannot be done, as Korsgaard believes, on the basis of an individualist, self-centred approach. Reasons and normativity do not originate out of an individual capacity, such as a capacity for reflectively choosing on one's own a course of conduct singled out as preferable to others; reasons and normativity are public through and through, from start to finish, and there is no point at which they can be viewed as individual; therefore, just as they arise out of a collective enterprise linking different persons together, so too, they must be justified on the same (public) basis. Normativity originates and unfolds in a thoroughly public space: it does not have its source in private conscience, for as much as this conscience may formulate and follow its own reasons, it cannot impose them on others or endow them in any relevant sense with normativity properly so called.

O'Day is saying in effect that normativity can only come about as the outcome of a legislating or law-making act and that this cannot be a private process. Private law-making is such that, by definition, the same person plays at once at least two roles, as both law-maker and law-abider. But this is a conceptual impossibility; it presents something of a conundrum. For, if the person empowered to set out normative standards is at the same time empowered to ignore them or leave them unenforced or even repeal them, then this person cannot really be regarded as subject to any standard at all: as legislator, 'it is open to you to undo your legislation and, furthermore, as the executive and judge you may decide whether or not to enforce it and if so how to interpret it' (O'Day 1998: 74). The activity of legislating, in other words, 'cannot be normative if it is constituted by the arbitrary contours of one's private practice' (O'Day 1998: 73). The moment we conflate into the same person the roles of maker, judge and enforcer of normative standards is the moment we have taken leave of normativity. And the reason for this is, on this view, that the standards so produced, without any collective process in which everyone has a role, will not exert any directive power: such standards will not have in them the potential to guide conduct. And the reason why they will not have this power is that no penalty is attached to them: self-legislated, self-imposed standards cannot possibly be backed by a penalty, and this circumstance alone can rob them of binding force and so of normativity.

---

[79] See, in particular, O'Day (1998).

There are two problems with this interpretation of the objection. The first of these is that the objection, so understood, seems to proceed on the assumption that a standard cannot be normative unless it can be enforced: a conceptual link is thus established between normativity and the availability of sanctions. But this is a mistake: a standard does not become normative by providing for a penalty that may be imposed for failing to comply with that standard. To claim otherwise is to conflate two concepts of what it means to be constrained to do something: on the one hand, there is the intangible or otherwise non-physical sense of being *obligated* to do something, and on the other, there is the more physical sense of being *obliged* to do something because forced to, in a way that makes it impossible for us to do otherwise even if we wanted to.[80] Only in the former sense is there an essential connection with normativity; in the latter sense, the connection may be there, but it may equally *not* be, which is to say that it is a contingent connection: a standard may well be normative even without an enforcement apparatus to back it up. To make enforcement a necessary component of normativity, as O'Day does, is to offer a variant of the sanction theory of normativity, under which our 'having an obligation' resolves itself into our 'being *forced* to comply with a standard'. My argument, by contrast, is that these two ideas ought to be kept distinct and that normativity belongs with the former—which is another way of saying that its connection with the former is conceptual, while its connection with enforcement and coercion is not: a standard not backed by an external system of pressures may well be less effective than one that is not backed up in this way, but it retains its normativity nonetheless. The distinction between these two ideas, then, is such that enforcement can *support* normativity but not *define* it. For this reason, enforcement is irrelevant to the question of whether human agency is normative, or to the question of whether it can ground the normativity of practical reason. It may well be that we cannot be *forced* to be human agents, but this has nothing to do with the *normativity* of human agency: it simply means that the constitutivist strategy does not see non-compliance with the standards of human agency as carrying with it a corresponding sanction. But this ought not to be viewed as a failure of the strategy; in fact it is a distinguishing feature, the whole point of the strategy being to account for the *foundation* of normativity. The basic premise of such a foundation cannot be arrived at simply by listing the sanctions that apply to different violations of the standards of practical reason.

---

[80] These two are *stipulated* senses of the participles 'obligated' and 'obliged' that have come into the common store of legal-philosophical language owing to Herbert Hart's statement of the distinction in *The Concept of Law* (1961). It bears mentioning, however, that in non-technical usage the two terms show a fair degree of overlap. *Merriam Webster's Dictionary of English Usage* describes in what way they do overlap and in what way they do not: 'in the sense of being bound or constrained legally or morally, *obligated* and *obliged* are essentially interchangeable . . . when the constraint is applied by physical force or by circumstances, however, *obliged* and not *obligated* is used' (emphasis added) (*Merriam Webster's Dictionary of English Usage* (Springfield, Mass., Merriam-Webster, Inc., 1994) 675, s.v. 'obligated, obliged'). It is in this second sense that *obliged* is being used here with respect to the distinction between what is normative and what is not.

The second problem with the objection is its inaccuracy, in the sense that the constitutivist strategy does, after all, provide for penalties for violating the standards of practical reason, only these are not penalties understood in a conventional sense as impositions brought to bear through an enforcement apparatus. To see what this means, we need only to go back to the conception of human agency introduced earlier, the conception forming the basis of the constitutivist account of normativity that is being considered here. It was observed in that discussion that human agency entails a capacity for principled conduct, that is, for conduct that can be qualified not only as spontaneous, reflexive and reactive but also as guided by general standards. And this enables human agents to behave in ways not controlled by what the inclinations say when engaged by a stimulus; in other words, it enables agents to choose to do otherwise. This ability to work the inclinations into an equation in which not the inclinations but reasoned standards explain why one course of action was chosen over another makes for a deeper and richer subjectivity than that which non-human agents can have, for in this latter case the alternative between different practical choices does not even arise. And the reason is that in this case, one faces a contingent form of subjectivity anchored to extemporary forces and heteronomous determinants, in such a way that one by and large fails to envision or to act on any plan of action different from what these external forces suggest or dictate. This in contrast to *human* agents, who do not behave exclusively by responding immediately to a circumstance but can take in a broader array of considerations, bringing into the equation of action an idea of the kind of person they want to be, a critical image of themselves and of the world in light of which they can evaluate a situation in different ways, seeing into it different possibilities, each of them acquiring meaning alongside the others. It is against the background of the possibilities so uncovered, brought to light and compared that human agents can be said to have properly *chosen* to behave in one way or another: the end result is a far deeper and more structured sense of the self than that which non-human agents can have, whose conduct cannot really acquire a meaning which fits into a broader vision and is backed by reasons for so behaving.

The thrust of these remarks is that we *do* stand to lose something by a decision to relinquish human agency: such a decision carries with it the consequence of depriving us of a complex of faculties without which we can only look to impoverished forms of practical life. There are in particular two ways in which we would stand affected by turning our backs on human agency, thereby ignoring practical reason and the normative requirements that flow from it: on the one hand, we would be discarding the menu of options that has become available to us by taking a critical assessment of the situation at hand (we would therefore be behaving as we do simply because we cannot choose to behave in any other way); and at the same time we would forgo the deeper and more complex subjectivity that such a wider spectrum of possibilities would open us up to, for (among other reasons) it would not be a meaningful mode of practical existence for us to behave as we do simply owing to an inability to conceive of or act on anything different from the course we happen to follow. This overall loss of potential and depth may not be a sanction in the strict sense of a penalty inflicted from the outside through a system for the enforcement of rules, to be sure, but it is precisely the point of the modified Kantian version of the constitutivist approach not to make normativity essentially dependent on the threat of sanction that comes with a failure to comply with normative standards; and, what is more, the loss in question still qualifies as a bad consequence that attaches to having failed to live up to a standard—that much it does have in common with traditional sanction theories of law, and its strength lies precisely in its *not* also sharing a coercive side with such theories. Indeed, rules enforced coercively from the outside render us accountable in the first place to *others* (and we may not care what others think, or we may not view the sanction posed as a real threat), but rules originating in human agency and enforced from the inside in the form of a reduced subjectivity make us accountable in the first place to *ourselves*. Moreover, there is no escaping from such a consequence either, as there is from the consequences of breaking the law (in that we might be able to fool an enforcement system, but we cannot fool ourselves). Hence, not only can the constitutivist strategy coherently claim that bad consequences will follow if we should violate the standards of practical reason, but it can render these consequences far more complete than those whose significance is exhausted in the likelihood of their being enforced, or in their harshness, in their perceived threat.

The second interpretation of the question 'Why be an agent?' poses a more serious challenge to the constitutivist strategy. Here, we are considering human agency not from the standpoint of its implications but from the standpoint of its normativity: we are being asked to consider not whether there are any *practical* consequences that follow from a decision to forsake human agency, but whether it makes sense to extract from human agency any *normative* consequences at all, and so whether normativity can legitimately be grounded in properties understood as constitutive and hence necessary. This second interpretation of the objection is given a full statement by Enoch, criticising the idea of the necessity of human agency or, rather, criticising the use made of this idea in the constitutivist strategy.[81] The idea is that human agency is constitutive of action—it forms a necessary part of what it means to act as a human agent—and this necessity and constitutiveness thereby impart normativity to human agency and practical reason, and so also to the standards drawn from the use of practical reason.

The problem here is that constitutive necessity is not continuous with normativity. Normativity belongs with the 'ought': a practical standard can be normative only in so far as it states or at least suggests what ought to be done. Constitutive necessity, by contrast, is concerned not with what *ought* to be but with what *has to* be, that is, with what has to be thus in order to count as an example of something: the traits constitutive of a kind are such that whoever or whatever lacks these traits is not a member of that kind; these traits are therefore not *normatively* but *epistemically* necessary, or definitional, in determining what it means to be something. Thus, while constitutive traits may *define* practical reason and enable us to

---

[81] See Enoch (2006: 187–92).

distinguish it from non-reason, they do not thereby make practical reason normative. This places a burden on the *source* of normativity (of practical reason), which has to exhibit its own normativity, showing that it is *itself* normative, since 'nothing short of an explicitly normative claim seems fit to settle normative questions' (Enoch 2006: 190). The normativity of practical reason cannot, then, be grounded in its constitutive necessity, the reason being that this necessity has to be of a normative kind: constitutive necessity can explain why something has to be the way it is, but it cannot *justify* this mode of being or show that something ought to be done. To suppose otherwise is to collapse the mode of what *ought* to be into the mode of what *has* to be, for this latter mode (the mode of constitutive necessity) can neither explain the former mode (the mode of normativity) nor justify it.[82] So the question 'Why be an agent?' should be understood here to mean: I understand that the properties of human agency are *constitutive* of human agency (for without them there would be no human agency at all and hence no practical reason) but how is this necessity supposed to make practical reason normative? What is normative about something necessarily having to be in a given way or having its own constitutive properties? And so, why should I be an agent and follow practical reason if my doing so only means that I qualify as an agent?

The problem just outlined (in connection with the second interpretation of the objection) has also emerged in the debate on the nature of regulative and constitutive rules,[83] and it will therefore be useful to consider this debate in formulating a reply. But first a brief introduction to these two types of rules: the essential difference between them is that regulative rules apply to *existing* practices, whereas constitutive ones *bring such practices into being* (or constitute them) and make them meaningful as practices of this type or that. What it means for regulative rules to come *after* the fact, or on top of an existing practice or conduct, is that such an activity can unfold independently of the rules by which it is regulated. The rules are thus said to be logically independent from the activity they regulate. And since the activity goes on anyway (that is, it makes sense even without such regulation) there must be some *other* role for these rules or some other point to them, or at least some other effect that they have on the activity: this is not to make the activity possible or meaningful, but to introduce into it an 'ought', and hence to impart to it a direction that may or may not be followed. Accordingly, the standard so introduced may be disregarded without thereby transforming the activity into something essentially different from what it is (the rules may be disregarded, and still the activity will be recognised as such, in the sense that it will still be said to continue as that kind of activity). Not so in the case of constitutive rules, whose objects do not exist beforehand but originate *with* the rules themselves, which in this sense can be understood as applying to otherwise inert matter, or to raw facts and prac-

---

[82] I would like to thank Corrado Roversi for discussing this point with me and providing valuable insights into the relation between what *ought* to and what *has* to be. If there is any error or failing in this discussion, however, I am entirely responsible for it.

[83] See Searle (1969: 33–42) on this.

tices that would have no meaning but for the rules that set them out as facts and practices of the specific kind described by the rules themselves. For this reason these rules typically occur in the form 'X counts as Y in context C'. Since X does not count as anything outside this context, the rule is said to have a transformative power, or a power by virtue of which something becomes recognisable as an object or practice within an institutional framework that (a) is brought into being through the connection established by the rule itself, and (b) endows the object or practice with a meaning where none previously existed.[84] Combining these two features is to say that the object or practice so constituted (or rather, brought into being through a rule constitutive of an institutional framework) cannot exist independently of the rule that describes (or constitutes) it. It follows that the rule cannot be disregarded without thereby returning the object or practice to its inchoate, unrecognisable state; which means, too, that there is a logical impossibility involved in the idea of 'disobeying' a constitutive rule. Two options are at hand: either we follow the rules by which an institutional framework is established, and in this way we can recognise one another as participants within this framework, or we do *not* follow these rules, but then we could no longer be said to operate within this framework. In this latter case, we are not just misapplying the rules: we are applying an entirely different set of rules, in such a way that others who *are* playing by the rules (and who are unfamiliar with the new set of rules) will not know what to make of our conduct. They will not think that we are 'playing' the system but that we might be operating under an unrelated system that they cannot interpret. Nor, for that matter, can they bring any judgement to bear on us, such as 'foul play' or 'blatant disregard for the rules', for they cannot locate our conduct within any institutional context of meaning. The point, then, is that constitutive rules do not belong with the 'ought', for the standard encapsulated in an 'ought' can be disobeyed as a constitutive rule cannot: a constitutive rule *can* be disobeyed, to be sure, but only in being transformed out of recognition. We thus say that a constitutive rule belongs not with what *ought* to be, but with what necessarily *has* to be in a certain way, failing which the object or practice to which the rule applies no longer ranks as an object or practice of that kind. But now the question arises: if constitutive rules have no traffic with the 'ought', in what way can they be described as normative, or as providing any practical guidance?

In reply to this objection we note, with Georg von Wright in his treatise *Norm and Action*, that constitutive rules actually play *both* roles at once, for in constituting an object or practice they thereby regulate it: it really depends on the point of view from which we look at the matter.[85] Thus, from the point of view of the practice

---

[84] Something so constituted becomes an institutional fact, on which see Searle (1969: 50–3). In legal theory, it is MacCormick who has pioneered a conception of the law based on the recognition of institutional facts: see MacCormick (1973a), MacCormick and Weinberger (1986), and MacCormick (2007a).

[85] This thought is briefly stated in von Wright (1963: 5–6). But when he returns to the same topic (1971: 151–2) he does not develop his earlier observation and indeed may even be seen as rejecting it.

as such—as a framework within which to engage in an activity—constitutive rules establish the conditions that make the practice possible and meaningful. This is their primary role: the constitutive rules of logic, for example, set the limits of cogent thinking by determining what an inference or a fallacy is, for example, just as the constitutive rules of chess make chess-playing possible, and so on. But in addition to determining the conditions for the possibility of the framework practice, constitutive rules can also be viewed from the standpoint of those *within* the practice, the standpoint of those who *use* the rules to make specific moves within the practice. These rules, so considered from the user's standpoint, state what is permitted, prohibited or obligatory within the practice. Thus, constitutive rules also serve a deontic function, and in this sense they ultimately also function as directives: in stating what counts as valid reasoning (thereby setting out conditions for the possibility of a reasoned argument), the rules of logic also state what specific inferences may or may not be made or have to be made; likewise, in defining the overall practice of chess (thereby making it possible for two players to play chess), the rules of chess also state what moves the players may or may not make, and ultimately when they ought to concede victory. So it is only in combination, as an overall framework, that the rules defining a practice actually *constitute* the practice (by bringing it into existence and setting it up as that kind of practice); when we shift perspective and consider the single move in relation to the specific rule or rules under which the move is made (this is the user's perspective), the rules play a different role, for in this case they allow or, indeed, compel us to make certain moves and prevent us from making others (failing which we can no longer be regarded as acting within the practice).[86] And it matters little that constitutive rules in this role do not take on any moral or advisory flavour whatsoever: they still prescribe, in one way or another, and for this reason they can properly be said to act as *normative* standards. We thus have a situation in which the same rules (constitutive rules) simultaneously exercise two kinds of force, depending on the relation with respect to which they are considered: collectively and in relation to the practice as a whole, they exercise constitutive force by stating the conditions subject to which the practice is possible, or under which it can exist at all; but in so doing they also individually exert a normative force in relation to those who take part in the practice, in that the rules instruct the players as to what moves they may or may not make and what moves they have to make. The meaning they acquire with respect to what the *players* are doing is, therefore, to state what moves are permitted, prohibited or obligatory, and this is properly understood as

---

[86] Von Wright so explains these two roles: 'from the point of view of the game itself, the rules determine which are the *correct* moves, and when viewed from the point of view of the activity of playing, the rules determine which are the *permitted* moves' (von Wright 1963: 6, emphasis added). This double nature of constitutive rules, with their primary constitutive role and their concurrent normative role, has also been pointed out by Searle in his observation that constitutive rules 'constitute (and also *regulate*) forms of activity whose existence is logically dependent on the rules' (Searle 1969: 55, emphasis added; cf Searle 1995: 48). Searle, however, does not develop the point or explain the double role so observed.

normative meaning owing to the prescriptive force of the rules, or to the deontic modalities they lay before the players.[87]

The bigger point here is that this property of constitutive rules—their acting in two roles at once—finds a parallel with the capacities constitutive of human agency, and this forms the basis for a reply to the second interpretation of the question 'Why be an agent?'. This is a two-part analogy, corresponding to the two roles in question, and we can therefore begin from the vantage point of the primary, or constitutive, role of the human capacities in parallel to the constitutive role of constitutive rules. This is quite straightforward: just as these rules define a framework practice and so make the practice possible (the practice would not be conceivable without these rules), so the constitutive capacities define human agency and in so doing establish the conditions subject to which human agency is possible (or failing which it would be inconceivable); just as we would not be able to make inferences without the rules of logic, and just as we would not be playing chess as we know it if we played by a different set of rules, so we could not act as human agents if we lacked the basic capacities for reflectivity, rationality and autonomy, and, just as importantly, we would not count as human agents if we switched to a different set of basic capacities. But now, in creating this possibility, the constitutive capacities also exert a normative force on human agents by framing the way in which they *ought* to think and act, and this is the second role of the constitutive capacities. This normative role works in essentially the same way as it does with constitutive rules, for in either case, whether we are human agents or participants in a practice, there are certain strictures we are subject to and ought to follow—strictures stating what may or may not be done or what ought to be done—if we are to qualify as members of the relevant class, or if what we do is to be recognised as consistent with human agency or with the relevant practice. So, the capacities of reflectivity, rationality and autonomy set forth prescriptions by stating how we ought to behave. What is more, they do this not just in the reduced style of the formally prescriptive 'ought' exhausted in the deontic modalities of permission, prohibition and obligation: they also make it possible for us to assess, for example, which of several permitted moves or courses of action best serves our interest as players (our interest in implementing a winning strategy), or our basic interest in preserving our integrity as human agents. This is something a bare constitutive rule cannot do but which a constitutive capacity can: a capacity is more plastic

---

[87] This normative meaning of rules should not be confused with whatever *psychological* meaning they may have. This is to say that the players or participants may well *experience* certain rules in certain ways, depending on the possibilities and restrictions the rules set out, but this 'experience' cannot be accounted as part of the normative force of the rules. Thus, eg, a player making a strategic move allowed by one rule or prevented from making a move prohibited by another rule might feel empowered by the first rule or move and hamstrung by the second, or a player might feel that some of the rules do not support the style of play he or she favours. But while these considerations might go into a 'psychology of rules', they do not account for the view defended here, namely, that constitutive rules have a normative meaning in relation to their users: this meaning owing to what rules *say* (what they prescribe), and hence to what they *do* (that is, what they allow, prohibit or require), and has nothing to do with how they are experienced or perceived.

than a rule, and so (consequently) is its guidance, which amounts to that of a full practical 'ought'.[88] But in any event, whether the guidance is formal or substantive, there is no doubt that the constitutive capacities of human agency lay out ways for human agents to behave. This is not their primary role, to be sure, but in stating what it is that makes someone a human agent, thereby serving as schemes by which to distinguish agents from non-agents (primary function), they also provide instructions for agents to follow (complementary function). What is more, these instructions, modes of conduct or standards come with a practical 'ought' attached to them, and so they are standards that can be acted on. In this respect, the standards can be regarded as pregnant with action, and so can, by extension, the concept of human agency from which these standards issue. In sum, the constitutiveness of constitutive rules and constitutive capacities alike is normatively laden: these rules and capacities can act not only in their primary (constitutive) role but also in a prescriptive role that makes them normative. This does not mean that the two concurrent roles are simultaneous in a *temporal* sense, for the normativity they can exert is engaged only when the relevant rule or capacity is called into play in the course of a game or in the course of practical decision-making. The dual role, in other words, can be appreciated by considering not *when* a constitutive rule or capacity becomes relevant, but the relation into which it enters: rules and capacities are *collectively* constitutive in relation to the overall practice or agency they define, and *individually* normative in relation to the people (players, participants, agents) to whom they apply, or in relation to the single moves or decisions they make acting within that practice or agency. The twofold force of reflectivity, rationality and autonomy thus depends on the different ways in which these capacities apply, or on their different objects. As we consider these different objects, we can appreciate how the same properties (reflectivity, rationality and autonomy) can be constitutive in some contexts and prescriptive in others: they are constitutive with respect to human *agency* and regulative with respect to human *agents*, acting as constraints necessary for human agency (what *has* to be in such and such a way) and as normative ones for human agents (what *ought* to be done).

In this way, constitutive necessity can be coupled with normativity. The significance of this coupling lies in the answer it provides to the question, 'Why be an agent if the capacities constitutive of human agency are just that—constitutive—and not also normative?'. This question rests on a assumption about constitutive features as merely defining features, or as features describing the 'nature' or 'essence' of something, in this case human agency understood as the source of the normativity of practical reason. I have offered arguments showing why this need

---

[88] This is the basic difference between a rule and a capacity: a rule is formal in a way that a capacity is not. A constitutive capacity of the sort we are considering can generate its own (regulative) rules—it can provide its own guidance—and the normativity of these standards is all the stronger for that reason, and closer to the agent, too: because the guidance issues from a *constitutive* capacity, and hence from a source considered central to what it is that makes us human agents to begin with, we tend to be correspondingly more invested in this guidance than in the guidance of bare permission, prohibition and obligation, which is a mere framework within which to move.

not be so: constitutive human capacities do have a guiding role enabling them to inhabit and shape the realm of the 'ought', not only formally but also substantively, thereby giving them the resources and the ability to ground the normativity of practical reason.

CONCLUSION

The overall aim of this chapter was to establish a foundation on which to ground the normativity of practical reason. It may not seem clear at first sight how this aim relates to the law, or to an inquiry into the normativity of law, but it does become clear once we take into account the basic thesis involved in setting out such an aim—the thesis of the unity of practical reason, under which practical reason is a single activity that develops in different ways as it is applied to one area or another, each such area being an instance of this single activity. Now, one of these areas is the law, and it follows that the specific normativity of law is rooted in the same foundation as the general normativity of practical reason. Once this overall foundation is arrived at, we can also appeal to our foundation for the normativity of law. The investigation carried out in this chapter into the normativity of practical reason is, therefore, a way of coming to terms with the grounding question that was set out in the previous chapter. And the grounding question in this chapter has been approached on the basis of a constitutivist strategy, so called because the normativity of practical reason is made to turn on certain fundamental capacities constructed as constitutive of human agency and hence as necessary prerequisites for anyone's being capable of carrying out actions, in the sense of 'action' specified earlier. The place of action in this construction is not irrelevant, for it implies the belief that action theory can enrich and enhance our understanding of normativity in the practical realm (or of what it is that confers normativity on our practical decision-making, as we take on the question of what ought to be done or what is the right course of action). The idea, then, is to base practical normativity on a concept of action, and since practical normativity, at this level of abstraction, is a subject usually reserved for metaethics, this approach essentially amounts to making metaethics dependent on action theory.

Now, this idea is not new: it has been explored by a number of writers, in particular, in the Kantian tradition of philosophy.[89] The one difference here is that the work done by contemporary Kantians is for the most part specifically concerned with the normativity of *morality*, whereas my enquiry takes a broader outlook, its concern being the normativity of practical reason generally (which is inclusive of, but not exhausted by, morality). But aside from this difference in scope, my attempt is conceptually akin to theirs: in both cases, the effort is to show how certain standards owe their normative force to the connection they have to a certain concept of action or of agency; which is to say that these standards or

---

[89] See, in particular, Gewirth (1978: 21–42), Korsgaard (2009) and Reath (2006: 67–91).

demands become normative by virtue of their drawing on features or ideals embedded into or constitutive of action or agency,[90] in such a way that any form of conduct or subjectivity that qualifies under such a standard as action or agency, respectively, is on that account considered normative. As we can see, the centrepiece in all these constructions is a concept of action or of human agency (or it is rather a twin concept of action *and* agency), forming a complementary pair regarded as the source out of which the normativity of a standard or a requirement arises. And in all of these constructions, the concept of human agency (with its accompanying concept of action) is forged from a roster of conceptual features or properties argued to be necessary to a practical account of what it means to be an acting subject (in such a way that no one can be considered an agent who does not embody these properties). Human agency is thus constructed as a *practical* concept (as against a metaphysical one) summarising certain *conceptual capacities* understood as essential (or necessary) and hence as independent of individual dispositions or inclinations, meaning that these capacities are common to all subjects who are capable of action, and who thereby gain the status of agents.

---

[90] The embedding process is such that the ideals or features in question are singled out on account of their being *necessary* to the concept of action or agency into which they are embedded, which is the whole point of the constitutivist approach, the alternative being to select features on account of their desirability under some other criterion, but this would amount to building normativity *directly* into the source concept of action or agency: what would then follow is an infinite regress, for we would then have to explain what it is that makes the source concept normative to being with. On a constitutivist approach, by contrast, we are left with the task of explaining not why the features singled out as constitutive are normative, but why they are necessary and in what way this necessity gives rise to normativity.

6
Grounding the Normative Claim and Force of Law

INTRODUCTION

IN CHAPTER FIVE, the essential traits of the modified Kantian approach were introduced as an account of the normativity of practical reason, an account revolving around the basic idea of human agency. We saw there that human agency through its three defining capacities—reflectivity, rationality and autonomy—shapes a minimal conception of the agent that no one can forego, for it provides the bare bones of our practical identity, meaning our identity as agents making our own decisions in the practical sphere, the sphere in which we deliberate about what to do or what the best course of action in this or that circumstance might be. One can step back at this stage and see an unbroken line running from human agency to practical reason, a line showing how practical reason ultimately borrows its *normativity* from the normativity of human agency: human agency is normative by virtue of providing us with a model, our practical identity, without which we could have no guidance in the practical sphere—precisely the guidance offered by practical reason. This conceptual chain (from human agency, to practical identity, to practical reason) is such that whatever normativity is found in human agency, as both a model and an enabling condition, making it possible for us to act meaningfully in the practical sphere, carries over to practical reason.

What is important here, as we move along, is that the normativity that practical reason takes up via human agency is transferable to any practice, framework or institution informed by practical reason. One of these practices is the law, and if we can qualify the law as a species of practical reason, we have a basis on which to make the normativity of practical reason relevant to the law: the essential features of the normativity of law can be determined by considering the normativity of those activities of which the law is a special case, namely, the activities of practical reason. In particular, this is a relation whereby the normativity of law can be grounded in the same way as that of practical reason: the law is and claims to be normative in essentially the same way and to the same extent as practical reason *qua* general sphere within which the law finds its own specification. That is to say that, just as the normativity of practical reason is grounded in human agency, so is the normativity of law.

The modified Kantian approach, then, in providing an account of the normativity of *practical reason*, makes it possible to ground as well the normative claim of *law*. And this was indeed the reason for introducing the approach in the first place. But now we can also appreciate, in adopting the approach, that consequences can be extracted from it that go beyond its stated purpose. That is to say that in explaining the normative *claim* of law, we also come to understand, on this approach, the functioning of the normativity of law in general, meaning its normative *claim and force*. It is to this broader question that we turn in this final chapter, considering, in particular, how the Kantian approach introduced in chapter five shapes an understanding of the normativity of law as a dimension including both its claim and force: this entire dimension I will call the *normativity* of law, while I refer to its two components (as discussed in the literature) as the *normative claim* of law and the *normative force* of law, the former referring to the *posture* that the law takes with respect to its normativity (how the law *presents* its own normativity) and the latter to its *influence*, or to the ability of the law to mould the behaviour of its addressees through its own normativity.

The argument will be unpacked as follows. I will first discuss the fundamental principle governing the normativity of law and further develop the thesis that this normativity is owed to the connection of the law with human agency, in such a way that the law can *be* normative or *claim* normativity only in so far as it in effect bears this relation to human agency. We will see that human agency, in its role as the source of the normativity of law, is an open-ended and flexible model: it works as a principle rather than as a rule, the difference being that a principle is to be optimised and fulfilled to the maximum degree possible, whereas a rule applies in an all-or-nothing fashion. We will also see that principles cannot be fleshed out in full—they cannot be filled with a content that show what, ultimately, they really mean—except through processes of concrete argumentation. And this brings out another hitherto unnoticed feature of the normativity of law. That is, once this normativity is acknowledged to have its source in human agency, and once this agency is acknowledged to act as a principle, then we can see that the normativity of law enters into a necessary connection with legal argumentation.

Once this basic connection is established, we will be able to focus on the more specific features of the normativity of law that the modified Kantian approach brings to light. These features I understand as adding to, rather than replacing, those that legal theory has attributed to the normativity of law (the features discussed in Part I), especially as these by and large relate to the normative claim alone. But there are a few distinctions that need to be introduced in order to comprehend the full complex of features. The most significant of these distinctions is that between *direct* and *indirect* normativity. This is a distinction that applies to the different directives and areas of the law but not to the legal system itself. A legal system owes its normativity (or its claimed normativity) to its ability (or its claimed ability) to foster human agency through an environment in which we can all freely exercise the basic defining capacities of human agency. This normativity is *direct*, and it is a property that can likewise be ascribed to the single provisions and branches of the law, in that they, too, can in their own right support us (or claim that they can support us) in exercising our distinctively human capacities. But unlike a legal *system*, its constituent *parts* (the different rules, provisions and branches of the law) can also be or claim to be *indirectly* normative, precisely by virtue of their being essential to systems that on the whole tend to promote human agency. At this point in the discussion there will still be some specific features of the normativity of law that need to be looked at: this will be done by considering, on the one hand, the content of the normative claim of law and, on the other, the content of its normative force. We will see that the normative force of a legal system functions in quite a different way than does the normative force of single provisions and branches of the law, and the two cases will therefore have to be considered separately. This provides an occasion to discuss in detail the normative force of provisions and areas of the law that are favourable, indifferent and contrary to human agency.

THE NORMATIVITY OF LAW: THE FUNDAMENTAL PRINCIPLE AND ITS IMPLICATIONS

The fundamental principle governing the normativity of law states, on the modified Kantian approach, that what is legal owes its normativity to its connection with the regulative idea of human agency. The basic assumption at work in this principle is that the normativity grounded in human agency irradiates across the entire domain of practical reason, in such a way that *any* use of practical reason (including those uses of it that are institutionalised, as in the law) owes its normativity to its commonality with human agency. It is from human agency that the institutions shaped by practical reason, such as the law, derive their normativity, and this normativity can only come about in so far as the relative institutions reflect in some way or support the defining capacities of human agency, these being reflectivity, rationality and autonomy. The capacities of human agency—its defining features—thus act as the measure of the normativity of law: the normative *claim* of law can be specified through its claim to support the reflectivity, rationality and autonomy of its addressees, just as the normative *force* of law can be said to rest with the functionality of the law in supporting, or at least not counteracting, the practical identity framed by human agency. The normative claim and force of law can, then, both be accounted for by looking to the relation of the law to human agency: only to the extent that the law takes an attitude supportive vis-à-vis human agency can it be said to have any normative claim, and only to the extent that human agency does in fact thrive under the law can the law itself be said to have any normative force.

This basic connection proceeds on an understanding of the law as an institutional framework grounded in practical reason: a framework based on an idea of practical rationality, and that takes among its defining objectives that of governing the interactions among human agents. As frameworks principally devoted to regulating social relations, then, legal systems are institutions necessarily concerned with human *agents*, and through this connection with human agency they necessarily incorporate a non-contingent practical dimension. This necessary practical dimension of legal systems brings the law within the general standards governing all institutions that relate to action and are shaped by practical reason. And as with any institution grounded in practical rationality, the law can exhibit normativity only to the extent that it is framed in such a way as to support the defining features of human agency.

The fundamental principle, then, is that human agency acts as the source of the normativity of all the instantiations of practical reason. The structure of human agency affects us in every aspect of our lives, extending its influence to the institutional frameworks in which we participate (including the institutions of the law as manifestations of practical reason). Now, clearly, our participation in an institutional framework or in any collective enterprise can affect our personal identity in a number of important respects, but not so far as to modify the basic traits and capacities framing our practical identity: these traits and capacities are logically prior to any role we might take up in an institutional setting (for they are enabling capacities) and so will operate independently of our participation in an institution.

This statement of the fundamental principle, as framed within the modified Kantian approach, with its idea of an independent standard of human agency as the necessary source of normativity, may strike some as an example of what Stanley Fish regards as the idea of the self *qua* a transcendental idea. According to this false conception, the self is conceived as an individual standing alone, an independent subject capable of moulding the environment to his or her satisfaction and re-engineering existing practices at will. It is Fish's contention that however appealing the conception of a free self may be (abstract and unconnected to anything or anybody), it will break apart on closer scrutiny. The cherished independence of the subject takes us only so far, for the social and cultural environment is *with* us. We *can* shape the environment, to be sure, but not as individual planners, and certainly not in a vacuum. Hence, the revised conception of the subject that Fish (1989: 346) calls for as a necessary premise, this before going on to develop a working 'set of methods for operating in the world' and a 'set of rationales and procedures for making judgements'. Fish's revised self is necessarily situated in a community, in a pre-existing social and political context and network of structures and interests of which he or she is a product and an extension (rather than this environment's being an extension of the self). At no time is the subject 'free to go his "own way", for he is always going in a way marked out by the practice or set of practices of whose defining principles (goals, purposes, interdictions) he is a moving extension' (Fish 1989: 13). The self is therefore not only inescapably embedded in history and society but is also shaped and defined by these very forces. By its constitution, such a socially constructed and locally determined self cannot possibly step outside itself to gain an external vantage point. The self and the environment are thus bound by a relation at once limiting and enabling: limiting, for the options made available by the environment are well-nigh all the options there are; enabling, for these options are malleable. Thus, although we come into an environment that is given, the same world is also plastic and fluid, making possible for us the 'moving extension' that Fish refers to.

This relation of necessity and possibility not only defines the self but also implies a conception of what it means to be impartial and objective in judgement and action. It is all written into the syntax of the relation itself in its constitutive and defining role; that is, we come into the world in a network of social, political and historical forces, and this is all material from which we can construct an identity but that concurrently defines who we are, thereby constituting our subjectivity. These forces are thus inescapable, but at the same time they are manifold and directional, forming a landscape that bristles with projects, ideas and points of view, an open landscape of choices and choice-making.[1] We must therefore move about in a world of locality and partiality, and since the forces at play are the very stuff of our existence, there is no way to transcend them, for this would amount to discarding what is constitutive of the subject. Identity will have to be constructed not by removing all the clutter from our surroundings, or retreating to a sequestered place affording shelter from all the currents that may pull in one direction or another, but rather by *engaging* with these elements and becoming part of the fabric of community and society, the very premise of our existence. To attempt otherwise—to set up the insular and hence independent and objective self, unbiased, value-neutral and impersonal—will paradoxically imply a *loss* of subjectivity and a specious standard of objectivity.

This criticism of an abstract notion of the self bears directly on the fundamental principle of the normativity of law as formulated in the modified Kantian approach. In characterising human agency, I set up what Fish would describe as a transcendental model of the self and so an objective normative standard from which to act; and I also argued that this standard extends its reach across the full spectrum of human activities. Fish would strongly oppose this abstract characterisation of human agency as resulting from a combination of reflectivity, rationality and autonomy. For Fish, what a human agent is cannot be formulated in such abstract terms, because our human agency is embedded in the communities of which we are members as extensions of the existing contexts and practices in which we take part. It follows that human agency must be accounted for by reference to the practices and communities through which we ultimately come to be who we are.

My reply begins with a concession. Fish is right to say that if we neglect to take into account our social backgrounds, attachments to particular persons and causes, and contextual bonds, we will inevitably end up with a deficient account of human agency and of the resulting practical identity. Still, this does not mean that

---

[1] On this idea of the double bind of context, whose forces we cannot escape, and which at the same time exert a definite pull on us, see Fish (1989: 26), who claims that the self is 'always and already constrained by the contexts of practice (interpretive communities) that confer on it a shape and a direction'. Cf Fish (1989: 323).

we cannot single out in the abstract the *essential* traits of human agency, meaning the elements on whose basis more specific and context-sensitive identities can be constructed. The reason why such a complex of essential traits can sensibly be worked out is precisely that they cannot exhaustively determine what a human agent is: they only serve as a *basis* for such a further build-up and specification of individual agency; they only identify *in a minimal way* what a human agent is, and so do not *replace* all the traits of individual agency but rather form the ground layer upon which to *add* the contextually determined traits specific to individual human agents defining themselves in different ways in action. It is only in this non-exhaustive sense that the essential traits of human agency are context-independent and can consequently be explained in abstract terms: they are abstract only in so far as their role does not go beyond their enabling us to take our place in the practical sphere. They establish in this sense a condition of possibility, in that they make it possible for us to operate in the practical sphere and be human agents, before we can be anything else: there is no way that we can move about in the sphere of action and make authentic decisions unless we have a capacity for reflection and for rational and autonomous conduct. Whatever else an X that is incapable of reflection, rationality and autonomy might be, this X will not be a human agent, for without these capacities we could not engage in action: we could *do* things, to be sure, but could not make of them meaningful examples of action, which is directional and guided by standards. Reflectivity, rationality and autonomy thus serve as essential enabling conditions, or as *conditiones sine qua non* of our being acting selves: they make it possible for us to perform action, and impossible for anyone to embark into action without them. In this way, they make it possible for us to take on all the further traits characterising our selves and self-conceptions as individuals. As enabling conditions for acting in the practical realm, these basic features of human agency must necessarily be general and abstract, not because they operate independently of any agent but, on the contrary, because no agent could be such without them. In this sense, they apply across the boards to *all* agents, serving as a common foundation, and for this reason they are forced into abstractness and generality, which is precisely the way in which the essential capacities for reflective, rational and autonomous conduct are framed. And not only are these capacities necessarily *abstract*: they are also necessarily *incomplete*, for in applying to everyone in general, they describe no one in particular, and particular agents are what we all necessarily end up being as real individuals defined through our social relations and institutional attachments developed in this or that context. Just as we cannot be human agents without the basic capacities for reflective and autonomous action, so we cannot be just that: we are still immaterial at this stage and need to complete ourselves in the weave of community. After all, a capacity—however complex it may be—is not yet an agent. Hence, the need for these two complementary stages: on an abstract level, we have the enabling conditions of human agency; on the concrete level, we have all that we become by building on these conditions to forge our individual identities as agents through the bonds of community and its social institutions.

Thus, on the modified Kantian approach, an acting subject is more than someone capable of reflective, rational and autonomous conduct, for no one really has a full identity (indeed no one can be anyone) without developing through the experience of particular attachments, institutional roles, social ties and other contextual means. At the same time, however, no one can develop in this way who does not have beforehand a capacity for reflectivity, rationality and autonomy and recognise others as having the same capacities. What makes these essential traits of human agency general and abstract is precisely their role as capacities that are both necessary and enabling. As *necessary* capacities, they simply cannot be dispensed with: we cannot renounce our reflectivity, rationality and autonomy and still pretend to take part in the practical sphere as performers of action. As *enabling* capacities, they form the ground layer for whatever other identities we may end up having through our specific life experiences. When we do forge such richer identities, as we must necessarily do in order to exist as complete agents, we are not bypassing the defining capacities of human agency—we are rather building on top of them. These capacities are context-dependent only to the extent that they guide us in the practical sphere, a context common to human agency in general; yet they are *not* context-dependent if this context is understood in any more specific way, as the communal and institutional context of living and experiencing that shapes our identity as individuals set in a developing narrative that makes each person unique and real.

Fish's remarks about the situatedness and social embeddedness of the self can be taken in this sense as a welcome reminder that human agency plays only a limited role in shaping the identity of acting selves: the conception of the self as an acting subject capable of reflectivity, rationality and autonomy only takes us so far in defining who we are, and so it is not exhaustive. What instead *is* objectionable about Fish's treatment is his attempt to radicalise the context-dependence of the subject to the point of denying that human agents can have any general traits or features, however minimal and non-exhaustive they may be, meaning traits not determined by an agent's membership in particular institutions or settings, and which define someone as an agent in contradistinction to a *non-agent* or someone incapable of action. No such radical understanding of the situatedness of the self can possibly be endorsed on the modified Kantian approach. This approach proceeds from precisely the opposite thesis: that the *fundamental* features of our identity can be framed without taking into account any of the particular institutions and practices in which different people take part. Hence, while we acknowledge that these practices are in their own way essential (we cannot have any particular identity without them), we must also acknowledge that our practical identity (the basic features of human agency) can and indeed have to be described in abstract and general terms without reference to the contexts of our social ties and attachments.

Again, this should not prevent us from recognising the specificity that different agents will ultimately forge for themselves, nor should it suggest that one's practical identity is *fully* described by the basic capacities of human agency, for these are precisely that, namely capacities, and we use them to round out our identities by taking part in particular institutions, understood as any social or collective practice framed by its own rules and principles. Our taking part in different institutions shapes our identity by placing us in different roles that deeply affect the way in which we perceive and conduct ourselves. Indeed, each institutional role we take up defines an ideal, and we end up changing who *we* are as we try to fit these ideals and fulfil their accompanying obligations. There is no denying, then, that we are who we are largely on account of the relations we enter into as members of this or that institution. Rather, what the modified Kantian approach does deny is that such institutions, practices and conventions determine in any exclusive fashion the features of our *human agency*. Granted, our participation in institutional frameworks will affect our identity as persons in the crucible of experience, but it will not fundamentally alter our identity as human agents. This is because the very institutions in which we take part are governed by practical reason, and so the specific identities we take on in participating in such institutions supervene, and so are subordinate to, the identity shaped by the minimally necessary self-conception. The practical identities conferred on us by specific institutions will therefore have no hold on us if they fail to cohere with the identity defined by human agency or if they fail to be instrumental in achieving the related features of reflectivity, rationality and autonomy. Then, too, whatever obligations an institution imposes on us are not exclusively determined by that institution. Institutions are not independent entities, rather they are the outcome of the interaction that takes place among those who bring them into being. It is true that an institution may develop somewhat independently of the individuals who create and take part in it, but not to the point that the institution ceases to make sense to these individuals as human agents, for it is the capacities of human agency that enable one to take part in an institution to begin with. Therefore, as much as an institution may be considered independent, no institution can aspire to be binding on anyone if it fails to build on human agency. The basis of institutional life therefore ultimately lies in human agency, and not the other way around: human agency sets the boundaries of institutional frameworks conceived as instances of practical reason, and in so doing it defines their scope and nature. Because it is only in a relative and limited way that institutions are insulated from those who take part in them, and because these individuals will first and foremost be human agents (whatever else they may be), any specific obligation that an institution may choose to impose on someone will be senseless if it cannot establish at least an indirect connection with the basic features of human agency.

In conclusion, while practical institutions can have a significant impact on human lives and can even make possible otherwise unthinkable achievements, it remains the case that their normativity derives from human agency and is conditional on it. No institution can advance any meaningful normative demand unless it claims at the same time to endorse the reflectivity, rationality and autonomy of its members; which is to say that no institution is binding unless it establishes some connection with the basic features of human agency. Therefore, only to the extent that the law can be conceived as an institution shaped by practical reason will it be endowed with normative properties, and it will be able to do so only for as long as it supports the human agency of its addressees (those who make, practice, interpret and comply with the law).

Essential to the normativity of law, then, is its capacity to support human agency. And this, in turn, makes the idea of *support* crucial in defining the fundamental principle of the normativity of law. But the idea of support requires some further specification, as do the contrasting ideas of indifference and opposition, here understood as signifying a *lack* of support. That the law 'supports' human agency may mean different things, for 'support' is a broad and wide-ranging notion. In general, it means that something (that by which support is provided) helps us in working toward a goal, ideal, person, practice or institution and so is favourable or conducive to the persistence and flourishing of such a person or thing.[2] Hence, the law can be understood to support human agency if its contents, structures and procedures are *functional* to the basic features defining human agency. So it is that they are suitable means to enable human agents to fulfil their basic and distinctive capacities. On this understanding, then, the notion of support in the law is an instrumental relation.[3]

The support of the law vis-à-vis human agency can take different forms. But these can be reduced to two basic forms, one strong, the other weak. We have the strong form when the law prescribes something that is already *built into* human agency (and so can be directly *deduced* from it), or when the law prohibits that which contradicts the built-in contents of human agency. This explains support as a relation working both positively and negatively, or as both upholding the defining features of human agency and not denying them. That is to say that the law can support human agency not only by proactively facilitating human agency but also by invalidating courses of conduct that are incompatible with our reflectivity, rationality and autonomy. For all practical purposes, then, the law can be understood as conducive to human agency whether it leads us to act as human agents or whether it prevents us from undermining our human agency. Accordingly, human agency can be defined by standards that either prescribe or proscribe certain courses of conduct (depending on how they relate to human agency itself). This is a *direct* operation of human agency, and the law can incorporate such prescriptions and proscriptions either by requiring us to act in a reflective, rational and autonomous way, or by prohibiting behaviour that runs counter to these features of action. Here, support points to a *logical* relation between the law and human agency.

---

[2] An introduction to this idea of support is provided by Green (1988: 9–16), who relies on Easton (1957).

[3] As such an instrumental relation, support fits into a likewise instrumental conception of the law whereby any value the law has is owed to its role in contributing to our fulfilment of human agency. In this instrumental role, the law has no value in itself, for its value derives from its being an adequate means by which to achieve certain valuable ends. To be sure, this view underlies the entire legal-positivist tradition, which has the merit of having consistently defended it; but our accepting this view does not thereby commit us to legal positivism.

A case in point might be a law that (a) prescribes a standard form for a certain kind of business transaction (a form specifying, for example, the number of witnesses that need to be present in a transfer of ownership for goods whose worth is beyond a certain threshold level), and that (b) renders invalid any such transaction that does not comply with the prescribed form. This form can be understood as assuring that both parties to a transaction take their acts with all due seriousness, so that they will not constrain their own freedom without a careful consideration of the matter at hand. If this interpretation is correct, and the law in question is in fact designed so that we will act only on reflection, the law can be said to support human agency in a strong sense, for it is prescribing something that is built into human agency from the start, namely, reflective action. Here, the content of the law can be directly *deduced* from human agency: human agency enters into a deductive relation with respect to the law.

We have a weaker form of support when, instead of prescribing what already forms a *part* of human agency, the law prescribes what is *justified* by human agency or prohibits what is not justified by it. The relation of human agency to the law is in this case a *justificatory* one. In addition to providing standards from which to *deduce* a legal directive, by direct operation of the standards of human agency themselves, human agency can also function as a repository of *justifying reasons* for a course of conduct. But if we are to recognise such a justificatory power, we will have to conceive of human agency as an overarching principle from which reasons for and against a given course of conduct can be inferred and weighed. And in making this assessment—using human agency as a justificatory criterion in evaluating whether a law coheres with its defining traits—we will be judging this law not against human agency directly but against a directive that can be justified on the *basis* of human agency.

For instance, in contract law the standard of autonomy justifies the rule that 'everyone ought to be free to enter into a contract', meaning that no one can be coerced into buying or selling anything (under threat of physical force or under mental duress, or indeed under any circumstance). But now, let us consider a hypothetical legal system establishing the rule that in certain circumstances (such as scarcity of certain goods, exclusive ownership of them by few persons, urgent need for the entire community to enjoy the same goods), you must, if you own any such goods, sell a certain quantity of them. The normativity of this legal rule (establishing an obligation to sell) should be determined by assessing the rule against the legal doctrine of freedom of contract, and in this assessment, the ideal of human agency does not exactly match the rule in question (the rule cannot simply be overlaid onto a defining standard of human agency) but rather stands in the background as a justificatory ground for freedom of contract. What distinguishes this justificatory relation of support from the logical relation just considered is its indirectness: in this justificatory relation, the law is no longer directly modelling a constituent of human agency (a defining trait) but is rather requiring us to behave in ways that can be justified by reasoning from such a defining trait (in this case, a capacity for autonomous action).

In both of these cases—logical derivation and justification—the law can be said to *support* human agency. But the relation of the law to human agency need not be one of support: it can also be one of indifference or even of opposition. The law is *indifferent* to human agency when it regulates forms of behaviour which are neither required nor prohibited under any defining standard of human agency, and which in this sense are merely permitted. In fact, as much as the directives derivable from human agency may cover a vast territory in the practical realm, human agency is not an all-embracing ideal: it is by no means true that we can look in every case to the practical standards of human agency in working out how we ought to behave. It is true that certain acts are instrumental to the fulfilment of our status as agents and others are inconsistent with it, but human agency falls short of covering the full spectrum of practical possibilities. There are areas in the practical sphere where human agency is silent, for there will be more than one course of conduct compatible with our agency, or there will be things we can do that will not affect our identity as human agents. In this entire middle range of what is permitted (neither required nor prohibited), the law enters into a relation of indifference with respect to human agency, for whatever we do or forbear from doing in these cases in compliance with the law will neither be functional to the defining features of human agency nor inconsistent with them. So, whenever a legal provision regulates a subject matter in such a way that our behaviour under such a provision makes no difference with respect to human agency (it will not affect our status as human agents), the relation of the law to human agency will be classified as one of indifference.

Finally, the relation of the law to human agency can be one of *opposition*. The relation of opposition can be understood by reference to the relation of support, which it denies and contradicts: the law opposes human agency whenever it prohibits what can be *deduced* from human agency or prescribes what cannot be so deduced, or whenever it prohibits what can be *justified* on the basis of human agency or prescribes what cannot be so justified. In all of these cases, the law turns itself into an institution contrary to human agency. Now, we should consider here a distinction between the kinds of opposition that are relevant to the normativity of law, especially as concerns its normative force. This distinction is based on how serious the contrast is between the law and human agency. This contrast may be shallow and partial, or it may be deep and extensive. In a *marginal contrast*, the fundamental features of human agency are only partially contradicted, and so the possibility of acting in the distinctive manner of a human agent (meaning the possibility of engaging in principled conduct) is affected only tangentially. Let us consider, in this regard, a legal provision framed under a scheme of strict liability.[4]

---

[4] An example of such a provision is the UK Wireless Telegraphy Act 1949, s1(1), which regulates the licensing of wireless telegraphy and states that 'no person shall establish or use any station for wireless telegraphy or install or use any apparatus for wireless telegraphy except under the authority of a licence in that behalf granted by the Postmaster General, and any person who establishes or uses any station for wireless telegraphy or installs or uses any apparatus for wireless telegraphy except under and in accordance with such a licence shall be guilty of an offence under this Act'. In *R v Blake* [1997] 1 All

This principle sets up objective standards of responsibility in the sense that someone may be found liable under the law (or legally responsible for an act) regardless of fault, that is, regardless of the mental state accompanying the act. Strict liability thus renders the subjective element (an agent's frame of mind) irrelevant in an assessment of whether an act may be qualified as unlawful: in this way, the relevant criterion becomes that of the *outcome* produced through an act, and someone can be deemed liable for such an outcome quite apart from any intended act. In strict liability, then, an action is understood as a quasi-natural event; it need not be willed or voluntary and it can be assessed solely on the basis of its consequences. This view does not sit comfortably with the conception of action defended by the modified Kantian approach, which defines action as principled conduct, meaning that the act must be purposive, intentional and planned, reflecting deliberation and requiring assessment not only in light of the implications it may have but also with an eye to the reasons that justify it. The doctrine of strict liability thus presents us with a behavioural model that is out of keeping with the modified Kantian paradigm: the way in which action is conceived under a system shaped by the principle of strict liability differs markedly from the way it is conceived under a system shaped by the regulative ideals of the modified Kantian approach. While this tension is undeniable it does not, however, amount to an outright incompatibility. This is because a system of strict liability does not, after all, *prevent* us from engaging in principled conduct. At most, it might *discourage* us from engaging in principled conduct, in that if we should have to make amends for situations that are beyond our control, we will not, in these cases, have a reason to use our reflective capacity to exercise control over our action, at least not for any purpose that has anything to do with the legal consequences of such action.

Furthermore, while strict liability can be ascribed regardless of fault, and so is detached from the subject's mental state, this person's capacities are not *totally* irrelevant in such an ascription. Under a system of strict liability, we can be deemed liable only if we can *understand* what we do and so can be said to have *chosen* to act: since in strict liability the focus is on the outcome of a course of conduct, it must be assumed that we are *capable* of such conduct in the first place, and this capacity therefore serves as a necessary condition for the ascription of strict liability. This kind of capacity to engage in a certain line of conduct is a general capacity whose only role in the ascription of liability is to qualify someone as having properly *done* something, and this is clearly a different kind of capacity from the threefold capacity (resulting from reflectivity, rationality and autonomy combined) enabling action understood as principled conduct. Even persons who are not *fully* reflective, rational and autonomous can engage in conduct for which they can be deemed responsible under the doctrine of strict liability. Still, we do need to see,

ER 963, the criminal division of the competent Court of Appeal found (per Hirst J) that the offence set forth under s1(1) falls under the doctrine of strict liability. The court dismissed on this basis the appeal of the defendant, a disk jockey whom the lower court had found guilty of using a station for wireless telegraphy without a licence, despite the defendant's argument that he was not aware he was transmitting and instead believed he was making a demonstration tape.

in these persons, at least some degree of reflectivity, rationality and autonomy before we can consider them capable of understanding what they do, and so before we can hold them liable for the results stemming from what they do. Hence, in so far as strict liability is associated with an ability to engage in the conduct whose outcome is the issue at hand, any system for the attribution of strict liability will make it necessary first to recognise someone as an able actor, and so as having capacities akin to those that on the modified Kantian approach define human agency.

In sum, from the modified Kantian perspective, a scheme of strict liability raises questions but is neither inconceivable nor deeply flawed. Because the compression of human agency that is brought about by way of a scheme of strict liability is marginal and limited, the corresponding violation or contradiction of human agency can be described as 'simple'. *Simple contradictions* of human agency are those whose contrast with the model of human agency is only superficial, and which therefore only compress, but do not entirely ignore, the requirements of reflectivity, rationality and autonomy.

Incidentally, this discussion, with its accompanying conclusion that strict liability and the modified Kantian approach are not *completely* at odds, also clarifies the notion that in adopting this approach, we are not thereby prevented from offering an *explanation* or even a *justification* of strict liability. One might be under this impression on the assumption that the modified Kantian approach is conceptually akin to and associated with the 'modern view of responsibility', in the form in which it has been reconstructed and criticised by Peter Cane in *Responsibility in Law and Morality*. On Cane's (2002: 23) account, the basic insight of the modern view of responsibility, which is 'often traced back to the work of Immanuel Kant' and has 'very influential contemporary followers' among philosophers as well as among legal theorists, is that 'responsibility is not something we ascribe or attribute to human beings but is, rather, intrinsic to, and part of what we mean by, being a human agent with free will'. The modern view of responsibility therefore focuses exclusively on agency and will: it depicts responsibility as a function of human agency, namely, with the effect that we can be held liable on the sole basis of having willed a course of conduct, and if it is determined that an appropriate mental state was associated with this conduct, this will suffice to hold us liable for any consequences stemming from such conduct. The modern view is led to the conclusion, on this basis, that personal responsibility is the only responsibility there is, a view that does not sit well with the idea of strict liability.[5] For this reason, given the link Cane establishes between this modern view and Kant's view, it may seem that the normativity of legal provisions setting up a scheme of strict liability cannot be fully explained or justified on the modified Kantian approach.[6]

This impression is not correct. There is little doubt that the modified Kantian approach does not easily co-exist with the paradigm of strict liability. If it seems,

---

[5] See Cane (2002: 22–5) for this criticism.
[6] I wish to thank Maksymilian Del Mar for bringing to my attention this possible interpretation of the modified Kantian approach.

however, that strict liability cannot be justified on the modified Kantian approach, this has little to do with any special connection that the approach has with the modern view of responsibility, if for no other reason that this approach cannot be catalogued as a modern view of responsibility. Indeed, on the one hand, the modified Kantian view does not deal directly with responsibility: it is instead framed in response to the problem of the normativity of law, and as such it is simply not a view of responsibility, modern or otherwise. On the other hand, it turns out on closer scrutiny that the principles behind the modern view of responsibility do not cohere with those underpinning the modified Kantian approach. In Cane's characterisation, the modern view explains responsibility exclusively in terms of the role played by the person who engages in the conduct at hand. This account pays no attention at all to the needs of those who are adversely affected by this conduct, whether it be an individual who stands affected or society at large. But this focus on the actor or wrongdoer alone is foreign to the modified Kantian approach. Granted, the approach is agent-centred, but it is so in a markedly different sense from that of the modern view of responsibility. On the modified Kantian approach, human agency does not apply exclusively to the subjectivity of those performing the act with respect to which liability arises: not only is the actor a human agent, but those on the receiving end of this behaviour are, too; and the modified Kantian approach also brings society into this relation, society understood as an aggregation of human agents.

The upshot of these remarks is that, if we were to work out an account of responsibility grounded in the basic concepts and principles framing the modified Kantian approach, the end result would be radically different from the modern view of responsibility, the reason being that on the modified Kantian approach we must take into account not only the actor (the individual responsible for the act in question) but also whoever is harmed or otherwise affected by the act, whether it be one or more persons or the society as a whole.[7] As a result, the problems and difficulties faced by the modern view of responsibility in accounting for strict liability are altogether different from the problems and difficulties that the modified Kantian approach might have to face once it is extended in order to deal with the question of responsibility in the law and morality. More specifically, since what prevents the modern view of responsibility from accommodating the paradigm of strict liability is its focus on the actor or wrongdoer, and since the modified Kantian approach is not constrained by this exclusive focus, there is nothing to suggest that once this approach is extended to the study of responsibility, it cannot

---

[7] This means that the standard arguments adduced in favour of strict liability are ones that in principle could just as well be defended by reasoning from the modified Kantian approach: on this approach, a scheme of strict liability can be justified by pointing to its ability to (a) make us safer from the threat of other people's harmful conduct; (b) find a compromise between the costs and benefits associated with activities undertaken because deemed useful to society at large, but which nonetheless carry risks; (c) fairly distribute the gains and losses deriving from good or bad luck, in such a way that one is not praised for something accomplished without merit or condemned for a bad turn of events that happened through no fault of one's own; and (d) contribute to important social and economic functions typically associated with the existence of the law.

account for the relationship between those who commit an act and the individuals or community affected by it, a relationship so central to an explanation of strict liability. In summary, if the relation between the paradigm of strict liability and the Kantian approach can in any sense be described as an uneasy one, this is owing to the distinct concepts of action involved: those underlying a system of strict liability on the one hand, and those underlying a system based on the modified Kantian approach on the other. When, by contrast, it comes to the ability of the modified Kantian approach to explain or justify strict liability, we do not have any sort of uneasy relation between the two.

To come back to the main argument, the contrast between the law and human agency is not always circumscribed and superficial, as happens with strict liability; it may also be extensive and deep. In these cases, the law renders it quite challenging for someone to engage in reflective, rational and autonomous conduct. An example is a legal system that makes it possible for people to be tortured, even if only in exceptional cases, in order to extract from them information deemed essential to provide for national security.[8] Even if the legalisation of torture is limited to exceptional cases, it flies in the face of human agency. Torture involves the intentional infliction of severe mental or physical pain or suffering on one who has not consented to such treatment and who is powerless to react. Its ultimate aim therefore is to break someone and to have this person abandon decision-making, at least in relation to some circumscribed area of life and for a limited period.[9] The institutionalisation of this practice affects the human agency of both the tortured person and the torturer.

The human agency of one who is tortured is contradicted by the direct suppression of autonomy involved in torture. Persons under torture are constrained not just physically but also in what concerns their capacity for self-determination: the condition of the tortured is such that any information they might offer will be owing not to an autonomous decision on their part but rather to making a mockery of their capacity for independent judgement.[10] As Seith Kreimer (2003: 298–9) very concisely puts it:

> torture seeks to shatter [the victim's] autonomy. Torture's evil extends beyond the physical; extreme pain totally occupies the psychic world; the agony of torture is designed to make choice impossible. Effective torture is intended to induce the subject to abandon her own volition and become the instrument of the torturer.

Thus, the victim's autonomy, and hence her capacity for reflective and rational conduct, are severely undermined, if not destroyed altogether.

---

[8] A critical introduction to the current debate on torture can be found in Kreimer (2003). See also Dershowiz (2003), Ignatieff (2004), Davis (2005), Tindale (2005), Sussman (2005), La Torre (2006), Posner (2006), and Belvisi (2009), where torture and the justification that may be offered for this practice are discussed from different theoretical perspectives.

[9] This is essentially the definition provided in the Convention Against Torture and Other Cruel, Inhuman or Degrading Treatment or Punishment, Art 1, GA res 39/46 of 10 December 1984, annex, 39 UN GAOR Supp (No 51) at 197, UN Doc A/39/51 (1984), which came into force on 26 June 1987.

[10] This is noted by Belvisi (2009: 67), among others, who claims that 'torture strikes at the very core of the citizen (as a person) and his capacity for independent decision-making'. See also Ignatieff (2004: 136) and Reemtsma (2005: 119–20).

Torture affects the human agency of the torturers, too. By treating the tortured as mere means to their goals, torturers make human status conditional on other values and interests rather than recognising it as a final and unconditional good. By so doing, torturers downgrade the status of the human agent in general— human agency is not regarded as an end in itself but is treated as an instrumental value. Torturers do not simply violate the human agency of those they *torture* but also debase their *own* status as human agents. The torturer thus engages in conduct the implications of which go beyond its immediate effects, namely, causing someone to undergo an excruciating experience and preventing this individual from exercising any capacity for reflection, rationality or autonomy; for in so doing the torturer diminishes the value of human agency itself, including the torturer's own agency. Once torture is legalised or otherwise institutionalised, the effects will then ripple through the system, for at the point at which we know it to be an accepted practice, we will have a different outlook on human agency, or at the very least we will know that it passes muster to understand human agency as something that can be dispensed with: the human agent occupies no special position in the practical sphere (at least not in the eyes of the law) and it thereby becomes inessential, as either a disposable value or one that can be sacrificed to something else (the welfare of society as a whole, or what have you). In summary, the ramifications of legalising torture cannot be contained: they cannot be kept within the bounds of the specific practice of torturing people (with whatever putative justification one might have for this practice), nor can they be kept within the bounds of the specific area of the law in which torture is permitted, nor can they be kept within the specific practical domain of which the law is an instance. They are instead far-reaching ramifications that sent their roots deep into the core of the practical domain as a whole, for once torture is legalised, we can no longer conceive of ourselves as having any inherent value or dignity.

It is therefore a real blow sustained by human agency at the hands of a legal system in which torture is permitted: real, for such a system collides head-on with human agency. I will call this an outright or *flat contradiction* of human agency (as against a marginal or simple one), occurring whenever any scheme or form of behaviour specifically designed to deny our capacity for reflectivity, rationality and autonomy is mandated or allowed by the law, to the effect that human agency is manifestly suppressed to an intolerable degree.[11] What makes a head-on collision with human agency intolerable is precisely its striking at the *defining* features of

---

[11] The distinction between a simple and a flat contradiction of human agency mirrors the distinction between injustice and extreme injustice theorised by scholars such as Gustav Radbruch and Robert Alexy. Radbruch distinguishes between 'unjust and inexpedient' legislation, on the one hand, and statutes conflicting with justice to 'an intolerable degree', on the other (Radbruch 1990: 89). Alexy (2002b: 47–8) makes this idea more perspicuous by connecting the threshold for an 'intolerable' or 'extreme' degree with the idea of a 'minimum moral requirement', one that 'encompasses the most elementary human rights'. Alexy (2002b: 48) also explains that this is something we have whenever, as in the Nazi regime, we witness an attempt to 'destroy physically and materially, in accordance with "racist" criteria, certain parts of one's own population, including women and children'. This criterion is a broad enough one we can borrow here and bring it to bear on this discussion, too.

agency (reflectivity, rationality and autonomy), for anyone who is subjected to treatment depriving him or her of these features can no longer be recognised as a human agent: it is this fact which makes the denial not only extreme but also unacceptable.[12]

As we move on, we need to qualify further and to develop the fundamental principle governing the normativity of law. The preceding remarks show that the normativity of law, or *normative law*, should take human agency as its regulative standard, with reflectivity, rationality and autonomy functioning as substandards. On the modified Kantian approach, then, human agency plays in relation to the normativity of law a role akin to the role that justice plays in natural law theory (in the uncompromising forms of it) in relation to the validity of the law. Just as in the strong variant of natural law theory, legality is defined in relation with justice (in such a way that a system cannot at the same time be unjust and legally valid),[13] so on the modified Kantian approach the normativity of law depends on an ability of the system to serve human agency by setting up an environment conducive to our exercise of the fundamental practical capacities. Therefore, the law cannot be (or otherwise *claim* to be) normative unless it can have (or otherwise *claim* to have) a supportive attitude toward human agency: in so far as the law contains directives incompatible with the reflectivity, rationality and autonomy of those it applies to, its normative claim remains unexplained and its normative force tenuous.

There is another way to characterise the relation between human agency and the normativity of law. This is to say that the regulative ideas governing human agency operate as general principles, or as optimisation commands understood in distinction to definitive and specific commands. The distinction between principles and definitive commands is one that Robert Alexy has introduced in his treatment of legal norms. Alexy claims that legal norms can take either of two forms: that of 'optimisation commands', as in the case of principles, or that of 'definitive commands', as in the case of rules.[14] By optimisation command, Alexy (2000a: 294–5) means a standard 'commanding that something be realized to the highest degree that is actually and legally possible'.[15] A definitive command, by contrast, consists in a directive that can either be complied with or disregarded: there is no leeway, no middle ground, for the command requires its addressees to do exactly as it says. Now, human agency operates as a *principle* rather than as a

---

[12] This is as precise a description as a general theory of normativity can provide of a flat or open contradiction of human agency. Any more specific description will be for the practice of rational argumentation to offer, for this is a practice that is always embedded in a concrete situation and therefore has a perspective enabling it to see things that one is not given to see by reasoning from a general theory. Hence, it is only in the course of a circumstantiated argument specific to this or that case that we can determine whether something should be qualified as a flat or as an oblique contradiction of human agency.

[13] For a recent reconstruction of this view and how it differs from the weak variant of natural law theory, see Murphy (2003).

[14] See Alexy (2000a) and Alexy (2002a: 44–69).

[15] See also Alexy (2002a: 47–8).

rule: it can be understood as encapsulating an optimisation command, and so as a directive that need not be complied with in full, but complied with only so far as is possible, or reasonable, depending on the context in which it is applied.[16] Human agency, then, does not establish rigid standards in the law: if it did, it would thereby renounce its status as a normative principle, requiring compliance of the all-or-nothing variety. Human agency should instead be understood as a set of *flexible* standards, which means that a specific law counts as normative not in so far as it comports with or fails to comport with human agency, but rather *in proportion to* the extent to which it comports with human agency.

This understanding of human agency as a standard whose realisation is subject to gradation is reflected in the composite make-up of human agency itself. Human agency is not a simple standard, rather it is a complex one encompassing a full range of substandards. These substandards can co-exist because they form a set comprehensive and flexible enough to allow for its constituents achieving consistency; but even so, these constituents (the substandards) can occasionally pull in opposite directions, in such a way as to have relationships that may need some explaining to show in what way they are coherent and harmonious.[17] Thus, for example, occasionally the conditions supporting our capacity for reflection may not just be different from those supporting our autonomy but also impossible to achieve without undermining autonomy. What ultimately makes them compatible is that human agency follows the logic of principles, subjecting its constituent standards to a procedure of weighing and balancing.[18] So the way to avert collisions between the different standards of human agency (and in particular between its defining features) is to determine the 'conditional priority of one of the colliding principles over the other with respect to the circumstances of the case' (Alexy 2000a: 296). Any priority a component of human agency is accorded over the others is thus conditional and can be overturned. This means that a defining feature of human agency will have greater weight than another in one set of circumstances and less weight in another: the feature carrying more weight will prevail over the one carrying less weight, but in any event there is no circumstance in which a feature yielding to another will thereby become invalid or subject to exception, not only because all of the defining features are (as the name suggests) essential to human agency, and so cannot be dispensed with, but also because a feature defeated in one set of conditions may prevail in another set.

[16] A caveat here is that principles are, strictly speaking, *deontological* statements prescribing what ought to be done or not done; this in contrast to human agency, which is instead *valuational*, for it incorporates an axiological statement as to what is good or not good. But this is not a difference that sets principles and values radically apart, since 'principles and values are only distinguished by their respectively deontological and axiological characters' (Alexy 2002a: 92). That is to say that, in the final analysis, an appeal to principles is not essentially different from an appeal to values: a transition from principles to values and vice versa is quite smooth, so much so that the two can be used interchangeably (on this point, see also MacCormick 1984a: 40–1). So, even though human agency is axiological rather than deontological, it can give rise to deontological statements and be used prescriptively to establish what ought to be done or not done.

[17] On the notion of contrasting but compatible principles, see Griffin (1997) and Burg (2000: 87–8).

[18] The balancing procedure is presented in detail in Alexy (2002a: 50–6).

A corollary of this framework is that the essential features of human agency are subject to the 'collision law' described by Alexy as governing the relation between principles. This law states that 'the conditions under which one principle takes priority over another constitute the operative facts of a rule giving legal effect to the principle deemed prior' (Alexy 2000a: 297). This makes reflectivity, rationality and autonomy subject to the tests of 'appropriateness', 'necessity' and 'proportionality in the strict sense'. Under the *principle of appropriateness*, a legal provision that undermines one standard of human agency in order to promote the other standards cannot be considered normative if it is in no way appropriate to promoting these other standards. If this provision can be abandoned at no cost to human agency, then optimisation requires one to qualify the provision as non-normative. Under the *principle of necessity*, a legal provision is devoid of normativity if there is an alternative provision that is (a) roughly as good in promoting a standard of human agency, but (b) does not undermine the same standard as extensively. As Alexy (2000a: 298) notes, 'the principles of appropriateness and necessity stem from the obligation of a realization as great as possible relative to the actual possibilities. They express the idea of Pareto-optimality'. By contrast, the *principle of proportionality in the strict sense* derives from an obligation to realise a standard as fully as possible relative to the other constituent standards of human agency. Whenever a standard or substandard of human agency can only be realised at the expense of another, we should weigh them against each other in such a way that the more we are forced to interfere with one standard, the more we should focus on achieving the other.[19]

An important methodological implication follows from qualifying human agency as an optimisation command. Because a flexible standard is open-ended and subject to balancing, it cannot be settled once and for all in relation to its object (for which it serves as a standard). Likewise, because human agency, in its role as the fundamental measure of the normativity of law, behaves not like a rule but like a principle, it cannot, on the modified Kantian approach, be constructed in such a way as to *predetermine* the relation between the law and normativity. Because human agency is such that we must optimise it, or realise it as best we can, we cannot state in general terms whether a single rule of the law supports human agency, but are required instead to consider the rule closely by going into specific details of the case. It is here that a general theory of normativity runs up against a structural limit. A general theory of normativity can establish the fundamental principle governing the normative component of the law, but it cannot on its own establish in each case whether a particular legal rule is normative. For this, we need to undertake contextual reasoning and employ arguments specific to the case at hand. It is at this point that general theory steps aside and argumentation moves in: there is no way to assess the connection between the law and human agency without entering the sphere of reasoning. We cannot assess the normativity of law unless we first go through the relevant argumentative procedures: only in this way

---

[19] On these three principles, see Alexy (2000a: 297–8) and Alexy (2002a: 44–69).

can legal argumentation be acknowledged as the privileged procedure by which the normativity of law is determined. The methodological implication is, therefore, that once human agency is constructed as an optimisation command, and so as a principle, and once we understand that principles require a balancing procedure for their application (this is part of the very concept of a principle), we have then opened up a space for legal argumentation.

The normativity of law is thus understood, on the modified Kantian approach, as a concept ultimately shaped by argumentation, or as conceptually connected with the practice of deliberation. We cannot fully account for the normative dimension of human activities unless we bring into the picture the idea of argumentation: deliberating, adducing and exchanging reasons, justifying and consolidating viewpoints by argument, not deciding on a course of conduct until we have assessed its pros and cons—all these are practices that cannot be bypassed in working out the details of the normativity of law. The arguments for and against a given legal system or provision should, accordingly, be regarded as the essential fabric from which the normativity of that system or provision emerges.[20] This point finds a recent statement in Sylvie Delacroix's (2006: 152) criticism of legal theories that fail to view deliberation as 'the unavoidable cornerstone of legal normativity'. Delacroix's theoretical assumptions (genealogy and practical constructivism) are in part different from the basic assumptions of the modified Kantian approach, to be sure. But there is one point with respect to which her genealogy and the modified Kantian approach are on common ground: they both uphold the argumentative structure of the normativity of law. This important point of agreement warrants bringing Delacroix's theory into play at this stage.

Delacroix rejects the view that to make normativity a variable dependent on reasoning reveals a mistaken understanding of how the law, in demanding that its addresses behave in certain ways, functions. On the view in question, the law functions through an act of imposition rather than through one of deliberation, and it can therefore require courses of conduct not supported by the best reasons. This understanding of the normativity of law may have intuitive appeal, to be sure, for it offers a straightforward account of the ability of the law to make a difference in our practical reasoning. It does so, that is, simply by having the last word. But in deriving the normativity of law exclusively from an act of authority, we thereby commit ourselves to understanding such normativity as a static concept. This is to subscribe to a serious misconception: normativity is not a static concept but a dynamic one, for its meaning and substance can only emerge from the human intercourse through which we exchange reasons. When dynamically constructed, the normativity of law will appear not as a fixed property but rather as one 'that needs rebuilding on a constant basis', the end-product of a continuing process of production and reproduction that 'occurs every time a person enters a practical deliberation aimed at balancing law's requirements with other types of demands, such as those of morality or prudence' (Delacroix 2006: 154). This openness to scrutiny in deliberation is

---

[20] On the relation between normativity and argumentation, see also Bertea (2004).

essential to the normativity of law, for it sets up a framework in which the demands of the law will not be followed in a perfunctory way, merely out of habit, but for a reason that forms a part of a public discussion, and in this way we avoid ultimately depriving the law of its normativity. Normativity 'ought' therefore to be viewed as an inherently argumentative idea; or, conversely, the practice of argumentation is the fabric out of which the normativity of law ultimately arises. This view of normativity as a dynamic concept shaped by argumentation can be regarded as a balanced attempt to steer a middle course between two extreme theses, each which is in its own way misleading and inaccurate: one is the thesis that assessing the normativity of law makes it necessary that each legal demand, on every occasion in which it comes to bear, be assessed; and the other is the thesis that in order for a legal provision to be normative, it must pre-empt deliberation in an exclusionary fashion. There is, therefore, a definite advantage to viewing the normativity of law as having an argumentative core: we secure the possibility of subjecting normative requirements to scrutiny without thereby implying that they need to be critically assessed on every occasion on which they are applied.

These remarks presuppose a certain conception of legal argumentation: that of legal reasoning as rational justification.[21] By *rational justification*, a process of deliberative reasoning, is meant a practice aimed at determining what the proper solution from a rational point of view might be. Legal reasoning is not a logical exercise, or an exercise in persuasion, or a political act in disguise: it is rather a process designed to satisfy an interest, namely, that of determining a rationally correct solution to a practical decision-making problem. This is something it seeks to do by setting up an exchange of communicative moves modelled on the ideal of a critical discussion aimed at the rational resolution of disputes and governed by rules, each of which is assigned a specific function in resolving controversies. The rule-governed structure of reasoning compels the participants to argue with reference to rational standards, and it counteracts the tendency to use legal argumentation as a tool for strategic positioning.[22] Legal argumentation ought accordingly to be understood as a practice structured around the principles of dialectical rationality, as distinct from both logical and rhetorical rationality. Logical rationality, requiring compliance with the rules of deductive logic, establishes an algorithmic ideal applicable in demonstrative argumentation. But legal reasoning is not exclusively demonstrative,[23] for it encompasses a number of

[21] This is a conception I have presented in some detail in Bertea (2002: 73–126).
[22] This is to say that argumentative structures, in framing legal argumentation in certain ways, by setting up a given method of justification, thereby curb our tendency to use argumentation in such a way as to have our own interest prevail. It may be objected here that this unduly restricts our discretion in settling the matter at hand: a code and a pre-established method of argumentation may so tie us up as to rule out a better solution available under a more relaxed system. This may well be. But at the same time, a complete freedom to argue any which way can make our decision-making arbitrary and irrational, if not impossible. Hence, the need for *structures* in legal reasoning: this can be considered part of the broader attempt to subject argumentative activities to rational control.
[23] In a coherently developed *logical* view, 'we "know" something (in the full and strict sense of the term) if-and-only-if we have a well-founded belief in it; our belief in it is well-founded if-and-only-if we can produce good reasons in its support; and our reasons are really "good" (by the strictest philosophical

activities, such as ascertaining, systematising, interpreting, weighing, applying and justifying legal norms, settling conflicts between directives belonging to the same legal system, following precedent, constructing statutes, and working out a legal classification of facts. These activities are all forms of deliberative reasoning, and this makes legal argumentation a *reconstructive* rather than a demonstrative activity, for it does not just *describe* the norms it works with—it contributes to *shaping* them, thereby transforming pre-existing law. Legal reasoning therefore incorporates elements that cannot be reduced to the syllogistic model.[24] But this should not suggest, at the other end of the spectrum, that we can account for legal reasoning as a form of *rhetoric*. The rhetorical approach attempts to widen the narrow logical view by redefining rationality as effectiveness, or persuasiveness, meaning the capacity to achieve a consensus among different participants. The foundational criteria of rhetorical rationality are sociological and anthropological, and this means that the standards for this kind of rationality are undeniably relative: whatever sort of justification may work in one case does not necessarily work in another. This relativity makes the rhetorical concept of rationality inadequate to account for the sort of rationality at work in the law.[25] While the rationality of the law (dialectical rationality) draws on both forms of rationality (logical and rhetorical), it cannot be equated with either, for it is instead a form of *communicative* rationality, a rationality framed by standards designed to govern discussion-moves in a critical exchange of arguments. The dialectical rationality of the law relies on communicative and interaction-shaped principles, such as coherence, generalisability, efficiency, testability, acceptability of consequences and sincerity.[26] To be sure, there is, strictly speaking, no need for these standards to be either logically binding or rhetorically persuasive. But they are rational in any case, in the sense that a failure to comply with them makes inconceivable any discussion aimed at resolving disputes among participants holding different views. The criteria of

standards) if-and-only-if we can produce a "conclusive", or formally valid argument, linking that belief back to an unchallenged and preferably unchangeable) starting point' (Toulmin 1976: 89; emphasis omitted).

[24] Contrary to logical-formal reasoning, legal argumentation does not unfold as a sequence of necessary steps, for it does not use a formal language or even a language that can entirely be transformed into a formal one: its language is rather pragmatic, and the reasoning proceeds from premises that are only probable. Legal reasoning should therefore not be understood as an algorithm 'for thinking or acting, which can be formulated as abstract rules' (O'Neil 1989: 18). For 'there can be no complete rules for judging and ... human reasoning is, as we may say, nonalgorithmic, down to bottom' (O'Neil 1989: 19). Insightful objections to the logical approach have been raised by Atienza (1993: 32–48) and Sartor (1997: 25–9). For a defence of logical reasoning as an essential part of legal reasoning, see Soeteman (1989).

[25] For a critical discussion of the rhetorical understanding of reason as a premise to a full-fledged theory of dialectical reason, see van Eemeren and Grootendorst (1988: 274–9).

[26] These criteria of dialectical rationality are set out in Aarnio, Alexy and Peczenik (1981: 266–70) and Aarnio (1987: 195–201). Dialectical rationality and its role in the law went through a period of neglect and then found renewed interest among legal theorists, philosophers and argumentation theorists about 30 years ago. In legal theory, the most important of these contributions are Aarnio (1987: 185–229), Alexy (1989a: 177–208), Peczenik (1989: 47–212), Wróblewski (1992), Viehweg (1993) and MacCormick (1994: 100–94); in philosophy and argumentation theory, we have Toulmin (1958), van Eemeren and Grootendorst (1984) and Habermas (1984; 1987).

dialectical rationality ought therefore to be considered rational to the extent that dialogue can serve as a rational strategy for settling controversies.[27]

A final point should be clarified in the context of a discussion of the general principles regulating the normativity of law. Not only is human agency a composite notion, but the law is, in turn, composite in so far as it presents different structural levels and can be approached from different perspectives. Two of these are particularly relevant here, the one atomistic and the other holistic. From the atomistic approach, the law is conceived of as a collection of separate provisions, some of which hold privileged relations and form specific clusters having a certain independence from other norms. But even then we would consider each of these separately, and so we would separately consider the normativity of specific legal items: of single legal directives or of particular areas of the law. And once we have discussed the normativity of these provisions and clusters, we will have explained the normativity of law itself and our investigation will come to an end. The normative claim of law will thus be explained (in this atomistic way) by explaining the way in which different legal provisions and branches of the law cohere with the standards of human agency; and the law itself will be recognised as having normative force once its provisions and branches are found to support human agency. To be sure, an atomistic analysis of normativity is an essential stage in any discussion of the normative component of the law: normativity is primarily and directly a property conferred on specific legal provisions and on particular branches of the law. But we must also consider the *systemic* structure of the law: doing so will reveal that to stop short, in our investigation of normativity, and see only as far as the different provisions and areas of the law will allow, is really arbitrarily to rest content with an impoverished account of the normativity of law, for we cannot aspire to any depth or comprehensiveness unless we also look at the law in a holistic way. Hence, the need for a holistic approach, which calls upon us to take into account the normativity of entire legal systems rather than the normativity of their respective provisions.

Thus, in this study of normativity I combine an atomistic approach, focused on the most basic legal items, with a holistic approach that considers the law as a system, gradually moving from a local view to a general one. This combination of perspectives is ultimately justified by the belief that single legal provisions and areas of the law cannot be fully understood unless they are seen in light of the

---

[27] The dialectical nature of legal reasoning has an important implication for the conception of the normativity of law. We saw that the normativity of law functions as a *variable* of legal argumentation and that the structure of legal argumentation is non-deductive: it follows from this that relying on human agency as the governing principle of the normativity of law means nothing like making such normativity conditional on the fulfilment of a supreme legal value from which all normative requirements can be deductively derived. Human agency does not come in as the single, overarching metaprinciple sitting on top of an axiological hierarchy and providing in algorithmic fashion the one right answer to all dilemmas concerning the normative component of the law. Nothing could differ more glaringly from the deductive model than the idea of dialectical rationality on which we are proceeding, because what we end up with in this case is a 'category of indeterminate reference' (Stone 1964: 263), a 'notion of variable content' (MacCormick 1984b: 131). It therefore cannot be formalised.

overall framework of which they form part. It does not matter how many norms and clusters of norms we consider singly, and it does not matter that they remain the basic constituents of the law: it is not by adding them all up that we can account for the normativity of law, nor, for that matter, can we account for the separate normativity of separate constituents simply by looking at the constituents themselves as self-sufficient entities. In fact, more often than not, their interpretation and justification is made possible only by reference to the broader system to which they belong. The system as a whole speaks not just to the way we interpret and justify legal norms and branches of the law: it speaks, too, to their normativity. If the normativity of the system as a whole comes to bear on the normativity of its parts, then we cannot account for the latter without considering the former.

These remarks should also be taken to mean, in regard to the normativity of law, that what applies to single legal provisions and areas of the law does not necessarily apply to the legal system as a whole. That is to say that while the basic principle of normativity in law may be the same throughout, its application is not: the principle does not apply to a legal system in the same way as it applies to its separate laws and branches of the law. We can appreciate this by considering the distinction between *direct* or individual normativity and *indirect* or systemic normativity. A legal form is (or claims to be) *directly* normative in so far as it is (or claims to be) supportive of human agency. Here, the normativity of law depends on its immediate connection with human agency. A legal rule, a branch of the law, or a system of law can each be directly normative (or can otherwise *claim* to have direct normativity). But this is not the only way to acquire normativity, directly from human agency; or, rather, it may be the only way for the system as a whole but not for the constituent provisions and branches of the law. For these can derive their normativity not only directly from human agency but also indirectly through their membership in a system that on the whole can be considered normative. By *indirect* normativity, then, is meant the normativity that a legal rule or area of the law borrows from the general framework of the law rather than from gains made on its own. Legal rules and branches of the law can be considered indirectly normative when, instead of being themselves functional to human agency, they form part of a system that is. More specifically, they *claim* indirect normativity if, rather than making the claim themselves, they owe it to the direct claim made by the system of which they are constituents. Then, too, a legal rule or branch of the law can be described as *being* indirectly normative: it will be so to the extent that it has no independent normative force but derives such force from the whole of which it forms a part. The reason why to single legal rules, provisions and areas of the law not one but two forms of normativity can be attributed (the one direct and the other indirect) is that there are two corresponding ways in which these rules, provisions and areas can contribute to supporting human agency: they can do so by prescribing directly behaviour that is consistent with the basic standards of human agency (reflectivity, rationality and autonomy) or by prohibiting behaviour that is inconsistent with these standards; or they can indirectly do so by contributing to a framework that is on the whole favourable to human agency.

Importantly, indirect normativity can only operate on the condition that a system of laws is taken to be itself capable, by virtue of its very existence, of providing a supportive environment in which we can exercise the basic capacities of human agency. This is a disputed assumption, to be sure, but it is nonetheless an assumption backed by reasons. I should mention just three of them here. The first is that legal systems can play a key role in securing coordination among people, for by channelling our behaviour, or stating what is out of bounds, a legal system helps us to form reasonable expectations about how most other people will behave (that is, in compliance with the law) and about what they can legitimately do.[28] This enables us to adjust our own behaviour accordingly, for if we can by and large assume that others will not break the law, or that they will be held accountable if they do, we can rule out certain scenarios as highly unlikely. Our ability to coordinate with one another will correspondingly be increased; and coordination, in turn, is functional to the full expression of our capacity to think and act rationally and autonomously. This way, by making coordination possible, legal systems not only preserve but also expand the sphere of rational and autonomous conduct based on reflection.[29] A second way in which the law supports human agency is through its expertise: legal systems provide the community they govern with bodies that are entrusted with tasks and goals that, to accomplish, require knowledge that may simply be unavailable to persons considered as so many separate individuals.[30] And this is knowledge that we can all rely on in working to make better use of our autonomy, for it helps us to reflect on the practical issues before us in such a way that we are less likely to make mistakes. Finally, legal systems can make available to their participants options and goods that are only affordable to a large-scale cooperative enterprise, and would otherwise be unavailable to us. The law is often perceived as limiting or even jeopardising our freedom of action as human agents, but at the same time, a legal system serves as a precondition for the achievement of goods and for the exercise of freedoms and capacities that we can hope to attain only by means of a cooperative effort, on a scale sufficiently large and flexible to imply that the law alone will be in a position to facilitate the effort.[31]

---

[28] For an introduction to this argument, see Green (1989: 804–8), among others.

[29] In particular, as Menendez puts it (2000: para 21), 'this allows us to realise that coercion does not only pose threats to autonomy, but at the same time can play an essential role in ensuring the conditions for its exercise, stabilising the expectations about the behaviour of other individuals with which we interact some way or another. This shows that we need law in order to constitute our autonomy, even if it coerces us, and even if we have to fight this same coercion which helps us to constitute our autonomy'.

[30] As Shapiro (2002: 388) frames this argument, practical authority is needed because 'the world is simply too complex for anyone to live one's life completely unaided by experts of one kind or another'.

[31] These few remarks are clearly not intended as an argument proper to show that legal systems generally support human agency. In fact, a powerful argument to the contrary has been put forward presenting the law as *incompatible* with human agency, and in particular with one of its defining features, autonomy. This is the argument presented in philosophical anarchism (see especially Wolff 1970). And though this view proceeds on a more robust conception of autonomy than that which I understand as a constituent of human agency, the challenge is one that is worth taking up. Philosophical anarchists say we cannot assume, as indirect normativity does, that legal systems operate by default in a way that is conducive to human agency.

THE NORMATIVITY OF LAW IN DETAIL

The general framework set out in the section above implies that a comprehensive study of the normativity of law should account for a number of basic distinctions. The most fundamental of those distinctions is the one setting the normative *claim* of law apart from the normative *force* of law. The normative claim of law refers to a *contention* that can be attributed to legal systems and provisions; the normative force of law, instead, individuates an actual *capacity* of legal systems and directives. The two—contention and capacity—differ, for a mere normative *posture* falls short of a normative *achievement*. Claiming to have the power to guide behaviour differs from possessing that power: one can purport to bind the addressees but at the same time fail to do so. The two basic dimensions of the normative component of the law should, therefore, be kept distinct and treated separately for at least some purposes and in certain respects. In the following sections I will take up these two dimensions of normativity in turn and consider them in relation to the other distinctions I have drawn above; in particular, the distinction between instances of the law favourable, indifferent and adverse to human agency, as well as the distinction between direct normativity and indirect normativity.

Normative Claim

In the preceding chapters I defined the normative claim of law and contended that it is a *classifying*, or *enabling*, requirement of the legal enterprise. Anything that fails to comport with a requirement of classifying significance does not merely fall short of fulfilling the regulative standards internal to its kind, and so is inherently faulty, but also abdicates the relevant status.[32] Hence, as far as the law is concerned, a requirement is of classifying significance if it determines the very legality of a directive, a practice or a system. When it is understood as an enabling requirement, the normative claim *defines* the legal domain, namely, it is an essential element of legality: a law that implicitly or explicitly does not even purport to be normative forfeits its legal quality. Accordingly, in so far as it is of classifying significance, the normative claim is a necessary property of the law and so an element of the concept of law, not a possible feature that only some instances of legal systems or directives may happen to have.

New light can be shed on these remarks by way of the statement that the normativity of law depends on the support the law can provide to human agency. This thesis, which was identified above as the fundamental principle governing the normativity of law, carries an important implication respecting the interpretation of the normative claim. The necessary normative claim of law consists in the

---

[32] On the notion of 'requirement of qualifying significance' as opposed to 'requirement of classifying significance' see Alexy (2002b: 26).

proposition that a part of the law aims at supporting the distinctive features of human agency. This holds true for both legal systems and individual legal provisions. Legal systems incorporate of necessity a normative posture, which the modified Kantian approach further specifies in terms of the necessity of endorsing and promoting the human agency of the concerned individuals. Legal provisions, in so far as they embody a directive aim either directly or indirectly, necessarily claim to connect up with the reflectivity, rationality and autonomy of their addressees. In sum, being supportive of human agency, and so causing no harm to the reflectivity, rationality and autonomy of the concerned individuals, is a necessary property of both the subset of orders for the social control that is designated as a *legal* system and the subset of provisions directing interactions that are taken to be *legal* directives. The necessary connection between the law and human agency, thus stated, is limited to the level of claims. A specific instance of a legal world could well fall short of actually cohering with, and being functional to, human agency without implying the loss of that instance's legal character. In other words, the assertion that legal provisions and legal systems alike are making may turn out to be false. We say that the normative claim of law is false whenever a legal instance in fact fails to live up to its normative contention, for example, by including directives that stand in contrast to the reflectivity, rationality and autonomy of the addressed individuals. Though possibly falsified in practice, the normative claim itself remains necessary to both the legal provisions and legal systems.

In the preceding remarks is a twofold pretence. First, in so far as legal instances of necessity make a normative claim, the concept of law can be defined as an institution that primarily concerns and directly addresses human agents. Secondly, and more importantly, by claiming to be normative, the law asserts that among its essential purposes there is the end of supporting the practical identity of its addressees. For conceptual reasons, the protection and the advancement of human agency, then, become an inherent regulative *ideal* of the law. Human agency is a legally relevant standard: reflectivity, rationality and autonomy are not external ideals whose respect determines, for example, the moral value of the law. Rather, they are legal ideals that contribute to a determination of what is legally valuable. This twofold pretence imparts to the law, in turn, an ideal dimension that integrates and complements its factual dimension. For conceptual reasons, then, the law cannot be reduced to a plain fact; it must be regarded as a practice consisting of both facts and values.[33] That the law comprises two levels—the factual level and the ideal level—has methodological consequences as well as substantial implications.

On the methodological front, the conclusion that the law is a mixture of factual elements and ideal features implies that some specific methodology (a non-naturalistic or crudely empirical one) is required to deal with legal issues. Whilst an empirical approach oriented to the external point of view is informative and so

---

[33] This is clearly stated by Alexy (2000b: 138). See also Dworkin's (1978: 48–58) argument for the view that the law is not a plain fact.

helpful to the understanding of the law in so far as the law includes a social dimension, such an approach is far from exhaustive, for it cannot do justice to the ideal dimension of the law. In consideration of the dual nature of the law, no account of the law can be deemed to be comprehensive unless it is based on a method that incorporates the internal point of view. The internal point of view conveys the understanding of the participants in legal practices. Its endorsement requires that one put oneself in the position of those who operate within a legal framework, use legal provisions, struggle to make sense of legal directives and acknowledge the soundness of the legal enterprise. Hence, once the modified Kantian perspective is taken on board, the internal point of view is regarded as a necessary component of any serious attempt to provide an account of the legal enterprise. The specificity of the law assured, on the modified Kantian view, by the combination of factual dimension and a strictly interwoven ideal side, is missed by an enquiry that fails to incorporate the internal point of view. In this respect, the modified Kantian approach converges on the methodology endorsed by mainstream jurisprudence ever since Herbert Hart's groundbreaking work.

Though widely endorsed, the method centred on the internal point of view is not unproblematic. Even among its supporters, the specific quality and scope of this legal methodology is disputed. A number of scholars have observed that the internal point of view, framed in terms of the participants' use of legal provisions and their acceptance of the legal system, is not univocal. There is a plurality of internal points of view as well as a multiplicity of accounts of the law that can be constructed in accordance with the methodology informed by the endorsement of the internal point of view.[34] This plurality and this multiplicity generate a specific problem for the advocates of the methodology based on the internal point of view: the problem of determining the privileged internal point of view within the multiplicity of potentially available internal points of view. In other words, the advocates of the method based on the internal point of view need to establish which version of the internal point of view is the most adequate to the understanding of the law. Especially in considering the alternative character that the various

---

[34] On this issue see Finnis (1980: 13) and Lucy (1999: 70–2), among others. Because of this plurality of internal points of view, the methodological implications of acknowledging that an ideal dimension is part and parcel of the law are not by themselves alone able to settle the dispute between legal positivism and non-positivism. For, on the one hand, the thesis of the primacy of the internal point of view coheres with Dworkin's emphasis on the need to embrace the point of view of a fully committed participant, which alone can enable us to make sense of 'what counts as a good or bad argument within [each given legal] practice' and so to grasp the character of the law as 'an argumentative social practice' (Dworkin 1986: 14). On the other hand, however, the evaluative dimension of the law can also be accounted for by (some of) the legal methodologies defended by the advocates of legal positivism. In particular, MacCormick's (1981: 34–40) 'hermeneutic point of view' and Kramer's (1999: 162–73) 'moderate external perspective' and 'simulative perspective' can be seen as valuable alternatives to the non-positivist characterisation of legal methodology in terms of the fully committed participant's point of view. Hence, whether one should prefer the fully committed participant's viewpoint (in the non-positivist fashion) or another of the other points of view is not a matter settled by the mere acknowledgement that the law incorporates an ideal dimension sitting alongside the factual dimension.

internal points of view proposed thus far present,[35] the mere acknowledgement that taking up the internal point is essential to the understanding of the legal domain is an unstable position. Thus, a choice is required. The modified Kantian approach cannot assist us in this choice for it has no specific methodological instruction directing one towards this rather than that interpretation of the methodology centred on the notion of the internal point of view. The claim that the law is a mix of factual elements and ideal features ultimately supports the thesis of the primacy of the internal point of view in legal studies, but it does not make possible a selection of one among the many possible alternative kinds of internal point of view. Hence, although the modified Kantian approach is not methodologically silent or indifferent, it does not provide a complete methodological position and it stands in need of integration in order to produce an exhaustive methodology.

From the substantive point of view, the ideal dimension is not only established but also delimited (up to a certain point) by the normative claim. In particular, the content of the ideal dimension is established by the values underlying human agency, as well as by any other value that is functional vis-à-vis the protection of the reflectivity, rationality and autonomy of the concerned agents. Thus, the ideal dimension of the law is fixed from the outset, although in broad terms: in so far as it cannot fail to account for human agency, the ideal dimension of legality is bestowed with a necessary content, which is ultimately fixed by the fundamental principle of the normativity of law. This principle implies that the normative claim of law, a claim that is a necessary component of the ideal dimension of the law, can be equated with the attempt to incorporate the defining features of human agency. The law meaningfully claims to be normative in so far as its content aspires to comply with the requirements set by the fundamental elements of human agency. In consideration of the necessary content of this claim, the fact that the law necessarily makes such claim establishes an indispensable connection between the concept of law and the endeavour to support human agency. The effort to safeguard the human traits of reflectivity, rationality and autonomy of the governed agents becomes a part of the very concept of law, a requirement that, in order to be qualified as law, any structure of social control must have. The attempt to operate within the framework of human agency is, then, to be considered an inherent quality of the law. Accordingly, an endeavour to support human agency is legally, and not just morally, required on the part of the law. Where this is brought together with the view that the normative claim is a part of the concept of law, the link connecting normativity and human agency makes of reflectivity, rationality and

---

[35] The options available are different, as are their further implications for the way legal studies are undertaken. Apart from the suggestions mentioned in n 34 (MacCormick's hermeneutical point of view, Kramer's simulative perspective and Dworkin's fully committed participant's point of view), other alternative characterisations of the internal point of view are theoretically important. Among these one should mention at least Raz's 'ordinary man's point of view' as well as his 'legal point of view', and Finnis's 'viewpoint of those who possess practical reasonableness'. On these further elaborations on the notion of internal point of view, see Raz (1970: 200) and Finnis (1980: 11–8).

autonomy the defining goals of legality. Hence, the specific definition of the law resulting from the embracement of the modified Kantian point of view: the law can be defined as a structure of social control enlisting among its necessary purposes the defence of the fundamental requirements of human agency. In consequence thereof, a necessary (broad) point is also imposed upon the law: for conceptual reasons the law exists in order to protect the reflectivity, rationality and autonomy of those addressed by legal norms. In this way, some aims that are quite independent of the decisions of those in power are imparted upon the law as essential aims.

In conclusion, the attempt to support the basic features defining human agency determines the status of an institution as distinctively legal and distinguishes it from other institutions that, although indistinguishable from the structural point of view, lack the goal of supporting human agency. A legal system is not just any system of social control. No structure of governance simply presenting law-like formal features can be qualified as legal: unless a system of governance performs an attempt to protect the distinctive practical identity of the individuals with whom it is concerned, there is no legal system in place. Systems that make no claim to afford protection to the distinctive traits of their addressees are not only legally defective but are, indeed, deprived of their legal character altogether. Or to put it in more dramatic terms, from the legal point of view institutions that do not take human agency seriously are non-existent; a practical institution that fails to claim to be functional to human agency has only a social existence, not a legal one. Legality, as a result, identifies a well-circumscribed subset of systems of social control.

Normative Force

In the modified Kantian approach, normative force should be seen as a qualifying requirement of the legal enterprise. A requirement is of qualifying significance for a phenomenon if it characterises, of necessity, the full-fledged instances of that phenomenon. Something that complies with all the requirements of qualifying significance fulfils the regulative standards internal to that kind: it is internally faultless and flawless. Hence, it passes any judgement that is based on the standards internal to, and defining of, that genre. This does not rule out the possibility of criticising that kind, or finding it wanting, once it is assessed by appeal to external standards of evaluation. Accordingly, the statement that normative force is a qualifying requirement of the law implies the view that, subject to the condition that all the other standards of internal soundness are fulfilled, a *normative* legal system is a flawless instance of the genre 'law', to wit, a form of law internally, or legally, non-defective. This qualification does not allow for the conclusion that a normative legal system is flawless *tout court*. A legal system that is correctly characterised as normative might nevertheless be an ineffective institution or an institution that causes the exploitation of some groups as well as discriminating arbitrarily between individuals. That legal system will, then, be criticised on the basis of non-necessarily-legal standards, such as the principle of efficiency and the principle of equality. To the extent that this criticism is successful, this legal system will be considered defective. But it will not be legally, or internally, defective; rather it will be externally defective, namely, it will be seen as wanting from the point of view of certain ideals that originate in non-legal domains. In a nutshell, a normative instance of the law can present defects of another nature (say, moral defects) but unless other internal standards of judgement are violated, it is not legally defective. Correspondingly, the failure of the law to manifest normative force results in a legal failure: a token of the law that does not meet the standards governing normative force is defective from the legal point of view itself. From this way of characterising the relationship between the law and normative force, it follows that we have less than a sound legal system if some of the provisions constituting that system cannot create obligations.[36]

Whilst an instance of the law lacking normative force is, however, legally defective, it does not thereby abdicate its legal status: it is still legal although not flawlessly so. The preservation of legal status on the part of those instances of the law that are bestowed with no normative force is warranted by the fact that there is no contradiction in terms, either logical or performative, in asserting that a provision or a system is legally valid but has no normative force. The expression 'law with no normative force' cannot be equated either with expressions such as 'married bachelor' and 'hot ice' (that are affined to logical contradictions) or with the decision handed down by Alexy's (2002b: 38) judge, who claims that 'the accused is sentenced to life imprisonment, which is wrong'—a case of performative contradiction. As a result, it is far from the case that for logical or pragmatic reasons, a legal system that is not bestowed with normative force is non-law. This shows that the law is not *intrinsically* supplied with normative force. Whereas the normative dimension is constitutive of legality in so far as no legal instance can refrain from adopting the normative posture, what is legal may lack normative force. Thus, the normative dimension inherent in legality is confined to an attitude and does not extend to either the power of generating special reasons to act or to that of imposing non-optional modes of conduct.

To summarise, normative force is a merely possible feature of the law, a property that (some instances of) the law may happen not to have rather than an inherent character of the law, an achievement conceptually linked with the existence of the law. In so far as the law is lacking normative force, its necessary normative claim neither disappears nor is devoid of meaning: it is simply false. Correspondingly, the law retains its defining conceptual features.

According to the fundamental principle governing the normativity of law, the merely possible normative force of law depends on the actual aptitude of the law

---

[36] From these remarks it follows also that legal soundness is a matter of degree. A legally sound system sets an ideal to strive for and is likely to be attainable only to a certain extent. We may have systems that are more or less legally sound depending on how many of their provisions have normative force and how important those provisions are.

in supporting human agency. Normative force is granted to the law subject to the condition that the content and form of the law comport with the requirements set by the elements that define human agency. On this basis, we can provisionally state that the law is legally flawless if, besides fulfilling the other possible standards of legal soundness, it is structured in such a way as to reflect the defining features of human agency. The law does not forfeit its nature simply because it fails to support the essential features of human agency, but it does forfeit its legal soundness in so far as it does not back them at all. Human agency, then, functions as a kind of inner standard of legal soundness. The actual inability of a given legal system to protect the reflectivity, rationality and autonomy of the human agents under its jurisdiction is not without consequences. Still, these consequences do not amount to the loss of legal character of that system. Rather, they imply a legal defect: legally defective instances of the law have an imperfect legal existence in that they may fail to create obligations.

These remarks set the general framework of normative force in a theory of law. But a detailed treatment requires a consideration of the distinctions introduced above, namely, the distinction between the law supporting human agency, the law unconcerned with human agency, and the law opposing human agency, as well as the distinction between direct normativity and indirect normativity. Moreover, no specific thesis on the normative force of law can be defended unless one deals separately with specific legal provisions and branches of the law, on the one hand, and legal systems, on the other. In the following sections I will address the various possible cases one by one.

Normative Force of Provisions and Branches of the Law

In the present context, legal provisions and branches of the law can be discussed together, for the functioning of their normative force is the same. Accordingly, henceforth I will take up only those cases of legal provisions where what is claimed about the normative force of legal provisions applies to the normative force of specific branches of the law, too. Legal provisions can be favourable, indifferent, simply contrary, or extremely contrary to human agency. The provisions *favourable* to human agency derive their normative force directly from their orientation toward human agency. A favourable attitude grants to legal provisions all the normative force they need. As a consequence, there is no need to appeal to any indirect notion of normative force. It is not that it would be wrong or conceptually impossible to refer the notion of indirect normative force to provisions supporting human agency. It is, however, practically speaking irrelevant whether or not a single provision that supports human agency is introduced into a system of laws maintaining an overall favourable attitude toward the defining features of human agency, for the provision in question need not find a systemic anchorage in order to generate special reasons to act. No matter whether the general framework into which a favourable specific directive is introduced confirms or disconfirms the attitude of that provision, the normative force of that directive will be generated.

A provision supporting human agency retains its independent normative force even though the system of which it is part is far from supportive of human agency.

In order to appreciate how the normative force of single legal provisions works, a concrete example may be of use here. Consider the original form of section 1(1) of the UK Race Relations Act 1976, which is meant to prohibit racial discrimination and provides that:

> A person discriminates against another in any circumstances relevant for the purposes of any provision of this Act if:
>
> (a) on racial grounds he treats that other less favourably than he treats or would treat other persons; or
> (b) he applies to that other a requirement or condition which he applies or would apply equally to persons not of the same racial group as that other but:
>   (i) which is such that the proportion of persons of the same racial group as that other who can comply with it is considerably smaller than the proportion of persons not of that racial group who can comply with it; and
>   (ii) which he cannot show to be justifiable irrespective of the colour, race, nationality or ethnic or national origins of the person to whom it is applied; and
>   (iii) which is to the detriment of that other because he cannot comply with it.

Whereas a definitive assessment of the normative force of this provision would require that one deploy an argument accounting for the way it has been interpreted and applied by courts, at first glance section 1(1) of the Race Relations Act 1976 supports, rather than contradicts, human agency. In particular, it adopts a supportive attitude towards the autonomy of subjects, for in so far as it bars unjustifiable discrimination, it avoids that the freely endorsed choice of individuals to act in accordance with the custom of their ethnic group is lawfully penalised. As a result of the enactment of the Race Relations Act 1976, one cannot lawfully discriminate against human agents when, in the exercise of their autonomy, they uphold a way of life that is characteristic of a given ethnic group.

The way autonomy is protected by section 1(1) of the Race Relations Act 1976 can be clarified by the decision in the case of *Mandla v Dowell Lee* [1983] 2 AC. In that case, an orthodox Sikh wished to enrol his son as a pupil at a private school, but the request was turned down, on the grounds that wearing a turban over unshorn hair (as the Sikh tradition requires) was deemed to conflict with the school rules on pupils' uniform. A legal action was then brought against the headmaster of the school on the ground that the refusal to admit orthodox Sikhs unless they were willing to give up a practice required by their membership of the Sikh group, in order to preserve the school uniform rule, was in violation of Race Relations Act 1976, section 1(1). Whereas both the Commission for Racial Equality and the Court of Appeal dismissed the case, the House of Lords stated that the behaviour of the headmaster led to indirect discrimination against Sikhs and such discrimination was unjustifiable under section 1(1). In the opinion of their Lordships (in particular, of Lord Fraser of Tullybelton, who wrote the opinion unanimously upheld), the unlawfulness of the 'no turban rule' set by the headmaster rested on the fact that it unjustifiably prevented orthodox Sikhs from attending the school. The justification for the ban on turbans adduced by the headmaster in order to bar the Sikh pupil from wearing a turban was that to allow pupils to wear symbols of their ethnic origin would emphasise the external differences between racial and social classes of the school population, as well as impairing the Christian image the school wanted to present to outsiders. This justification, however, was regarded as unsatisfactory, for it allowed discrimination against pupils in ethnic groups for whom exhibiting symbols was an essential requirement. As a result, the ban on turbans was to be considered discriminatory. Importantly, it can be shown that the prohibition by the headmaster stands in contrast with the protection of autonomy to be afforded to human agents, for it implies a limitation on the autonomy of those individuals willing to act as orthodox members of the Sikh group in so far as it forces them to choose between their membership of the ethnic group of their origin and their freedom to attend the school of their choice. No matter which of the options is taken, the autonomy of choice of the concerned individuals suffers a significant blow. This example illustrates how section 1(1) of the Race Relations Act 1976 can be regarded as having, overall, a supportive attitude toward human agency. In turn, such a supportive attitude undergirds the direct normative force of that provision. This assessment settles the question concerning the normative force of Race Relations Act 1976, section 1(1), and therefore makes, practically speaking, irrelevant a further judgement needed to establish the quality of the legal system in which that provision is included, and so the possible indirect normative force of that provision.

Matters are more complex when one considers the case of provisions that are *indifferent* to human agency. These provisions are not directly normative, for indifference to human agency implies the inability to support human agency. Since in the modified Kantian view such support is the ultimate justification of the normative force of practical reason, provisions indifferent to human agency are by themselves alone unable to create specific obligations. Still, they can be acknowledged to have normative force, although only normative force derived indirectly, namely, as a result of their membership in a normative system. In so far as the provisions indifferent to human agency are either *essential* or *useful* to the maintenance of a legal system that is overall supportive of human agency, they derive normative force from the support they provide (not to human agency but) to the system favourably oriented to human agency. In other words, as long as a legal directive does not support human agency, as a matter of principle it cannot by itself create obligations. Nonetheless, its normative force can be preserved indirectly in so far as it is a part of a system that supports as a whole the basic features of human agency. Hence, even legal provisions that do not substantiate human agency can have normative force. The justification of the indirect normative force of provisions indifferent to human agency lies in the fact that, in being either essential or instrumental to the preservation of a framework helping agents to behave reflectively, rationally and autonomously, indifferent provisions ultimately link up with human agency, which still remains beyond their direct scope. Thus, albeit indirectly, the existence of provisions indifferent to human agency may have a favourable impact on the prospect of protecting human agency by virtue of the networking of these provisions with the overall legal system. In this way, the systemic connection obtaining between indifferent provisions and human agency grants to these provisions the normative force that they would not possess on the basis of their own direct merit.

Finally, legal provisions *contrary* to human agency should be further distinguished and, as a consequence, two subcases can be fashioned: the case of provisions perpetrating a simple infringement of human agency, and the case of provisions that stand in sharp contrast to the features defining human agency. Legal provisions opposing human agency in a merely superficial and partial way are affined to the directives indifferent to human agency, although they hinder the prospect of fulfilling human agency in a more serious way. Accordingly, they enjoy no direct normative force: by failing to support human agency they have no access to direct normativity. Their opposition to human agency is, however, relative, not absolute. As a result, it is less significant on the whole than the support to human agency they can possibly provide in so far as they contribute to the continuation of a system that is overall supportive of reflectivity, rationality and autonomy. Therefore, legal provisions perpetrating simple infringements of human agency can be acknowledged to have (indirect) normative force whenever they happen to be *essential* to the preservation of a system that provides for the safeguarding and enhancement of human agency. In other words, in principle, directives inconsistent with human agency should be denied normative force on the ground that they tend to undermine human agency. But if their tendency to undermine human agency is compensated by the indirect aid to human agency that they ultimately offer as part of a wider system, this tendency can be 'forgiven', as it were. The principle conditioning normative force vis-à-vis the capacity to support human agency can be compressed in so far as its uncompromised application is ultimately more harmful than helpful to human agency. Provisions superficially infringing on human agency fulfil this condition. Therefore, their lack of normativity can be disregarded. The ultimate reason for the ascription of normative force to those legal directives is that by drawing them away from the normative force altogether, one would jeopardise the overall framework of which they are part. And the damage to human agency that can stem from the collapse of a system that, even though it includes some unfavourable provisions, nonetheless supports on the whole the reflectivity, rationality and autonomy of the governed individuals, is greater than the damage determined by the simple infringement of human agency caused directly by some of its provisions. As a consequence, it seems opportune to put into place a rescue strategy in the very interest of that human agency from which normativity stems. Importantly, the scope of the indirect normative force of provisions opposing human agency is more limited than the scope of the indirect normative force of provisions indifferent to human agency. In consideration of the fact that, by itself, the provision is not only extraneous to the realm covered by human agency but also hostile to the features distinctive of our practical identity, the mere functionality of the directive to the persistence of the system does not suffice. It is required that the legal provision in question be not only *functional* and *useful* but indeed *essential* to the system supporting human agency. This marks a key difference from the indirect normative force of indifferent legal directives.

An example can be of use here, in order better to understand the concrete functioning of the indirect normative force of provisions superficially infringing human agency. An instance of this sort of provision is supplied by the UK Anti-terrorism, Crime and Security Act 2001, which deals in Part 4 with those suspected of international terrorism and enables the Secretary of State to issue a certificate by means of which people merely suspected of putting the national security at risk and of being international terrorists can, among other things, be refused leave to enter or remain in the United Kingdom, or be issued a deportation order, or be detained (sections 21–23).[37] The power to sanction on the basis of the mere suspicion that one is involved in a plot and is under the influence of people aiming at 'the commission, preparation or instigation of acts of international terrorism' (Anti-terrorism, Crime and Security Act 2001, section 21(3)(b)) contrasts with the full recognition of human agency; for such power implies that one's sphere of action may possibly be limited, and so one's human agency, notwithstanding the fact that it has not been shown that one has acted unlawfully. Correspondingly, conferring the power to punish suspects implies that, in principle, someone may be sanctioned although the party is neither subjectively nor objectively accountable for any unlawful action. This means that the acts one freely undertakes in consequence of independent deliberation are not decisive in legal judgments. The very idea of the human agent as a reflective, rational and autonomous subject is affected here. Sections 21–23 of the Anti-terrorism, Crime and Security Act 2001, which introduce a form of accountability based not on facts but only on beliefs, should, then, be considered as contrary to human agency. However, the contrast between those provisions and human agency is lessened by the requirement that the belief on the basis of which a suspect is punished should be reasonable (section 21), and the sanction issued by the Secretary of State can be challenged before another state power, the Special Immigration Appeals Commission (sections

---

[37] In particular the latter provision—that which confers on the Secretary of State the power to order the detention of a suspected international terrorist even for an indefinite period—has raised serious concerns among human rights activists ever since its enactment. Notwithstanding these concerns, the provision has been used to sanction a number of suspected international terrorists and was renewed with the Anti-terrorism, Crime and Security Act (Continuance in Force of Sections 21 to 23) Order 2004 before being declared in contravention of the European Convention on Human Rights by the Law Lords on 16 December 2004 in so far as it allowed indefinite detention without charge and targeted exclusively non-British citizens (by so amounting to a patently discriminatory measure). Whilst the provision remained in force all the same under the terms of the Human Rights Act 1998, it was finally changed by Parliament with the Prevention of Terrorism Act 2005, which replaced the power to issue detention orders with the power to issue control orders, ie orders directed to restrict an individual's liberty—under a number of respects, such as the possession and use of specified objects, substances, services and facilities, the place of work and residence, the activities one can carry out, the rights of association and communication, the freedom of movement etc—in forms falling short of imprisonment.

25–27). Arguably, the limitations to which the discipline contrary to human agency contained in the Anti-terrorism, Crime and Security Act 2001 is subjected suggest that sections 21–23 of that Act perpetrate a simple infringement on human agency rather than an extreme one. Therefore, whereas sections 21–23 are not supplied with normative force by themselves, they can derive normative force from their membership in the legal system in force in the United Kingdom, provided that one can show that the Anti-terrorism, Crime and Security Act 2001 should be considered essential to the maintenance of the relevant legal system and the relevant legal system overall supports human agency.[38]

Concluding this discussion of the normative force of legal provisions perpetrating a simple infringement of human agency, it is important to emphasise that indirect normative force does not stand on an equal footing with direct normative force. Indirect normative force presents itself only if direct normative force proves to be unavailable. This subsidiary quality of indirect normative force is due to the fact that indirect normative force derives from, and supervenes upon, qualities external to the directive in question. These further qualities become relevant only if the directive by itself does not hamper (directly) human agency more than it (indirectly) supports human agency. This condition can hardly be fulfilled by means of provisions commanding conduct that is extremely adverse to human agency. Those provisions are far too damaging to human agency to be rescued indirectly. An extremely inhospitable attitude towards human agency blocks the indirect supervening effect and hinders the systemic mechanism that allows us to save the normative force of non-particularly meritorious legal directives. No overturning is possible in such a case, for the support that, by virtue of its systemic connections, a directive strongly opposing reflectivity, rationality and autonomy can provide to human agency cannot be enough to counterbalance the extreme infringement of human agency that it directly causes. Thus, an extreme infringement of human agency deprives the standard of any normative force. Correspondingly, a system comprising directives that infringe human agency to an extreme degree is locally deprived of normative force.

An example may be of use here. In the period when eugenics was in its heyday, the General Assembly of the State of Virginia passed a series of laws aimed at combating a development that at the time was perceived as leading to the 'suicide' of the 'Anglo-Saxon race', to put it in Theodore Roosevelt's terms. Among the relevant statutes, on 20 March 1924, the Senate passed Bill 219 entitled An Act to Preserve Racial Integrity (hereinafter, the 'Racial Integrity Act'). This Act required the racial make-up of individuals to be recorded at birth. To that end, the Racial Integrity Act first distinguished the different races acknowledged at the

---

[38] For instance, one could argue that the Anti-terrorism, Crime and Security Act 2001, ss21–23, are meant to protect national security, which in turn is essential to the existence of the legal system in force in the United Kingdom. Moreover, one could appeal to the fundamental human rights on which the legal system in force in the United Kingdom is based in order to show that, overall, such a system is supportive to human agency. Clearly, these scant notes fall well short of an argument and are included here only to invite attention to a possible argumentative route, rather than to pursue it.

time to exist, namely, 'Caucasian, negro, Mongolian, American Indian, Asiatic Indian, Malay, or any mixture thereof, or any other non-Caucasic strains' and, secondly, prescribed the competent authorities to issue a registration certificate stating 'the racial composition of the parents and other ancestors' of each individual (section 1). In addition, the Racial Integrity Act introduced a ban on miscegenation by making it 'unlawful for any white person in [Virginia] to marry any save a white person, or a person with no other admixture of blood than white and American Indian' (section 5). For the purpose of the Racial Integrity Act, the term 'white person' applied 'only to the person who has no trace whatsoever of any blood other than Caucasian; but persons who have one-sixteenth or less of the blood of the American Indian and have no other non-Caucasic blood shall be deemed to be white persons' (section 5). The Racial Integrity Act is a paradigmatic example of a legal provision that stands in sharp contrast to the features defining human agency. A ban on interracial marriages prevents agents, upon rational deliberation, taking autonomous decisions respecting their conjugal life. As a result, it denies those concerned the distinctive features of human agency; for the *reflective capacity* of those addressed by the ban is undermined and delimited in so far as they are not allowed to take into consideration the whole range of available options when they come to the decision as to whom they marry. Moreover, they are shorn of their *rationality*, for the Racial Integrity Act is in fact based on a general negative evaluation of miscegenation, and this general evaluation makes the individual assessment of the reasons for and against interracial marriages on the part of each subject irrelevant. Finally, they are deprived of their *autonomy*, for they are not left free to choose independently of external coercion the person whom they wish to marry. For all these reasons, the Racial Integrity Act forces on some people a pattern of behaviour that betrays their distinctively human agency. The degree of the violation of human agency determined by the Racial Integrity Act is made more serious by the fact that the Act concerns a dimension—the choice of a partner—that is essential to human life. The infringement on human agency of provisions like the Racial Integrity Act is, then, to be qualified as extreme. Therefore, not only should the Racial Integrity Act be seen as having no direct normative force, but it should also be considered without any prospect of acquiring normative force indirectly from the system of which it is part. Even if, in the 1920s, the legal system of the State of Virginia might have arguably been overall supportive of human agency, the Racial Integrity Act would have to have been considered not binding all the same: its opposition to the reflectivity, rationality and autonomy of the concerned individuals was too great to grant to it any possibility of its normative force being rescued indirectly.

Normative Force of Legal Systems

The discussion of the normative force of legal systems requires us to analyse a smaller number of cases, for in this context the distinction between direct normative force and indirect normative force disappears. Legal systems can only be directly normative. In so far as legal systems are not directly normative, they are not normative at all. The cases to be discussed, then, are just three in number: legal systems favourably oriented to human agency; legal systems indifferent to human agency; and legal systems opposing human agency. The application of the fundamental principle regulating the normative force of the law to these cases does not present particular difficulty. Legal systems are invested with normative force in so far as their existence contributes to implementing the practice of reflection and the exercise of rationality, as well as autonomy, among the agents they address. Conversely, legal systems that incorporate contents and take forms indifferent to or incompatible with the distinctively human predicaments fail to achieve normative force. In the absence of any supportive link to the idea of human agency, there is no longer enough left over in a legal system to create duties. Having completely betrayed their rational nature, such legal institutions lack normative force altogether. In sum, the failure to acknowledge the status of human agents to the individuals they address amounts to a barrier that prevents legal systems from having binding force; the functionality of legal systems to human agency is a necessary condition of their normative force.

This is tantamount to claiming that legal systems bestowed with normative force emerge with certain necessary features attached to them. Some limits are imposed upon normative legal systems by the necessary connection obtaining between normative force, on the one hand, and reflectivity, rationality and autonomy, on the other. The limits set by the requirement that reflectivity, rationality and autonomy be implemented in legal institutions are, indeed, quite broad. To be sure, the substance and form of legal systems endowed with normative force may vary considerably. But the freedom of law-making powers is not absolute; rather, constraints are at work. The legal contents and forms compatible with the possession of normative force are restricted to those that are contrary to the defining features of human agency. Therefore, in so far as they can generate special reasons to act, legal systems neither incorporate any content whatsoever nor take whatever form best suits those in power. Some types of contents and certain forms deprive legal systems of normative force. Accordingly, a system that incorporates such content or takes on such forms is legal but not binding.

Two examples can clarify the points just made. Both make reference to ideal-types of legal system, as opposed to legal systems as they are deployed in fact. The choice of focusing on ideal-types in this context is dictated by reasons of simplicity. As will be explained further below, the analysis of actual legal systems is extremely complex and requires technical competence as well as considerable knowledge of the specific legal system under consideration. Ideal-types, by contrast, are of more immediate presentation and general apprehension. A focus on ideal-types will enable me to elucidate the views just expressed in a clearer and more simplified form. This is to say that the task of extending the analysis to concrete cases of actual legal systems will be left to the reader. The first example brings into the picture the idea of democracy, which especially in its deliberative forms can be constructed as an ideal-type of a legal system oriented favourably towards human agency. The second example appeals to the notion of the governor system, which is argued to be a paradigmatic instance of a legal system inconsistent with the practical requirements set by human agency.

Gradually emerged in the 1980s as an alternative to the models of aggregative democracy, agonistic democracy and pluralist democracy, deliberative democracy is a normative paradigm and is arguably capable of responding to the crisis of democracy denounced by elitist theorists.[39] Deliberative democracy can be summarised as the view that 'public deliberation of free and equal citizens is the core of legitimate political decision making and self-government' (Bohman 1996: 401). The model of deliberative democracy, then, sets an ideal of political arrangement emphasising the role that rational reasoning, exchanging arguments, discourse and discussion among citizens has in public decision-making.[40] In this view, collective argumentation taking place under ideal conditions (such as full information, equal opportunity for political influence, impartiality, sincerity and absence of time-constraints) has a central place in political life and replaces strategic behaviour (for example, voting and bargaining) as the pivotal mechanism used to reach decisions on issues of public concern. In a system shaped by the ideal of deliberative democracy, keys to political life are the rational processes aimed at reaching a consensus among all the potentially interested parties, which are taken to be free and equal, through the force of the better argument rather than through simple compromise, irrational persuasion, mere negotiation or bargaining equilibrium. A public matter will thus be legitimately settled with this model only if the selected settlement is one that everyone can accept or, at least, not reasonably reject. This way, deliberative democracy individuates an ideal that is critical, oppositional and reformist in respect of the standard practices of liberal constitutional democracy as deployed in the Western world, central to which are procedures for making laws that provide citizens with equal rights to register their preference through voting and procedures for making decisions that are based on majority rule. The paradigm of deliberative democracy, in other words, indicates what political institutions should be, rather than describing what they actually are, in the fashion of an explanatory model, for it relies on a number of idealising assumptions that set it apart from the democratic systems with which we are familiar.

This ideal coheres to a very high degree with the notion of human agency. Democratic institutions, when shaped by the deliberative model, can be regarded as supportive of the idea of human agency, for in principle they are so structured as to lend to reflectivity, rationality and autonomy an opportunity to flourish. Democracy supplies agents with the possibility of fulfilling their *autonomy* in so far as it grants to them a fair chance to discuss public issues and to have their reasons

---

[39] The phrase 'deliberative democracy' was first used by Bessette (1980), who introduced the idea to oppose the elitist interpretation of the United States Constitution. The ideal of deliberative democracy, which found early formulations in the works of Jean-Jacques Rousseau, John Dewey and Hannah Arendt, was successively consolidated in Elster (1986), Cohen (1989), Dryzek (1990), Bohman (1996), Gutmann and Thompson (1996), Habermas (1996) and Nino (1996), among others.

[40] See Cohen (1996: 99–100).

weighed in the process of common will-formation.[41] And having been given an opportunity to have a voice in the process leading to a decision is a precondition of regarding that decision as an autonomous act. Moreover, the idea of equal participation, which is conceptually associated with the existence of institutions approaching the ideal of deliberative democracy, is essential to the possibility of handling public questions *rationally* and *reflectively*. Especially by virtue of its egalitarian and participatory dimension, deliberative democracy can be interpreted as the institutionalisation of collective reflection regulated by rational standards in the universe of the individuals whom the relevant decision concerns. By structurally allowing an extensive confrontation among the subjects that are affected by each particular decision, democracy, understood along the lines of the deliberative model, sets a procedural paradigm of sound deliberation on public issues.[42] Within democratic institutions, the interests of different parties can be heard and the reasons for and against each possible alternative course of action can be compared, discussed and weighed. This has the potential to contain the significance of selfish interests and the power of opposite factions, as well as to increase the basis of knowledge on which decisions are taken.[43] As a result, institutions modelled by the ideal of deliberative democracy, central to which is the notion of *rational* and *autonomous deliberation*, provide strong support to the rationality, autonomy and reflectivity of the subject concerned.[44] Therefore, democracy should be qualified as a procedural ideal-type of a legal system that is favourably oriented to human agency, and the issuances of democratic legal systems are to be regarded as provided, prima facie, with normative force.[45]

---

[41] Incidentally, the discussion of democracy is relevant also because it shows most clearly that among the factors determining the normative failure of the law, some have to do with the content of a system and others are related to its form. The relevance of the content of the law is immediately understandable: there exists conduct so inconsistent with the basic features of human agency that any provision prescribing or failing to forbid such conduct is less than normative. Legal forms and procedures might appear less significant at first sight. But they are relevant, too. Some kinds of forms and procedures are by themselves incompatible with human agency and so are insurmountable obstacles to the emergence of the normative force.

[42] For a similar interpretation of democracy, see in particular Nino (1996: 117–43).

[43] This point is extensively made by those who defend the epistemic justification of deliberative democracy. See, eg, Cohen (1986) and Estlund (1997), who in a nutshell claim that public deliberation is the most reliable procedure for knowing the right political decision. The epistemic reliability of rational public deliberation is due to the fact that deliberation favours the exchange and sharing of information, thereby increasing the degree of knowledge available, improves the chance of detecting mistakes in reasoning, contributes to controlling, lessening, filtering and even overcoming the impact of emotional factors and irrational preferences, and makes the manipulation of information more difficult. For clear and concise statements of the epistemic virtues of deliberative democracy, see Freeman (2000: 384–9), Warren (2002: 192–6) and Lafont (2006: 8–14).

[44] To put it in Samuel Freeman's (2000: 390) terms, the ideal deliberation sitting at the core of democratic regimes shaped by the deliberative model 'respects citizens' *autonomy*, because it encourages the exercise of their deliberative capacities and the formation of preferences as a result of deliberation'. This point is made and elaborated on also in Cooke (2000: 954–6).

[45] Importantly, the fulfilment of the democratic principle is not a sufficient precondition for an institution to achieve normative force. To be sure, democratic regimes can fail to possess normative force in so far as the content of the directives enacted within them departs from human agency as far as the substantial point of view is concerned.

The second case study requires the introduction of a kind of legal system, the 'governor system', discussed by Alexy (2002b: 33–4) in his treatment of the concept of law. The governor system designates a system in which the rulers exploit the governed community 'according to a rule-driven practice' (Alexy 2002b: 33). This system is constructed as a development of a system of social control that Alexy (2002b: 32) calls 'senseless order'.[46] In a senseless order, 'a group of individuals is ruled such that the consistent purposes of the ruler or rulers are not discernible nor is a long-term pursuit of a purpose by the ruled possible'. The rulers issue arbitrary and even contradictory commands that may well be unstable and impossible to fulfil. Whereas, in Alexy's view, such a system cannot be considered legal, it can be turned into a legal system by an effort, on the part of the rulers, to acquire a modicum of legitimacy. This result is achieved by incorporating into the order a claim to the effect that the system of exploitation is correct and functional vis-à-vis the general interest or any other valuable end. This way, a senseless order is transformed into a governor system. The governor system has the same structural characteristics of a senseless order save for the addition of a claim to be correct and functional to the interests of the people ruled. This claim remains completely unfulfilled, for the system is in fact instrumental to the exploitation of the governed. Yet, its existence is not without consequences: it implies, at the very least, that the exploitation is lawful only if it is alleged to fit the ends institutionally set. On this basis, Alexy (2002b: 34) argues that the governor system is severely unjust but deserves the qualification of legal system. Being an unjust legal system, the governor system falls short of an ideal law and is, indeed, recognised by Alexy as legally defective (2002b: 35). The modified Kantian construction allows us to clarify further the extent of the legal defect displayed by the governor system. Whereas in Alexy's framework the content of that defect is left vague, in the framework shaped by the modified Kantian approach the defectiveness at stake can be specified as the absence of normative force. The governor system is legal but has no normative force, for it is a paradigmatic instance of a system that conflicts with human agency, as in a governor system some capacities defining human agency remain unfulfilled. On the one hand, in consideration of the instability and the arbitrariness of the commands issued by the governors, there is no point in the governed agents assessing the legal qualification of their conduct. Reflection is discouraged, for it does not help the governed to steer clear of legal sanctions. On the

---

[46] Strictly speaking, the closest kin of the governor system is not the senseless order but the ideal-type of evil regime, where the governmental officials pass legal directives that, like the directives passed in the governor system, can find no moral justification and, in addition, contrary to what it is the case in the governor system, are not even claimed to be justifiable. A specific instantiation of this kind of evil regime is Despotia, introduced and discussed in Kramer (1999: 88, 90–2), namely, a system in which officials sustain their lavish lifestyles by imposing crushingly heavy taxes on citizens without concerning themselves with the justification of their directives (though they might find it strategically wise to explain their decisions in terms of citizens' alleged legal duties). From the modified Kantian perspective, a Despotia-like evil regime is an example of a *non-legal* system that is closer to the defective *legal* system shaped by the model of the governor system.

other hand, the individuals concerned with the governor system, apart from those forming the ruling class, have no possibility of exercising their autonomy. The negative attitude that the governor system holds towards two of the main features of human agency—reflectivity and autonomy—deprives that system of binding force.

The relatively simple casuistry concerning the normative force of legal systems is counterbalanced by the remarkable conceptual complexity surrounding the assessment of the normative force of legal systems. This complexity can be appreciated best if one considers the composite procedure involved in determining the relation between a given legal system and human agency. Whilst determining whether a single legal provision maintains a supportive, indifferent or adverse attitude towards human agency is a relatively straightforward operation, the same assessment is enormously more complicated when it involves the whole system of legal directives and procedures. For the assessment of the relation between a given legal system and human agency implies an account of the fundamental principles of that system, as well as the analysis of its most fundamental statutes and leading cases. One should, then, embark on an enterprise that is roughly similar to the task awaiting Dworkin's judge Hercules.[47] This task involves a number of complicated operations, ranging from the identification of the authoritative body of the law to the attribution of meaning to the enacted law, and to the detection of the justifications underlying the directives of the system and the imposition of a set of wide-ranging and integrated points in the disparate bits and pieces of legal material.[48] As a whole, these operations require reflection on the rationale encompassing the various branches of the law, as well as discussion of the relationships among the different components of the legal system. In this way, a more detailed and comprehensive knowledge of the system is obtained and a rough map of the entire legal system can be constructed. On this basis, the overall relationship obtaining between human agency and the legal system in question can be determined by pitting the legal material that fits well with the basic requirements of human agency against the enacted laws that contrast with human agency, and by assessing the importance of each.

Arguably, an ideal of coherence stands behind this approach.[49] However, the ideal of coherence underlying it is not imperialistic. In this view, there is no special connection between coherence and unity: the coherence test has nothing to do with a showing that many or all of the issued legal directives within a system fall into the same line and are encompassed by a single principle whose application

---

[47] See Dworkin (1978: 105–30).
[48] Some of these operations are discussed by Dworkin (1986: 65–8).
[49] Among the legal theorists who have dealt with coherence are Levenbook (1984); Dworkin (1986: 164–275); Alexy and Peczenik (1990); Hurley (1990); Peczenik (1990); MacCormick (1994: 152–94); Alexy (1998a); Peczenik (1998); Rabinowicz, (1998); Rodriguez-Blanco (2001); Schiavello (2001); and Soriano (2003). For a critical approach to coherence in the law, see Raz (1994: 277–325) and Kress (1999: 533–52).

provides a unified explanation of the entire body of posited laws.[50] On the contrary, coherence should be regarded as an ideal that assists us in making sense of the diversity of the law. Making the law intelligible along the lines of a coherence-based approach cannot, without distortion, be equated with a denial of the complex nature of the law. Appealing to coherence is compatible with taking pluralism seriously and striving to impose an order on an entity that is inherently plural. Therefore, coherence does not commit us to ignoring the complexity of the law or to espousing an unrealistic model of a legal system that manifests no tension.[51] Accepting coherence as an important value in the law is not incompatible with the recognition that the law reflects pragmatic compromises, and reflects, too, the disparate ideologies and interests of the changing political forces that govern the country at different times.

A final point addresses the significant difference that sets the normative force of legal systems apart from the normative force of single legal provisions. By itself, the claim that a system of laws is normative cannot be equated with the assertion that each and every single provision of that system is normative. A legal system that is deemed to have normative force may well happen to list non-normative provisions among its components. Hence, that a system is normative merely means that the system in question can ascribe indirect normative force to those of its provisions that both lack direct normativity and do not infringe human agency in the extreme. The normative force of the system does not go beyond the possibility of rescuing those directives that do not perpetuate an extreme infringement of human agency. To put it otherwise, a statement of the normative force of a legal system is not a shortcut that allows us to recognise an obligation-generating capacity in all the elements of that system, thereby sparing us from assessing the normative force of each and every specific piece of the law. The systemic nature of the legal phenomenon can, at most, provide a safety net vis-à-vis those specific legal provisions that do not in themselves support human agency. Conversely, provisions that are directly normative do not lose their normative force owing to their membership in a system that is not provided with normative force, this as a consequence of its indifferent or inhospitable attitude towards human agency. As the normative force of legal systems fails to irradiate to their specific directives and branches equally, so the lack of normative force of a system does not by itself negatively affect the normative force of its parts. If a legal directive supporting human agency is included in a system that overall hampers its addressees from fulfilling the require-

---

[50] The drive to eliminate as much contingency and complexity as possible stems from the very idea of the law. To some extent, then, the aspiration to unity is inherent not only in coherence, but also in the legal domain per se. When driven to extremes, however, this search for simplification, unity and certainty becomes a false idol. On these issues, see Bańkowski (2001: 27–42).

[51] Raz is right in this regard to criticise coherence-based theories of law, at least to the extent that they 'underestimate the degree and implications of value pluralism, the degree to which morality itself is not a system but a plurality of irreducibly independent principles' and to the extent that they 'idealize the law out of the concreteness of politics' (Raz 1994: 298). But coherence-based approaches to law do not necessarily do all of that. They can be consistent with the thesis that the lawhave to be rendered intelligible in their plurality.

ments set by human agency, and so has no normative force, the normative force of the provision in question remains unaffected. Therefore, the directives that make up a system endowed with normative force and those that are introduced into an order lacking normative force stand on an equal footing where their direct normative force is concerned: they both must display a supportive attitude towards human agency to be directly normative. As far as normative force is concerned, the advantage of being a member of a system certified as having normative force consists only in the availability of the systemic rescue effect.

Conclusion

IN THIS BOOK I discussed in some detail the normative claim of law and, by submitting it to critical scrutiny, it has been my intention to contribute to the understanding of the normative dimension of the law. My discussion focused on four key areas: meaning, status, essential features and grounds of the normative claim of law. I argued that the *meaning* of the normative claim of law is fixed by the notion of normativity. Since normativity in the practical realm refers to a mix of action-guidance and justificatory potential, the normative claim should likewise be defined as an assertion that aims to guide and to justify conduct. In consideration of its generality and abstractness, this account of the normative claim of law should be uncontroversial enough to warrant a starting point, for the discussion of status, features and the foundation of the normative claim of law, that enjoys a consensus. The *status* of the normative claim of law has been debated at some length in the legal literature. I therefore assumed that this issue can be settled by engaging in the relevant ongoing debate within legal theory. In this context, I took a position against the view that presents the normative claim of law as a merely fictitious and optional contention. I showed, instead, that the normative claim is an actual contention that is made of necessity, sometimes directly and sometimes indirectly, by legal instances, even if only implicitly. Determining the *essential features* of the normative claim of law called for a more articulated argument and a systematic discussion of the treatment that that claim has undergone within analytical legal positivism. The advocates of (some versions of) analytical legal positivism have correctly grasped some fundamental traits of the normative claim of law—its practical orientation, reason-relatedness, necessity, moral character, generality of scope, linkage with authority—but have also failed to realise that the reasons that the law claims to generate follow a dialectical logic, are content-dependent, and stem from instructions to be depicted as reinforced requests—as opposed to being exclusionary, content-independent and preemptive reasons. Finally, a significant portion of the book was devoted to the discussion of the *grounds* of the normative claim of law. The attempt to provide a theoretical justification of the normative claim of law has been eschewed by most legal theorists, who have denied either the need for or the general significance of the source of the normative claim of law. I argued that this reluctance to engage with foundational issues is misplaced and that no comprehensive treatment of the normative claim of law can be arrived at unless the grounds of that claim are established. In order to address the grounding question, I expanded upon the framework set out by some contemporary practical philosophers who, following Kant, anchor the normative experience not in the world but rather in the subject, understood primarily as a pragmatic unity, that is, an acting self. On this basis, I also showed that the normativity and normative claim of law have the same source as the normativity of practical reason: human agency.

The conclusions of the argument deployed throughout the book have two important implications that cannot be explored in details here, but ought to be mentioned by way of conclusion, this in order to reinforce the thesis that a study of the normative claim of law is of general theoretical significance. First, the discussion carried out in the book supports the conclusion that the traditional schools of legal thought have not provided a comprehensive theory of the normative claim of law. Legal theorists have grasped some of the key traits of the normative claim of law but they have not been concerned to provide a theoretical justification of the normativity of law. Because the grounding question is a genuine philosophical problem (which is the assumption underlying, for example, the lively philosophical debate concerning the practice of following a rule), the existing legal-theoretic accounts of the normativity of law have failed to reach a sufficient level of comprehensiveness. Accordingly, we cannot produce a general theory of the normative claim of law unless we go beyond the approaches defended by the traditional schools of legal thought and embark on a genuinely interdisciplinary enterprise, gathering together the contributions from different areas of practical philosophy, such as metaethics, theory of action and moral theory. In dealing with the normative question, in other words, legal theory meets its structural limits and needs to be integrated with the views, conceptual frameworks and tools found in other disciplines.

Secondly, the theses defended in this book bear on the study of the concept of law and frame the law in terms that can be shown to be altogether distinguishable from the positivist account. The non-positivist quality of the concept of law stemming from my treatment of the normative claim of law is warranted by the combination of the necessary status of the normative claim of law and its specific features and contents. The necessary status entitles us to regard the normative claim of law as an element of the concept of law, an ingredient that something needs to possess in order to be qualified as a distinctively legal instance. By virtue of this connection obtaining between concept of law and normative claim, the features and contents of the normative claim address the issue of the nature of law. This account will be non-positivist owing to two distinct sets of considerations: those concerning the relationship between that normative claim and the authority of law, on the one hand, and those concerning the link between normativity, normative claim and human agency, on the other. I might briefly elaborate on these two points.

In chapter three, I argued that the notion of authority contributes to a settlement of the basic features of the normative claim of law, and so enters the characterisation of that claim. By virtue of the necessary link between normative claim and concept of law, authority should be acknowledged also as being an element of the concept of law: being incorporated into the normative claim of law as a fundamental feature, authority, too, becomes a component of the concept of law in so far as the normative claim of law is constitutive of the concept of law. In addition,

I claimed that there is a conceptual connection between authority—its definition and working—and the moral arguments justifying the existence of authoritative structures (this being the basic principle underlying the dialectical model of authority). But so long as substantive moral reasons necessarily permeate the authoritative directives emanating from the law, it cannot be defined, identified and explicated in morally neutral terms. The connection between the law (authoritative directives) and morality (justificatory reasons) holds true at every level, including the level of which the law is identified, for once incorporated into the normative claim—an essential element of the law—authority is made constitutive of the very concept of law and so authority-related considerations affect, among other things, the way the law is identified. In other words, the permeability of form and substance that on the dialectical model characterises authoritative structures is such that the law, like every other authoritative institution, cannot be identified without recourse to moral considerations. In so far as it is shaped by the notion of authority, the law is a morally coloured practice, for authoritative standards and justificatory moral reasons inhabit realms that are not radically separate or distinct from each other. The dialectical relationship between the different elements of practical reasoning makes it impossible even to identify authoritative provisions without recourse to substantive considerations. Thus, the positivist explanation of the nature of law, centred on the thesis of the conceptual separation of law and morality, finds no support in the theory of authority. On the contrary, once authority is characterised along the lines of the dialectical model, reflections on the normative claim of law force upon us a concept of law that is distinct from any account based on the positivist thesis of the conceptual separation of law and morality. Therefore, the discussion of the normative claim of law discloses an important truth relative to the concept of law: the characterisation of the normative claim of law in terms of authority, combined with the theses both that such a claim is definitive of the legal domain and that the adequate model of authority is dialectical, brings with it a non-positivist conception of the nature of law.

Similar conclusions can be drawn from the assertion that a conceptual link obtains between normativity, normative claim and human agency. This link makes possible the presentation of the normative claim of law as the contention that the law needs to make an attempt to comply with (namely, to protect and promote) the requirements set by the defining features of human agency. This characterisation of the normative claim is relevant for our conceptualisation of the law, for the normative claim is a classifying trait of the legal enterprise and so determines the legality of a statement or practice. As a result, the protection and promotion of human agency should be recognised as inherent purports of the law, purports that any structure of social control must make room for in order to be qualified as law. This conclusion has three different implications, and all of them converge in so far as they disqualify the concept of law that is defended by legal positivism. First, the incorporation of human agency among the distinctively legal aims narrows the insularity of the legal realm. Human agency has been constructed as a general concept produced by philosophical reflection on action. As such, it instantiates an extra-legal notion in the twofold sense, namely, that it is neither defined by legal practice nor produced by specifically legal reflection. To the extent that human agency, an extra-legal notion, enters the very concept of law, the autonomy of the legal domain suffers a blow: an external notion is found at its very heart. Thus, far from being a sealed and self-contained universe, as legal positivism depicts it,[1] the legal world is an environment irremediably open to external influences and inputs to the effect that the existence, contents and force of the law are determined by standards that make reference to extra-legal considerations, and so legal discourse cannot proceed without engaging non-legal arguments. Secondly, the link between the law and human agency implies that the legal domain is not merely affected by external considerations but also deeply informed by them. In order meaningfully to purport to support human agency, the law must adopt certain values and mechanisms (and rule others out). This necessary inclusion (and exclusion) constrains the forms and contents that legal provisions and legal systems may take up, as well as the kinds of procedures that legal institutions are allowed to use in their regulative effort: forms, contents and procedures that are radically incompatible with the requirements stemming from human agency are legally unavailable. This conclusion runs counter to the positivist picture of the law as a practice that is exhausted by the decisions of those in power and so can assume the most disparate contents (and, indeed, potentially any content).[2] In the picture framed by my treatment of the normative claim of law, the law and power are indeed interlinked, but not in the unconstrained way that emerges from positivist studies of the nature of law. Finally, the preceding remarks also show that a merely structural, or formal, definition of the law is not a sound basis for articulating the concept of law. The concept of law stems from a combination of structure, function and substance. This is clearly not the place to elaborate on this statement to arrive at an exhaustive formulation of the concept of law. But, by way of gesturing at a research direction rather than pursuing it, it should be noted that no system fits into the legal category unless it incorporates certain structural traits. We are hardly willing to treat a social system as a legal system unless it consists (at least) of institutions empowered with the task of legislating, adjudicating and executing the provisions issued by officials. In addition, the system must be

[1] In the positivist view, the law pertains to an autonomous sphere of practical reason and consists mainly of norms which institutions having appropriate competence produce in observance of proper procedures. This statement entails a picture of the law as a self-contained universe, wherein laws are valid only in so far as they meet certain systemic and procedural criteria, regardless of whether any extra-legal requirements are fulfilled in so doing. To put it in Jeremy Waldron's (1992: 160) words, 'law can be understood in terms of rules and standards whose authority derives from their provenance in some human source, sociologically defined, and which can be identified as law in terms of that provenance. Thus statements about what the law is—whether in describing a legal system, offering legal advice, or disposing of particular cases—can be made without exercising moral or other evaluative judgement'.

[2] This picture emerges paradigmatically in Kramer's qualification of monstrous systems certain people set up just to exploit all the other citizens as a legal order, notwithstanding the fact that such systems make not even an attempt to be just or to operate in the interests of all the concerned parties. See Kramer (1999: 83–92).

invested with the broad function of channelling conduct by impinging on the practical reasoning of the concerned people, and must be oriented in such a way as to implement the fundamental features that define and specify the idea of human agency. This sketchy and preliminary formulation of the lines along which research concerning the concept of law needs to unfold is enough to give an idea of the difference between the positivist conceptualisation of the law and the likely outcomes of research into the concept of law that is undertaken in accordance with the principles inspiring the treatment of the normative claim of law as reflected in this book. Whereas the positivist concept of law is shaped solely by structural concerns,[3] my reflection on the normative dimension suggests that structural elements are just one factor among several factors that contribute to a determination of the nature of law.

To summarise, whereas this work is confined to a discussion of a specific aspect of the normative dimension of the law and, accordingly, has no ambition to bear directly on the longstanding debate between positivism and non-positivism with respect to the concept of law, the theses argued for throughout this book are not neutral or agnostic in respect of that debate. By endorsing the dialectical model of authority, denying the insulation of the legal domain, and emphasising the partiality of a merely formal characterisation of the law, the views defended here support a non-positivist approach to the concept of law, which cannot be fully and soundly accounted for unless a critical stance towards the positivist paradigm is taken.

---

[3] This purely formal conceptualisation of the law is defended by Kramer (1999: 92–101), among others.

Appendix

The Modified Kantian Account and Kant's Legal Philosophy

THE ACCOUNT OF the normative claim of law defended in this book rests in part on Kant's account of practical philosophy and, in particular, on his view of the normativity of practical reason as grounded in the idea of humanity. Humanity was then reinterpreted as human agency, and that yielded the modified account, whereby the law owes its normativity to the force of practical reason, understood as embodying an idea of human agency. On the modified Kantian account, thus, the normativity of law is an *instance* of the normativity of practical reason, and it can be presented as such an instance on the basis of an argument for the *unity* of practical reason.[1] In my treatment I referred for the most part to Kant's *Groundwork of the Metaphysics of Morals* and to his *Critique of Practical Reason*, for it is these two works that set out the core of his practical philosophy. Yet neither of these two works deals specifically with the law, a subject that is treated instead in *The Metaphysics of Morals*, which also sets out Kant's basic view of morals,[2] drawing a line of continuity to the *Groundwork*.[3] It stands to reason, then, that *The Metaphysics of Morals* should play a prominent role in any attempt to work out a Kantian account of the law: not only does Kant offer in this work the only *systematic* statement of his legal philosophy, but he does so by building on and developing to maturity ideas first presented in *Groundwork*, a development that also marks this as his *definitive* statement.

And yet *The Metaphysics of Morals* is kept very much in the background throughout this discussion of the modified account. So the question arises: why should an account of the normativity of law that describes itself as Kantian (in however modified a way) choose largely to disregard the one work that Kant specifically devoted

---

[1] This is the view of practical reason as a single activity devoted to different subjects in different spheres of reasoning between which there is significant overlap: the spheres of practical reason are in this sense distinct but not separate, their contiguity being owed to their sharing some fundamental principles.

[2] For Kant, *morals* is any discipline that takes for an object not nature but freedom of choice (see Kant 1996 AK 6:216, for example). Morals thus cover a number of subjects, including legal philosophy, political theory, moral philosophy, moral anthropology, moral theology and the philosophy of history.

[3] As Kant explains, the *Groundwork* had originally been conceived as an introduction to *The Metaphysics of Morals*. Indeed, the foundation and critique of practical reason 'was to be followed by a system, the metaphysics of morals, which falls into metaphysical first principles of the *doctrine of right* and metaphysical first principles of the *doctrine of virtue*' (Kant 1996 AK 6: 205).

to legal philosophy? Why treat Kant's legal philosophy as secondary and focus mainly on his account of practical reason? And if that restriction does not seem puzzling enough, what are we to make of it in the context of a conception of the law and morality as connected entities,[4] in direct contrast to the view set out in *The Metaphysics of Morals*, in which the law and morality are instead kept separate as entities governed by mutually independent principles pertaining to spheres in need of separate treatment? One might suspect that this contrast on the question of the normativity of law, with one account upholding what the other denies, is precisely the reason why the former account keeps the latter out of the picture. The suspicion, in other words, is that Kant is being interpreted as if he did not really mean what he says, this on 'the unspoken assumption' that 'in distinguishing between law and ethics Kant misunderstood the significance of his own ideas and that this misunderstanding can be remedied by inserting ethical considerations where he deliberately excluded them' (Weinrib 1987: 472).

It will be argued in this appendix that the modified Kantian account of the normativity of law, with its endorsement of the connection thesis, remains faithful to Kant's legal philosophy and assumes nothing that Kant rejects in *The Metaphysics of Morals*. The argument will be based on a close reading of Kant's text and will proceed by bringing out the shortcomings of the perspective opposite to that of the connection thesis as worked into the modified account. Thus, I will introduce two contemporary legal theories whose authors, George Fletcher and Ernest Weinrib, draw on Kant's account of the law for the opposite thesis, namely, that the law exists apart from morality, and I will then show that *The Metaphysics of Morals* does not warrant the radical distinction between the law and morality that Fletcher's and Weinrib's theories need for their respective separation theses. Indeed, while Kant does set out a basic distinction between the law and morality—between the spheres of right and virtue, as they are referred to in *The Metaphysics of Morals*—he also understands them as overlapping in several respects by virtue of their being specific instances of practical reason. He does so even in his final statement of practical and legal philosophy, *The Metaphysics of Morals*, in which an account of the law is presented that, far from rejecting the connection thesis, leads to it by casting the normativity of law as a special case of the normativity of practical reason, the very source that also grounds the normativity of morality, which, too, can thereby be understood as a special case of practical reason. Thus, the argument for the connection between the law and morality rests here on an account of Kant's practical philosophy that does not in any way relegate to an inferior status his legal philosophy as set out in *The Metaphysics of Morals*, offering instead a view that is very much *consistent* with this latter statement.

A number of contemporary legal theorists have looked to Kant's legal philosophy for insight into the nature of law, as well as into specific aspects of the law, finding a clear-cut separation between the law and morality in the account of them

---

[4] This is the connection thesis, described by Alexy (2002b: 4) as the view that 'the concept of law is to be defined such that moral elements are included'.

that Kant presents in *The Metaphysics of Morals*. This view is, therefore, not solely the purview of Fletcher and Weinrib. Still, they do give the matter a stronger statement than most other theorists in the same group, and that explains my focus on their statements. In an influential article, Fletcher (1987: 534) finds that Kant's view of the relation between the law and morality has received less attention than it deserves, and he argues that 'while the prevailing view today treats law and morality as intersecting sets of rules and rights, the Kantian view treats the two as distinct and nonintersecting'. Kant, on Fletcher's interpretation, understands the law and morality as independent owing to the different spheres they regulate, those of *external* and *internal* freedom respectively. The internal freedom of morality is a condition attained as the outcome of a process by which we gradually pull away from the influence of the subjective inclinations: this gives us morality proper, or a capacity and freedom 'to act exclusively according to reason' (Fletcher 1987: 537). The law, by contrast, protects the external freedom to behave in one way or another, the 'freedom to act on one's choices' (Fletcher 1987: 535). Different people can make different choices, choices that may well result in conflicting courses of action, the reason being that these 'need not express the dictates of reason. They need not be morally sound choices. They are subjectively contingent choices, reflecting the divergent purposes of concrete individuals' (Fletcher 1987: 535).

Thus, internal freedom delimits the sphere of objectivity, sameness and oneness; external freedom, that of subjectivity, difference and plurality. The former is the subject of morality and the latter of the law. So long as it stays that way—with morality concerning itself only with internal freedom and the law only with external freedom—the two spheres will remain divided by a separation of roles that may be complementary, to be sure, but certainly do not admit of any overlap; not only because none exists between what is internal and what is external, but because the problem involved in the former case is completely different from that involved in the latter. Indeed, morality is entrusted with *abstracting* from our subjective choices (from our preferences and sensual determinations), thus enabling us to behave independently of them and find 'our identity as beings endowed with univocal reason' (Fletcher 1987: 543). The law, by contrast, is entrusted with *reconciling* the subjective choices of different agents so as to make these choices in some way compatible and to maximise each agent's external freedom. This can be achieved only if the law does not cross over into morality and take on a moral role; that is, only if the law refrains from ranking choices or singling out any particular choice as prior or as having a special status, since the point of having a system of laws in place is not to help us choose among different courses of action but to make possible many such courses. Kant's view is, therefore, that the law can neither endorse nor enforce moral values: it simply 'acknowledges our concrete particularity and seeks to harmonize our divergent purposes' (Fletcher 1987: 543). On this reading, then, the law and morality are understood by Kant as practices 'unfolding on distinct normative planes' (Fletcher 1987: 549), and any attempt to bridge the gap between the two would amount to a distortion such that Kant can no longer be recognised. This would happen not only if we took Kant to hold the stronger view that makes two identical sets out of the law and morality, but also if, less demandingly, we understood his view of morality as either a side-constraint on the law or a subset of the law, with the law providing a framework for moral conduct.[5] A more emphatic statement of the separation of the law from morality is scarcely imaginable.

Weinrib finds a similar separation. He ascribes the contrary view (namely, the view of a connection between the law and morality in Kant) to the tendency in contemporary legal theory to pay more attention to Kant's moral philosophy than to his legal philosophy. Weinrib starts out by acknowledging that Kant constructs the law and morality as both originating in practical reason. Reason provides us with a unified framework for ordering and systematising concepts.[6] Some of these concepts 'relate to what we bring into being through an operation of will' (Weinrib 1987: 481): these concepts are practical, and so is the reasoning that deals with them, the sphere they inhabit, the sphere of freely chosen actions or of actions purposely carried out rather than causally connected. Yet what governs in this sphere, the practical sphere of purposive conduct, are principles established by morality, on the one hand, and the law, on the other. So, while morality and the law both guide conduct by the use of practical reason, they do so in different ways. Morality is concerned with the goodness of actions, for it 'considers action from a standpoint internal to the actor' (Weinrib 1987: 490) and so looks at the will from which an action originated. The law, by contrast, is concerned not with the inherent goodness or rightness of actions but with their interaction: with the way in which one agent's action might affect another agent's freedom of action. In this sense, the law can be understood as 'the articulated unity applicable to the external relationships of freely willing beings' (Weinrib 1987: 500), or as 'the union of externality and freedom' (Weinrib 1987: 487), for it is the very point of the law to make everyone's action (externality) consistent with everyone's *freedom* of action, regardless of whether the outcome conforms to any principle of morality.

Hence, on this concept of law, as Weinrib understands it from his reading of *The Metaphysics of Morals*, the law plays an essentially *non-moral* role as a framework within which to act on various *moral* grounds. This clearly makes for a bold separation of roles, one that Weinrib further specifies by noting that moral conduct is autonomous, just as law-abiding conduct is not:[7] it is only in so far as what we do is of our own choosing and is based on our own reasoning (practical reason governing from *within*) that we can be considered moral agents, in contrast to what we

---

[5] Fletcher considers each of these views specifically before coming to the conclusion that under no circumstances should we satisfy 'the yearning for a union between Kant's moral and legal thinking' (1987: 553–7), since 'if the two sets collapse into one, the result is either a fascist distortion of law or a liberal distortion of Kantian morality. If morality is a side constraint, an intersecting set, then, the state must engage in the task of enforcing moral precepts and thereby undermine the possibility of self-legislated moral action. If freedom and the Right exist merely to facilitate a subset of moral acts, then freedom can no longer claim to be an intrinsic value' (Fletcher 1987: 557).

[6] See Weinrib (1987: 478–81).

[7] See Weinrib (1987: 488–91).

do as law-abiders, which is not chosen at all but is coerced (practical reason governing from *without*). And though we may at any time be acting in both roles at once, as both moral agents and law-abiders, the law need not concern itself with the question of whether what we do in compliance with it is something we would do in any case as moral agents, that is, as agents acting autonomously on the basis of moral reasons that specify an obligation to act. Indeed, it makes no difference to the law *why* its addressees act legally, so long as they *do* act legally. In this sense, the law can be said to deal with the *form* of action, in contrast to morality, which concerns itself with the *content* of action or with the will behind an action, and so with purposive action and with the reasons for acting in one way or another. As Weinrib (1987: 501) puts it, the law and morality 'differ in the incentive that each holds out: in law the actor responds to the prospect of external coercion, whereas in ethics the idea of duty itself motivates the action'. This ultimately makes the law an 'essentially conceptual, abstract, or self-contained' entity that is both independent of morality and 'somehow prior' to it: it does so by providing a framework within which morality can unfold, in the sense that legal relationships 'actualize the capacity for purposiveness that underlies the specification by ethics of the obligatory objects of free choice' (Weinrib 1987: 501–2).

For Fletcher and Weinrib alike, then, Kant's legal philosophy establishes a radical separation between the law and morality. This reading ascribes to Kant the legal positivist thesis of the conceptual separation between the law and morality, thereby also disqualifying as inconsistent any appeal to Kant's philosophy as a means of defending the connection thesis in legal theory. But let us look now at *The Metaphysics of Morals* and try to see clearly into Kant's separate treatment of the law and morality. To anticipate: we will see that, while they cannot be equated, they cannot be regarded as insulated from each other either. Their relation, therefore, ought properly to be constructed as one of conceptual overlap.

In *The Metaphysics of Morals*, Kant works out some implications of the fundamental principle of practical reason as expounded in the two foundational works on practical philosophy written in the 1780s, *Groundwork of the Metaphysics of Morals* and *Critique of Practical Reason*. Like these earlier works, *The Metaphysics of Morals* undertakes a conceptual rather than an empirical investigation. Indeed, in Kant's terminology, a metaphysical account is an entirely a priori or purely conceptual account aiming to establish those principles that can be known by reason alone.[8] Accordingly, *The Metaphysics of Morals* presents a detailed system of principles that can be worked out independently of any empirical considerations.[9] A system of

---

[8] On this meaning of metaphysics see, eg, Kant (1996 AK 6: 215–18).

[9] Although Kant (1996 AK 6: 205) does hope to achieve a comprehensive and reasonably specific ethical system of pure concepts, he nonetheless recognises that such a theoretical undertaking can only fall short of its own ideal: the resulting system (in essence, a moral metaphysics) cannot stand on its own. This can be appreciated as we pass from the fundamental principle of practical reason to the more specific principles into which the system expands. The initial statement is highly theoretical and can be framed by reason alone, but the more we specify it and work out its detail, the more we must rely on empirical considerations, or on what we can learn from experience, including the experience of applying the principle to understand how it works and what it ultimately means. As Kant (1996 AK 6: 217)

this sort can be divided into two main parts, these being on the one hand, a 'doctrine of [law]', concerned with legality, or with 'the mere conformity or [lack of] conformity of an action with law, irrespective of the incentive to it', and on the other hand, a 'doctrine of virtue', which is concerned with morality, where 'the idea of duty arising from the law is also the incentive to the action'.[10] This point is further elaborated by Kant (1996 AK 6: 214) who clarifies that the laws of freedom, which constitute the object of 'morals', are:

> called *moral* laws. As directed merely to external actions and their conformity to law they are called *juridical* laws; but if they also require that they (the laws) themselves be the determining grounds of action, they are *ethical* laws, and then one says that conformity with juridical law is *legality* of an action and conformity with ethical laws is *morality*.

This scheme not only makes it clear that the law and morality are distinct but also spells out the basis of their distinction. This basis, providing the rationale for the two parts into which the metaphysics of morals is divided, revolves around the idea of an incentive, meaning the incentive to action provided in law-giving. For (Kant 1996 AK 6: 218):

> in all lawgiving (whether it prescribes internal or external actions, and whether it prescribes them *a priori* by reason alone or by the choice of another) there are two elements: first, a *law*, which represents an action that is to be done as *objectively* necessary, that is, which makes the action a duty; and second, an incentive, which connects a ground for determining choice to this action *subjectively* with the representation of the law.

It is, then, this second component of law-giving, its incentive to action, that accounts for the specific difference between the law and morality (Kant 1996 AK 6: 219):

> that lawgiving which makes an action a duty and also makes this duty the incentive is *ethical*. But the lawgiving which does not include the incentive of duty in the law and so admits an incentive other than the idea of duty itself is *juridical*.

In short, what distinguishes the law from morality is the different sorts of compliance that each requires. In morality, the *motive* for complying with a requirement is just as important as the *action* of complying: if we are to count as moral agents, we must not only do what is (morally) required of us but must do it for the right reasons, too (that is, for moral reasons). Our actions may be morally correct as far as their external expression is concerned, but if they are done for non-moral

says: if we are to show 'what can be inferred from universal moral principles', we must necessarily take into account 'the particular nature of human beings, which is cognized only by experience'. It follows that 'a metaphysics of morals cannot dispense with principles of application'. This is not to say that moral anthropology, on Kant's view, forms the basis of the metaphysics of practical reason. On the contrary, it is the metaphysics of practical reason that grounds moral anthropology (and on the weakest hypothesis can be said to *apply* to it). So, as much as Kant may recognise the need to supplement the conceptual basis of his ethical system with empirical considerations, he is careful to maintain these two orders of reasoning separately. Moral metaphysics are established independently of any moral anthropology, and the distinction between these two domains should therefore be maintained, despite their tendency to merge in certain circumstances. Similar remarks can also be found in Kant 1996 AK 6: 215.

[10] See Kant (1996 AK 6: 219). Cf Kant (1996 AK 6: 205, 214).

reasons, such as self-interest, they cannot be considered moral. Not so in the law, where no compliance is required other than the external compliance of our outward behaviour. An action will be considered legal (comporting with the law) so long as it coheres with what is permitted or required under the provisions of the law (as duly enacted by the appropriate legal institutions), regardless of whether such compliance was wholehearted or not, and so even if the only reason for complying was fear of the threat of coercion stemming from the legal system. The motive for compliance, meaning the incentive to action, is thus irrelevant to the legality of a conduct. Hence, whereas morality speaks to agents who share certain attitudes and values, and so is aimed at setting up a kingdom of ends by which those agents are bound, the law does not necessarily address a community held together by shared ends and values. The realm of the law cannot be analogised to the moral kingdom of ends, since legal systems represent fields in which a plurality of views and purposes co-exist.

Clearly, the line that Kant draws between the law and morality rules out any possibility of equating them: we cannot, on Kant's approach, make any claim that the law and morality coincide or even any claim that one is fully incorporated into or subordinate to the other. The textual evidence shows this clearly: there is no way, on Kant's view, that either the law or morality can be made to collapse into the other, the reason being that they pertain to independent spheres. Thus, whereas morality unfolds in the internal sphere of freedom, the law is concerned 'only with the external and indeed practical relation of one person to another, in so far as their acts, as deeds, can have (direct or indirect) influence on each other' (Kant 1996 AK 6: 230). Again, morality considers the way in which the different components of the self relate to one another, and it seeks to order them by regulating their mutual claims—its sphere is therefore *internal* to each person. The law, by contrast, is aimed at harmonising the actions of different people and so at removing such external obstacles as may prevent persons from acting on their own advice. This is the *external* sphere of freedom of action, wherein different persons can pursue different ends, and the law accordingly considers the way in which one person's conduct may affect another's freedom of action.[11] The law is thus concerned with *social* relations, those that hold among different agents, rather than among the different components of a single agent. This sphere, the sphere of social interaction, is reflected in the concept of law as defined by Kant, namely, as 'the sum of the conditions under which the choice of one can be united with the choice of another in accordance with a universal law of freedom' (Kant 1996 AK 6: 230).

Incidentally, this way of drawing the distinction between the law and morality—as pertaining to independent spheres—means that morality depends for its existence on the very possibility of confining the law within the sphere of external freedom. That is because morality, on Kant's view, can only flourish in a context of freedom and autonomy: there can be no morality except as the outcome of an agent's free and autonomous choice. Yet there can be no autonomy in any situa-

---

[11] See Kant (1996 AK 6: 214). Cf Kerstin (1992: 344–8).

tion in which a moral standard is imposed (from the outside) on an agent. A legal system that forced moral ends and values on its citizens would thereby jeopardise the very existence of morality. It is therefore inconsistent with Kant's approach to hold that the law should incorporate *moral* duties and punish citizens for failing to live up to them. A legal system is not a moral system supplemented with sanctions, for in that case we would end up with a system for the enforcement of morality, or at least a system in which moral values were enforced simply by virtue of their incorporation within the system. Yet that would amount to compelling agents to be moral under the threat of sanction, and hence to undermine Kant's whole idea of morality as the realm of autonomy. It follows, on Kant's view, that legal systems must leave, for us, as many options open as possible, giving us the freedom to act as we choose, including the freedom to act immorally if that is what suits us. A legal system will fail in this respect to the extent that the content of its laws takes up the content of morality.

This distinction between the law and morality is reflected in their two governing principles. Under the basic principle of the law (Kant 1996 AK 6: 231):

> any action is right if it can coexist with everyone's freedom in accordance with a universal law, or if on its maxim the freedom of choice of each can coexist with everyone's freedom in accordance with a universal law.

This first principle shares with the first principle of morality the form of a universal law. Under the universal law of morality, you must 'act only on that maxim through which you can at the same time will that it should become a universal law' (Kant 1959 AK 6: 421). So the two basic principles, that of the law and that of morality, are both based on an idea of universal action, directing each agent to act in ways that all others would accept for themselves as well as for everyone else considering what would happen if everyone were to act in the same way.[12] But while the two principles may have the same form, they each have their own content and subject matter. As Wolfgang Kerstin (1992: 346) puts it, the basic principle of the law governs the 'coexistence of symmetrical freedom for human beings who live in spatial relations' and so 'defines the domain that each may consider his own, occupy as he pleases, and defend against injuries to its boundaries'. The basic principle of morality, by contrast, is concerned not with co-existence (an 'outward' matter) but with the inward sphere of the self, requiring that each agent make the rational component of the self prior to its non-rational component: this is a principle of reason over the natural inclinations. We can see, then, that the fundamental principle of the law cannot be considered an instance or a specification of the fundamental principle of morality.

The distinct content of the two basic principles of the law and of morality is reflected in their respective natures, the one being analytic and the other synthetic. The basic principle of the law is an analytic proposition (Kant 1996 AK 6: 396):

---

[12] See Kant (1996 AK 6: 226).

it is clear in accordance with the principle of contradiction that, if external constraint checks the hindering of outer freedom in accordance with universal laws (and is thus a hindering of the hindrance to freedom), it can coexist with ends as such. I need not go beyond the concept of freedom to see this; the end that each has may be whatever he will.—The supreme *principle of* [*the law*] is therefore an analytic proposition.[13]

The basic principle of morality is, by contrast, a synthetic proposition: its justification is not contained in its constituent terms, and it therefore requires a specific argument, like the one that Kant discusses at length in *Groundwork of the Metaphysics of Morals* and *Critique of Practical Reason*.[14] This, too, is a feature that marks the distinction between the law and morality: the law is a practice whose basic organising principle is given by an analytical proposition; morality, by contrast, is informed by a synthetic proposition. This is another reason why the law and morality cannot be equated: to do so would be tantamount to equating two sorts of propositions (analytic and synthetic ones), neither of which can be reduced to the other.

So construed, the main thesis defended in *The Metaphysics of Morals* supports Fletcher and Weinrib in their claim that Kant's framework does not justify any attempt to either moralise the law or make morality subordinate to it. That is to say that one is not justified in treating either the law or morality as enjoying primacy: on the one hand, we cannot, on a Kantian approach, understand morality as the necessary source for the justification of the law, nor can we equate legal requirements with moral duties, a move that would amount to representing the law as the coercive side of morality. On the other hand, we cannot, on the same approach, view the law as the indispensable framework which makes moral action possible, or without which the existence of morality would be impossible. Thus, any attempt to establish a hierarchical relation between the law and morality is misleading: the two realms stand at the same level, a level ultimately subordinated to practical reason but not internally structured in a vertical fashion. But, for Fletcher and Weinrib, these differences between the law and morality justify a view of them as separate entities: Kant's account of the law and morality as distinct entities enjoying a good deal of independence from each other is understood by Fletcher and Weinrib to imply a *separation* between the law and morality. However, this radical interpretation finds no textual support in Kant: nowhere in his work does Kant deny that the two spheres overlap, and nowhere is this overlap presented as contingent or merely possible.[15] In fact, it is presented as conceptual and necessary, in that Kant sees the law and morality as parts of the same conceptual whole, as defined by practical reason. And they are so defined because

---

[13] This also means that the imperatives set forth in a legal system need not be categorically binding. Unlike morality, which proceeds from a synthetic proposition and binds us categorically, the law is governed by an analytical proposition, and its imperatives apply neither unconditionally nor objectively.

[14] See especially Kant (1996 AK 6: 396–8).

[15] One area of overlap concerns the duties and obligations they each establish: 'ethics has its special duties as well (e.g. duties to oneself), but it also has duties in common with right; what it does not have in common with right is only the kind of *obligation*' (Kant 1996 AK 6: 220).

they are two specifications of practical reason, meaning that both are rational enterprises shaped by the rational legislative capacity of human agents. Kant thus understands reason as the common ground of both the law and morality.[16] Even though reason can take different forms, it ultimately remains one.[17] The same holds for the law and morality: as two specifications of practical reason, they cannot be made into two separate entities, each completely independent of the other, for they both issue from the same conceptual whole and are therefore best viewed as two species of the same genus. The distinction between them does not work itself out into a disconnection: just as they do not fully overlap, so likewise they do not stand in fully mutual independence either, for both are instrumental to human agents, enabling them to devise and carry out life plans in accordance with reason. It is thus a single principle, a principle of reason, that prompts us to submit to the requirements of both the law and morality and that indeed justifies such submission. The law and morality may have different contents, may provide different incentives, and may belong to different spheres of human experience; still, as much as they may diverge in these respects, they will always and necessarily retain their rational nature as two forms springing from the same source.

In sum, there is nothing about the mutual independence of the law and morality in Kant that would prevent them from sharing a common conceptual framework: their distinction does not imply any separation or disconnection; in fact, it is a distinction that would not even make sense were it not for the connection between the law and morality as two activities that both respond to the demands of reason. On a Kantian approach, then, one should be careful neither to equate the law and morality nor to regard the two as unrelated, as if their mutual independence justified driving a wedge between them that prevented any communication at all, this along the lines of the separation thesis. Kant's view of the relationship between the law and morality rejects both of these extremes: morality and the law neither coincide nor exist in complete isolation. In fact, the view charts a middle way: that of partial overlap and mutual influence, both features deriving from the connection thesis as defended throughout this book. The connection thesis does not undermine the distinction between the law and morality, it simply claims that the law is not cut off from morality or vice versa: they each act in ways that affect the other. The overlap, however partial it may be, is framed by Kant as a necessary feature of the relation between the law and morality. For this reason, Kant's view can be considered a paradigmatic statement of the connection thesis, the two facets of which—necessary overlap and mutual influence—are very much consistent with Kant's legal philosophy as framed in *The Metaphysics of Morals*.

---

[16] The idea of the law as a rational enterprise grounded in practical reason is stated in Kant (1996 AK 6: 221, 251, 306, 312–16 and 371–2), among other places. Compare on this point Kerstin (1992: 342–4).

[17] Thus, while legal and moral rationality differ in the important ways we have seen, they cannot contradict each other, either, precisely because that would amount to an internal inconsistency within reason itself and would cause reason, whatever its form, to turn into something other than reason. And while the common root of the law and morality (their root in practical reason) establishes a connection between them, it does not go so far as to make them identical, precisely because each of them develops into its own form of practical reason. On the unity of reason, see, eg, Kant (1996 AK 6: 207).

Appendix: The Modified Kantian Account and Kant's Legal Philosophy 287

Finally, and most importantly, Kant's legal philosophy, on this reading of it, supports the view that the law and morality owe their normativity to the same source, this being their rational nature as activities born of and guided by practical reason. It is Kant's view that only reason can give rise to obligations: a demand can have normative force only in so far as it is an expression of reason. And reason, in turn, owes its binding force to its being a defining feature of humanity, which thus emerges as the only possible source for the normative force of any demand of practical reason. The law and morality are both conceived in reason and owe to this source their capacity to give rise to obligations. The argument showing morality to be rational in the sense specified is put forward in the *Groundwork*, where Kant explains that the normative force of morality is ultimately traceable to its basis in humanity. And the same is true of the law. Its normativity is not inherent, rather it comes to the law from the outside, and specifically from its being the outcome of a rational activity. The law is a specification of practical reason and derives its normativity therefrom, that is, from the normativity of practical reason in both its hypothetical and its categorical forms. The duties prescribed by the law may well differ *in content* from those prescribed by morality, but the source of their normative force remains the same.

This idea can be restated, following Allen Wood, by observing that the law is invested with normativity owing to its role in regulating, and hence in making possible, free action in the public sphere.[18] This role—that of protecting the external expression of freedom—is in turn instrumental to human autonomy, the ability of humans to establish their own ends in action. Hence, the law is not inherently valuable but derivatively so: its value stems from its role, a necessary one, in supporting autonomy, which for Kant is a defining feature of humanity. Humanity is inherently valuable as the seat of human autonomy and reason, and it bestows its inherent value on the forms of reason into which it develops. This is especially true of practical reason, and of the law and morality as two instances of practical reason. This has the further consequence that if humanity were any less valuable, then the law and morality would correspondingly lose their normative force. And if the value of humanity were not inherent, but merely transferred, then the normativity of law and morality might not be constructed as deriving from a single source. These remarks are perfectly in keeping with the account of the source of normativity offered in this book, for I have argued that the law and morality have the same source but develop into different practices with different contents. On my modified Kantian approach, the law is distinct from morality but can obligate us only in so far as it embodies a concept of human agency. This, it seems to me, is precisely the position that Kant not only expounds in his foundational works of the 1780s, but also restates in his final account of practical philosophy.

---

[18] See Wood (1999: 321–3).

Bibliography

Aarnio, A (1987) *The Rational as Reasonable: a Treatise on Legal Justification* (Dordrecht, Reidel)
Aarnio, A, Alexy, R and Peczenik, A (1981) 'The Foundation of Legal Reasoning' 21 *Rechtstheorie* 133
Adams, R (1997) 'Things in Themselves' 57 *Philosophy and Phenomenological Research* 801
Alexander, L (1990) 'Law and Exclusionary Reasons' 18 *Philosophical Topics* 153
Alexy, R (1989a) *A Theory of Legal Argumentation* (1978, Oxford, Oxford University Press)
—— (1989b) 'On the Necessary Relation between Law and Morality' 2 *Ratio Juris* 167
—— (1996) 'Discourse Theory and Human Rights' 9 *Ratio Juris* 209
—— (1998a) 'Coherence and Argumentation or the Genuine Twin Criterialess Super Criterion' in A Aarnio *et al* (eds), *On Coherence Theory of Law* (Lund, Juristfoerlaget) 41–9
—— (1998b) 'Law and Correctness' in M Freeman (ed), *Legal Theory at the End of the Millennium* (Oxford, Oxford University Press) 205–21
—— (1999a) 'My Philosophy of Law: the Institutionalisation of Reason' in LJ Wintgens (ed), *The Law in Philosophical Perspective* (Dordrecht, Kluwer) 23–45
—— (1999b) 'The Special Case Thesis' 12 *Ratio Juris* 374
—— (2000a) 'On the Structure of Legal Principles' 13 *Ratio Juris* 294
—— (2000b) 'On the Thesis of a Necessary Connection between Law and Morality: Bulygin's Critique' 13 *Ratio Juris* 138
—— (2002a) *A Theory of Constitutional Rights* (1986, Oxford, Oxford University Press)
—— (2002b) *The Argument from Injustice* (1992, Oxford, Clarendon)
—— (2003) 'On Balancing and Subsumption: a Structural Comparison' 16 *Ratio Juris* 433
—— (2007) 'Thirteen Replies' in G Pavlakos (ed), *Law, Rights and Discourse* (Oxford, Hart) 333–66
Alexy, R and Peczenik A (1990) 'The Concept of Coherence and its Significance for Discursive Rationality' 3 *Ratio Juris* 130
Allison, H (1998) 'Morality and Freedom: Kant's Reciprocity Thesis' in P Guyer (ed), *Kant's Groundwork of the Metaphysics of Morals: Critical Essays* (Oxford, Rowan & Littlefield) 273–302
—— (2004) *Kant's Transcendental Idealism* (New Haven, Yale University Press)
Alston, W (1964) 'Linguistic Acts' 1 *American Philosophical Quarterly* 1
—— (1977) 'Sentence Meaning and Illocutionary Act Potential' 2 *Philosophy Exchange* 17
—— (2000) *Illocutionary Acts and Sentence Meaning* (Ithaca, Cornell University Press)
Ameriks, K (1992) 'The Critique of Metaphysics: Kant and Traditional Ontology' in P Guyer (ed), *Cambridge Companion to Kant* (Cambridge, Cambridge University Press) 249–79
Atienza, M (1993) *Las razones del derecho. Teorias de la argumentacion juridica* (Madrid, Centro de Estudos Constitucionales)
Aune, B (1980) *Kant's Theory of Morals* (Princeton, Princeton University Press)
Austin, JL (1954) *The Province of Jurisprudence Determined* (London, Weidenfeld and Nicolson).
—— (1975) *How to Do Things with Words* (1962, Oxford, Clarendon)
Bańkowski, Z (2001) *Living Lawfully: Love in Law and Law in Love* (Dordrecht, Kluwer)

Belvisi, F (2009) 'The Ticking Bomb Scenario as a Moral Scandal', in B Clucas, G Johnstone and T Ward (eds), *Torture: Moral Absolutes and Ambiguities* (Baden-Baden, Nomos), 61–72
Bentham, J (1970) *Of Laws in General* in JH Burns (gen ed), *Collected Works of Jeremy Bentham* (1782, London, Athlone)
Bertea S (2002) *Certezza del diritto e argomentazione giuridica* (Soveria Mannelli, Rubbettino)
—— (2004) 'On Law's Claim to Authority' 55 *Northern Ireland Legal Quarterly* 396
Bessette, JR (1980) 'Deliberative Democracy: the Majority Principle in Republican Government' in R Goldwin and W Schambra (eds), *How Democracy is the Constitution* (Washington: American Enterprise Institute) 102–16
Beyleveld, D and Brownsword R (1986) *Law as a Moral Judgement* (London, Sweet & Maxwell)
Black, M (1969) 'The Gap Between "Is" and "Should"' in WD Hudson (ed), *The Is-Ought Question* (London, Macmillan) 99–113
Blackburn, S (1984) *Spreading the Word* (Oxford, Clarendon)
Bohman, J (1996) *Public Deliberation: Pluralism, Complexity and Democracy* (Cambridge, Mass., MIT Press)
Broome, J (unpublished typescript) 'Reasoning'
Burg, E (2000) *The Model of Principles* (Amsterdam, Universiteit van Amsterdam)
Burton, S (1989) 'Law as Practical Reason' 62 *Southern California Law Review* 747
Cane, P (2002) *Responsibility in Law and Morality* (Oxford, Hart)
Christodoulidis, E (1999) 'The Irrationality of Merciful Legal Judgement: Exclusionary Reasoning and the Question of the Particular' 18 *Law and Philosophy* 215
Clarke, S (1978) 'A Discourse concerning the Unalterable Obligations of Natural Religion and the Truth and Certainty of the Christian Revelation' in *The Works of Samuel Clarke* (1705, New York, Garland)
Cohen, J (1986) 'An Epistemic Conception of Democracy' 97 *Ethics* 26
—— (1989) 'Deliberation and Democratic Legitimacy' in A Hamlin and P Pettit (eds), *The Good Polity: Normative Analysis of the State* (Oxford, Blackwell) 17–34
—— (1996) 'Procedure and Substance in Deliberative Democracy' in S Benhabib (ed), *Democracy and Difference* (Princeton, Princeton University Press) 95–138
Coleman, J (1982) 'Negative and Positive Positivism' 11 *Journal of Legal Studies* 139
—— (1998) 'Incorporationism, Conventionality, and the Practical Difference Thesis' 4 *Legal Theory* 381
—— (2000) 'Constraints on the Criteria of Legality' 6 *Legal Theory* 171
—— (2001) *The Practice of Principle* (Oxford, Oxford University Press)
—— (2002) 'Conventionality and Normativity' in E Villanueva (ed), *Legal and Political Philosophy* (Amsterdam: Rodopi) 157–75
Cooke, M (2000) 'Five Arguments for Deliberative Democracy' 48 *Political Studies* 947
Cooter, R (1984) 'Prices and Sanctions' 84 *Columbia Law Review* 1523
Copp, D (1997a) 'Does Moral Theory Need the Concept of Society?' 19 *Analyse and Kritik* 189
—— (1997b) 'The Ring of Gyges: Overridingness and the Unity of Reason' 14 *Social Philosophy and Policy* 86
—— (2001) *Morality, Normativity, and Society* (1995, Oxford, Oxford University Press)
—— (2004) 'Moral Naturalism and Three Grades of Normativity' in P Schaber (ed), *Normativity and Naturalism* (Frankfurt, Ontos Verlag) 7–45
—— (2005) 'The Normativity of Self-Grounded Reason' 22 *Social Philosophy and Policy* 165

Cornell, D (1992) *The Philosophy of the Limits* (London, Routledge)
Cover, R (1986) 'Violence and the Word' 95 *Yale Law Journal* 1601
Cunliffe, J and Reeve A (1999) 'Dialogic Authority' 19 *Oxford Journal of Legal Studies* 453
Dancy, J (2000) 'Editor's Introduction' in J Dancy (ed), *Normativity* (London, Blackwell) vii–xv
Darwall, S (1982) 'Scheffler on Morality and Ideals of the Person' 12 *Canadian Journal of Philosophy* 247
Davis, M (2005) 'The Moral Justification of Torture and other Cruel, Inhuman, or Degrading Treatment' 19 *International Journal of Applied Philosophy* 161
Delacroix, S (2004) 'Hart's and Kelsen's Concepts of Normativity Contrasted' 17 *Ratio Juris* 501
—— (2006) *Legal Norms and Normativity* (Oxford, Hart)
Derrida, J (1990) 'Force of Law: the "Mystical Foundation of Authority"' 11 *Cardozo Law Review* 920
Dershowiz, M (2003) *Why Terrorism Works: Understanding the Threat, Responding to the Challenge* (Melbourne, Scribe Publications)
Detmold, MJ (1984) *The Unity of Law and Morality* (London, Routledge & Kegan Paul)
Dryzek, J (1990) *Discursive Democracy* (Cambridge, Cambridge University Press)
Dworkin, R (1978) *Taking Rights Seriously* (1977, London, Duckworth)
—— (1986) *Law's Empire* (Cambridge, Mass, Harvard University Press)
—— (2006) *Justice in Robes* (Cambridge, Mass, Harvard University Press)
Easton, D (1957) 'An Approach to the Analysis of Political Systems' 9 *World Politics* 383
Eemeren van, F and Grootendorst, R (1984) *Speech Acts in Argumentative Discussions* (Dordrecht, Foris)
—— (1988) 'Rationale for a Pragma-Dialectical Perspective' 2 *Argumentation* 271
Elster, J (1986) 'The Market and the Forum: Three Varieties of Political Theory' in J Elster and A Hylland (eds), *Foundations of Social Choice Theory* (Cambridge, Cambridge University Press) 103–32
Enoch, D (2006) 'Agency, Schmagency: Why Normativity Won't Come from What is Constitutive of Action' 115 *Philosophical Review* 169
Estlund, D (1997) 'Beyond Fairness and Deliberation: the Epistemic Dimension of Democratic Authority' in J Bohman and W Rehg (eds), *Deliberative Democracy: Essays on Reasons and Politics* (Cambridge, Mass, MIT Press) 173–204
Finnis, J (1980) *Natural Law and Natural Rights* (Oxford, Oxford University Press)
Fish, S (1989) *Doing What Comes Naturally* (Oxford, Oxford University Press)
Fitzpatrick, W (2005) 'The Practical Turn in Ethical Theory: Korsgaard's Constructivism, Realism, and the Nature of Normativity' 115 *Ethics* 651
Fletcher, G (1987) 'Law and Morality: a Kantian Perspective' 87 *Columbia Law Review* 533
Flew, A (1969) 'On not Deriving "Ought" from "Is"' in WD Hudson (ed), *The Is-Ought Question* (London, Macmillan) 135–43
Frankfurt, H (1971) 'Freedom of the Will and the Concept of a Person' 68 *Journal of Philosophy* 5
Freeman, S (2000) 'Deliberative Democracy: a Sympathetic Comment' 29 *Philosophy and Public Affairs* 371
Friedman, R (1990) 'On the Concept of Authority in Political Philosophy' (1973, now in J Raz (ed), *Authority*, Oxford, Basil Blackwell, 56–91)
Fuller, L (1969) *The Morality of Law* (New Haven, Yale University Press)

Gauss, C (1981) 'The Normativity of Law and its Coordinative Function' 16 *Israel Law Review* 333

Gaut, B (1997) 'The Structure of Practical Reason' in G Cullity and B Gaut (eds), *Ethics and Practical Reason* (Oxford, Oxford University Press) 161–88

Gavinson, R (1991) 'Comment: Legal Theory and the Role of Rules' 14 *Harvard Journal of Law and Public Policy* 727

Gewirth, A (1978) *Reason and Morality* (Chicago, University of Chicago Press)

Gibbard, A (1999) 'Morality as Consistency in Living: Korsgaard's Kantian Lectures' 110 *Ethics* 140

Gillet, G (1987) 'Reasoning about Persons' in A Peacocke and G Gillet (eds), *Persons and Personality* (London, Blackwell) 75–88

Goldsworthy, J (1990) 'The Self-Destruction of Legal Positivism' 10 *Oxford Journal of Legal Studies* 449

Green, L (1985) 'Authority and Convention' 35 *Philosophical Quarterly* 329

—— (1988) *The Authority of the State* (Oxford: Oxford University Press)

—— (1989) 'Law, Legitimacy, and Consent' 62 *Southern California Law Review* 795

—— (2002) 'Law and Obligations' in J Coleman and S Shapiro (eds), *The Oxford Handbook of Jurisprudence and Philosophy of Law* (Oxford, Oxford University Press) 514–47

Grice, H (1989) *Studies in the Way of Words* (Cambridge, Mass., Harvard University Press)

Griffin, J (1997) 'Incommensurability, What's the Problem?' in R Chang (ed), *Incommensurability, Incomparability, and Practical Reason* (Cambridge, Mass, Harvard University Press) 35–51

Gutmann, A and Thompson D (1996) *Democracy and Disagreement* (Cambridge, Mass, Harvard University Press)

Guyer, P (2000) *Kant on Freedom, Law, and Happiness* (Cambridge, Cambridge University Press)

—— (2005) *Kant's System of Nature and Freedom* (Oxford, Oxford University Press)

Habermas, J (1984) *The Theory of Communicative Action* (1981, Boston, McCarty) vol I

—— (1987) *The Theory of Communicative Action* (1981, Boston, McCarty) vol II

—— (1996) *Between Facts and Norms* (Cambridge, Mass, Polity)

Hacker, P (1973) 'Sanction Theories of Duty' in A Simpson (ed), *Oxford Essays in Jurisprudence* (Oxford, Clarendon) 131–70

Hare, RM (1952) *The Language of Morals* (Oxford, Oxford University Press)

Hart, H (1982) *Essays on Bentham* (Oxford, Clarendon)

—— (1983) *Essays in Jurisprudence and Philosophy* (Oxford, Clarendon)

—— (1990) 'Commands and Authoritative Legal Reasons' (1982, now in J Raz (ed), *Authority*, Oxford, Basil Blackwell, 92–113)

—— (1994) *Concept of Law* with a Postscript (1961, Oxford, Clarendon)

Heidemann, C (2005) 'Law's Claim to Correctness' in S Coyle and G Pavlakos (eds), *Jurisprudence or Legal Science?* (Oxford, Hart) 127–46

Hill, TE (1998) 'Kant's Argument for the Rationality of Moral Conduct' in P Guyer (ed), *Kant's Groundwork of the Metaphysics of Morals: Critical Essays* (Oxford, Rowan & Littlefield) 249–72

Himma, KE (2001) 'Law's Claim of Legitimate Authority' in J Coleman and S Shapiro (eds), *Hart's Postscript* (Oxford, Oxford University Press) 271–309

—— (2002) 'Inclusive Legal Positivism' in J Coleman and S Shapiro (eds), *The Oxford Handbook of Jurisprudence and Philosophy of Law* (Oxford, Oxford University Press) 125–65

—— (2005) 'Conceptual Jurisprudence and the Intelligibility of Law's Claim to Obligate' in M O'Rourke, J Keim-Campbell and D Shier (eds), *Topics in Contemporary Philosophy: Law and Social Justice* (Cambridge, Mass, MIT Press) 311–26

Holmes, OW (1897) 'The Path of the Law' 10 *Harvard Law Review* 457
Honnefelder, L (1996) 'The Concept of a Person in Moral Philosophy' in K Bayertz (ed), *Sanctity of Life and Human Dignity* (Dordrecht, Kluwer) 139–60
Hubin, D (2001) 'The Groundless Normativity of Instrumental Rationality' 48 *Journal of Philosophy* 445
Hudson, H (1994) *Kant's Compatibilism* (Ithaca, Cornell University Press)
Hume, D (1888) *A Treatise of Human Nature* (1739–1740, L Selby-Bigge (ed), Oxford, Oxford University Press)
Hurd, H (1991) 'Challenging Authority' 100 *Yale Law Journal* 1611
Hurley, S (1990) 'Coherence, Hypothetical Cases, and Precedent' 10 *Oxford Journal of Legal Studies* 221
Hutcheson, F (1971) *An Essay on the Nature and Conduct of the Passions and Affections, with Illustrations on the Moral Sense* (Cambridge, Mass, Harvard University Press)
Ignatieff, M (2004) *The Lesser Evil: Political Ethics in an Age of Terror* (Princeton, Princeton University Press)
Kant, I (1902) *Religion within the Boundaries of Mere Reason* (1793–1794, New York, Harper)
—— (1930) *Lectures on Ethics* (1775–1780, London, Methuen)
—— (1956) *Critique of Practical Reason* (1788, Indianapolis, Bobbs-Merrill)
—— (1959) *Groundwork of the Metaphysics of Morals* and *Critique of Practical Reason* (1785, Indianapolis, Bobbs-Merrill)
—— (1965) *Critique of Pure Reason* (1781 1st edn, 1787 2nd rev edn, New York, Macmillan)
—— (1968) *Enquiry concerning the Clarity of the Principles of Natural Theology and Ethics* in GB Kerferd and DE Walford (eds), *Kant: Selected Pre-Critical Writings and Correspondence with Beck* (1763, Manchester, Manchester University Press)
—— (1974) *Anthropology from a Pragmatic Point of View* (1798, The Hague, Martinus Nijhoff)
—— (1996) *Metaphysics of Morals* (1797, Cambridge, Cambridge University Press)
Kelsen, H (1950) 'Causality and Imputation' LXI *Ethics* 1
—— (1967) *Pure Theory of Law* (Berkley, University of California Press)
—— (1992) *Introduction to the Problems of Legal Theory* (1934, Oxford, Clarendon)
Kerstin, W (1992) 'Politics, Freedom, and Order: Kant's Political Philosophy' in P Guyer (ed), *Cambridge Companion to Kant* (Cambridge, Cambridge University Press) 342–66
Kornhauser, L (1999) 'The Normativity of Law' 1–2 *American Law and Economics Review* 3
Korsgaard, C (1996a) *Creating the Kingdom of Ends* (Cambridge, Cambridge University Press)
—— (1996b) *The Sources of Normativity* (Cambridge, Cambridge University Press)
—— (1997) 'The Normativity of Instrumental Reason' in G Cullity and B Gaut (eds), *Ethics and Practical Reason* (Oxford, Oxford University Press) 215–54
—— (2009), *Self-Constitution: Action, Identity, and Integrity* (Oxford, Oxford University Press) available at www.people.fas.harvard.edu/~korsgaar/#Publications
Kramer, M (1999) *In Defense of Legal Positivism: Law without Trimmings* (Oxford, Oxford University Press)
—— (2004) *Where Law and Morality Meet* (Oxford, Oxford University Press)
Kreimer, S (2003) 'Too Close to the Rack and the Screw: Constitutional Constraints on Torture in the War on Terror' 62 *Journal of Constitutional Law* 278
Kress, K (1999) 'Coherence' in D Patterson (ed), *A Company to Philosophy of Law and Legal Theory* (Oxford, Blackwell) 533–52
La Capra, D (1990) 'Violence, Justice, and the Force of Law' 11 *Cardozo Law Review* 1065

La Torre, M (2006) 'Juristen, boese Christen: Thinking on Torture and its Legality', seminar given at workshop held at Juristisches Seminar of the Christian-Albrechts-Universitaet zu Kiel, 24 to 29 July 2006

Ladenson, R (1980) 'In Defense of a Hobbesian Conception of Law' 9 *Philosophy and Public Affairs* 134

Lafont, C (2006) 'Is the Ideal of Deliberative Democracy Coherent?' in S Besson and JL Martí (eds), *Deliberative Democracy and its Discontents* (Aldershot, Ashgate) 3–25

Lagerspetz, E (1995) *The Opposite Mirrors* (Dordrecht, Kluwer)

Leiter, B (2002) 'Naturalism in Legal Philosophy' in EN Zalta (ed), *The Stanford Encyclopedia of Philosophy*, available at http://plato.stanford.edu/entries/lawphil-naturalism/

Lenman J (2006) 'Moral Naturalism' in EN Zalta (ed), *The Stanford Encyclopedia of Philosophy*, available at http://plato.stanford.edu/archives/fall2006/entries/naturalism-moral/

Levenbook, B (1984) 'The Role of Coherence in Legal Reasoning' 3 *Law and Philosophy* 355

Lucy, W (1999) *Understanding and Explaining Adjudication* (Oxford, Oxford University Press)

Lyons, D (1977) 'Principles, Positivism, and Legal Theory' 87 *Yale Law Journal* 415

—— (1987) 'Comment: the Normativity of Law' in R Gavison (ed), *Issues in Contemporary Legal Philosophy* (Oxford: Clarendon) 114–26

MacCormick, N (1973a) 'Law as Institutional Fact' 90 *Law Quarterly Review* 102

—— (1973b) 'Legal Obligation and the Imperative Fallacy' in A Simpson (ed), *Oxford Essays in Jurisprudence* (Oxford, Oxford University Press) 100–30

—— (1981) *H.L.A. Hart* (Stanford, Stanford University Press)

—— (1982) *Legal Right and Social Democracy* (Oxford, Clarendon)

—— (1984a) 'Coherence in Legal Justification' in W Krawietz and H Schelsky (eds), *Theorien Der Normen* (Berlin, Duncker & Humblot) 37–59

—— (1984b) 'On Reasonableness' in C Perelman and R Vander Elst (eds), *Les Notions a Contenu Variable en Droit* (Bruylant, Bruxelles) 131–56

—— (1993) 'Argumenation and Interpretation in Law' 6 *Ratio Juris* 16

—— (1994) *Legal Reasoning and Legal Theory* (1978, Oxford, Oxford University Press)

—— (1997) *Institutions of Law* (Oxford, Oxford University Press)

—— (2005) *Rhetoric and the Rule of Law* (Oxford, Oxford University Press)

—— (2007a) *Institutions of Law* (Oxford, Oxford University Press)

—— (2007b) 'Why Law Makes No Claim' in G Pavlakos (ed), *Law, Rights and Discourse* (Oxford, Hart) 59–68

MacCormick, N and Weinberger, O (1986) *An Institutional Theory of Law* (Dordrecht, Reidel)

Marmor, A (2001) *Positive Law and Objective Values* (Oxford, Oxford University Press)

—— (2002) 'Exclusive Legal Positivism' in J Coleman and S Shapiro (eds), *The Oxford Handbook of Jurisprudence and Philosophy of Law* (Oxford, Oxford University Press) 104–24

Menendez, A (2000) 'Complex Democracy and the Obligation to Obey the Law', ARENA Working Papers, available at www.arena.uio.no/publications/working-papers2000/papers/wp00_25.htm

Mian, E (2002) 'The Curious Case of Exclusionary Reasons' 15 *Canadian Journal of Law and Jurisprudence* 99

Michelon, C (2006) *Being Apart from Reasons* (Dordrecht, Kluwer)

Miller, D (1981) 'Constitutive Rules and Essential Rules' 39 *Philosophical Studies* 183

Moore, GE (1903) *Principia Ethica* (Cambridge, Cambridge University Press)

Moore, M (1989) 'Authority, Law and Razian Reasons' 62 *Southern California Law Review* 830

Murphy, M (2003) 'Natural Law Jurisprudence' 9 *Legal Theory* 241

—— (2006) *Natural Law in Jurisprudence and Politics* (Cambridge, Cambridge University Press)

Nagel, T (1979) *Mortal Questions* (Cambridge, Cambridge University Press)
Nino, CS (1996) *The Constitution of Deliberative Democracy* (New Haven, Yale University Press)
O'Day, K (1998) 'Normativity and Interpersonal Reasons' 1 *Ethical Theory and Moral Practice* 61
O'Neil, O (1989) *Constructions of Reason* (Cambridge, Cambridge University Press)
Palmer Olsen, H and Toddington, S (1999) 'Legal Idealism and the Autonomy of Law' 12 *Ratio Juris* 286
Parfit, D (2006) 'Normativity' 1 *Oxford Studies in Metaethics* 325
Paulson, S (1992) 'The Neo-Kantian Dimension of Kelsen's Pure Theory of Law' 12 *Oxford Journal of Legal Studies* 153
—— (1998) 'Four Phases in Hans Kelsen's Legal Theory? Reflections on a Periodization' 18 *Oxford Journal of Legal Studies* 153
Pavlakos, G (2006) *Our Knowledge of the Law* (Oxford, Hart)
Peczenik, A (1983) *The Basis of Legal Justification* (Dordrecht, Reidel)
—— (1989) *On Law and Reason* (Dordrecht, Reidel)
—— (1990) 'Coherence, Truth and Rightness in the Law' in P Nerhot (ed), *Law, Interpretation and Reality* (Dordrecht, Kluwer) 275–309
—— (1996) 'Jumps and Logic in the Law' 4 *Artificial Intelligence and Law* 297
—— (1998) 'A Coherence Theory of Juristic Knowledge' in A Aarnio *et al* (eds), *On Coherence Theory of Law* (Lund, Juristfoerlaget) 7–16
Perelman, C and Olbrechts-Tyteca, L (1969) *The New Rhetoric: a Treatise on Argumentation* (1958, Notre Dame, Notre Dame University Press)
Perry, S (1987) 'Judicial Obligation, Precedent and the Common Law' 7 *Oxford Journal of Legal Studies* 215
—— (1989) 'Second-Order Reasons, Uncertainty and Legal Theory' 62 *Southern California Law Review* 913
—— (2001) 'Hart's Methodological Positivism' in J Coleman (ed), *Hart's Postscript* (Oxford, Oxford University Press) 311–54
Pink, T (2004) 'Moral Obligation' in A O'Hear (ed), *Modern Moral Philosophy* (Cambridge, Cambridge University Press) 159–87
Posner, R (2006) *Not a Suicide Pact* (Oxford, Oxford University Press)
Postema, G (1982) 'Coordination and Convention at the Foundations of Law' 11 *Journal of Legal Studies* 165
—— (1987) 'The Normativity of Law' in R Gavison (ed), *Issues in Contemporary Legal Philosophy* (Oxford, Clarendon) 81–104
—— (1991) 'Positivism I Presume? . . . Comments on Schauer's "Rules and the Rule of Law"' 14 *Harvard Journal of Law and Public Policy* 797
—— (1998) 'Jurisprudence as Practical Philosophy' 4 *Legal Theory* 329
—— (2001) 'Law as Command: the Model of Command in Modern Jurisprudence' 11 *Philosophical Issues* 470
Prauss, G (1974) *Kant und das problem der Dinge an sich* (Berlin, de Gruyter)
Price, R (1974) *A Review of the Principal Questions in Morals* (1787 3rd edn, Oxford, Oxford University Press)
Rabinowicz, W (1998) 'Peczenik's Passionate Reason' in A Aarnio *et al* (eds), *On Coherence Theory of Law* (Lund, Juristfoerlaget) 17–27
Radbruch, G (1990) 'Gesetzliches Unrecht und übergesetzliches Recht' in *Gesamtausgabe*, vol III, *Rechtsphilosophie III* (1946, A Kaufmann (ed), Heidelberg, Müller) 83–93
—— (2006) 'Statutory Lawlessness and Supra-Statutory Law' (1946) 26 *Oxford Journal of Legal Studies* 1

Railton, P (2000) 'Normative Force and Normative Freedom: Hume and Kant' in J Dancy (ed), *Normativity* (London, Blackwell) 1–33
Rawls, J (1999a) *A Theory of Justice* (1971, Cambridge, Mass, Harvard University Press)
—— (1999b) *Collected Papers* (Cambridge, Mass., Harvard University Press)
Raz, J (1970) *The Concept of a Legal System* (Oxford, Oxford University Press)
—— (1975) *Practical Reason and Norms* (London, Hutchinson)
—— (1979) *The Authority of Law: Essays on Law and Morality* (Oxford, Oxford University Press)
—— (1984) 'Hart on Moral Rights and Legal Duties' 4 *Oxford Journal of Legal Studies* 123
—— (1986a) *The Morality of Freedom* (Oxford, Oxford University Press)
—— (1986b) 'The Purity of the Pure Theory' in R Tur and W Twinning (eds), *Essays on Kelsen* (Oxford, Clarendon) 79–97
—— (1989) 'Facing Up: a Reply' 62 *Southern California Law Review* 1153
—— (1994) *Ethics in the Public Domain: Essays in the Morality of Law and Politics* (Oxford, Clarendon)
—— (1999) *Engaging Reason* (Oxford, Oxford University Press)
—— (2003) *The Practice of Value* (Oxford, Oxford University Press)
—— (2004) 'Incorporation by Law' 10 *Legal Theory* 1
Reath, A (2006) *Agency and Autonomy in Kant's Moral Theory* (Oxford, Oxford University Press)
Reemtsma, J (2005) *Folter im Rechtsstaat?* (Hamburg, Hamburger Edition)
Regan, D (1987) 'Law's Halo' 4 *Social Philosophy and Policy* 15
—— (1989) 'Authority and Value' 62 *Southern California Law Review* 995
Rodriguez-Blanco, V (2001) 'A Revision of the Constitutive and Epistemic Coherence Theories of Law' 14 *Ratio Juris* 212
Rosati, C (1995) 'Naturalism, Normativity, and the Open Question Argument' 29 *Nous* 46
—— (2003) 'Agency and the Open Question Argument' 113 *Ethics* 490
Sartor, G (1997) 'Logic and Argumentation in Legal Reasoning' 15 *Current Legal Theory* 25
Scheffler, S (1982) 'Ethics, Personal Identity, and the Ideals of the Person' 12 *Canadian Journal of Philosophy* 229
Schiavello, A (2001) 'On "Coherence" and "Law": an Analysis of Different Models' 14 *Ratio Juris* 233
Schiffer, S (1972) *Meaning*. (Oxford, Clarendon)
Schneewind, JB (1998) 'Natural Law, Skepticism, and Methods of Ethics' in P Guyer (ed), *Kant's Groundwork of the Metaphysics of Morals: Critical Essays* (Oxford, Rowan & Littlefield) 3–25
Searle, J (1968) 'Austin on Locutionary and Illocutionary Acts' 77 *Philosophical Review* 405
—— (1969) *Speech Acts* (Cambridge, Cambridge University Press)
—— (1971) 'What is a Speech Act?' in J Searle (ed), *The Philosophy of Language* (Oxford, Oxford University Press) 39–53
—— (1979) *Expression and Meaning* (Cambridge, Cambridge University Press)
—— (1995) *The Construction of Social Reality* (London, Penguin)
Searle, J and Vanderveken, D (1985) *Foundations of Illocutionary Logic* (Cambridge, Cambridge University Press)
Setiya, K (2003) 'Explaining Action' 112 *Philosophical Review* 339
Shafer-Landau, R (2003) *Moral Realism: a Defence* (Oxford, Oxford University Press)
Shapiro, S (2000) 'Law, Morality, and the Guidance of Conduct' 6 *Legal Theory* 127
—— (2001) 'On Hart's Way Out' in J Coleman (ed), *Hart's Postscript* (Oxford, Oxford University Press) 149–91

—— (2002) 'Authority' in J Coleman and S Shapiro (eds), *The Oxford Handbook of Jurisprudence and Philosophy of Law* (Oxford, Oxford University Press) 382–439
Sidgwick, H (1967) *The Methods of Ethics* (1874, London, MacMillan)
Skorupski, J (1998) 'Rescuing Moral Obligation' 6 *European Journal of Philosophy* 335
Smith, M (2006) 'The Law as a Social Practice: Are Shared Activities at the Foundations of Law?' 12 *Legal Theory* 265
Soeteman, A (1989) *Logic in Law* (Dordrecht, Kluwer)
Soper, P (1977) 'Legal Theory and the Obligation of a Judge: the Hart/Dworkin Dispute' 75 *Michigan Law Review* 473
—— (1984) *A Theory of Law* (Cambridge, Mass, Harvard University Press)
—— (1989) 'Legal Theory and the Claim of Authority' 18 *Philosophy and Public Affairs* 209
—— (1996) 'Law's Normative Claims' in R George (ed), *The Autonomy of Law* (Oxford, Clarendon) 215–47
Soriano, LM (2003) 'A Modest Notion of Coherence in Legal Reasoning: a Model for the European Court of Justice' 16 *Ratio Juris* 296
Stavropoulos, N (1996) *Objectivity in Law* (Oxford, Clarendon)
—— (2003) 'Interpretivist Theories of Law' in EN Zalta (ed), *The Stanford Encyclopedia of Philosophy* (Winter 2003 edn), available at http://plato.stanford.edu/archives/win2003/entries/law-interpretivist/
Stone, J (1964) *Legal System and Lawyers' Reasoning* (London, Stevens)
Strawson, P (1964) 'Intention and Convention in Speech Acts' 73 *Philosophical Review* 439
Stroud, S (1998) 'Moral Overridingness and Moral Theory' 79 *Pacific Philosophical Quarterly* 170
Sussman, D (2005) 'What's Wrong with Torture?' 33 *Philosophy and Public Affairs* 1
Thomson, J (1969) 'How Not to Derive "Ought" from "Is"' in WD Hudson (ed), *The Is-Ought Question* (London, Macmillan) 163–7
Tindale, Ch (2005) 'Tragic Choices: Reaffirming Absolutes in the Torture Debate' 19 *International Journal of Applied Philosophy* 209
Toulmin, S (1958) *The Uses of Arguments* (Cambridge, Cambridge University Press)
—— (1976) *Knowing and Acting: an Invitation to Philosophy* (London, Macmillan)
Velkley, R (1989) *Freedom and the End of Reason: On the Moral Foundations of Kant's Critical Philosophy* (Chicago, University of Chicago Press)
Velleman, D (1989) *Practical Reflection* (Princeton, Princeton University Press)
—— (1996) 'The Possibility of Practical Reason' 106 *Ethics* 694
—— (2000) *The Possibility of Practical Reason* (Oxford, Oxford University Press)
—— (2004) 'Replies to Discussion on *The Possibility of Practical Reason*' 121 *Philosophical Studies* 277
Viehweg, T (1993) *Topics and Law* (1953, Frankfurt am Main, Lang)
Waldron, J (1992) 'The Irrelevance of Moral Objectivity' in R George (ed), *Natural Law Theory* (Oxford, Oxford University Press)
Waluchow, W (1994) *Inclusive Legal Positivism* (Oxford, Clarendon)
—— (2000) 'Authority and the Practical Difference Thesis: a Defence of Inclusive Legal Positivism' 6 *Legal Theory* 45
Warren, M (2002) 'Deliberative Democracy' in A Carter and G Stokes (eds), *Democratic Theory Today* (Cambridge, Polity) 173–202
Watkins, E (1998) 'Kant's Antinomies: Section 3-8' in G Mohr and M Willaschek (eds), *Kooperativer Kommentar zu Kants Kritik der reinen Vernunft* (Berlin, Akademie Verlag) 445–62
Wedgwood, R (2006) 'The Meaning of "Ought"' 1 *Oxford Studies in Metaethics* 127

Weinrib, E (1987) 'Law as a Kantian Idea of Reason' 87 *Columbia Law Review* 472
Williamson, T (2000) *Knowledge and its Limits* (Oxford, Oxford University Press)
—— (2005a) 'Contextualism, Subject-Sensitive Invariantism, and Knowledge of Knowledge' 55 *Philosophical Quarterly* 213
Williamson, T ((2005b) 'Knowledge, Context and the Agent's Point of View' in G Preyer and G Peter (eds), *Contextualism in Philosophy* (Oxford, Oxford University Press) 91–115
Willigenburg van, T (2004) 'Being Bound by Reasons: Practical Identity and the Authority of Self-Legislation' in M Sie *et al* (eds), *Reasons of One's Own* (Aldershot, Ashgate) 39–55
Wolff, P (1970) *In Defense of Anarchism* (New York, Harper & Row)
Wood, A (1999) *Kant's Ethical Thought* (Cambridge, Cambridge University Press)
Wright, von G (1963) *Norm and Action: a Logical Enquiry* (London, Routledge)
—— (1971) *Explanation and Understanding* (Ithaca, Cornell University Press)
Wróblewski, J (1992) *The Judicial Application of Law* (Dordrecht, Kluwer)

Index

accountability, 126, 260
acts and actions, 191–96
   guidance, and, 160–63, 195
   human agency, and, 189–204
   meaning, 191
   moral reasons *see under* reasons
Alexy, Robert, 1, 2, 3, 17–18, 128–29, 242, 255
   claim to correctness, 15, 32
   claim-making capacity, 30
   collision law, 243
   governor system, 266
   special case thesis, 173
Alston, William, 125
analytical legal positivism, 2, 3–4, 12, 67, 69, 70
coercive mechanisms and law, 81–82
   definition, 12–13
   exclusive positivism *see* exclusive positivism
   inclusive positivism *see* inclusive positivism
   reductive thesis, 142–45
   shared cooperative activity *see* shared cooperative activity
animality, 183
Anti-terrorism, Crime and Security Act [2001], 260–61
apartheid, 81
appropriateness, principle of, 243
argumentation *see* reasons and deliberations
assertive illocutionary acts, 56, 58, 60
atomistic approach, 247–48
attributive claims, 33–36, 48, 63, 64
Austin, John, 40, 145, 147
authoritative standards and provisions, 61, 69, 101, 103–104, 108–21, 127–31
authority:
   argument from, 106–107
   autonomy, and, 125–26
   exclusionary dimension of, 108–121
   legal, 104–105, 121–32
      meaning and nature, 2, 103–104
   myth, as, 150–51
   normative claim of law, and, 121–32
      reasons, and, 125–26
   obligations, 101, 125
   power, and, 151
   reason-giving, 127
   requests, and, 124–27
   thesis, 104–105
   see also law
autonomy and self-determination:
   discrimination, 257–58, 261–62

human agency, and, 176, 200–202, 206–209, 211–13, 221–22, 225
   defining trait of, 201–202
   normativity of law, and, 227, 229–34, 237, 239–43, 251–54, 265, 267
   meaning, 200–202
   normative claim of law, and, 109, 111, 116, 117, 125–27, 143
   practical reasons, and, 175–76, 182–83
   reductive thesis, 143
   terrorism, 260–61

behaviour *see* conduct
Bentham, Jeremy, 40, 143–45
Bohman, J, 264
branches of law, normative force and, 262–69
Bratman, Michael, 74
Broome, J, 20
Burton, Steven, 61

Cane, Peter, 237–38
categorical imperatives *see under* imperatives
causation, 42, 179–80
choices:
   exclusive positivism, 112–13
   inclusive positivism, 88, 93
   metaphysical question, 45, 61
   normativity, 22–23, 165, 229, 239, 253, 257–58, 262–63
   practical reason, 178–81, 186, 188, 198–202, 209, 279, 281–84
Christodoulidis, Emilios, 116–17, 119 132
citizens, 11, 68
   attitude towards law, 95–96, 123, 124, 129
   claims on, 94–95
   democracy, 264
   game-modelled view of legal normativity, 85–86
   imperatives, and, 77, 80–81, 83–84
   institutions, and, 122–23
   needs and interests, 92, 105–106
   obligations, 81, 88, 89, 95
   see also people and individuals
civil disobedience, 24
claim to justice, 2, 17, 18
coercion and force:
   authority, and, 151
   deconstuctionist theory, 148–51
   factual, 158
   law, and, 172, 234

coercion and force (cont.):
  obligations, and, 95
  organised, 81
  power, 147–48
  regimes, 77, 81–82, 83–85
  rules and human agency, 217
coherence test, 267–68
Coleman, Jules:
  grounding question, 134–35, 136
  inclusive positivism, 67, 68, 69, 71, 72, 73–76
  rejection of practical difference thesis, 79–80
  scope of normative claim of law, 94
  shared cooperative activity, 86–89
collision law, 243
command theory of law, 122, 124, 127, 147
commands, definitive, 241–44, 261
Commission for Racial Equality, 257
commissive illocutionary acts, 55, 60
commitments, 3, 44, 60, 69, 74, 86–87, 93–96, 164, 207, 213
common moral cognition *see* Kant, Immanuel, and Kantian philosophy
Concept of Law (Hart), 69, 72–73, 146
conceptual role semantics, 25–26
conduct:
  autonomous subjects, 202
  commanding *see* commands
  explanation, 42
  guidance, and *see* guidance of conduct
  normative claim of law, and, 17
  see also normative claim of law
  performatively contradictory, 207
  principled, 193–94, 196, 197, 201–202, 216
  reactive, 192–96, 216
  reasons, and, 27–28, 199–200
  reflexive, 194, 196, 216
  regulating, 42
  spontaneous, 191–92, 196, 216
  standards, 12, 61, 216
see also will
constitutive rules, 218–22
constitutivist strategy, 212–23
content-dependence, 12, 108
content-independent reasons *see under* reasons
continental normativism, 152–59
conventional morality *see* positive *under* morality
conventionalism, 99
Copp, David, 140, 163–69, 201
Cornell, Drucilla, 148–51
correctness, claim to, 2, 15, 32
critical morality *see under* morality
Critique of Practical Reason (Kant), 7, 177, 179
Cunliffe, John, 125–26, 127

Dancy, J, 21
decision-making, 26, 173, 239, 245, 264
declarative illocutionary acts, 55, 57–58, 60

deconstructionist theory, 148–50
defectiveness, 254–56, 266
definitive commands, 241
Delacroix, S, 20, 24, 95, 244–45
deliberation *see* reasons
deliberative and executive stages, 112–14
democracy, 264–65
deontic considerations, 21–22, 23, 161, 220, 221
dependence thesis, 103–104
Despotia, 81, 83
dialectical rationality *see under* rationality
directive illocutionary acts, 50–55, 56, 59–62, 64, 79, 125
directive speech acts, 125
directiveness, 21–25, 28, 68
discontinuity, thesis of, 90–91
discrimination, 257–58, 261–62
discursive logic and character, 12
discursive model of legal authority, 121–31
duty *see* legal duty; obligations
Dworkin, Ronald, 69, 89, 267

efficacy and validity of law *see under* law
empirical positivism, 142–43
endorsement, concept of, 3, 21, 78, 93, 96, 133, 140
  internal point of view, and, 73, 252–53
Enoch, David, 214, 217, 218
essentialism *see* foundationalism
ethical naturalism *see* practical naturalism
eugenics, 261–62
evaluative considerations, 21, 22, 23
exclusionary dimension of authority, 108–21
exclusionary reasons *see under* reasons
exclusive positivism, 13, 67, 70
  argument from authority, 106–107
  authority thesis, 104–105
  conventionalism, form of, 99
  defined, 99
  dependence thesis, 103–104
  exclusionary dimension of authority, 108–21
  guidance and authority, 100–102, 103–107
  practical difference thesis, 76
  Raz's theory, 100–108
    criticised, 108–14
    objections and counter-objections, 114–21
    key theses, 107–108
executive and deliberative stages, 112–14

facts, 136, 140, 162–63, 170
  facticity, 148, 156–58, 162, 170
  see also reductive thesis; social facts
fair-play based considerations, 88
fascism, 81
final reasons *see under* reasons
first-order reasons *see under* reasons
Fish, Stanley, 147, 148
  authority, 151

foundationalism, 145–46
  self, 228–29, 231
Fletcher, George, 7
force *see* coercion and force
force of law, normative *see* normative force of law
foundational violence, 149, 150
foundationalism, 145–46, 150, 171
free will *see under* will
Fuller, L, 123–24
fundamental principle of normativity of law, 227–49, 250–51, 255–56

game-modelled view of legal normativity, 74, 85–86, 72, 96, 222
general scope of normative claim of law, 94–96
Germany, 81
governor system, 2, 264, 266–67
grounding question, 134–37, 139–70
  irreducible core of normativity of law, 152–70
    legal-theoretical considerations, 152–59
    metaethical considerations, 135, 141, 142, 160–69
  reductive thesis, and, *see* reductive thesis
grounding normative claim of law, 225–69
  direct normativity, 226–27, 248–49
  force of law, normative, 226, 227, 250, 254–69
    legal systems, 262–69
    provisions and branches of law, 256–62
  fundamental principle of normativity of law, 227–49, 250–51
    human agency, and, 225
      democracy, 264–65
      law contrary to, 227, 235–36, 250, 256, 259–62
      law favourable to, 227, 233, 248, 250, 256–58
      indifference of law to, 227, 234, 250, 256, 258–592
      legal systems, and, 262–69
      source of normativity of law, 226, 227–49
      standards of, 241–44
      support of law, 233–34, 250–51, 255–62
      torture, 239–41
    indirect normativity, 226–27, 248–49
    modified Kantian approach, 225, 226, 227–44, 258, 266–67
grounding normativity of practical reason, 171–224
  human agency and practical reason, 204–12
    objection to, 212–23
  Kant, normativity source of practical reason, and, 171, 175–88
    criticised, 184–88
  modified Kantian account, 188–223

Groundwork of the Metaphysics of Morals (Kant), 7, 177–78, 188
guidance of conduct, 2, 12, 20–21
  action, and, 160–63, 195
  actualised, 23–25
  autonomous subjects, 201
  directiveness, 21–25
  exclusive positivism, and, *see* exclusive positivism
  law, by, 24, 27–28, 72, 75–76, 81
  illocutionary acts, and, 60
  imperatives, and, *see* imperatives
  normative claim, and, 49–50, 52, 170
  proffered, 22–25
  reasons, and *see* reasons
  standards, 61, 139, 140, 143, 147–48, 222
    applicability without acquiescence, 160–64

Hacker, Peter, 159
hard positivism *see* exclusive positivism
Hart, Herbert L.A, 1, 12, 13, 134, 252
  guiding function of law, 79
  inclusive positivism, 67, 68, 69, 72–73, 75, 76, 80, 83
  law and reasons, 82
  reductive thesis, and, 144–45, 146–47, 148, 159
Heidemann, Carsten, 2, 16
  claim to correctness, 32
Himma, Kenneth Einar, 2, 16
  unitary claims, 36–38
holistic approach, 247–48
human agency, 6–7, 118–19, 176, 180–81, 182–83
  action, and, 189–204
  autonomy, and, *see* autonomy and self-determination
  constitutivist strategy, 212–23
  definition, 196–97, 202
  law, and, *see under* grounding normative claim of law
  legal systems, and, 262–69
  minimally necessary self-conception, 206–10, 212, 213, 232
  nature of, 190–91, 203
  non-human agents, 214–17, 222
  normativity, and, 204–212
  performative contradictions, 107
  practical concept, as, 202
  practical reason, and, 204–12, 225
  see also practical reason
  rationality essential to, 200
  reflectivity, founded on, 202
  source of normativity of practical reason, 205–11
  standards of, 241–44, 251
  torture, 239–41
  traits of, 197–203, 205

humankind and humanity, 6, 182–84, 186–88, 189, 211
  see also Kant, Immanuel, and Kantian philosophy
Humeans, 211
hypothetical imperatives *see under* imperatives

ideal dimension of law and legal systems, 252–53, 263–66
illocutionary acts, 45–48, 52–54, 64
  claim-making entities, as, 46–48
  conditions, 46–47, 48, 49, 50, 54, 55
    success and non-defectiveness conditions compared, 56–59
  components, 46, 47, 50–51
  directive *see* directive illocutionary acts
  legal systems, and *see under* legal systems
imperatives, 76–77, 80–85, 124
  categorical, 76, 176, 182–84, 186, 212, 287
  hypothetical, 176, 182, 184–86, 212, 287
  imperative fallacy, 82–83
impersonal claims *see* attributive claims
inclinations, 193, 194–95, 196, 216
  reflexivity, and, 199, 202
inclusive positivism, 13, 67–68
  failure of, 68, 78–96
    general scope of normative claim of law, 94–96
    moral nature of normativity of law, 85–93
    non-contingent status of normative claim of law, 78–85
  necessity of normative claim denied, 68
  normative claim of law, and, 69–78
incorporationism *see* inclusive positivism
injustice *see* justice
intention and claim-making *see under* capacity to make claims *under* law
intentional agents:
  claim-making capacity, 30–31, 33, 34–35, 63
  legal systems, and, 30
internal point of view, 73, 154, 252–53
institutions, 8
  authoritative and legal, 104–107, 122, 123, 127–28, 131, 228, 254, 263
    directives, 127–28
    guiding action, 75
  democratic, 265
  element of law, as, 28, 43
  impersonal, 90
  individuals and human agency, 90–92, 122–23, 231–33
  law, 28, 107, 109, 122, 127, 131, 172, 176, 227–28, 235, 251
  legal system, 254–55
  normative claim, and, 15, 27–28, 29–30
  normativity of law, and, 24
  obligations, 232
  political, 263, 265

power, 90, 126
public, 90–92
social, 231–33
subjectivist view, and, 31–33
instrumental reasons *see under* reasons
insulation thesis, 109–121
irreducible core of normativity of law, 152–70
'is' category *see under* 'ought' category
Italy, 81

judges, 78, 87
jurispathetic violence *see* law-conserving violence
justice, 15, 19, 129
  law, and *see under* law
  normative claim to, 17–18
justifiability and justification, 18, 25–28, 89–93, 129–32
  grounding question, 134–36
  reductive thesis, 135–36, 150

Kant, Immanuel, and Kantian philosophy, 5, 6, 7, 139, 152, 167, 237
  normativity of practical reason, 171, 175–88, 205, 211–12, 217, 223
  criticised, 184–88
  practical constructivism, 136
  see also modified Kantian account
Kelsen, Hans, 139, 142–43, 152
Korsgaard, Christine, 118, 135, 211, 212, 214
Kramer, Matthew:
  imperatives, 80–85
  inclusive positivism, 67, 68, 69, 71, 75, 76–78
Kreimer, Seith, 239

language and law, 41–48, 64
  claim-making capacity, 43–48
  legal language as normative, 72–73
  reasons, and, 172
law:
  atomistic approach, 247–48
  authority, 72, 75, 77–78, 104–105, 131
    see also guidance
  capacity to make claims, 16, 27–48
    attributive claims, 33–36, 63
    claims attributed to legal state of affairs, 35–36
    elements in definition of, 61
    intention, and, 30–33, 36
    legal systems and unitary claims, 36–41
    objectivist view, 31
    performative claims, 33–35, 37
    subjectivist view, 31–33
  citizens, and, *see* citizens
  deliberative rational activity, as, 172–73
  directive illocutionary acts, and, 60, 64
  efficacy and validity, 152–59, 170
  essential functions, 75, 79
  foundations, 124

guiding action *see* guidance of actions
holistic approach, 247–48
human agency, and *see under* grounding normative claim of law
ideal dimension, 252–53
illocutionary acts, and *see* illocutionary acts
institution, as *see under* institution
justice, and, 18–19
language, representation through, 41–48, 64, 172
   claim-making capacity, 43–48
legal systems *see* legal systems
minimal normative claim, and *see* minimal normative claim
morality, and, *see* morality
nature of, 12–13, 172
normative claim of *see* normative claim of law
normative force, and *see* normative force of law
normativity *see under* normativity
practical enterprise, as, 16, 23, 49, 61, 64–65
practical reason, and, 61, 85, 90, 94, 172–75, 225, 227–28
praxis, as, 172
reasons for acting *see* reasons and deliberations
social institution and practice, as, 28, 69
structural levels, 247–48
unitary system, represented as, 39–41, 63–64
validity and efficacy, 152–59, 170
see also reasons
law-conserving violence, 149, 151
legal defects *see* defectiveness
legal duty, 1, 85–86, 88
see also obligations
legal fictions, 37
legal obligations, 75, 76, 81, 85–86, 88, 96, 255–56, 258, 268
legal officers *see* officials
legal positivism *see* analytical legal positivism
legal provisions, 8
   claim-making capacity, and, 30–32
   directive illocutionary acts, and, 60–61
   imperatives, and, 77
   force of law, and, 256–62
   indirect outcome of law, 79–80
   law, as part of, 29
   normativity *see under* normativity,
   practical difference claim *see* practical difference thesis
   principle:
      appropriateness, of, 243
      necessity, of, 243
      proportionality, of, 243
   reasons, and, 4
   validity, 128–29

legal systems:
   claims making *see* capacity to make claims *under* law
   conduct guiding, 12
   de facto authority, 1–2
   direct outcome of law, 79–80
   directive illocutionary acts, and, 59–62
   elements of, 29–30
   force of law, and, 262–69
   governor system, 264, 266–67
   ideal, 263–65
   illocutionary acts, as, 45–46, 48, 59–62, 64, 79
   imperatives, and, *see* imperatives
   legal authority, 2
      officials speaking for, 31–33
   normativity *see under* normativity
   practical difference claim *see* practical difference thesis
   practical nature of, 61
   structure, 77–78, 81, 83, 84, 122–24
   subjects of intention, as, 30
   unitary claims, and, 36–41, 63–64
   unjust, 266–67
legal theory, 1, 16–17, 19, 40, 135–36, 226, 256
   deliberations on, 245–45
   Kant *see* Kant, Immanuel, and Kantian philosophy
   legal-theoretical considerations, 152–59
   modified Kantian account *see* modified Kantian account
   metaethical considerations, 135, 141, 142, 160–69
   reductive thesis *see* reductive thesis
legality, boundaries of, 2
legitimate authority, 15, 19
   claim to, 17–18, 77–78
   exclusive positivism, and, 100–102, 103–107
   meaning, 18
   see also law
lies and unjustified assertions, 56, 58, 59
logical rationality *see under* rationality
Luhmann, N, 117, 118, 132

MacCormick, Neil, 2, 16
   imperative fallacy, 82–83
   law and reasons, 82
   law not claim-making subject, 33
Mandla v Dowell Lee [1983], 257–58
Marmor, Andrei, 22, 70, 99
meaning and status of normative claim of law, 11–65
   definitions and theories of normative claim, 15–16
   metaphysical question *see* metaphysical question
   semantic question *see* semantic question
metaethical considerations, 135, 141, 142, 160–69

metaphysical question, 11, 28–62
  law, claim-making capacity of, 16, 27–48, 62–65
    attributive claims, 33–36, 63
    claims attributed to legal state of affairs, 35–36
    intention, and, 30–33, 36
    legal systems and unitary claims, 36–41
    objectivist view, 31
    performative claims, 33–35, 37
    subjectivist view, 31–33
  necessity of normative claim, 28, 48–62
    non-defectiveness conditions *see* non-defectiveness conditions
    speech acts theory, 43–47, 48–49, 52, 55, 62
    structure and components of normative claim, 49–50
      aim-specific component, 49–51, 53, 59–60, 62
      mode-specific component, 49–51, 59, 62
      success conditions *see* success conditions
  possibility of normative claim, 28–48
    entitlement to make claims, 30
    law, claim-making capacity *see above*
Mian, E, 114
minimal normative claim:
  meaning and status, 15–20, 27–28, 62–65
minimally necessary self-conception, 206–10, 212, 213, 232
mistakes, 114–16
modern view of responsibility, 237–39
modified Kantian account, 188–223, 225, 226
  fundamental principle of normativity of law, 227–44
  normative force, and, 254–69
  see also Kant, Immanuel, and Kantian philosophy
moral:
  correctness, 19
  defects, 255
  naturalism *see* practical naturalism
  normative claim to, 17–18
  obligations, 89, 99, 106, 182, 184
  reasons *see under* reasons
Moral Naturalism and Three Grades of Normativity (Copp), 163
morality:
  critical, 92, 93
  duties, 95
  exclusive positivism, and, 99–100, 132
  legal validity dependent on, 69–71
  justification, 89–93
  meaning, 166
  moral correctness *see* moral correctness
  moral nature of normativity of law, 85–93
  neutral elements and definition of law, 83
  normative nature, 163–69

  positive, 92–93
  promises and pacts, 74, 87–89
  reasons *see under* reasons
  separability thesis, and, 13
  will, and, 178–79
Murphy, Mark, 55–59

Nazis, 81
natural law theory, 2
  weak natural law thesis *see* weak natural law thesis
natural necessity, 20, 21, 163, 179, 181, 187–88
necessity:
  normative claim, of *see under* normative claim of law
  principle of, 243
need thesis, 166
non-defective conditions, 46–47, 48, 49, 54
  success, and, 56–59
non-contingent status of normative claim of law, 78–85
non-intentional entities, 34–35
non-positivism, 2, 70, 81, 83
Norm and Action (von Wright), 219
normative claim of law:
  authority, and, 121–31
  content *see* semantic question
  directive force, 68
  see also directiveness
  fundamental traits, 11–12
  general scope, 94–96
  grounding *see* grounding normative claim of law
  human agency, and *see under* grounding normative claim of law
  irreducible core, 152–70
  meaning and status *see* meaning and status of normative claim of law
  modified Kantian approach *see* modified Kantian approach
  morality, and *see* morality
  necessity of, 1–2, 28, 48–62, 68, 79
    challenges to, 79–85
  non-contingent status, 78–85
  normative force of law *see under* grounding normative claim of law
  normativity *see under* normativity
  possibility of *see under* metaphysical question
  practical nature, 17, 68
  reason-related, 68
  see also reasons
  traits, 67, 99, 100
normative force of law, 226, 227, 250, 254–69
  legal systems, 262–69
  provisions and branches of law, 256–62
normativity:
  direct *see under* grounding normative claim of law

foundationalism, and, 146–47
grades or modes of, 165–67
human agency, and, 204–212
indirect *see under* grounding normative claim of law
law:
  fundamental principle, 227–49
  grounding normative claim *see* grounding normative claim of law
  human agency, and *see under* grounding normative claim of law
  irreducible core, 152–70
  legality, constituent element of, 1, 2, 250
  modified Kantian approach *see* modified Kantian approach
  normative force of *see* normative force of law
  object, normativity as, 85
legal provisions, 7, 17, 226–27, 248, 251
legal systems, 226–27, 248–49, 251
practical reason, 26, 50, 68, 72, 76, 79–80, 82, 96, 171–88, 205–206
  grounding *see* grounding normativity of practical reason
  modified Kantian approach *see* modified Kantian approach
see also analytical legal positivism; law

obligations, 1, 24, 215, 221, 232, 243,
  authority, 101, 125
  Bentham's concept of, 143–45
  coercion, 95
  directives, 99, 129
  individuals, 91, 96
  institutions, 232
  legal, 75, 76, 81, 85–86, 88, 96, 255–56, 258, 268
  moral, 89, 99, 106, 182, 184
  notion of, 106
  promises and pacts, 88
  practical reason, and, 22–28, 176–77, 258
  public offices, 99
  shared cooperative activity, 74, 88–89
  statements of, 73
see also legal duty
O'Day, Ken, 214, 215
officials and legal officials, 3,11, 35
  beliefs and legitimate authority, 78
  directives, and, 123
  illocutionary acts, and, 45–46
  imperatives, and, 77–78, 80–81, 83–84
  inclusive positivism, and, 68, 73–75
  institutions, and, 90–92
  justification, and, 90–93
  legal fictions, and, 37
  objectives, 95–96
  obligations on, 88, 89
  power, 151

practical reasons, 94, 96
prescriptions, and, 84–85
rule of recognition, and, 70, 73–74, 94
sanctions and penalties, 144
shared cooperative activity, 86–87, 88, 95–96
subjectivist view, and, 30–33
'ought' category, 162–63, 203–204, 217, 218, 221–22
  imperative fallacy, 82–83
  'is' category, and, 139, 142–43, 148, 151, 152
  normativity as an 'ought', 20–21, 25–28
  power, and, 145
  prescriptions, 76
  reasons, 26
optimisation commands, 241–44

pacts and promises *see* promises and pacts
Palmer Olsen, H, 175
Parfit, D, 141
penalties *see* sanctions
people and individuals:
  claims by, 34
  conduct *see* conduct
  intentional agents, as *see* intentional agents
  machinery of law, as part of, 8, 29, 38, 43, 63
  officials *see* officials
see also citizens
performative:
  claims, 33–35, 37, 63, 207
  contradictions, 207
Perry, Stephen, 1, 120–21
personal claims *see* performative claims
Peru, 33–34
plain normativity *see* minimal normative claim
positive morality *see under* morality
positivism *see* analytical legal positivism
possibility of normative claim of law *see under* metaphysical question
power, 16, 17, 24, 29, 31, 48, 76, 101, 115, 120
  authority, and, 151
  law, and, 172, 173
  meaning, 151
  normativity, as, 141
  reductive thesis, 141–51
practical constructivism, 136
practical difference thesis, 76, 79–80, 131
practical naturalism, 141–42, 163–69
practical rationality *see* rationality
practical reasons and reasoning, 1–7, 12
  action, and, 171–72
  authority, and, 130–31
  Despotia, and, 81
  directive illocutionary acts, 51, 62
  discursive conception, 115, 121, 131
  guiding conduct, 7, 84, 99, 100, 132
  exclusionary component, and, 103–108, 110–13, 117, 119–121

practical reasons and reasoning (*cont.*):
  grounding normativity *see* grounding
      normativity of practical reason
  human agency, and, 204–12, 225
  see also human agency
  internal point of view, 73
  law, and *see under* law
  legal officials, 75
  minimal normative claim, 27–28
  minimally necessary self-conception, 206–10, 212, 232
  normativity *see under* normativity
  obligation-creating power, 176–77
  rationality informing, 172–73
  Raz's theory, 101–103, 104, 105, 108, 109, 119, 120
  simplifying, 129–30
  weak natural law thesis, and, 55
predatory order, 2
prescriptions, 76, 80, 84–85, 96, 99, 160, 164, 221, 233
principled conduct *see under* conduct
promises and pacts, 74, 87–89
proportionality, principle of, 243
protected reasons *see under* reasons

Quinean, 161

Race Relations Act (1976), 257–58
Racial Integrity Act (1924), 261–62
Radbruch, G, 128–29
Railton, P, 21
rapacious order *see* predatory order
rationality, 6, 93, 167–69
  dialectical, 246–47
  human agency, 176, 179, 202, 206–208, 210–13, 221–222, 225
    normativity of law, and, 227, 229–33, 237, 239–41, 243, 251–54, 265
    terrorism, 260–61
  instrumental, 182, 185
  logical, 245–46
  practical reasoning, and, 173, 175
  rational justification, 245–46
  reasons, and, 199–200
  rhetorical, 246
  will, 178–79, 187–88
Rawls, J, 88
Raz, Joseph, 1–4, 15, 17–18, 67, 122, 129–32, 205
  exclusive positivism, theory of, 100–108
    argument from authority, 106–107
    criticised, 108–14
    exclusionary dimension of authority, 108–121
    objections and counter-objections, 114–21
    grounding question, 134, 135, 136
    law, nature of, 39, 40, 97, 99

normativity and reasons, 26–27, 76–78
reactive conduct *see under* conduct
reasons and deliberations:
  action, for:
    exclusive positivism, 100, 102, 105, 114, 120
    inclusive positivism, 72, 76, 82, 95
    metaethical considerations, 160, 165
    metaphysical question, 49, 61–62
    moral *see* moral *below*
    normative claim of law, 2, 11, 12, 127, 130–31, 172
    semantic question, 22, 27–28
  authority, and, 125–26, 127
  conduct, and 199–200
  content-independent, 72, 78, 101, 105, 108–12, 119
  deliberations, value of, 26, 52, 62, 75, 79–80, 112–14 129, 262, 264–65
  deliberative and executive stages, 112–14
  endorsed patterns, 73–74
  exclusionary, 102, 113, 114, 117, 120–21
  final, 90–91, 92
  first-order, 102, 120, 121
  genuine, 72
  guidance, and, 49–50, 52, 61, 72–73, 75, 77, 79
  human agency, 234
  see also human agency
  imperatives, and, *see* imperatives
  inclinations, and, 199
  instrumental, 90, 92, 174, 186, 211, 212
  mistakes, 114–16
  moral, 12, 72, 83, 77, 81, 90, 92, 106, 174, 186, 212
  new, 130
  normativity, and, 25–28, 244–47
  peremptory, 72, 78
  practical *see* practical reasons
  practical difference thesis *see* practical difference thesis
  prescriptions creating, 76
  protected reasons, 100, 101, 103, 105, 114
  prudential, 77, 81, 90–92, 106, 174, 175, 185, 186, 212
  public nature, 214
  rational thinking, 167–68
  sanctions, and, 82
  second-order, 102, 105, 121
  self-grounded, 167
  standards for citizens, 89, 95–96
  reweighing, 120–21
  theoretical, 90
Reath, A, 201
reductive thesis, 5, 135–36, 139, 140–51
  authority, idea of, 150–51
  criticised, 152–59, 160–69

foundationalism, 145–46
normativity, 146–50
Reeve, Andrew, 125–26, 127
reflectivity, 6, 176
   human agency, 197–99, 202, 206–209, 212–13, 221–222, 225
      normativity of law, and, 227, 229–33, 237, 239–43, 251–54, 265, 267
      terrorism, 260–61
reflexive conduct *see under* conduct
regulative rules, 218
requests, 122–31
   authority, and, 124–27
Responsibility in Law and Morality (Cane), 237
reweighing reasons, theory of, 120–21
rhetorical rationality *see under* rationality
Roosevelt, Theodore, 261
rule of recognition, 70, 73–74, 75, 87, 94, 99
rule-governed behaviour, 1
rules, 218–22

sanctions and penalties, 80–81, 82, 83, 94–95, 144, 145
   normativity, and, 158–59, 214, 215–17
Searle, J, 47, 50–54, 57
second-order reasons *see under* reasons
self-conception, 6, 167–69, 176, 230
   minimally necessary self-conception, 206–10, 212, 213, 232
self and self-consciousness, 198–203, 206, 211, 214, 216, 228–31
see also will
self-determination *see* autonomy
self-grounded reasons *see under* reasons
semantic question, 11, 17–28
   minimal normative claim, 15–20, 27–28, 62–65
   normativity, constituent elements:
      directiveness, 21–25, 28
      justification, 25–28
   normativity, 'ought', as, 20–21, 25–28
senseless order, 2, 266–67
separability thesis, 13
Shapiro, S, 76
shared cooperative activity, 74, 86–89, 95–96
'shmagency', 214
Sidgwick, Henry, 159
Smith, Matthew Noah, 86–87
social facts, 5, 12–13, 69–70, 141–42, 146, 149, 152, 154–58, 161, 169–70
   facticity, 148, 156–58, 162, 170
see also facts; reductive thesis

social institution, law as, 28
social source and legality of norms, 69, 74–75
soft positivism *see* inclusive positivism
Soper, Philip, 1, 2, 3, 15, 17–18, 31
South Africa, 81
special case thesis, 173
Special Immigration Appeals Commission, 260
speech acts theory *see* theory of speech acts
spontaneous conduct *see under* conduct
standards:
   authoritative standards and provisions, 61, 69, 101, 103–104, 108–21, 127–31
   citizens, for, 89, 95–96
   conduct, 12, 61, 216
   guidance of conduct, 61, 139, 140, 143, 147–48, 222
      applicability without acquiescence, 160–64
   human agency, 241–44, 251
strict liability, 235–39
subjectivist view of claim-making, 31, 63
success conditions, 46–47, 48, 49, 52–53, 54, 55, 61, 64
   non-defectiveness conditions, and, 56–59
system-membership, 154
systems theory, 117, 118, 119, 132

terrorism, 260–61
theoretical justifications *see* grounding question
theory of speech acts, 16, 43–47, 48–49, 52, 55, 62, 64, 207
Toddington, S, 175
torture, 239–41
transcendent morality *see* critical *under* morality

unitary claims and legal systems, 36–41
United Kingdom, 260, 261

validity and efficacy of law *see under* law
Vanderveken, D, 47, 52, 54, 57
Velleman, D, 192

Waluchow, Will, 69
weak natural law thesis, 55–59
Wedgwood, Ralph, 25, 26
Weinrib, Ernst, 7
will, 178–79, 181, 183, 185, 211, 237
   free will and determinism, 179–81, 186
see also self and self-consciousness
willed normative statements, 21
Wolff, Robert, 126
Wright, George von, 219